STATELY MANSIONS

Eighteenth Century Paris Architecture

Frontispiece. R . DE COTTE : Grand Hôtel du Maine, 1715:
façade facing the Seine, slightly modified about 1770.
Painting by J. A. Knip (Rijksmuseum Amsterdam).

Michel Gallet

STATELY MANSIONS

Eighteenth Century Paris Architecture

PRAEGER PUBLISHERS
New York · Washington

BOOKS THAT MATTER

Published in the United States of America in 1972
by Praeger Publishers, Inc., 111 Fourth Avenue,
New York, N.Y. 10003

© 1972 in London, England, by Michel Gallet

Library of Congress Catalog Card Number: 75–166512

Designed by Michael Carter

Printed in Great Britain

Contents

Illustrations   vii

Drawings and Plans   xi

Introduction   xiii

1   Paris in the 18th century   I
The appearance of Paris – Public buildings under
Louis XV – Urban development after 1763 – Development
of the Champs-Elysées

2   Building   9
Finance – Building regulations – Contracts and valuations –
Role of the contractors – Labour – Obstructed streets and
accidents

3   Architects   18
Role and remuneration of architects – The architect and
the client – The Architect in Society

4   The connoisseur   26
Taste among the nobility – Financiers and eccentrics –
The middle class

5   Artistic evolution   37
The tradition of Mansart – The origins of rococo – Baroque
survivals – Parisian rococo – Classical nostalgia – The
architecture of reason – Palladianism – The influence of
Robert Adam – The transition of styles – Dreamland

6   The middle-class home   63
The plan of apartments – Dwellings in large groups –
Neo-classical façades

7   The nobleman's hôtel   69
Its evolution in the course of the century – The covered
entrance – Staircases – Court ceremonial and private life –
Grands salons – Salons de compagnie – Eating-rooms – State
bedrooms – Galleries – Presentation of works of art –
Chapels

8 Pavilions and folies   95
Legend and truth – Architecture of the pavilions –
Classical and pre-romantic gardens

9 Artists' and writers' houses   104

10 Comfort and decoration   109
The art trade and the craftsmen – Privacy – Warmth –
Bedrooms – Sanitary installations – Panelling and carved
ornamentation – Decoration in relief during the Louis XVI
period – Printed fabrics and wallpapers – Decorative
painting – Illusionism – Mythological painting

Register of Architects   139

Illustrations

Frontispiece. R . DE COTTE : Grand Hôtel du Maine, 1715: façade facing the Seine, slightly modified about 1770. Painting by J. A. Knip (Rijksmuseum Amsterdam).

N . DESÈGRE

1 Hôtel Pujol, 5 Rue Béranger, 1715: *œil-de-bœuf* from inside. One can see part of the Hôtel de Polisy, built by Sébastien Buirette.
2 Hôtel Pujol: the garden front.
3 Hôtel Pujol: *œil-de-bœuf.*
4 Hôtel Pujol: detail of doorway.

P .-A . DELAMAIR

6 Design for Hôtel Soubise, 60 Rue des Francs-Bourgeois, 1705 (Munich Library).
7 Elevation of the Hôtel de Rohan – on the courtyard, 87 Rue Vieille-du-Temple, 1704 (Munich Library).

CLAUDE III AUDRAN

8 Ceiling of the Hôtel de Flesselles, Rue de Sévigné (now in the Musée des Arts décoratifs in Paris).

A . WATTEAU

9– Decorative panels from the Hôtel de Poulpry,
10 Rue de Poitiers.

P . FR . GODOT

11 Eynaud house, Rue de l'Arbre-Sec, 1717.

J .-B . BULLET DE CHAMBLAIN

12 Hôtel Dodun, 21 Rue de Richelieu: front door.
13 Hôtel Dodun: the staircase.
14 Hôtel Dodun: design for the staircase (Stockholm Museum).
15 Hôtel Dodun: bas-relief of children on the staircase.
16 Hôtel Dodun: design for the front elevation (Stockholm Museum).

OPPENORD

17– Sketches for decorations (Stockholm
18 Museum).

19 Engraving of a detail of the courtyard of the Hôtel de Saint-Albin, Place des Victoires – after 1723 – demolished 1785.
20 Engraving of the salon of the Hôtel de Chavaudon, Rue des Francs-Bourgeois.

TIERCELET

21 Plan of a town house, after Tiercelet, 1738.

C .-N . LEPAS DUBUISSON

22 House, 151 Rue Saint-Jacques, 1721.
23 Hôtel, 120 Rue du Bac, 1713–15. Carving by Louis Dupain.

L . HERPIN (decorator)

24 Design for a dining-room for the Hôtel Soubise.

R . DE COTTE (architect), VASSÉ SR . (decorator)

25 Gallery of the Hôtel de la Vrillière, now the Banque de France.
26 Engraving of the Gallery of the same.

COURTONNE

27 Hôtel de Noirmoutier, 138 Rue de Grenelle, built by Courtonne in 1722: detail of the decoration – the hen with the golden eggs.

ARCHITECT UNKNOWN

28 Wall decoration in the Hôtel de Boullongne, Place Vendôme, painted by Nicolas Lancret.

JULES-MICHEL HARDOUIN (architect), MICHEL LANGE (sculptor)

29 Trophy in the Grand Salon of the Elysée, 1722.

SULPICE GAUBIER (and another architect)

30 Hôtel de Choiseul, Rue Saint-Romain.

PIERRE DE VIGNY

31 Front door of the Hôtel de Chenizot, 51 Rue Saint-Louise-en-l'Ile, 1726.
32 Hôtel de Chenizot: bannister of the staircase by Nicolas Viennot.
33 Fabulous beast above the doorway of the Cour du Dragon (now in the Musée du Louvre).

DENIS QUIROT THE ELDER (architect)

34 Hôtel de Bersan, 110 Rue Vieille-du-Temple, 1731: bannister of the staircase, by Fr. Lesquillier.

35–36 Hôtel de Bersan: details of the same.

37 Hôtel de Bersan: the front door, carved by Fouquier and Stangué.

LOUIS FOURCROY (architect), VARIN (sculptor)

38 The front door of the Hôtel Jacques Samuel Bernard, 46 Rue du Bac, 1730.

39 Front door of the Hôtel Langlois de La Fortelle, Rue des Francs-Bourgeois.

CH. BERNARD

40 Hôtel Cul-de-sac de Ménars, 1732: design.

41 Rondet house, 35 Rue de la Harpe, 1730.

ALAXANDRE JOUASSE (sculptor)

42 Front door of the Hôtel de Mortemart, 14 Rue Saint-Guillaume, 1731.

P. DESMAISONS

43 Hôtel de Jaucourt, 2 Rue de la Vrillière, 1733.

THIERRY-VICTOR DAILLY

44–45 Designs for the Hôtel Lelièvre de la Grange, 4 and 6 Rue de Braque, 1737.

MARTIN GOUPY

46 Robillard house, 15 Rue Montorgueil, 1729.

47 Dubuisson house, 29 Rue de la Parcheminerie, 1736.

ARCHITECT UNKNOWN

48 Design for a pair of houses, Rue de la Chanvrerie.

Attributed to H.-Q. DESBEUFS

49 Dalençon-Dorville apartment house, 70 Rue des Gravilliers, 1737.

H.-Q. DESBEUFS

50 Bonin apartment house, 17 Rue Sainte-Croix-de-la-Bretonnerie, 1734.

51 Moreau de Saint-Just apartment house, Rue de la Monnaie, 1745.

JACQUES V GABRIEL (?)

52 Camuset house, 14 Rue François Miron, 1737.

JACQUES VINAGE

53 Houses in the Place Baudoyer (4 to 12 Rue François Miron), 1734.

FR. DEBIAS-AUBRY

54 Hôtel de Bouillon, 17 Quai Malaquais, 1740 – now the Ecole des Beaux-Arts.

55 Cotelle house, Rue Saint-André-des-Arts, 1737.

LOUIS JOUBERT

56 Design for the elevation of 7 Rue Maître Albert, 1741.

JEAN AUBERT

57 Plan of Hôtel Peyrenc de Moras.

PIERRE-JEAN VARIN

58 His house, 57 Rue de Seine, 1740.

J.-B. VAUTRAIN

59 Belon-Vatard house, Rues Poissonnière and de Cléry, 1740.

60 Belon-Vatard house: detail of the same.

J.-B.-A. BEAUSIRE

61 Hôtel d'Ecquevilly ou du Grand Veneur, 60 Rue de Turenne, 1734: bannister of the staircase by Lebrun and Daguinot.

62 Hôtel d'Ecquevilly ou du Grand Veneur: trophy of gardening implements.

63 Hôtel d'Ecquevilly ou du Grand Veneur: blazon under the staircase.

CHARLES and PIERRE BOSCRY

64 Hôtel d'Orrouer, 87 Rue de Grenelle, 1731: the garden front.

65 Hôtel d'Orrouer: doorway, present state.

66 Hôtel d'Orrouer: design for the same.

67 Hôtel d'Orrouer: Nicolas Pineau (decorator) – design for the chimney-piece of the Grand Salon.

68 Hôtel d'Orrouer: relief above the chimney-piece, present state.

MICHEL TANNEVOT

70 His house, 26 Rue Cambon: panelling by Nicolas Pineau (decorator).

J.-B. LEROUX (architect), N. PINEAU (decorator)

71 Engraving of the gallery of the Hôtel de Villars, 116 Rue de Grenelle, demolished.

CHARLES and PIERRE BOSCRY

72 Hôtel de Feuquières, 58 Rue de Varenne, 1736: design for the façade.

N. PINEAU (decorator)

73 Sketch for the decoration of the same façade.

CL. BONNOT (architect), N. PINEAU (decorator)

74 Hôtel de Marcilly, 18 Rue du Cherche-Midi, 1738: the courtyard façade.

75–76 Hôtel de Marcilly: details of the bannister on the staircase.

77 Hôtel de Marcilly: design by N. Pineau for the staircase.

78 Hôtel de Marcilly: details of the bannister on the staircase.

79 Hôtel de Marcilly: design by N. Pineau for the staircase.

J. HARDOUIN MANSART DE SAGONNE (architect), N. PINEAU (decorator)

80 Clostrier house, 56 Rue des Francs-Bourgeois, 1752.

JEAN AUBERT and J.-B. LEROUX (architects)

81 Design for *portes cochères* of the Palais Bourbon and the Hôtel Mazarin (demolished).

JEAN HARDOUIN MANSART DE JOUY

82 Engraving of designs for a chimney-piece.

UNKNOWN ARCHITECT

83 Hôtel de Luteaux, 27 Rue Lhomond, 1736: the garden front.

PIERRE DE VIGNY

84 House de la Barre de Carroy, 42 Rue François Miron, 1742.

BOFFRAND

85–
87 Hôtel Soubise: the oval salon, 1734.
88– Salon at the Arsenal decorated by the
89 architect Dauphin. Detail.

SAINT-MARTIN (architect), LANGE (sculptor)

90– Paintings by Huet, Dutour and Crépin, in the
91 *salon des singes*, Hôtel de Rohan, 87 Rue Vieille-du-Temple.

QUIROT LE JEUNE

92 His house, 2 Rue de la Jussienne, 1752.

CH. E. BRISEUX

93 Hôtel d'Augny, Rue Drouot, 1752 – engraving of the garden front.

94 Engraving of a design for a salon.

SERVANDONI

95 Design for the staircase for the Hôtel d'Auvergne, Rue l'Université, 1740

96 Staircase of his house, Place Saint-Sulpice, 1757.

CONTANT D'IVRY

97 House of Choiseul-Gouffier, Rue Etienne Marcel, 1738: carving by Casimir Duhamel.

98 Staircase of the Hôtel de Thiers, 19 Place Vendôme, 1747.

99–
100 Staircase of the Palais-Royal, about 1765.
101 State bedroom of the Palais-Royal.
102 Palais-Royal façade.

ANTOINE-MATHIEU LE CARPENTIER and GUILLAUME COUTURE LE JEUNE

103– Pavilion of the Boissière, Rue de Clichy,
104 1751–70: engravings of the plan and the façade.

SAINT-MARTIN

105 Design for restoration of house of the Maréchal de Richelieu à Clichy.

CHEVOTET

106 Pavillon de Hanovre, 1757: design. (Destailleur coll.)

107 Pavillon de Hanovre: the actual building, now in the Parc de Sceaux.

GAETANO BRUNETTI

108 Staircase of the Hôtel de Luynes, 1748, now in the Musée Carnavalet.

SERVANDONI

109 His house, 6 Place Saint-Sulpice, 1754–57.

UNKNOWN ARCHITECT

110 House *à la grecque*, Rue Saint-Honoré.

L.-F. TROUARD

111 His house, 9 Rue du Faubourg Poissonnière, 1758.

112 His house: detail of the bannister.

PIERRE-LOUIS MOREAU-DESPROUX

113 Design for Hôtel de Chabanne, Boulevard du Temple, 1758.

CHERPITEL

114 Design for the Hôtel d'Uzès. (Rejected.)

LEDOUX

115 Hôtel d'Uzès, Rue Montmartre, 1767–69: engraving of the courtyard façade.

116 Hôtel d'Uzès: engraving of the plan.

117– Hôtel d'Uzès: decorative panels in the salon
118 ('Europe', 'America') carved by Boiston.

ROUSSET

119 Design for the salon of the Hôtel d'Uzès. (Rejected.)

LEDOUX

120 Design for Hôtel d'Hallwyl, Rue Michel-le-Comte, 1766.

CHERPITEL

121 Courtyard of the Hôtel du Châtelet, 127 Rue de Grenelle.

122 Design for the Hôtel d'Harcourt, Rue l'Université.

123 Design for the Hôtel du Châtelet – elevation of the courtyard façade and plan (British Museum).

124 Architect's sketch of garden front of the Hôtel du Châtelet (British Museum).

125 Dining-room in the Hôtel du Châtelet.

MOREAU-DESPROUX

126 Room from the Hôtel de Luynes, now in the Musée du Louvre.

CHALGRIN

127 Hôtel de La Vrillière, Rue Saint-Florentin: drawing by Chambers.

128 Hôtel de La Vrillière: sculpture by Gois in the courtyard.

129 Hôtel de La Vrillière: view of the staircase.

130 Hôtel de La Vrillière: details of the bannisters.

JACQUES-DENIS ANTOINE

131 Hôtel Brochet de Saint-Prest, 28 Rue des Saints-Pères, 1774: detail of the staircase.

JEAN-CHARLES DELAFOSSE

132 Engraving of a decorative vase.

133 Hôtel Delbarre, 58 Rue du Faubourg Poissonnière: decorative vase, 1774.

134 Hôtel Delbarre, details of the staircase.

135 Hôtel Goix, 60 Rue du Faubourg Poissonnière: the garden front.

136 Hôtel Goix: detail of the oval boudoir.

137 Maquette of a stove.

BOULLÉE

138 Hôtel de Brunoy – façade on the Champs-Elyseés: engraving.

139 House of M. de Monville: engraving.

BERNARD POYET

140 Design for the house of the painter Callet, Quartier Montparnasse, 1775.

141 Watercolour of the house of the Princesses d'Orléans at Bellechasse, 1778.

CHARLES DE WAILLY

142 Hôtel d'Argenson, Rue des Bons-Enfants: sketch by Chambers of the dining-room.

BRONGNIART

143 Hôtel de Sainte-Foix, Rue Basse du Rempart: engraving.

144 Hôtel de Bourbon-Condé, 12 Rue Monsieur, 1785.

145 Decoration of the Hôtel de Monaco (Musée Carnavalet).

ANDRÉ AUBERT

146 House, 4 Rue Caumartin: design for the façade.

147 House, 4 Rue Caumartin: the façade today.

148 Hôtel Deshays and Hôtel d'Aumont, Rue Caumartin: engraving.

UNKNOWN PAINTER

149 Oval ceiling in the Hôtel Vassal de Saint-Hubert, Rue Montmartre.

CHEVALIER DE BEAUREGARD

150 His house at Chaillot.

CELLERIER

151 Summer dining-room in the house of the Maréchal de Soubise, Rue de l'Arcade, 1786.

JEAN-ARNAUD RAYMOND

152 Design for the house of Mme Vigeé Lebrun, 8 Rue du Sentier, 1785.

PIERRE ROUSSEAU

153– Hôtel de Salm, 1785.
157

Attributed to LEDOUX

158 Design for decoration for the Hôtel Hallwyl, 1766.

LEDOUX

159 Hôtel Thélusson, Rue de Provence, 1782: general view.

160 Hôtel Thélusson: plan.

161 Hôtel Thélusson: elevation.

162 Hôtel Thélusson: two sections.

163 Hôtel Thélusson: detail of a door.

164 Hôtel de Montmorency, 1770: plan, original design.

165 Hôtel de Montmorency: elevation, original design.

166 Hôtel Montmorency: decoration of the salon, original design.

167 Hôtel de Montmorency: section, original design.

168 Hôtel de Montmorency: two panels from the salon, carved by Métivier, now in the Boston Museum.

LEMOINE LE ROMAIN

169 Hôtel Beaumarchais, 1790.

BÉLANGER

170 House of Mlle Dervieux, Rue de la Victoire: the dining-room, 1787.

171 Pavilion of the Hôtel de Brancas, Rue Taitbout, 1771.

172– Designs for the garden of the folie Sainte-
173 James, after 1777.

174 Bagatelle: design for the elevation, 1777.

175 Bagatelle: bedroom of the comte d'Artois.

176 House in the Rue Joubert, 1785.

HAPPE and SOBRE

177 Cour Batave, 60 Rue Saint-Denis: design, 1792.

Drawings and Plans

All the drawings are by the Author and all are elevations unless otherwise stated

1   Pierre de Vigny: Hôtel de Chenizot,   3
    51 Rue Saint-Louis-en-l'Ile, 1726.

2   Three houses in the Rue Montorgueil: 7
    No. 15 – Martin Goupy: Robillard
    house, 1729;
    No. 17 – Martin Goupy: Chenot house,
    1730;
    No. 19 – Treffeuille: Gobin house, 1776.

3   Pierre de Vigny: Entrance to the Cour du   11
    Dragon, 50 Rue de Rennes (demolished
    about 1950), 1732.

4   Hôtel de Luteaux, 27 Rue Lhomond, 1736.   13

5   Jacques-Richard Cochois and J.-B.-A.   20
    Beausire: Claude Aubry house, Rues
    Saint-Denis and Grenéta, 1732.

6   Victor-Thierry Dailly: Hôtels Le Lièvre   27
    de La Grange, 6–8 Rue de Braque, 1737.

7   J.-B.-A. Beausire: Hôtel d'Ecquevilly ou   30
    du Grand Veneur, 60 Rue de Turenne,
    1734.

8   J. Hardouin-Mansart de Sagonne: House   34
    of the Dames de Saint-Chaumont,
    151 Boulevard de Sébastopol, 1734.

9   J.-R. Cochois: Nourry house, 115 Rue   39
    Saint-Honoré, about 1735.

10 F. Debias-Aubry: Cotelle house, 52 Rue   42
    Saint-André-des-Arts, 1737.

11 Ironwork designs by F. Debias-Aubry: 44
    (a) Balcony facing the quay – Grand
    Hôtel de Bouillon, 17 Quai Malaquais,
    1740;
    (b) Cotelle house, 52 Rue Saint-André-
    des-Arts, 1737;
    (c) Debias-Aubry house, 131 Rue
    Saint-Martin, 1729;
    (d) Juliennet house, 45 Rue de la
    Harpe, 1740. Also a house at 11 Rue

Daguesseau (no longer standing), the
Hôtel de Gesvres, 23 Rue Croix-des-
Petits-Champs (no longer standing),
and a house at 16 Rue Saint Sauveur,
these latter three buildings being
attributed to F. Debias-Aubry;
(e) A house at 47 Rue de la Harpe –
attributed to F. Debias-Aubry, 1735;
(f) Hôtel Thoynard, 9 Rue du Coq
Héron, attributed to F. Debias-Aubry,
1735;
(g) Cotelle house, Rue Saint-André-
des-Arts, 1737;
(h) Petit Hôtel de Bouillon, 15 Quai
Malaquais, 1745.

12 J.-R. Cochois: Hôtel, 47 Rue Saint-   47
    André-des-Arts, 1741.

13 J.-R. Cochois: Plan of Hôtel de Marcillac,   51
    Rue Sainte-Avoye (now demolished), 1747.

14 J.-B. Vautrain: Hôtel du Tillet, 31 Rue   56
    des Francs-Bourgeois, 1740.

15 Martin Goupy: His own house, Rue des   58
    Prouvaires (no longer standing), 1740.

16 Fourcroy and other artists: Hôtel Jacques   62
    Samuel-Bernard, 42 Rue du Bac, 1730–40.

17 Pierre de Vigny: House of La Barre de   65
    Carroy, 42 Rue François Miron, 1742.

18 Contant d'Ivry: Hôtel de Thiers, 19 Place   68
    Vendôme (plan), 1747.

19 Pierre Quirot le Jeune: His own house,   71
    Rue de la Jussienne, 1752.

20 J.-R. Cochois: Plan of his house, Rue du   72
    Bouloi (now demolished), 1754.

21 J.-R. Cochois: The same house, street   74
    and garden elevation.

22 Claude-Louis Daviler: Simonnet house,   77
    27 Rue Saint-André-des-Arts, 1754.

23   Ironwork designs which corroborate   78
attribution of several houses to J.-R.
Cochois:
   (a) Cochois house, 29 Faubourg Saint-
Martin, 1740;
   (b) Claude Aubry house, 1732;
   (c) 47 Rue Saint-André-des-Arts, 1740;
   (d) Central balcony, 47 Rue Saint-
André-des-Arts, 1740;
   (e) Aulard house, Impasse des Trois
Visages, from an old photograph as are:
a house, 11 Rue de la Ferronnerie and
Nourry house, 115 Rue Saint-Honoré
(the latter two attributed to Cochois);
   (f) Nourry house, first floor.

24   Mouret: Hôtel d'Estiaux, 1 Rue de Lille   81
(plan), 1754.

25   House in the Greek taste, 12 Rue de la   83
Lune (house of the Sœurs de la Charité,
now Ecole d'Electronique), about 1760.

26   L.-F. Trouard: His house in the Greek   85
taste, 9 Rue du Faubourg-Poissonnière,
1758.

27   L.-F. Trouard: Banisters in the same   87
house, 1758.

28   L.-E. Boullée: Hôtel Alexandre, 16 Rue   88
de la Ville l'Evêque, 1763.

29   J.-J. Lanoue de La Couperie (Architect)   92
Jacques Lucotte (Ironsmith): Banisters of
the Hôtel de l'Hôpital, Boulevard du
Temple (demolished), 1762.

30   F. Franque: de Crillon house, Rue du   94
Renard (plan), 1768.

31   S.-N. Lenoir-le-Romain: Hôtel Rigoley de   96
Juvigny-Giambonne, Rue de Bondy (now
Rue René Boulanger, demolished), 1776.

32   Cellerier: Plan of an Hôtel Chaussée-   98
d'Antin, 1776.

33   Brongniart: Pavillon de Valence –   99
Timbrune, Rue de la Chaussée-d'Antin,
demolished, 1776–7.

34   Neveu: His own house, 12 Rue de   101
Tournon, 1776.

35   Blève: Apartment house, Rue Vieille du   106
Temple and Rue de Bretagne – plan of
first floor, 1776–7.

36   Blève: The same: elevation on the Rue de   111
Bretagne, 1776–7.

37   Joseph Métivier: House of the master-   114
ciseleur Gouthière, 6 Rue Pierre Bullet,
1780.

38   H. Piètre: Salon of the Hôtel d'Orléans,   116
Rue de la Chaussée d'Antin, about
1780.

39   E. Fr Legrand: Hôtel de Gallifet (today   119
the Italian Embassy), 73 Rue de Grenelle
– garden front, 1784.

40   Fr Soufflot le Romain: Hôtel de   120
Montholon, 21 Boulevard Montmartre,
1785.

41   J.-A. Raymond: House of Mme Vigée-   121
Lebrun, circular court, 8 Rue du Sentier
(demolished), 1785.

42   P. Rousseau: His house, 25 Rue de La   122
Rochefoucauld.

43   Hôtel de Botterel-Quintin, 44 Rue des   125
Petites-Ecuries (plan), 1785.

44   Hôtel de Botterel-Quintin. The dining-   126
room.

45   J. Métivier: His own house, Boulevard   128
Saint-Denis, 1789.

46   E. Damesme: Brasserie Weel, Rue Richer   131
– a Greco-Gothic building, (demolished),
1793.

47   Brongniart: Hôtel de Sainte-Foix   132
(plan).

48   Raymond: House of Mme Vigée-Lebrun   133
(plan).

49   Bergevin and Mellan: Cour d'Aligre, Rue   135
Bailleul, 1782.

50   Jean Courtonne: Hôtel de Noirmoutier,   137
138 Rue de Grenelle, 1721.

Introduction

We are watching the desperate efforts of cultivated people to save the few old parts of the city which have not completely succumbed to vandalism. Admirable as this awakening has been, it comes very late. For too long interest in architectural history was confined to Classical Antiquity and the Middle Ages without regard for more recent times. Our generation has been the first to realise that the entire legacy of the past matters; that a villa by Le Corbusier or an octroi-house by Ledoux deserves as much to survive as a Romanesque church in Périgord. The admirer of classical art may deplore that eighteenth-century buildings are still to a large exter deprived of official protection and that the efforts expended on their behalf are too often ineffective. Baron Haussmann's clearances and a proliferation of characterless buildings may well have destroyed or engulfed half the fine houses of the period. A significant proportion of the survivors have been stripped of their internal appointments. Scattered over two continents, Parisian panelling has drifted into the hands of collectors who usually know nothing of its origin. From this mutilated legacy it is our job to identify the essential features and the evolution of the domestic ideals of the eighteenth century. We must examine the residue and reassemble the scant fragments. Evidence of what has disappeared can be found on plans and from engravings, in artists' biographies, and from contemporary records and accounts in old guide-books. But many important buildings are unmentioned.

In the very small world of scholarship, interest in the domestic architecture of Paris was long restricted to the houses of the nobility and the financiers. Our acquaintanceship with these homes owes much to the pertinacity of a few investigators working at the beginning of this century, who reconstructed the chain of successive ownerships, a difficult task at a time when the archives of the hundred property registries of Paris were not yet concentrated in one place, as they are today. Subsequently, this patiently accumulated information was subjected to copious second-hand exploitation by writers who enlivened the history of these houses by recalling their illustrious occupants and by tales of gallantry and intrigue, neglected by the original investigators. Neither expert research, however, nor popularisation has thrown much light on the artistic character of the houses; the deeds of sale establish the genealogy of a property, but ignore the work of construction and embellishment carried out during the intervals of change. We must therefore turn to other sources.

Archives offer us guide-lines to fresh information upon the private architectural work of the time. Taxation records, deeds of succession, building authorisations and agreements between neighbours, duly attested, disclose dates of construction. More thorough research into notarial documents reveals dealings between landlords and tradesmen. The irrefutable evidence of such records confirms and excels that of engravings, biographies and old guide-books. It illuminates the activities of private individuals of every condition, introducing us both to the princely residence and to the dwellings of ordinary people, which thus assume their proper place in the city's evolutionary pattern. It always gives the names of contractors, who held sole legal responsibility at this period, and often those of architects, whose designs may be attached to the contracts. The master-smith, who fashioned the ironwork, appears among the subcontractors. The decorative sculptors and carvers, worthy academicians of Saint-Luc, are a little more difficult to discover. Their work was not entered in the general estimate for the building. They were the subject of private agreements which have rarely come down to us. The bill of quantities only included the amount of building stone needed before the intervention of the artist.

By such accidents of research, the fruits of private architectural work emerge gradually from anonymity. In one district and another the buildings of one particular architect or the mannerisms of the same craftsman are seen to correspond. Although destruction prevents us from identifying many of the creations of these forgotten designers, distinct personalities take shape and are presented here for the first time.

In recent years art history has become a matter of international synthesis. We have seen the old chronological classifications broken and the chauvinistic postures which once obsessed historians disappear. For many, the terms 'classical', 'baroque', 'romantic', no longer indicate periods, but particular attitudes more or less coexistent at all times. As for the stylistic labels – Louis XIV, Louis XV and Louis XVI – it has long been recognised that they do not correspond to the duration of these reigns. The coming of the Louis XV style was perceptible about 1690, that is to say not long after the zenith of Louis XIV's sovereignty. It flourished around 1730 and declined after the middle of the century. Drawing its inspiration from nature, this style is – with Gothic – the most original in French art. But where did it come from? Its very originality poses a much debated aesthetic problem. Is it simply a province of rococo, or alien to it? Was rococo itself born in the salons of Versailles, in Piedmont, or elsewhere? Is it really a mutation of baroque? Did it wither exhausted by its final flowering or thwarted by the archaeological reaction and the rationalism of the 'philosophes'? To these problems, a limited investigation, like the one undertaken here, may supply the rudiments of an answer, but no solutions.

The period of the Seven Years' War marks the great division of the century. Architectural activity ceased, while the theorists kept their counsel and artists prolonged their sabbaticals in Italy, where archaeology was uncovering new aspects of Antiquity. The architecture which followed the peace of 1763 was inspired by a desire for grandeur and the return to the Graeco-Roman tradition, honoured in Louis XIV's reign. Louis XV lived another eleven years and saw the birth of an art designated by posterity with his successor's name. But the social conditions which enabled the Louis XV style to thrive remained the same until the Revolution. The floral inspiration of the decoration, the sense of theatre in the setting, optical illusions and tricks with mirrors lingered for a long time, and the many survivals of this convention have provided a justification for certain German-speaking historians to embrace almost the entire century with the term 'rococo'. The indolent teacher is thus disappointed to find that movements do not succeed each other, but proceed simultaneously. If the dates 1715 and 1792 may be chosen as points of beginning and ending, no chronological division can be considered absolute. The analysis of any phase in history entails as much returning to the past as venturing into the future.

1 *Paris in the 18th Century*

As Louis XIV's reign drew near to its close, the nobility, gathered by royal command at the court, abandoned the corridors of Versailles for town-houses in Paris. Their return gave a strong impetus to private architecture, and the Faubourg Saint-Germain soon rivalled in luxury the Quartier Richelieu, the home of finance. In 1715 the Regent installed the seat of government in the Palais-Royal. The pleasures of fashionable life, the intellectual vitality and the art trade made Paris one of the most frequented cities in Europe. The conurbation continued to spread, and the absolute monarchy failed to impose a limit to the process. The declaration of July 1724 had defined a perimeter, beyond which building was forbidden. The decision was justified on the grounds that the expansion of the town caused rises in food prices and excessive consumption of material. The old houses were forsaken for apartments on the outskirts. The long distances hampered the course of business and the task of the police. The plan then drawn up bore the device 'Nec plus ultra', but soon appeared inapplicable. The financiers of the Faubourg Saint-Honoré, and then the guildsmen of the Bièvre, obtained exemptions, all the more willingly granted because they enriched the Treasury. From this time no government measure has been able to check a movement, which today poses almost insoluble administrative problems.

The appearance of Paris

The three-quarters of a century from 1715 to the Revolution transformed the face of Paris. Contemporary artists have recorded various, but always limited, aspects of the town. The monuments, the gardens and the banks of the Seine inspired Rigaud's engravings, and the paintings of De Machy, Noël and Raguenet, but these minor artists' names are little known. No artist of high talent tackled the Paris panorama as a whole. Were Montmartre and Chaillot too distant as vantage-points to afford an accurate impression? The Venetian masters of townscape, Antonio Canale and Bernardo Bellotto, travelled through Europe in the middle of the century, depicting the monuments and skies of Venice and Vienna, Dresden and Warsaw, St Petersburg and London, with a nice combination of exaggeration and exactitude. Thus 'Europe of the Capitals' acknowledged her painters, but Paris did not invite them.

We may therefore applaud the initiative of the Prévôt des Marchands Turgot, father of the great minister, who had a plan of the city engraved, more instructive and curious than genuinely artistic. A bird's-eye view, drawn by the architect Bretez in 1734, it gives a fairly good idea of the appearance of the Paris bequeathed by the great urbanists of Louis XIV. Like the topographers of the past, Bretez put his foreground in the north-west, near the present Boulevard Malesherbes, to show the portals of churches liturgically turned towards the setting sun. The architect-perspectivist had received official permission to enter private properties, and one of the attractions of his plan lies in the illusion which it conveys of penetrating the secluded gardens of religious communities and of noblemen's hôtels. The plantations laid out in quincunxes, the formal bedding, palmettes and arabesques of French gardens imprint their elegant pattern between the flowing lines dividing the plots of ground. We can thus appreciate the extent of the green spaces, which freshened the Paris atmosphere. The author's concern for clarity excuses a few liberties taken with the classic rules of perspective. The scale is always the same, whatever the distance between objects on the plan. To show the height of façades, Bretez arbitrarily widened the streets of the central areas, which none the less struck foreign visitors by their narrowness and congestion.

After Louis XIV's death official architecture suffered an eclipse and Paris witnessed the construction of no major public buildings. The Louvre still lay engulfed in its decrepit surroundings, but the avenue opened by Le Nôtre through the groves of the Champs-Elysées improved the view from the Tuileries. On the periphery were deployed the great foundations of the last century: the Jardin des Plantes, the Salpétrière, the Gobelins, the Observatory and the Invalides; but the scheme for the boulevards of the south of Paris, planned to link them together, was not to be completed under the Ancien Régime. On the north side, flat and planted with trees, the walls of the city of Charles V were pierced by the gates of Saint-Antoine, Saint-Martin and Saint-Denis, triumphal arches dedicated to Louis XIV's victories. In the verses of the *Pauvre Diable*, Voltaire names the contractor Outrequin as responsible for maintaining the highway and plantations of these *grands boulevards*.

Public buildings under Louis XV

In the course of the century the problems entailed in the health and agreeable development of the city became matters of public concern, on which the opinions of the Abbé Lubersac, Voltaire, the Père Laugier and Blondel were to be heard. The architects Delamair and Moreau-Desproux submitted general plans. The construction of public buildings was to provide opportunities for creating pleasing prospects and improving the adjacent areas. In a celebrated pamphlet, *L'ombre du grand Colbert*, La Fond de Saint-Yenne deplored the abandonment of the Louvre and the wretchedness of its surroundings.

After the Peace of Aix-la-Chapelle, for the last time in the history of the old monarchy, Louis XV launched a great architectural campaign. Several provincial towns devoted public 'squares' to the glory of the sovereign. These included Rennes, Rouen, Reims and Bordeaux, while in Paris the project was elaborated, which was to give birth to the Place de la Concorde. A first competition was concerned with the choice of a site. The architect Soufflot proposed to link the Cité and the Ile Saint-Louis by solid ground, upon which the new *place* would be built. Boffrand, anticipating certain ideas of our own day, wanted to establish a vast esplanade in the locality of the Halles. Another planner

2

advocated a circus of converging roads at the Carrefour Buci. The multiplicity of these proposals, all of them interesting, embarrassed the Prévôté des Marchands, who referred the problem to the King's scrutiny. Each of the schemes benefited a populous area, but entailed great expense. Louis XV evaded the difficulty by offering the city a site on his own property, between the Champs-Elysées and the Tuileries.

In 1753 the members of the Academy of Architecture were invited to submit designs for a formal 'square' for erection on this site, but the mediocrity of the results merely indicated the end of an aesthetic era and the sterility of a particular school. None of the projects was retained, and the King commissioned Gabriel to prepare another incorporating, if possible, the more felicitous ideas of his colleagues. In practice, the two palaces bordering the *place* borrow the proportions of their upper storeys and Corinthian galleries from the colonnade of the Louvre, of which Claude Perrault is the supposed author. After the Places des Vosges, Vendôme and des Victoires, this was the last of the great Parisian set-pieces conceived as a frame for a statue of the monarch. At a time when a taste for natural beauty was beginning to spread, the architect avoided the masking of the Seine landscape by buildings. Ditches, now filled in, sufficed to define the esplanade. Bisecting the palaces, the Rue Royale led to the new church of the Madeleine, under construction to Contant d'Ivry's designs. This was one of the operations which committed the western districts of Paris to a future

1 Pierre de Vigny: Hôtel de Chenizot, 51 Rue Saint-Louis-en-l'Ile, 1726

of wealth and elegance. The opening of the Carré Marigny extended the views from the garden of the Elysée, at the period when Madame de Pompadour sometimes resided there. Adopting an idea of Mme de Châteauroux, she encouraged the building of the Ecole Militaire, in order to unite the old nobility to the crown when the loyalty of other classes was flagging. Although the chapel of the Ecole Militaire testifies to Gabriel's ability, his name was not associated with any major religious building. The influential circle of Madame de Pompadour put forward a rival in Soufflot, and Gabriel expressed his resentment when the newcomer, a man of genius, but 'very circumspect in his behaviour', received the commission to design the great church offered by Louis XV to the canons of Sainte-Geneviève.

In the building of Greek-cross plan, Soufflot dreamed of reconciling the majesty of Roman architecture and the lightness of gothic. Successive schemes show that he first intended a fairly low dome before imparting its soaring height. Thanks to him Sainte-Geneviève had been given a church worthy of her long protection of Parisians, although later obliged to pardon the Constituants for assigning the building to the cult of France's great men.

Urban development after 1763

The privations imposed on France by the Seven Years War reduced activity on the royal building sites and discouraged private clients. The difficulties were aggravated after French defeats and few fine houses were built around 1760. The sack of Hanover, it is alleged, provided the Maréchal de Richelieu with the elegant pavilion which took the name of that province, but this was a brash exception. After 1763 the pace of building in Paris quickened, stimulated by commercial recovery, the enterprise of financing societies and, to some extent, government initiative.

In 1767 the Duc de Croÿ, making his way through the city in the company of Soufflot, remarked upon the scale of building work: 'It showed that there was money about and what peace could do. But Paris was perhaps better off than the rest of the kingdom.' In the plain of Gentilly, giant wheels were exhausting the limestone quarries; cranes bristled along the approaches to Sainte-Geneviève, in the district of the Madeleine and on the Seine-side wharfs, where Conflans stone was piled, on the very threshold of the Louvre, on the quays of Saint-Nicolas; slate and brick was unloaded on the Quai des Mira-moines, facing the chevet of Notre-Dame; and timber went ashore on the Ile Louviers, in front of the Arsenal. In the streets heavy wagons and stone-cutting operations obstructed movement.

About 1785 Sébastien Mercier expressed the view that a third of Paris had been rebuilt in thirty years:

> Huge blocks of dwellings rise from the ground as if by magic and new districts of the most magnificent houses take shape. The building mania gives an air of grandeur and majesty to the city.... The speculators cry out for the contractors who, with a plan in one hand and a contract in the other, bring balm to the hearts of the capitalists.

This activity transformed the inner districts of the city, and thrust them outward beyond the old boundaries. The overpopulated areas at the centre were insanitary. In the summer heat the drains and butchers' stalls diffused a noxious exhalation which infected food. The dead were still piled in charnel-houses in the very heart of the city of the living. In 1780 the ossuary of the Innocents burst its walls and overflowed into the cellars of adjacent houses. The well-to-do classes forsook such areas. The aristocracy abandoned the Saint-Antoine district, where under the Valois the presence of royalty had been a magnet, and the neighbourhood of the Louvre to which they had been attracted by the Bourbons. The old hôtels were now subdivided into modest dwellings. In 1750 the *beaux quartiers*, as they were called, were the Faubourg Saint-Germain, the resort of the nobility, and the Faubourg Saint-Honoré and the Richelieu quarter, favoured by finance. The Marais, where the great legal families lived until the Revolution, was considered unfashionable. 'I am not criticising anybody's tastes,' wrote a contemporary, 'but in this bailiwick there are some ghastly dowagers who have become congealed with the cushions of their armchairs and can no longer be detached.' Every increase in rents, like the one at the end of 1754, to which the Marquis d'Argenson drew attention, was first felt in the *beaux quartiers*, spreading thence to the Marais and the University quarter. Fashion, snobbery and the influx of provincials and foreigners contributed to this rise in prices which does not seem to have stopped under Louis XVI, in spite of the large number of new houses.

Public works cleansed and modernised the old Paris. The architect Moreau-Desproux, the last '*Maître des bâtiments de la Ville*', was an urbanist of precise views. In 1796 he submitted a scheme to the King, which provided for the construction of new quays on the left bank, the extension of the parvis of Notre Dame, the building of *places* in front of Saint-Eustache and the Palais-Royal, and the demolition of the houses lining the bridges and hiding the riverscape of the Seine. Many of these proposals were carried out. Paris was transformed under the combined control of the Maître des Bâtiments, the Lieutenant de Police and the Directeur des Bâtiments du Roi. The erection of a number of public buildings led to the building of groups of dwellings round them. The finance societies and their architects realised these schemes in accordance with official directives. The first of these benefited the district of the Halles. In 1763 a society convened by Oblin acquired land bordering the former Hôtel de Soissons. Built by Lecamus de Mézières, the circular structure of the Halle au Blé, which resulted, was surrounded by apartment buildings completed by six contractors in three years.

In 1770 Moreau submitted his design for the Place du Palais-Royal, which had hôtels built on its approaches. In 1781 the establishment of the Théâtre Italien in the old gardens of the Hôtel de Choiseul involved a major operation. Four projects were offered to the former minister and his adviser Laborde. The plan of the architect Louis-Denis Lecamus, which was preferred to those of his rivals, Jacquin, Cellerier and Lenoir, incorporated into his scheme the houses surrounding the theatre (later to become the Opéra-Comique). On the other bank, Peyre and de Wailly, architects of the Théâtre Français, disposed in front of the building a half-moon-shaped open space, and along the roads radiating from it rose handsome apartment housing, which sometimes suggests the influence of Ledoux. On the Place du Palais Bourbon, laid out by Bélisard, hôtels were built in which Palloy, who demolished the Bastille, seems to have had a hand. Desmaisons arranged a semicircular *place* in front of the Palais de Justice and entirely transformed the quarter.

Prosperous middle-class families came to live in these new houses, but the period also produced its inexpensive dwellings. In the Marais, the scheme realised by a certain Caron on the lands of the Prieuré Sainte-Catherine still shelters people of modest means in somewhat cramped accommodation. Some people seem to have deplored the disappearance of the old homes demolished to make way for the new; but, Métra tells us, 'sensible people replied that, since the mania for building had so vastly extended the frontiers of this monstrous town, it was right to clear out the accumulation at the centre'.

· The more elegant residences were to be found in the continuously expanding outskirts. Financiers, noblemen, fashionable artists and theatrical stars responded to the lure of the countryside which, on the north side, reached to the *grands boulevards*, established upon the ramparts of Charles V. To the west, the urban aggregation of the Faubourg Saint-Honoré merged with the village of Le Roule during the reign of Louis XVI.

When Gabriel, architect of the two palaces of the Place Louis XV, had brought order to the Rue Bonne-Morue (Boissy d'Anglas) and laid out the Rues Royale and Saint-Florentin, business men like Le Tellier and Vavasseur-Despérières built large apartment blocks along them.

Development of the Champs-Elysées

The development of the Champs-Elysées led to the appearance of fine houses to the north of the present gardens and along the perimeter of the Grand Cours. The Pavillon de Langeac and the Hôtel de la Reynière have disappeared, but the Hôtel de Montsauge has been more fortunate. It was moved in 1930 to the Faubourg Saint-Jacques, where it accommodates the meetings of the Société des Gens de Lettres. At 38 Avenue Gabriel, nineteenth century flats obscure the Pavillon d'Argenson, the last of the old houses to survive hereabouts. To extend the view from the Elysée, her Paris residence, Madame de Pompadour opened up the Carré Marigny, where there was a group of restaurants and pleasure gardens. Not far from here Jean-Jacques Rousseau planned the first Café des Ambassadeurs, and the Restaurant Ledoyen appeared in Louis XVI's time. Close to the Elysée, Boullée built a hôtel for Madame de Brunoy in the form of a temple dedicated to Flora (Pl. 138). During the Consulate, the architect's biographer wrote: 'Which of us has passed through the Champs-Elysées without feeling a kind of sensuous delight in the enchanting abodes which adorn them?'

Near the latter-day Rue La Boétie, The Comte d'Artois, Louis XVI's brother, tried to split up the former royal nursery plantation into building plots. The new monastery of the Capucins d'Antin gave birth to the present Rue Joubert and the district around it. In dividing up these sites, which he had acquired from a M. Sainte-Croix, Louis XVI exempted the tenants from billeting the Gardes-françaises and from building taxes. The Rue Caumartin and its neighbourhood were built by the speculator Sandrier, and the architects Hébert and Aubert, on land leased from the Mathurins. The hôtels of the Rue Basse-du-Rempart, on the site of the Opéra, rivalled in luxury those of the Chaussée d'Antin, built to the plans of Cellerier, Brongniart and Boullée. Towards the Rue de Provence, the area called La Planchette was developed by the banker Laborde, in association with the architects Bélanger, Perlin and Ledoux. In the same district the gastronome La

Reynière and the financier Bouret de Vézelay were aided in their speculations by a young lawyer, who was to become miserably notorious in 1793, Fouquier-Tinville.

Along the road to Clichy, the financiers Boutin, La Boissière and Meulan set their homes in the midst of landscaped gardens, which the Duc de Chartres, heir to the House of Orléans, was soon to copy in his *folie* of Monceau, while some highly unusual 'pavilions' were scattered about the foot of Montmartre, set against a background of windmills and quarries, which the romantic painter Georges Michel exploited in his landscapes. At the Nouvelle-France (today Faubourg Poissonnière) a certain Benoist de Sainte-Paule and the architect Goupy developed the former nursery gardens of the Filles-Dieu. Further to the east, when the Comte d'Artois, Grand Prior of Malta, had disposed of most of the precinct of the Temple, large apartment

2 Three houses in the Rue Montorgueil:
No. 15 – Martin Goupy: Robillard house, 1729
No. 17 – Martin Goupy: Chenot house, 1730
No. 19 – Treffeuille: Gobin house, 1776

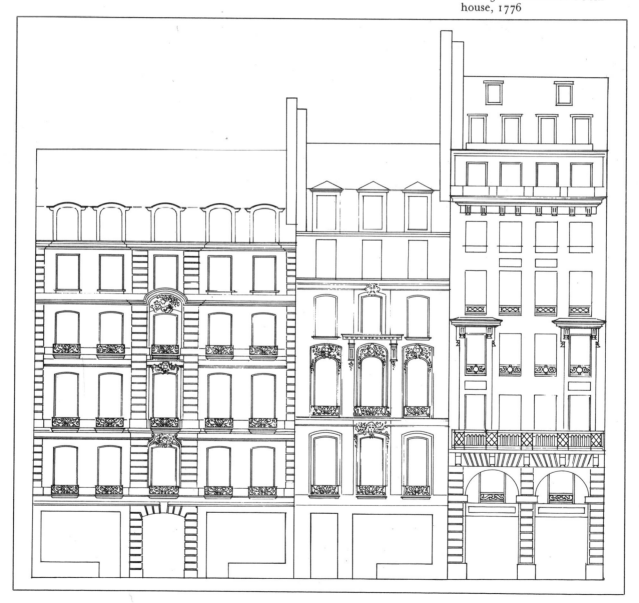

houses lined the Rues de Bretagne, de Crussol and des Fossés, extending the Faubourg du Temple and bringing a new youthfulness to the historic heart of the Marais.

Hôtels appeared on the boulevard from the Madeleine to the Porte Saint-Antoine. The more monumental façades which, in the hôtels of the past, were only displayed to those in the private garden, now faced the avenue, exposed to the admiration or censure of passers-by. Chéradame succeeded Outrequin, as the contractor responsible for planting along the boulevard. Here and there stood an Oriental pavilion by a terraced garden. Art and luxury conspired to beautify this long avenue, fashionable at the Madeleine end, plebeian at the Porte du Temple. Hôtels, theatres, *cafés turcs*, *jeux de paume* and Chinese bathing establishments lay cheek by jowl. Carriages swept by at full gallop, only slackening their speed at theatre time. None the less, this was one of the most frequented places in Europe and a principal sight for foreigners. Kings would have renounced their capitals to live there. Gustavus III of Sweden sent for the plans of a hôtel which he wanted to acquire.

On the left bank, the development of the southern boulevards was completed about 1760, the district remaining quiet and little visited. A few *folies* appeared between the Rue Notre-Dame-des-Champs and the Boulevard du Montparnasse. Between the esplanade of the Invalides and the Champ de Mars, the development of the Gros-Caillou quarter involved the creation of a new parish. In 1785 it was decided to restore the octroi-wall around Paris. The architect Ledoux proposed to house the offices of this organisation in some sixty buildings which were, to use his expression, the Propylaea of Paris. Only four of these toll-gates remain, but this ring marked a new stage in the city's development and determined the course of the boulevards which now pass through the Villette, the Place de la Nation, the Place Denfert-Rochereau and the Etoile.

2 Building

Regulated by royal and municipal authority, the real-estate boom relied for the most part on the wealth and initiative of private people.

The influx of provincials, the long prosperity of bankers, backed by the establishment of Swiss companies in Paris, and the guarantees granted by Louis XV's government on building loans were the driving forces behind an architectural vitality which did not falter for almost a century. Two difficult periods for the French economy, the liquidation of the Law system and the Seven Years War passed almost unnoticed. In the other direction, Philibert Orry's sound financial management in the 1740s seems to have strengthened the confidence of capitalists. During the brief ministry of Turgot in 1775 the number of building projects undertaken reveals the most sanguine hopes among the enlightened and privileged for the capabilities of the young Louis XVI and his enterprising minister. After 1776 the boom resisted the short recession caused by the great economist's disgrace and the 'guerre des farines'. Neckèr's expedients and his appeal for foreign capital, while fixing the date of the monarchy's bankruptcy, were to allow another decade of commercial prosperity and artistic brilliance. Meanwhile the building industry rode on the crest of the wave. Certain passages devoted by Sébastien Mercier to the Paris of Louis XVI evoke in another century those pages from César Birotteau and La Curée, in which Balzac and Zola depicted the property speculations of their day.

Making our way through eighteenth-century Paris, we have met a few business men for whom the expansion of the city meant fat profits. In earlier years, men like Payen, Charlot, Barbier and Villedo had been engaged in such activities, similar to those of our property developers. The religious communities, watching the mounting costs of their vast horticultural estates, were glad enough to part with them as building sites. Long leases assured them a modest rent and, after ninety-nine years, the ownership of the tenement houses built on their lands. An engraved prospectus acquainted the public with the development plan and the address of the architect or notary to whom application for lots could be made. Letters patent signed in the King's council authorised the opening of roads and decided their width.

9

Finance

At a time when the construction of an apartment house was not beyond the means of the private individual, the financial conditions were much the same as those which prevailed until the First World War. For a shopkeeper of the Rue Saint-Martin, the rebuilding of his paternal home was a profitable investment of savings from a lifetime of work and hardship. For a contractor, an architect or a group of financial backers, a new road or the building of a new quarter was often a most advantageous speculation. The case of the nobility was different. For a gentleman, to build a hôtel was first and foremost to fulfil the duties of his rank. He would set aside for his Paris residence part of the income from his estate. For his house in the Rue Pagevin, the Comte de Choiseul sold a wood at a place called Le Buisson, and the La Grange family felled a section of forest to pay for their house in the Rue de Braque. A business man's loan to a gentleman would be secured by the revenue from his property in the country. It is common to find on the same building contract the names of a Parisian contractor and of a farmer who would pay him certain instalments at the end of the agricultural year. But the unforeseen often occurs. Harvests were unpredictable and payments were spread over ten or twenty years, even when the amount of the payments was not arbitrarily reduced by the architects' auditors or the estate's agents. In the course of his long career, the Maréchal-Duc de Richelieu strained the patience of his creditors in his many undertakings. The widow of the Chevalier Servandoni had difficulty in obtaining the settlement due to her husband for the ice-house and temple of Gennevilliers, built twelve years before. During the Seven Years War the Maréchal had another pavilion built and the public accused him of pillaging Hanover to pay for his wild spending. He tried to justify himself to his intimates, but his sole excuse was that he had listened too much to his architect: 'Were those hundred thousand écus which Carpentier* cost me so far beyond my means to justify malicious gossip?'

Under Louis XVI major architectural programmes were completed with bank loans. When the Duc de Chartres, Philippe-Egalité, decided to build the shopping galleries bordering the garden of the Palais-Royal, Giambone and Co., the powerful representatives of the Bank of Genoa in Paris, obtained for him an initial loan of a million. Kornmann of Strasbourg and Bontemps and Mallet of Geneva procured the rest. The revenues of the House of Orléans and the sale to the Queen of the Château of Saint-Cloud enabled Philippe-Egalité to honour his commitments. The operation enriched Swiss capitalists and left the prince on the verge of ruin.

The Marquis d'Orrouer, the Comte de Gouffier and the master-ciseleur Gouthière ruined themselves by their building enterprises. The goods of the financier Bouret were seized in Paris on the very day that he offered a peach to Louis XV in his pavilion of Croix-Fontaine. The Prince de Salm inaugurated his palace (Pls. 153–6) with a grand ball, at which he knew barely half the guests. The next day he declared himself bankrupt and, to cancel his debt, was on the point of marrying off his nephew to the daughter of the contractor Thévenin. Tradition sanctioned the preferential rights of lessors, contractors and architects over the properties which they had combined to build. Thus P. Rousseau,

* A slip by the narrator for Chevotet.

the Prince de Salm's architect, if he did not actually take possession of the palace, as legend alleges, appropriated the dependent buildings. A judgement of 1766 recognised the ancient custom by ensuring the state's guarantee to privileged creditors. This wise decision revived building activity and made its benefits felt up to the eve of the Revolution.

Building regulations

The powers, often competitive, of the royal administration and the City Office, subjected urban construction to rigorous controls. The general regulations governing frontage lines, formulated by the Grands Voyers (Surveyors) of the Généralité de Paris (City Treasury), were transmitted to the Inspector-General of the roads of Paris and the suburbs. Any person preparing to build along the public highway applied for a private building line. The placing of scaffolding and shores entailed a tax payable to the royal treasurers. There were also liabilities on the

3 Pierre de Vigny: Entrance to the Cour du Dragon, 50 Rue de Rennes (demolished about 1950), 1732

11

projecting parts of buildings and arched canopies. After 1744 all window-sills were taxed. The tax on doors and windows, which only disappeared in 1920, seems to have originated from fiscal burdens imposed by the War of the Austrian Succession, on the eve of Fontenoy. The construction of balconies was the occasion for an inquiry 'de commodo et incommodo' conducted by the Commissaire Voyer (Surveyor-Commissioner) of the city, who invited the views of neighbours and specified the positioning of consoles 'properly anchored to the wall face for their own security and the public safety'. An ancient prerogative entitled the court of the Châtelet to verify the siting of corner-houses determining the alignment of streets and to fix the extent of the wall surfaces cut off. When the Cotelle house (Pl. 55 and Fig. 10, p. 42) was built at 52 Rue Saint-André-des-Arts, the contractor Martin Lepas was forced to demolish walls already completed, to provide a deeper set-back for the rotunda.

The Chambre des Bâtiments (Chamber of Buildings), which sat successively in the Rue Bardubec and Rue de la Verrerie before its establishment at the Palais, exercised an active control over Parisian building sites. Periodic visits used to disclose infractions of Parisian customary laws or faulty workmanship which might result in accidents. A strict rule required the reinforcement of the heads of party walls at their junction with the street façade. This thickening, called *jambe étrière*, can still be seen in entrance passages and front shops of old buildings. The projecting stones of entablatures, which often fell out and caused fatal injuries, had to be secured by iron cramps. It was forbidden to extend cellars beneath the public way. A regulation of 1667 prohibited gables on the street side and limited the height of façades to eight *toises* (a little less than sixteen metres), whatever the width of the road. It remained in force until 1783. Payment of a tax, however, permitted building above this height with a timber frame and rubble infill, an advantageous concession for the revenue, but one which multiplied certain abuses of Louis XVI's day deplored by Sébastien Mercier:

> A limit had to be set to the excessive height of Paris houses, for some individuals had in practice built one house on top of another. The height is restricted to seventy feet, excluding the roof. Unfortunately people in some districts have neither air nor sunlight. Some are ill from having to scale daily stairs as long as Jacob's ladder. The poor who live in such places for economy's sake pay more dearly for the delivery of wood and water, while others must light candles at noon to prepare their meals. This prodigious height contrasts oddly with the paralysis of our streets. . . .

None the less it was advisable not to load the ground beyond certain limits, for subsoil resistance varied according to the district. In the Chaussée d'Antin quarter, the water-table, which was later to cause much concern to the architect of the Opéra, obliged Nicolas Ledoux to build the Hôtel Thélusson (Pls. 159–63) on a raft, i.e. a slab carried on piles and cross-members, as found under Amiens cathedral, and the Rialto bridge and the church of La Salute in Venice. Along the *grands boulevards* on the east side, the defensive embankment established by Etienne Marcel was subsiding imperceptibly beneath buildings with faulty foundations. The quarries of Montrouge and Gentilly, exploited since the Middle Ages, extended their galleries under a considerable part of the left bank. At mid-century several houses in the Faubourg Saint-

Jacques foundered, and this greatly disturbed Parisians and persuaded the royal government to create an inspectorate of quarries.

Contracts and valuations

Depending on the particular case, contractors could enter into engagements with owners by three sorts of engagement. The *Devis et marché* vouched for by a notary, offered good guarantees to the contracting parties. It promised the client faithful execution of the specification and of the plans prepared by his architect. It ensured payment to the contractor on stipulated dates. The agreement by *seing privé*, if it entailed no registration fees, exposed the signatories to possible disputes. The third form was the *devis judiciaire*. This applied in every case in which the clients were not owners in the full legal sense: minors under guardianship, joint heirs and purchasers, or commendatory abbots managing the properties of their abbey. Two appraisers or 'experts' and a clerk of the works from the Chambre des Bâtiments calculated the costs and quantities and returned to the site on completion of the work.

The big speculations of Louis XVI's reign made general a procedure which ensured a legal guarantee to the lessors; the deposition with

4 Hôtel de Luteaux, 27 Rue Lhomond, 1736

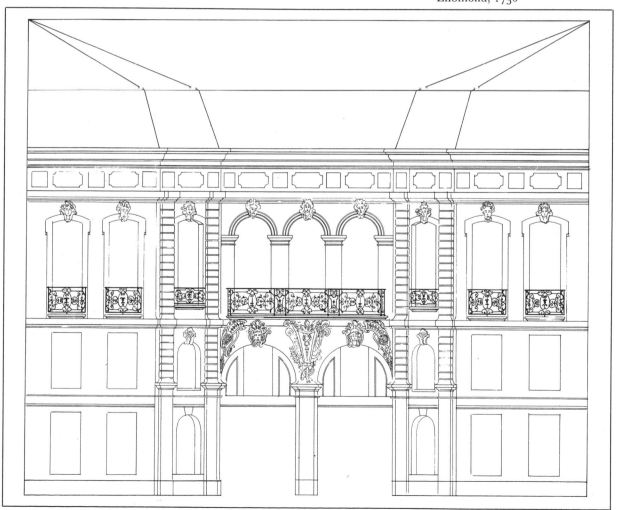

the Chambre des Bâtiments of the project drawn up by an architect of the client's choice; the estimate of costs and quantities; and due acceptance on completion by the officers of the Chambre. This system of registration has preserved for us many schemes, some of buildings now disappeared. Until the simplification of French law brought about by the Revolution and the Empire, our ancestors remained as litigious as Racine and Boileau made them out to be. All litigation to which property ownership might be prone was settled by the Parlement through the 'experts' of the Chambre, builders turned lawyers, whose office was venal and susceptible to manipulation. The assessment of rents and legacies, the valuation of rentable assets and visits to 'contentious places' were there commonest jobs. If, at a conference of two 'experts', one was challenged by his colleague, the name of a third would be drawn 'from a hat' among senior members of the Chambre. If the problem involved the examination of a chimney flue, the 'experts' would send up a sweep's boy and record his statements.

Joint occupation of buildings obliged the owner to use an 'expert', when walls were rebuilt, for agreements were needed to fix the share of each party. Often, moreover, the client's expert was none other than his architect. Meetings were held with representatives of adjacent properties. Documents establishing very ancient rights would then be produced, and a clerk would draft and deposit with the Chambre des Bâtiments the minutes of such meetings.

Besides these commonplace tasks, their wide competence sometimes required the 'experts' to pronounce upon objects of artistic consequence. We find them estimating for the ladders ordered by the Abbé Bignon from one of the Boulle family for the King's library, the draft by Bretez for the plan de Turgot, some ottomans by Delanois, Boullée's decorative schemes for the Elysée and the pulpit of Saint-Sulpice designed by de Wailly. The 120,000 documents which they have left us throw an interesting light on the architectural history of Paris. Well-known architects like Boffrand, Antoine and Desmaisons performed the duties of 'experts' until admitted into the first class of the Royal Academy. Others like Payen and the Goupy family left reputations as jurists. Nevertheless, Sébastien Mercier, a morose observer of Louis XVI's Paris, did not spare these men 'with their devious processes'.

Role of the contractors

The term *entrepreneur* embraced men of widely differing quality. Most were business men, but knowledge and skill raised some of them to the level of artists, and the names of these deserve to survive. The exacting tests guarding entry to the mastership of the craft preserved the secrets of stone-cutting among the masons. So long as descriptive geometry was confined to scholars – for Monge had many precursors in this field, from Pierro della Francesca to Tschirnhausen – the science of vaults, pendentives, volutes, voussoirs, etc., in short everything implied by the Greek term of stereotomy, remained empirical.

Under Louis XV, the audacity of several architects, imbued with baroque sympathies, inspired staircases suspended on cloister vaults or rampant arches, like that of the Hôtel Matignon, executed by the master-mason Pierre Lafon. Blondel described as startling the effect of this mass of stone overhanging a void. Main parts of buildings were floated on squinches. The corbelling of the Hôtel de Jaucourt, 2 Rue de la

Vrillière, was designed by the young architect Desmaisons and became the masterpiece of the mason Pierre-Jean Varin (Pl. 43). On the other hand the Regent's architect, Gilles Oppenord, was more brilliant as a decorator than as a structural expert. Not knowing how to build a squinch, he carried the *grand salon*, constructed over an angle of the Palais-Royal, on fragile consoles which caused biting comment. However, we find the contractor Morin and his foreman-mason paying several visits to the office of the architect Vautrain to resolve the problem posed by a projecting element and balcony of the Hôtel du Tillet. The entablature installed by Matias Pasquier on the portal of Saint-Eustache still carries its load, defying the theories of Legrand, who forecast its collapse. The foreman-mason Bénard was a valued ally of Servandoni and Gabriel.

The Brunet family were esteemed in Louis XVI's time for the care evidenced in the execution of Saint-Philippe du Roule and the Cour du Mai frontage of the Palais de Justice. If Nantes and Nancy possessed splendid ironworkers, the balustrades of Parisian staircases do as much honour to the master-smiths who forged them as to the decorators and architects who designed them. The name of Corbin is connected with the staircase banisters of the Palais-Royal (Pl. 99), while those of the Ecole Militaire are so sumptuous that the bill for 17,000 livres presented by the master-smith Fayet raised a storm in the school's council. Viennot, Brochois and Daguinot forged some of the finest rococo balconies in Paris. The Louis XV screen of the Palais de Justice is a luxuriant work by Bigonnet.

In the eighteenth century the arts of building did not undergo any great technical changes, like the ogival system in the Middle Ages, or prefabrication, lift-slab construction or mobile shuttering in our own day. But the use of prefabricated elements, especially in decoration, was no novelty to eighteenth-century architectural practice. A Venetian observer reported that in 1760 a palace façade was for sale in separate units at a marbler's in the city. We also find mass-moulded decorative panels being used in Paris. The stucco-workers who, like D'Hollande or Goutheinze, made this their speciality, were protected from imitations by royal privilege or patent. Another factor making for uniformity, the simplified masses which, after 1750, marked the transition from rococo to neo-classicism may have led to a decline in the art of stone-dressing, until that time so skilled, but the period also had its great constructors. The engineer Perronet boldly depressed the arches of his bridges, and Rondelet, Soufflot's collaborator, used an iron-strengthened rubble infill foreshadowing reinforced concrete. The use of metal was increasing. Certain schemes disclose iron braces hidden in the bracket supports of balconies and the cavities below floors.

About 1780 the high price of structural timber, and the attention paid by architects to Renaissance buildings, revived certain systems of carpentry combining strength and lightness with economy in wood. The dome of the Halle au Blé was executed by the employees of Roubo fils and Albouy in remarkably safe conditions, despite the absence of scaffolding and modest price. For the Opéra at Versailles, Abraham Guerne created one of the most admired roof-trusses of the eighteenth century. It goes without saying that, before being applied to royal buildings, technical improvements were first tested on private jobs. Pierre Damun, the City Architect, tried out a fireproof roof on a house in the Poissonnière district. Raymond, son of a Toulouse carpenter, exploited a method of his own invention in the hôtel of Madame Vigée

Lebrun: 'The trusses constructed there by this architect . . . to roof a picture gallery . . . would be worth looking at, were they exposed.'

Labour

In Louis XVI's reign the big contractors became gentlemen of consequence, who speculated in the newly developing areas, held a share of the real estate capital, and came by carriage 'to review their plastery regiments'. The building labourers came from the Marche and the Limousin, and we may surmise that their existence was already what Martin Nadeau described in the 1830s, in the early days of the social movement. They lodged together in garrets, and each winter took their scanty savings home. The monetary value of certain materials tempted these poor men; and the roofers, especially, used to steal lead. To do this, they worked in pairs. One of the accomplices would drop it from the roof into the court of an adjacent house, where the other gathered it up, safe from the eyes of the foreman. The dealer in stolen lead was one of the petty traders who enlivened the contemporary street scene.

Names and surnames of workmen appear in the archives of the Maison du Roi on the ceremonial occasions, when His Majesty 'stood treat'. When Louis XV laid the first stone of Sainte-Geneviève, a bonus was distributed according to each man's qualifications. The foreman-mason received more than the cementer, and the cementer more than the labourer. When a private house was finished, the traditional bouquet offered by the workmen was a calculated compliment to a generous client.

Obstructed streets and accidents

If a Juvenal or a Boileau reappeared among us, they would find plenty to say about the tribulations of city life in our time; but Parisians of the eighteenth century lived amid the din of building operations and streets obstructed by the transport of materials. Saint-Aubin's sketches and De Machy's paintings have recorded the brisk world of the building sites. At the Salon, Diderot stopped in front of one of these pictures which, he tells us, might have been thrown on to a screen by a magic lantern to amuse children: 'Scaffolding, cranes, turmoil.' In those days there was no pavement and materials were heaped in the roadway. During the construction of the Hôtel de la Grange, Rue de Braque, an account refers to the obstruction of adjoining streets caused by the cutting and trimming of building stone. Constant difficulties arose between the contractors and the local commissioners responsible for public order. The architect Franque wrote to the Comte de Crillon:

> During the last few days I have received the letter which you did me the honour of writing to me about your building. I go there every day and do all I can to see that it progresses. What holds us back is the refusal to allow us to put stone in the Rue de la Potterie. I have been several times to Commissioner Moricot, but without obtaining his permission. I was with him yesterday on my way from the building, and after telling him that if he did not want to allow me, I should go and ask the Lieutenant de Police, he gave in. . . .

An accounts item appearing in the papers of the same job reveals that accidents had happened to workmen during building works: 'Additional expense, gratuities from M. le Comte to compensate workers injured during the construction of the house. . . .' The figure has been left blank. The victims and their families were not assisted by the state, but by charitable institutions and private generosity. In 1721 a gallery and half a pavilion of the Hôtel Crozat, Rue de Richelieu, collapsed. The contractor François Roquet had made a wall only nine inches thick instead of the specified thirty. Pierre Crozat had to provide pensions for the victims and widows. The financier behaved generously. In the past Colbert had operated a form of paternal compensation for the loss of men's lives on the royal building sites.

3 Architects

For two centuries architecture had assumed the character of a liberal profession, and a legal and social distinction had been established between the architect and the contractor. During the Renaissance, rendered illustrious by men like Philibert Delorme and Pierre Lescot, the artistic activities of builders had evaded the hierarchical system of the craft guilds. The De Brosse, Lemuet and Le Vau clans had brought glory to their profession; but, as in the past, many contractors drew their own designs and several reputable architects did not disdain the contractor's role. Many people therefore confused, or pretended to confuse, the status of the two. Thus, the Premier Président (of the Parlement) Harlay had insolently replied to Jules Hardouin-Mansart, who had solicited the office of 'Président à Mortier' for one of his colleagues: 'Sir, do not mix your mortar (mortier) with ours. . . .'

Role and remuneration of architects

A phenomenon of humanism and Italian court life, the architect had at first been the friend of princes, rewarded by gifts or the benefices of abbeys. In the seventeenth century the gentry had generally adopted him, but the middle-class merchant, more reactionary in outlook, still entrusted the job of designing and building his house to a mason, assisted by Savot's manual and Lemuet's engravings. In the early eighteenth century, when the merchant class resorted to the services of the architect, it did so as much to ape the nobility as to protect its purse from the trickery with which it was all too familiar.

The liberal practice of architecture did not conflict with speculation in building sites. At the beginning of the century, Hardouin-Mansart, Boffrand and Gabriel had grown rich from the development of the Place Vendôme and the Faubourg Saint-Germain. After 1770, Brongniart conducted operations of this kind round the Invalides and in the Chaussée d'Antin. A tacit understanding linked architects and speculators, who divided up plots surrendered for trivial sums by impoverished communities. When a merchant sold a building lot, he also foisted his architect on the purchaser. Behind Bélanger, Cellerier and Ledoux were men of means, some of whom we have met: Sandrier, Machet de Vélye, Laborde and Benoist de Sainte-Paule. Lenoir, the range of whose business was considerable, was backed by his father-in-law Riboutté, director of an insurance company, the Royale Incendies, and by the banker Kornmann, whose private life was attacked by Beaumarchais.

18

Often the architect himself sold the ground on condition that it was built upon. If he had capital, he put up hôtels at his own expense in expectation of handing them over to the newly rich, who had only to add their coat of arms. The forms of property investment vary with the period and the structure of society. In the eighteenth century, capitalists and monastic communities were the 'bare owners' of hôtels, in which the life interest had been allocated to noblemen already specified before construction began. In such cases the architect's role was to reconcile the wishes of the contracting parties. In 1713, Jacques Lepas-Dubuisson built for the Seminary of Foreign Missions the two hôtels situated at 118 and 120 Rue du Bac, taking scrupulous care of his clients' interests, visiting the quarries of Saint-Leu, and the woods which provided the structural timber. Lepas showed an equal concern for the future occupant of the two houses, the Abbé Colbert de Seignelay, calculating the extent of his library – the Colbert family were great bibliophiles – in order to provide the space and installations needed to accommodate it in his new home.

In 1778 the financier Laborde was 'bare owner' of a hôtel which the architect Perlin adapted to the requirements of its tenant, the Comte de Mercy-Argenteau, ambassador to the Empress of Austria. The record of a visit introduces us to a hôtel under construction at the corner of the Boulevard and the Chaussée d'Antin: 'Present was the said Sieur de Mézières [Lenormand de Mézières, 'bare owner'], accompanied by M. Ledoux, his architect, who also acts for Mgr le Prince and Madame la Princesse de Montmorency, with whom we conferred on many subjects relevant to the completion of the works. . . .' We may suppose that the new occupants were satisfied with the fine sculptured trophies (Pl. 168) which are today in Boston. We do not know if the statues of the Connétables de Montmorency were already in place along the cornice of the building. Carved at their feet was the inscription 'Hotel de Montmorency', but so high up that one needed 'a good telescope' to read it.

The architect and the client

The architect often assumed total responsibility for a building, from buying the site to the disposition of the furniture. He prepared a mass of drawings, especially for the decoration. Chevotet filled a portfolio with them for a house in the Rue Saint-Martin and Boullée made some 200 for rooms in the Elysée, when they were occupied by Beaujon. An expert's report speaks of the quantity of designs usually rejected by clients before their final choice.

The designs of this period were submitted on laid paper from Holland (e.g. Blauw and Zoonen). The architect used graphite fitted into a slender holder, a drawing-pen or a quill. Elevations and sections might be touched up with water-colour mixed from a palette containing smalt blue, green earth, yellow lake, gallstone, carmine and bistre. An exacting master, Le Geay, brought a new discipline to architectural draughtsmanship, and the designs of his pupils – Boullée, de Wailly, Moreau – are characterised as much by their accuracy as by elegance. To impress those unresponsive to the abstract nature of plans, the architect turned to mock-ups or models, which might be of limewood, service-tree or walnut, cardboard or Montmarte soapstone. Several craftsmen were famed for their skill in making these miniature structures: Lombard, Méreau, Pichon, Fouquet and François (known as Tourangeau).

Soufflot kept a model of Sainte-Geneviève on his bedroom chimney-piece. Ledoux, who took such care with his first commissions, presented to M. and Mme d'Hallwyl a model of their hôtel in the Rue Michel-Le Comte. Later, he made another of a circular house for M. de Witt, who refused to pay for it. Raymond had one made of the Cardinal de Brienne's apartments, while we still have the model of the Chinese pavilion of the Hôtel de Montmorency, Boulevard Montmartre. The theorist Blondel recommended the use of models, for 'nothing is better calculated to instruct minds not yet capable of visualizing'. The taste for models seems to have declined in the nineteenth century, while an improved technique in perspective enabled architects to foresee the visual effects of their constructions. Perhaps, like Fontaine, they thought that 'a model says too little to the professional and too much to the layman'.

At a time when tracing was rare and photo-copying unknown, draughtsmen had plenty to do. Not only had plans to be provided for the contractors and the notary, but also for a bureaucracy as demanding as our own. The Inspector-General of Roads, the Maître des Bâtiments of the City, the Office of the Grands Voyers, the Police Lieutenancy, the Chambre des Bâtiments, the Magistracy of Montmarte and still other authorities retained such documents in their archives. On a plan for apartments made in Lenoir's office, the following instruction to the draughtsman can be read: 'A similar copy required tomorrow at 11 a.m.'

The architect used to visit his clients, but the grander people would sometimes go to him to examine cumbersome models. Papillon de la Ferté, in his *Journal des Menus-Plaisirs*, reports that he went with the

5   Jacques-Richard Cochois and
    J.-B.-A. Beausire: Claude Aubry
    house, Rues Saint-Denis and
    Grenéta, 1732

Ducs de Duras and d'Aumont to the architect Damun. A few architects' houses can still be identified. At the north corner of the Rues Saint-Martin and de Venise stands the residence of François Debias-Aubry, a very active architect in Louis XV's reign. In the Rue Montorgueil, a carved sign announces the 'planning office' of the architect Trouard. Two partners, Legrand and Molinos, practised at No. 6 Rue Saint-Florentin, where their initials are stamped on two capitals of the façade. In the hall two pseudo-antique bas-reliefs proclaim the nature of the place. In the court are mouldings after Jean Goujon. As a contemporary, Le Camus de Mézières, noted, the architect had to be at once firm, courteous and conciliatory in dealing with the authorities, his clients and, especially, their neighbours, too often inconvenienced by the hubbub of site operations and the indifference of some contractors. The architect would go to the workshops of the carvers and metal-craftsmen to see that his designs for the staircases and wainscots were faithfully executed. If he was building in the outskirts of Paris or the country and did not want to leave the city, he sent a job-architect. For the Château de Champs, Bullet de Chamblain prepared many designs (which we still have), but was represented on the site by a colleague, the architect Sébastien Buirette, who spent three years in the village. 'He sends for materials, handles the worksheets, calculates quantities and keeps the papers in cardboard boxes.' At the other end of the century, Ledoux maintained one or two inspectors on the site of the Hôtel Thélusson:

> M. Trosson goes there every morning, works out material requirements with the quantity surveyor, is present at every weighing of iron and lead, keeping a private record of this, does not allow workmen to handle the 'broches' [iron cramps for reinforcing masonry] unless they understand their use. . . . He is the one who draws the details for the craftsmen to follow.

Such was the force of medieval tradition that legislation practically ignored the architect, unless he held the position of 'expert'. The contractor was alone responsible before contemporary law. The fairly rare disputes between clients and architects, which we know about, were settled empirically by the 'experts', but always to the advantage of the second. For a long time architects' fees were not fixed by a legally authorised scale. In 1685 Mme de Grignan consulted Libéral de Bruant, architect of the Salpêtrière and the Hôtel des Invalides, about modernising some fireplaces in her apartment of the Hôtel Carnavalet. She questioned her mother, who turned for advice to an uncle, the 'Bien Bon' Abbé de Coulanges: 'As for M. Bruan,' concluded Mme de Sévigné,' 'the Bien Bon says he is not the sort of man to take a pistole for a conference, and to give him two would be too much: one must find out from M. Le Cour, who has often consulted him and M. de la Trousse, who will not pay him until his building is finished.'

By about 1730, architects, like lawyers, were paid according to the number of their attendances. J.-B. Vautrain, architect of the Vatard house, Rue de Cléry (Pls. 59 and 60), after helping with the acquisition of the site, made 1,004 'attendances' in the course of managing the job, which suggests that he went (or was represented) there at least twice a day. 'He gave this house the taste and form which could be wished for, drew the details and full sizes, directed all the work of carving, joinery and gilding . . . particular care being devoted to the painting of the big first-floor drawing-room.' But the client wanted a noble establishment on too small a site. She deplored the restricted staircase and the exiguous court, in which carriages could hardly turn. Vautrain, however, got his merited 4,000 livres for this house, one of the prettiest of the Poissonnière quarter in the Louis XV style. Towards the middle of the century, fees took the form of a percentage of the total of all accounts duly settled and audited. The rate of one sol per livre, or five per cent, became customary under Louis XVI and was to be recognised by a decree of Pluviôse in the year VIII. But an architect's reputation and the importance of the decorative work might justify fees higher than the normal. The 'expert' of the celebrated Desgodetz convinced Mme Lombard d'Ermenonville of the rights of a 'person of his merit accomplished in architecture holding, by right, the King's diploma as an architect, and in addition professor of the academy of architecture'.

Ledoux openly boasted of ruining his clients. Boullée, his rival, had more modest pretensions. For seven years of work for the financier Beaujon, he asked less than 60,000 livres. For two hôtels in Paris and a villa at Pantin, Delafosse received 56,592 livres. His wife was also offered a gold box and case, which the couple seem to have refused. On the other hand, Soufflot accepted a snuff-box from the Prince de Condé, and the young Chalgrin was given a watch by the Comte de Saint-Florentin, for arriving late for the inauguration of his hôtel.

The Architect in Society

Socially and culturally, Parisian architects were representative members of the cultivated middle class, of the same standing as lawyers, many of them provincials, whose conception of justice and eloquence guided the Revolution to success. They were skilled craftsmen for the most part, versed in the building trades. Many of them emanated from the guilds, whose traditions were handed down from father to son. This was the case with the dynasty represented by the Mansart family and their kin. Jules Hardouin, who rose to the rank of the nobility and to ministerial responsibilities, had made a humble beginning at the beck of Libéral Bruant; but a staircase installed under his care in the Hôtel de Vendôme had brought him to the notice of the connoisseurs. Although he possessed a library of art books, he had never made an Italian tour, regarded as indispensable to a good architect's education. Robert de Cotte and Jacques (V) Gabriel, his relations and successors in the office of Premier Architecte du Roi, made the journey together and have left us a detailed account. With ciceroni to guide them, they drew and accurately measured more than 100 buildings; and if, despite the dawning age of enlightenment, their general education was still slight, it was linked to an intense desire to fathom the origins of their art and to extend its possibilities. It could have been said of them, as of Poussin, that they had neglected nothing to perfect their work. With them the technique of the mason had come before the training of the artist.

Others, however, were humanists and had studied theory before entering practice. Until the foundation of the Royal Academy, no institution had taught architecture, so that the aesthetic appreciation of the art often remained the province of scholars. Claude Perrault, a doctor, and N.-F. Blondel, a mathematician, figured as great architects without ever having been masons. The type of the cultivated architect was to spread in the course of the century, in which the aesthetic image assumed great importance. The number of publications on theory was considerable. Courtonne, who taught at the Academy, had the plans of his hôtels engraved. In the manner of Palladio, he used to give discreet hints about the standing of his clients and his dealings with them. Boffrand, who was the nephew of Quinault, presented his works and artistic convictions in Latin. The public lectures of Jacques-François Blondel attracted in the middle of the century a whole generation of French, Dutch and British students. At the end, the impassioned reflections of Ledoux, whose long and obscure text, pierced with occasional dazzling flashes, like lightning in a night sky, was as much a portent of Saint-Simonian socialism as of the aesthetic philosophy of our own day.

As men of taste, architects were often art collectors. Oppenord and Cartaud were among the first practical admirers of Gillot and Wattcau. Their colleagues, Dullin, Le Carpentier, Pierre de Vigny and Debesse preferred the old masters. In Louis XVI's reign, Clérisseau, Raymond, Paris and Cherpitel collected the sketches of Hubert Robert and Fragonard, companions of their years in Italy.

Employed by the nobility and gentry, architects assumed their tastes and way of life, being sometimes privileged by their friendship: 'I visited the site works of Arnouville managed by my friend Contant', wrote the Prince de Croÿ. Twenty persons of quality signed the marriage contract of Chevotet, son of a mere purveyor of mineral waters of the Faubourg Saint-Marcel, who was one of the architects of château, *folies* and gardens most in favour with the nobility at mid-century. The biographers of Le Carpentier, Girardin, and even the very expensive Ledoux insist on the integrity gladly accorded to them by contemporary society. The friendship of writers helped in their promotion. Fontenelle recommended Pierre de Vigny to the approbation of the Royal Society in London and Elie Fréron publicised the young Victor Louis in his *Année littéraire*. Diderot conversed on architecture with Prosper Doucet. Thiéry, author of several travellers' almanacs and a celebrated guide, used to question architects about their projects and publish the interviews. Louis appeared at Mme Geoffrin's 'Wednesdays' and was introduced by her to the King of Poland. The great lawyer Gerbier supported Pierre Damun's pseudo-antique design for the Théâtre Français. An enduring liaison, if somewhat stormy and punctuated with reciprocal infidelities, united the agreeable Bélanger with Mlle Arnoult of the opera. This lady, who had ensured the success of Gluck in France, introduced the architect to her dear Charlot, the Prince de Ligne, and to the Comte de Lauraguais 'who had given her two million kisses and made her shed more than four million tears'.

Le Camus de Mezières and his two brothers, one a doctor, the other an iron-merchant, staged plays in their house at Charonne. Cellerier had a clientèle of actresses, theatre directors and fashionable restaurateurs. With his friend Carle Vernet and the impresario Barré, he was still a habitué of the Café de Foy, at the Palais-Royal, during the Empire. The construction or rehabilitation of a theatre was a stiff public test for an architect. The opening of the new opera of the Palais-Royal in 1770 earned Moreau-Desproux a brilliant ovation. Lenoir, who later built the Porte Sainte-Martin theatre, was rewarded when he handed to Marie-Antoinette the key of her box. But when the new Théâtre Français (Odéon) was inaugurated, the ladies of fashion considered the excessively light colours of the auditorium disastrous to their complexions and dresses.

A little before the middle of the century, the Society of Arts and Sciences, founded by the Comte de Clermont, brought artists and amateurs together. Its meetings took place every Sunday at the Petit Luxembourg, and the architects Jean Aubert, de Vigny, Boffrand and

Chevotet received their colleagues from abroad there. After the foundation of the Grand Orient by the Duc de Chartres, forming a bridge between the aristocracies of birth and talent, freemasonry encouraged the nobility and artists to meet. About forty architects were affiliated: Brongniart to the lodge of Saint-Jean d'Ecosse du Contrat Social, Bonnet de Boisguillaume to that of the Neuf Sœurs, Blève to the Harmonie, and Chalgrin and de Wailly to the Cœurs Simples de l'Etoile Polaire.

Under Louis XV gentlemen like the Beausire family, Servandoni and Mansart de Sagonne practised architecture in the grand manner. Quick to draw their swords in artists' quarrels, they were notable for their reckless living. To escape his creditors, Mansart de Sagonne had to take refuge with the Prince de Conti in the precincts of the Temple and may have gone to Portugal, where Lisbon awaited reconstruction after the catastrophic earthquake of 1755. Jérôme Beausire had to flee to San Domingo, where he ended his days. The debts accumulated by Servandoni were discharged by the superintendent of the Menus Plaisirs in Louis XV's name. Diderot, we remember, forgave him for them and wrote movingly of his brilliant gifts.

All these remarkable men mingled sufficiently in the society of their time to inspire lively comment in letters and memoirs. The character of Jacques-François Blondel, evoked by Casanova, contrasts oddly with his disciplined buildings and teaching. Without censuring the architect, the adventurer, who had been Blondel's rival with the alluring musician, Marie-Anne Balletti, attributed to his cousin La Mothe a three-storey house without a staircase. There were less serious shortcomings which eighteenth-century society overlooked in men of talent. Chalgrin, who had been the pupil of Blondel, was as vague in everyday affairs as he was prudent in building practice. Not only did he arrive late for the inauguration of his first hôtel, as we have noted before, but he submitted imprecise estimates to the Comte de Provence: 'M. Chalgrin often hands me very inaccurate statements. . . .' Worse, he neglected the interests of the ageing Voltaire at the time when he was buying for himself and his niece one of the two adjoining houses of M. de Villarceaux in the Rue de Richelieu. In one of the last notes of his immense career as a letter-writer, the patriarch takes Chalgrin affectionately to task:

> It seems, Sir, to have been forgotten that the life purchaser, who is simply a leaseholder, benefited from the common well serving both houses, without which the leased house would become uninhabitable and the servants would never have anything with which they might even clean the horses' hoofs, so soon as the owner had placed a wall between the well and the leased house.
>
> It is very astonishing that such an essential clause was left out.
>
> M. Chalgrin is implored to remedy this serious inconvenience and lose no time in reassuring M. de Voltaire and Mme Denis, who have unlimited confidence in his abilities and are most sincerely attached to him.

The Tronchin family, friends of his Vernet in-laws, probably introduced Chalgrin to the philosopher. Mme Chalgrin was to die, a victim of the Terror, on the sole grounds of having candles in her home bearing the mark of the house of Provence, a fate which recalled an earlier comment of Voltaire: 'Without her, only "chagrin" remains.'

On the eve of the Revolution, decorators and architects of talent enjoyed, in the view of all contemporary observers, such wide consideration that the vainer spirits disdained to flatter princes: 'I see', said Ledoux to the Landgrave of Hesse-Cassel, 'that your excellency is not rich enough to have an architect like me.' In 1782 the Czarevitch, son of Catherine the Great of Russia, visited Paris under the name of the Comte du Nord and made the acquaintance of artists. The architect Clérisseau, who had worked for the Czarina, found some reason to reproach the Comte, ending his outburst with 'I shall write to your mother!' The financier Grimod de la Reynière, in whose house the row occurred, was overcome with confusion.

4 *The connoisseur*

The prestige attached to the artistic professions is easily explained in an environment full of well-informed amateurs of the fine arts. In the eighteenth century artistic education had its place in a nobleman's training. Private collections grew rich and multiplied, while Paris became, like London, one of the capitals of the art trade. The Enseigne de Gersaint, which combined in the same surroundings worldly elegance and a taste for painting, was the perfect image of the social circle where Watteau was fêted. Manuals of good manners and dictionaries of conversation rubbed bindings with vocabularies of arms, hunting and law. An educational treatise warns against confusing the architect with the mason, and the sculptor with the stone-cutter, at the risk of seeing the arts fall once more 'into their past barbarism and revive the Gothic taste'. Another exhorts gentlemen to employ artists and pay them well, but 'the ornaments of a house should not drain those resources needed for purposes more closely linked to the duties of their station'. A third counsels visits to the King's pictures, accompanied by an authority, to compare the gallery of Lebrun at Versailles with Mignard's at Saint-Cloud (*sic*) and that of Rubens at the Luxembourg. In architecture the reading of Perrault is recommended and of the first Félibien, both of them classics of Louis XIV's reign, which long maintained their reputation with teachers. When Mme du Châtelet and Voltaire undertook the modernisation of Cirey, the philosopher requested a correspondent in Paris to obtain for him 'a book on architecture illustrated with figures from which one can find the proportion of the five orders well drawn; whether the book is by Perrault, Blondel, Scamozzi, Palladio or Vignola does not matter'.

Taste among the nobility

In the tale of Jeannot and Colin, Voltaire attributes this view to a pedagogue:

> A young nobleman of fortunate birth is neither painter, nor musician, neither architect, nor sculptor; but he makes all these arts flourish through his munificence, for it is probably more valuable to support, than to practice, them. It is enough for my lord to have taste, and only right for the artists to work for him. Thus there is good reason for saying that persons of quality (I mean those who are very rich) know everything without having learnt

anything, because they genuinely know how to appreciate all the things which they commission and pay for.

Letter-writers and commentators have left us evidence in various records of the pleasure taken by the aristocracy of the Ancien Régime in building and decorating their houses. The generation of the Précieuses had seen Mme de Rambouillet draw the plans of her celebrated hôtel, and Mme de Sevigné's circle took pride in advising the great architect Libéral Bruant. When the question of modernising the chimney-pieces of the Hôtel Carnavalet arose, a friend intervened to submit his plan: 'He has taken such an interest in this little improvement of ours that he wants to be the architect.' Soon Mme de Grignan had become involved, and her mother wrote to her: 'We shall have to provide rather more substantial support for the chimney-piece of the room; it is amusing that Bruant did not think of this and that your idea from Provence should have put it right.'

The reign of Louis XIV saw the emergence at the court of the '*grands amateurs*', well able to leave their imprint on a building and set the pattern of taste. All had gained their knowledge from the residences of the Great Kings, and some had been all over Europe. The Président de Mesme was a 'true connoisseur', and M. de Langlée used to advise his friends upon their building projects: 'There was not a house built or bought without him directing the way it should be fashioned, adorned and furnished.' The Marquis de Béchameil interposed in the work at Saint-Cloud and caused some offence to Mansart. The Duca di Fornaro, a Sicilian from Messina, designed a staircase at Liancourt and at several hôtels in Paris: 'He drew to perfection and had much knowledge of architecture and an exquisite taste in all sorts of building. . . . The

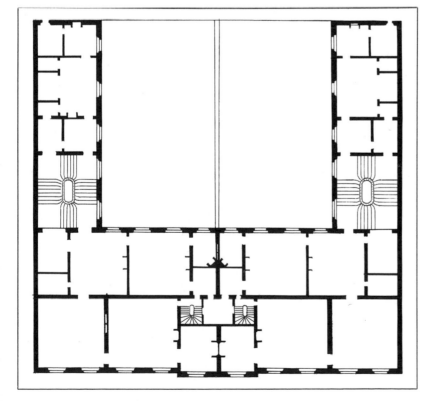

6   Victor-Thierry Dailly: Hôtels
Le Lièvre de La Grange, 6–8 Rue
de Braque, 1737

king sometimes spoke to him about his buildings and fountains.' His personality made a great impression on the Swedish minister: 'He makes the whole fraternity of architects tremble, with his imperious manner and learning in architecture.' A Marquis de Coatnizan wrote a treatise on the art of building staircases. When the Marquis de Lassay undertook the construction of his hôtel, today the Présidence de l'Assemblée Nationale, and rebuilt his Château de Moncanisy, he exploited his own experience. He had travelled in Hungary, admired the Villa d'Este and the Vigne Pamphili, and had advised the Duchessa in her splendid gardens of Bracciano. Perhaps it was he who suggested to his sister-in-law, a legitimatised daughter of Louis XIV, to invite an Italian to plan the Palais Bourbon.

There were many such characters in eighteenth-century international society, men like Paolo Falconieri and Abbot Farsetti in Italy, and the Earl of Burlington and Horace Walpole in England. With the British indeed, practising the arts might sometimes lead to a rise in social rank: an inscription on a plate at Sutton Scarsdale, a house in Derbyshire, describes Francis Smith and the English and Italian decorative artists, who were employed on the building, as 'gentlemen'. The Italian Algarotti was a connoisseur of international repute, who helped Augustus III to establish his Dresden gallery, wrote learnedly on architecture, reluctantly witnessed the decline of rococo and accepted the return to a simple, nobler, manner of building, to which the Carmelite friar Lodoli showed him the way. He was ennobled by Frederick II.

In the reign of Louis XV, Louis Petit de Bachaumont was the arbiter of Parisian taste. He advised the Duc de Bouillon on work for the Château de Navarre, the Marquis de Belle-Isle at Bissy, and M. du Châtel on the modernisation of the Hôtel Crozat. He compiled forms of directive, which have come down to us. Here is his reply to the Maréchal d'Isenghien, who had consulted him, possibly for his house at Suresnes:

> Get Messrs Contant and Cartaud for large parks and gardens, M. de la Chapelle, Le Nôtre's best apprentice, for shrubs, beds and other pretty features. For the inside and outside adornment of a house, when sculpture is entailed, like chimney-pieces, sideboards, shells, marble tops for an eating room, carved panelling, cornices, table-legs, fire-baskets, fire-dogs, the jambs of fire-places, candle-sticks and chandeliers in gilded bronze and suchlike, vases in stone, bronze, lead, terra cotta or pewter, marble inlays also, privies and other internal subjects for sculptural treatment, you should employ Messrs Slotz, sculptors to the King, who live at the Louvre, men of honour and probity, not expensive or self-interested, and opposed to the fripperies so much in vogue nowadays. For marble statues, try Bouchardon, Lemoyne junior, the brothers Adam, La Datte. . . . The best sculptors for frames are Morisan and Le Sueur; next to them Charny and Cailleux, and, for ordinary ornamental borders, apply to the Sr de Launay, Quai de Gesvres, at the Star.

Present experience seems to suggest that architecture is among the least appreciated of the arts, and is regarded with relative indifference by educated people. This was not the case in the eighteenth century, when architectural masterpieces roused the deepest wonder in intelligent tourists. Jefferson embraced with an equal admiration the Maison Carrée at Nîmes, the brand-new Hôtel de Salm and the *folie* built at Chaville by Boullée for Mme de Tessé. He was indignant at the sight of a road paved with stones from the theatre at Orange, in which Louis XIV had recognised 'the finest wall' of his kingdom.

As M. Pierre Verlet has shown, the monarchs at Versailles, in daily contact with artists, were the greatest connoisseurs of their day. Louis XV loved architecture, discussed it with his intimates and was a good judge. Ledoux recalled the first royal visit to the pavilion of Louveciennes, where the colonnade had been critcised by some of the envious: 'Louis XV, seeing from a distance a peristyle of columns which I had erected in a private building, said: "They are not bad at all; when one gets closer, they are good."' The King used to advise his courtiers. The Duc de Croÿ went to talk to him about a hunting lodge, which he wanted to build in Artois. At an intersection of forest glades, he proposed a central salon, from which a view would extend down four avenues, a scheme similar in intention to that of the Pavillon Français de Trianon, where the plan is in the form of a St Andrew's cross:

> The King was very fond of buildings. He took me into his pretty pavilion of Trianon and made me realise that this was the taste in which one should build. He instructed M. Gabriel to give me two plans which they had made together in the same taste and, asking for pencil and paper, I did a sketch of my situation for him; he spent quite a time putting these ideas into drawings, both on his own and with M. Gabriel, pondering long over the one which seemed to interest him most.

The Marquis de Marigny, Mme de Pompadour's brother and Director of the King's Buildings, built lavishly on his own account. He scrutinised with a connoisseur's eye the drawings of Soufflot, who had acquainted him in Italy with the monuments of antiquity:

> I will bring you tomorrow, Sir, the plans which you have made for my house at Le Roule. With regard to the decoration. . . . I look to you for the same good taste which you have given me on the façade. I think you have the plan you need for designing the two pavilions. I am sending what I have roughed out for you to look over; you are used to understanding me.

The Marquis disclosed his fears to the anxious Soufflot: 'I am always nervous that the cornice of my salon in Paris may be too heavy. You will probably have foreseen the effect, and I leave it to you.' It was also the cornice of her *grand salon* in a hôtel of the Rue Saint-Dominique, which disturbed the Princesse de Monaco. When the work was finished, she wanted the ovoli shifted so that there should be one in a vertical line with each modillion, something which the ornamentalist Cauvet had not noticed. Architects were often asked to incorporate older ornament in a new design. The Comte d'Andlau wished to make use of panels of arabesques in his hôtel in the Faubourg Saint-Honoré. These had been painted by Oudry for the Château de Voré, which he owned. He wrote to his agent: 'My architect is M. Cherpitel, Architect of the King's Buildings, c/o M. Lacassaigne, apothecary, Rue du Bac, near the University . . . I forgot to tell you that the exact dimensions of the arabesque paintings of the Italian salon must be sent to M. Cherpitel, to see if they can be adapted for furnishing the dining-room in my new house.' Elsewhere, architects and decorators had to satisfy less justifiable demands. Le Carpentier, working for the financier Bouret, 'complained that his compliance might well damage his reputation. The bad taste of clients only too often conflicts with artists' intentions.'

Building a town-house or château was a matter in which a gentleman gladly involved his intimate circle. M. Dupré de Saint-Maur, Intendant of Berry, was heard to regret one day that a plan by Louis for his house had gone astray: 'It would have been a great pleasure for me to argue it out with my wife.' The witty Mme d'Epinay depicts her husband engrossed in having the Château de La Chevrette transformed by the architect Lefranc; 'M d'Epinay is in ecstasy with his plans and projects, and talks to us of nothing else.'

7 J.-B.-A. Beausire: Hôtel d'Ecquevilly ou du Grand Veneur, 60 Rue de Turenne, 1734

Thus, everyone has always prided himself in being his own architect. Jules Hardouin-Mansart knew this, when he submitted 'imperfect plans' to Louis XIV to give him the pleasure of finding the solution himself.

'All clients', wrote Blondel, 'regard themselves as architects, so much so that a man with the urge to build would prefer not to do so, rather than follow the advice of a qualified fellow who might cramp his tastes.' Marigny and Soufflot wanted to dissuade Dufort de Saint-Leu, Marshal of the Diplomatic Corps, from acquiring the Château de Cheverny, of which one pavilion was subsiding. Dufort took no notice and proceeded to embellish his new home: 'M. de Cypierre brought me his architect, but I felt I knew enough to do without him.' The Prince de Ligne, contemplating his own work as a gardener at Belœil, reflected in unrestrained terms about the professionals: 'An author of books on gardens, a painter, an architect or an anglomaniac would have turned all Belœil upside down to create grand effects.' He consulted Bélanger, however, over the gardens which Chevotet had beautified in his late father's time.

One of the *Contes Moraux* of Marmontel is entitled 'Le Connaisseur'; at the Théâtre Français, Barthes gave *L'Amateur*, a character returned from Italy; the Abbé de a Porte staged *L'Antiquaire*; and, in the Empire period, Krafft was to emphasise the extent to which travel had transformed architecture. Cultivated members of the nobility, like the Prince de Ligne and the Ducs d'Harcourt and de Nivernais, showed themselves receptive to the most progressive aims of archaeologists and artists.

When the Comte de Caylus wanted to bring back into favour the Graeco-Roman method of encaustic painting, it was first tried out at the Hôtel d'Harcourt. The Marquis de Girardin, the Duc de Nivernais and the Duc d'Harcourt were among the first to promote landscape gardening in France. The Prince de Ligne, another garden enthusiast, regarded the evolution of the arts with the eyes of a travelled European. Here is what he advocated for the elevations of a place in the country: 'It can be of one or two storeys, the roof hidden by a balustrade. An extreme neatness is the proper thing, not magnificence; no columns, but bas-reliefs, a long rectangle with recesses for busts, with a broken chevron above' – the Prince was mixing heraldic with architectural terminology here – 'a few pilasters at most. The colour a uniform pale yellow, or rather light grey.' As the Prince rarely stayed in Paris, to avoid meeting his creditors there, he has not left us his views about town-houses; but the decoration which he recommends for the country is exactly that of the finest Parisian façades of Louis XVI's reign. During his long life the Prince de Ligne had been able to watch fashions change even more quickly than political régimes. He had detested rocaille and been bored with the Arabian, Etruscan, Chinese and Gothic tastes, at one time preferring 'the Turkish and the Moldavian'. On the subject of decoration, he commented:

> My distaste is also apparent for those supposedly fine papers with flowers, ornamental patterns or branches of foliage, with which people think to beautify a salon. I relegate them to the cloak-rooms, with the framed prints, for which I do not care either. The papers which I have recommended are the galleries of the Vatican, the Palazzo Farnese, Herculaneum, Pompeii. . . .

The Prince has given us his conception of the home, whether palace or cottage, and summarises his tastes thus: 'simplicity, modernity, grace'. His book is akin to those agreeable, sometimes novelettish, treatises which provided fashionable people with an initiation into architecture. The *Guide de ceux qui veulent bâtir* and the *Génie de l'architecture*, published about 1780 by Le Camus de Mézières, are the work of a well-read architect, imbued with the philosophical ideas of Condillac. But the oddest work dates from the end of the rococo. This is Bastide's *La petite maison*, a novel which first appeared in 1752 and expresses the conception of domestic luxury and comfort in vogue in the middle of the century, naming several fashionable decorators. In the company of the Marquis de Trémicour and the pretty Mélite, and preceded by a Negro who lights the lamps and chandeliers before them, we visit the most delightful dwelling imaginable to a contemporary of Mme Leprince de Beaumont, Marivaux and Laclos.

Twenty years later, in association with the architect Blondel, Bastide published *L'homme du monde éclairé par les arts*, but the novelist and his characters were now older. It is now the Comte de Salleran who describes to his friend, Mme de Vaujeu, the gardens of Marly and, in her company, visits sone new sights, like the School of Surgery, the royal furniture repository, and the pavilion of Mlle Guimart. A young architect shows them round a large hôtel, which he has just finished transforming for a soldier. We recognise the Hôtel d'Uzès and Ledoux, whom Blondel had no wish to mention, for his pupil's success roused the old master's malice:

> He follows you complacently everywhere, when you come to look at the hôtel, and is at pains to show you that the capitals of his orders are finely carved; that the statues are by so-and-so; that here he has been faithful to decoration in the antique manner, and there to Grecian forms; and, in short, that he has known how to break away from the commonplace.

None the less the society which read such works welcomed the innovations. An Alsatian, Mme d'Oberkirch, who visited Paris every summer, followed the architectural progress of the finest houses, and in her memoirs takes us to see them. The Prince de Condé made his pavilion 'the prettiest trinket in the world', furnished 'with a delicious refinement, but perhaps not splendid enough for what it contains. There are whimsicalities and curios here, as at Mlle Dervieux's place.' As for Mme Thélusson's house, 'it attracted all Paris at the time. One needed tickets to get in. It seemed to me more bizarre than beautiful; but the details are in the best taste. The staircase is superb. . . . Everywhere nothing but columns to be seen' (Pls. 159–63).

In architecture, and especially in decorative art, the part played by women of taste should not be ignored. Mlle de Bourbon directed the works at the Château de Vanves and la Grande Mademoiselle was proud to have had the elder Gabriel as her architect. In Louis XV's time, the Duc de Luynes claimed that his wife was the first to have had the idea of heightening the effect of wainscot carving by colouring it green against a white background. Architects and ministers sometimes studied designs for two hours in Mme du Barry's presence without her interest flagging, while there is a floral manifestation of the Louis XVI style, to which the name 'style Marie-Antoinette' may be applied.

The fact is the history of taste is as much that of the amateurs as of the artists. Between two people, one of whom submits a design and the other agrees to finance its execution, a subtle relationship is established, and the mysterious evolution of style is influenced by every such contact.

'It is the client who, so to speak, gives the key to the architect' (Boffrand). A connoisseur advises the first in the choice of the second, and here are the terms in which Louis Petit de Bachaumont recommends to his noble friends the architect Cartaud:

> He is an intelligent, educated man, who enjoys his work. He is neither grasping, nor obsequious. . . . If he turns it down, I suggest Le Bon, a young architect fresh from Rome, clever and a gentleman, who has Cartaut's backing and guidance. M. Cartaut has already sent Le Bon to several of his old clients, who were well satisfied, most recently to My Lord Cardinal de Rohan, for work at Saverne and Strasbourg. . . . M. Le Bon follows sound principles and is particularly opposed to the rubbish so much in fashion today.

Was his advice always followed? For the job at Bissy, he had recommended Cartaud to the Marquis de Belle-Isle, who preferred Contant d'Ivry. 'M. Contant has been chosen', noted Bachaumont, 'and a good choice has been made. He is a very sound chap.' About 1745 Bachaumont was acknowledging the merits as artistic consultants of Messrs de Caylus, Mariette, Berger, Sevin, Jullienne, de Gravelle and Vallory.

> If you want to do a perfect job [wrote Boffrand] take the advice of a candid connoisseur. He will tell you frankly that the apartment does not make the best of the view. . . . Your staircase needs more room; why do you have to take the left side up, when you can take the right? This decoration is overburdened with ornament. Tone it down.

A close collaboration grew up between the patron and the architect of his choice. When the Prince de Croÿ worked with Chevotet and his son-in-law Chaussard, he recorded his satisfaction in having the advice of the best artists:

> I also finished the plan of the surroundings and the way round the house (Château de l'Ermitage) with young Chaussard, a lad full of talent, and – what is more – I worked with the famous Chevotet, so that I had the ideas of all the great masters of Paris. . . . In Paris, I found the salon finished: it was superb and in good taste, and that had not been easy, for we had had to grope our way to success, my son and I being obliged to get M. Chaussard to change many things. All was well in the end: the pictures in bas-relief, medallions and doors are the things which do us credit. The large adjoining room, differently furnished and adorned with fine pictures, cleaned, and the altered anteroom complete a splendid apartment.

The too brilliant design, which might prove disappointing in practice, was to be distrusted. An admirer of Oppenord, the amateur d'Argenville could not resist writing that his schemes did not produce the same effect when executed, and the same comment was made about Meissonier. To avoid surprises, the architect proposed a repetition of the arrangements successful in another building. According to the contract concluded for the construction of the Hôtel de Polisy, the banisters of the great staircase were to be the same as those made for M. Poyrier's house in the Rue Thévenot. Occasionally, however, the artist had the chance of creating, during the progress of building, a decorative effect difficult to foresee on paper. When Servandoni submitted to the Cardinal d'Auvergne a design for a staircase to be built in his hôtel, he reserved the right to introduce into mouldings and sculpture a few changes 'which can only be seen at a certain stage in building', and at an earlier period François Mansart had asked Colbert if he could 'do and undo, until he achieved a building to his liking'. But an artist's indecision could raise costs to an unexpected figure. Financial forecasts were not very reliable, and we have already spoken of the slowness of payments and the monetary problems of the nobility, a delicate episode in human relations at the end of the Ancien Régime.

Financiers and eccentrics

The taste for fine architecture had long spread from the court to the new gentry and the very rich. When Antoine Crozat's apartment property of the Cour du Dragon was being built, he wrote from the country to the architect, Pierre de Vigny, 'to get on with the job'. The foreman-mason must be sent the design for the arcades, and the wing facing the

8   J. Hardouin-Mansart de Sagonne: House of the Dames de Saint-Chaumont, 151 Boulevard de Sébastopol, 1734

34

Rue de Sépulcre (Rue du Dragon), in which twenty rooms on each floor were to be let, had to be roofed before winter. Madame Crozat, whose handsome portrait by Aved has come down to us, was concerned, like her husband, over the scheme for the main entrance which, in particular, needed to be widened to allow for the slope of the street (Fig. 3, p. 11).

As in the time of La Bruyère and La Fontaine, 'every tradesman wants to build like a lord' and as soon as he had made himself a palace, is so dazzled by it that he hardly dares live there. According to a contemporary, a certain Le Maître, grown rich in the cloth trade, put on slippers and gloves to pass through the salons of his château in the Marais. Beaujon was less startled by his own magnificence. In his apartments of the Elysée, charming ladies whom he called his 'cradle-rockers' helped the sick man to find sleep by talking and reading to him. To beautify the house, he requested innumerable sketches from the already famous Boullée, whom Beaujon boasted to have raised 'to the top jobs'; but the philanthropist, so well known for his charitable endowments, disputed the architect's fees. Boullée sued him, and exhibited 200 drawings to the experts, which Beaujon attributed to subcontractors: the trellis-workers Langelin and Crosnier, the stove-maker Bertolini, and the ornamentalist Cauvet. His arguments, comprehensively set out in the evidence, reduced the architect 'to a mere cipher'.

An eccentric of the end of the century, M. de Monville, 'did not profess to be an architect, but he had the bent and the taste: he even had new ideas of his own and always very agreeable ones'. In the wilderness of Retz, he contrived one of the strangest landscape gardens of the pre-romantic age. He claimed its paternity and allowed it to be engraved under his name, but a court directive disclosed the identity of the architect as Barbier, who worked on the Chinese pavilion (still standing), of which an admirable drawing is preserved in Stockholm, and the antique temple, the aviary and the baths. We see Barbier visiting friends of the owner, making a sketch of a vase at M. d'Invau's house, one of a trellis in the Faubourg du Temple, and a tent in M. de Montsauge's garden of La Bretêche. But Monville asserted that he had only used him as a draughtsman 'to put on paper the ideas which he provided for him'.

The middle class

In the course of the century, the pursuit of architectural beauty had extended to the lower ranks of the middle class, as many apartment buildings bore witness. In 1700 the author of the *Lettres d'un Sicilien* was still speaking of houses in Paris 'built by philosophers rather than architects, to judge by their clumsy exteriors', but a large number of the apartment properties in the central areas were rebuilt under Louis XV, and the old gothic gables disappeared. The owners were tradesmen, builders, lawyers and notaries, few apparently being doctors. The architects of the bourgeoisie were what a contemporary, the Président de Frémin, ironically called the coxcombs of the profession: 'They imagine they have scaled the heights of excellence, when they have told a tradesman that his staircase will have landings. It is a tradesman's pleasure and flatters his self-esteem to say to his neighbour that he is building . . . and his wife maintains that her architect is the handsomest man in town.' In their apartments, panelling and mirrors were no longer a luxury. The eighteenth-century bourgeois, 'that social outcast', held the purse strings, but found himself deprived of a leading role, although conscious of his part in advancing those standards and values which brought prosperity to his station. Following the gentry's example, he was not reluctant to appear in the guise of amateur and patron of the arts. The salon of 1739 displayed the portrait of a 'M. Suhard holding a design for panelling'. A widow of the Quartier Poissonnière showed, according to her architects, 'a decided taste for the beautiful'. Gudin de la Brenellerie wrote in 1775: 'Nowadays the pettiest burgher disdains an undecorated apartment.'

5 *Artistic evolution*

We must return to the climactic years of Louis XIV's reign to find the
source of the principal streams animating French art in the first half
of the eighteenth century. In their interpretation of form, as in their
philosophical attitudes, the 1680s were decisive. For the government
of Louis XIV, architectural activity, the commercial prosperity of the
arts and the establishment of academies were among the necessary
manifestations of political supremacy. From the beginning of his
personal rule, one of the concerns of the King and of Colbert had been
to free French art from its long subordination to Italy. The realisation
of a new independence inspired the endeavours of artists and the theoretical disputations of connoisseurs.

As far back as 1665 the competition for the main façade of the Louvre
had offered a test for architects. Confronted with Louis Le Vau's
failure and the hesitations of the ageing François Mansart, Louis XIV
and Colbert reluctantly turned to the Italians. They welcomed Bernini
to Paris with princely honours, but the challenge of his presence inspired the Colonnade, a collective manifesto of French originality in
adapting antique forms. François d'Orbay directed for some years
an intensely active building programme at Versailles. Jules Hardouin-
Mansart succeeded him, enlarged Saint-Cloud and Meudon, and
brought Marly and Trianon into being. At Versailles, Le Vau's transient
fairyland gave place to the enduring dispositions of Mansart. The
gilded aviaries, the shell-work deities, the grottoes, the stalactites and
the water organs, all the tinsel paraphernalia disappeared, and between
the lure of Italy and the classical reaction of *grand goût* a fruitful rivalry
arose. The second Versailles of Louis XIV achieved a dynamic harmony,
to which a variety of talents contributed under the guidance of a single
hand, and the taste of the King, who was in a position to choose, had
been refined by its influence. Meanwhile Blondel, Bruant and Bullet
gave a majestic order to Paris, where their works were to inspire a
simple beauty.

Classicism was less the effect of a spontaneous evolution of the arts
than an attempt to awaken in the subjects and rivals of Louis XIV a
sense of the grandeur and clarity of purpose animating his government.
Classical proportions and the proper employment of columns exercised
the same authority as the harmony of rhythms and the fitness of words
upon writers of prose. For some years elementary geometrical figures
comprised the entire interior decoration in the palaces of a monarchy
under the spell of reason. And yet, whether it occurs under Pericles,

in the reign of Saint-Louis or under the pontificate of Julius II, the classical phase of a style endures hardly the space of a generation. Soon the ageing king and the princesses of his circle were hearkening to the seductions of a new style to charm and divert them. Almost imperceptible mutations were guiding the decorative art of Versailles into the imaginative reaches of rococo. Among the painters, the triumph of the Rubénistes over the Poussinistes bore witness to the victory of sensibility over sense, exposing new horizons of poetry and generating a manner of its own, to which Watteau was to bring lustre at the end of the reign. In the meantime, the Revocation of the Edict of Nantes signalled the virtual and final failure of absolutism. Without his contemporaries fully realising it, the autocratic action of Louis XIV unleashed a crisis in Europe, which would initiate the intellectual movement of the century of enlightenment. In a few years, behind the majestic façade of the Great Reign, were crystallised the forms, the feelings and the ideas which determined the artistic and intellectual direction of the eighteenth century.

The tradition of Mansart

Jules Hardouin-Mansart, Louis XIV's premier architect and superintendent of his buildings, died in 1708, seven years before the sovereign whose favour he had successfully won and retained. Since the Peace of Nijmegen, his activities had been deployed in urban design and landscape. While the dome of the Invalides and the façades of the Place Vendôme were nearing completion, the construction of the royal chapel had concluded the operations at Versailles. In preserving the supremacy of the French style, of which his uncle, François Mansart, had been one of the creators, Hardouin had also been able to gratify the predilection which Louis XIV secretly felt for Italian art. He had imitated Palladio at Marly, where the King liked to take refuge with his favourite courtiers from the ceremonial of Versailles. Sansovino was his inspiration for the lofty windows of the Galerie des Glaces, designed to reflect the shimmering water of garden pools, as their Venetian model mirrored the Grand Canal. The polychrome marbles of the *grands appartements* and the Colonnade, the terraces of Versailles and Trianon, and the fairyland of the maze, inhabited by fantastic animals, afford equal proof. The eighteenth century did not grudge its admiration for the elegance of this Versailles compromise. La Dixmerie complimented Mansart for having introduced into architecture a blend of magnificence and civility, while the Marquis d'Argenson contrasted the refined French architecture of his school with the ponderous majesty of the Italian. The hôtels de Noailles at Saint-Germain and of Lorges in Paris represented Jules Hardouin-Mansart's contribution to the architecture of town-houses, a field in which his uncle François had so distinguished himself. Their tradition was perpetuated in the hôtels built after 1700, on both banks of the Seine, in which Jules Hardouin's brilliant assistants set the standard.

None the less, whether their names were Robert de Cotte, Gabriel (senior), Delamair or Lassurance, the grand town residence subjected their talent to solutions, in which respect for convention suppressed originality. A tranquil rhythm, discreet projections, and a sober use of columns, such are the ingredients of these harmonious façades. Decorative sculpture, economically applied, enlivens the keystone of certain arches and the tympanum of a pediment. But no two compositions are identical, and ingenious variations on a similar theme reveal original qualities to which other programmes offered a freer rein. A few words about each of these architects will be enough to place

9 J.-R. Cochois: Nourry house, 115 Rue Saint-Honoré, about 1735

them in the context of their time and to suggest the differences distinguishing their work.

Robert de Cotte, architect of the Hôtel du Maine, was responsible for the felicitous designs of the episcopal palaces of Verdun and Strasbourg. Jules Hardouin-Mansart's brother-in-law, he made a journey to Italy, from which his diary survives. The antiquities disappointed him, but he tells us of his interest in the slender proportions of the nymphs of Giovanni Bologna, the painting of Guercino, and the already baroque architecture of Pietro da Cortona. All academic art was thus foreign to his temperament.

Boffrand, who can be admired in Paris for the oval court of the Hôtel de Gournay, was the master who, with recollections of Versailles, built in one go the palace of Lunéville for Léopold de Lorraine.

Jean Aubert, the architect to whom the Hôtel Biron must be exclusively ascribed, built the grand stables bordering the lawns of Chantilly for the Duc de Bourbon. Of this palace, designed for horses (and hounds), it has been said that its creators must have believed in metempsychosis. The stables at Chantilly are the finest buildings of the Régence, and the work of a prince of architecture for a prince of the realm. We shall not be surprised, therefore, to rediscover the splendid uninhibited inspiration of Jean Aubert in the former doorway of the Palais Bourbon (Pl. 81).

One of the few architects to have devoted all their abilities to the building of hôtels was Lassurance, Dessinateur des Bâtiments du Roi, whose talent, Saint-Simon and Dangeau declare, was exploited by Mansart and Robert de Cotte. His position as Comptroller at the Invalides, however, enabled him to extend his activities into the Faubourg Saint-Germain. The able schemes which he conceived for the Hôtels de Rothelin and de Lassay were to be copied after him. During the Régence Parisian originality did not lie so much in the architecture as in the appointments and decoration of the rooms. This was a domain in which individual aspirations came into their own, when the man of fashion had already imprinted on the exterior of his house the marks of his rank.

The origins of rococo

Examined by M. Alfred Marie, 2,000 portfolios of documents from the Maison du Roi have disclosed the activities of the 'Bâtiments' under the direction of Jules Hardouin-Mansart, Robert de Cotte and the Gabriel family. Fiske Kimball, the American scholar, relied on this material for his description of the evolution of interior decoration in the royal residences, from the years of Louis XIV's splendour to the patronage of Mme de Pompadour. Avoiding the traditional designations of the Louis XV and Louis XVI styles, which do not coincide exactly with the duration of the reigns, he accepted no more willingly the equally traditional term of 'rocaille'. His preferences lay with 'rococo', a word which can be traced back to the young days of Ingres and seems to be a corruption of 'rocaille' and 'barocco'. At one time bearing a depreciatory meaning, the word was applied by Stendhal to the Rome of Bernini, by Hugo to the Grand'Place of Nancy, and by the Académie française to the style of the ornamentalist Oppenord. Adopted by German historians, it referred to the art of Central Europe and the Latin countries in the first half of the eighteenth century. By applying it to French art, Kimball ruffled a few national susceptibilities.

But for him, the rococo was born in France, free from any foreign influence, long before 1715. Its manifestation owed nothing to the militant return of Flemish and Italian tendencies, for long rebuffed by the artistic hierarchy of Louis XIV. It was not, as Gurlitt, Brinkmann, Hans Rose and other German-language historians accepted it, a development of baroque art.

The evolution of form, which gave birth to rococo, was accomplished after 1680 in the vast field of experiment offered to decorative invention by the royal apartments. Louis XIV had melted down his silver furniture, and renounced the stupefying luxury which had shocked Europe and failed to dazzle the Doge of Genoa, summoned to Versailles. The financial strain imposed by the War of the League of Augsburg limited the decorative use of precious metals. The Sérancolin marble quarry was exhausted. In rooms of less impressive dimensions than hitherto, oak panelling was often preferred to inlaid marble. Work in wood and stucco became customary again, and the possibilities afforded by these materials broadened the sources of the ornamentalist's inspiration. In 1685 the departure of Le Brun, as a result of the political circumstances, meant that decorative painting would no longer celebrate in heroic terms the exploits of the Sun-King. The younger generation of royalties – Monseigneur, the Duchesse du Maine, the Duchesse de Bourgogne, the Duc de Vendôme – assumed the mantle of patronage. Jean (I) Bérain and Claude (II) Audran were invited to ply wainscots and ceilings with adornments of gossamer grace, scrolls, flowers and chimeras, and a symbolism bereft of all political allusion. Thus a new vitality rejuvenated the arabesque, a decorative device imitated from ancient Rome, which the studio of Raphael, the school of Fontainebleau, and the circle of Vouet and Charles Errard had each in their turn enriched.

From 1685 to 1708 several designers worked in Mansart's offices, whose decorative schemes bear their master's signature, but are recognisable by their distinctive styles. The two most original, Lassurance and Pierre Lepautre, produced hundreds of drawings for Versailles, Trianon, Marly and Meudon. They transformed chimney-pieces, lowering the mantelpiece to breast height, deepening the mantelshelf, and ornamenting the overmantel with a pier-glass enclosed in a richly decorated frame, instead of with the paintings placed there before. Between fireplaces and bay openings an interplay of elementary figures, rectangles, circles and ovals had until then sufficed to enliven panelling. As M. Alfred Marie has shown, Lassurance, and especially Pierre Lepautre ingeniously translated into this decoration of carved wood the motifs developed by Bérain and Audran in their painted arabesques. Bérain's mirrors and baldacchini carried basket-arch heads. Ceilings and panels evolved from delicate rosette centres and C-scrolls and hawk's bills soften the angles. Pierre Lepautre returned to the repertoire of motifs compiled by his father Jean Lepautre, but relieved the luxuriant scrolls and chimeras with swirls of acanthus. In the course of the process now beginning, rococo decoration was to exhaust the whole vocabulary of nature as well as exploiting the abstract possibilities of interlaces, the treasury of every artist. At its apogee, rococo distributed branches, dangled garlands and framed a mirror with a palm-tree. It disseminated on all sides these supple vegetal forms, heightening or constraining the momentum of their growth, and opposing the spontaneous energy of living forces to the static laws of architecture.

Thus, according to Fiske Kimball, the style of mural decoration progressed imperceptibly from Le Brun's classicism to the flowering of rocaille. Rococo was born in France; it grew up there, prospered abroad and died about 1755, under the effect of neo-classical reaction.

Baroque survivals

In spite of the evident independence of this development, it was impossible for France to disregard tendencies which had already penetrated her soil and triumphed elsewhere. Masters like Cucci, Temporitti and Meissonier, Oppenord senior, Sibrayque and the Slodtz family infused into French art the bountiful vitality of Italy and Flanders. The work of Pierre Francastel, Bernard Teyssèdre and François Souchal showed the effects of Italian expressionism upon the sculpture of Versailles. In the manner of the Bolognesi, Santerre had painted for the royal chapel a scene so profane in character that the priests refused to celebrate the sacrament in front of it. In architecture, the Académie Royale upheld the correct employment of the orders and instanced as examples to students the buildings of F. Blondel and Perrault. But several artists betrayed their sympathy for the inventive planning, decorative exuberance and pathos of Borromini. The competition for the portal of Saint-Sulpice, in which Servandoni's classical design was confronted by baroque schemes from Oppenord and Meissonier, illustrates the conflict.

Italianism took refuge in more modest experiments. The goldsmith Thomas Germain, who had done architectural work at Livorno, gave to Saint-Louis du Louvre a portal characterised by Borrominian undulations. The baldacchino of the Val-de-Grâce, for which Bernini

10 F. Debias-Aubry: Cotelle house, 52 Rue Saint-André-des-Arts, 1737

may have prepared the drawings in 1665, was copied all over France for almost a century. The mannerist motif of the cartouche had long been known in France and made a fresh appearance in rococo. The palms of Bernini's fountains, the heraldic dragon of the Borghese, Borromini's seraphs, their wings drawn back '*en espagnolette*', and many other features of high baroque were tirelessly repeated, transformed or modified. The characteristic bestiary of rococo is almost the one which Sarrazin's verses described in the time of Louis XIII and classicism rejected:

> *Sphinx, dragons, elephants, chimeras, rams with wings,*
> *Dogs, sirens, griffins, fantastic monstrous things . . .*

The baroque aesthetic was present on every joyful or spectacular occasion. In inspired the scenery, the staging and the costumes of the Opéra. It embellished public holidays. Illuminations and water entertainments on the Seine, given on the occasion of royal marriages, needed floating rocks, temples of Hymen and river-borne buffets. The Slodtz family and Beausire (father and son) lavished their decorative invention upon these ephemeral structures. After Fontenoy, the triumphal ornamentation with which the theorist Blondel clothed the Porte Saint-Martin combined all the strident effects which he condemned in his writings. We have seen that Servandoni chose the side of classicism in architecture. He was also a theatrical designer and left a reputation as a brilliant illusionist. Occasionally, too, he would turn his hand to decorating private houses, like that of the financier Samuël Bernard for his daughter's marriage to the Président Molé. This 'aesthetic of the ephemeral', as it has been called by M. Roger-Armand Weigert, offered ever fresh inspiration to eighteenth-century decorative art.

Parisian rococo

The interior decoration of Parisian houses evolved under such influences. Ornament became so important that the architect was often obliged to entrust part of his programme to a specialist designer. Jacques-François Blondel pointed with disdain to several architects who, capable only of making plans, turned for help to leading decorators. Such collaboration was common and no secret. We must therefore give some further consideration to the role of masters of ornament, like Toro, Oppenord and Pineau senior, who inspired their contemporaries, for their personalities assume a new significance, as the extent of their influence emerges.

Among the immediate successors of Bérain and Audran, Bernard Toro was one of the strangest characters of the Régence. Although schooled on the work of Puget, this Provençal created a world filled with the tenuous forms and delicate graphic contrivance of the mannerists. Cupids lead sea-horses with unicorns' heads. A faun torments a sphinx with a cock's head. A young satyr suckles a winged goat. Children tame lion cubs. Helmets are crowned with hippogriphs. The baldacchini and valances recall Bérain. Among the scrolls and roundels, and the cartouches set askew as with Meissonier, writhe fearsome dragons. About 1715, the architect Cl.-N. Le Pas-Dubuisson (the elder) invited Toro to Paris and supervised the engraving of his *Livre des tables*. Dubuisson was at this time building, for the Seminary of Foreign Missions, the two hôtels at 118 and 120 Rue du Bac (Pl. 23), and it seems clear that

11 Ironwork designs by F. Debias-Aubry:

(a) Balcony facing the quay – Grand Hôtel de Bouillon, 17 Quai Malaquais, 1740

(b) Cotelle house, 52 Rue Saint-André-des-Arts, 1737

(c) Debias-Aubry house, 131 Rue Saint-Martin, 1729

(d) Juliennet house, 45 Rue de la Harpe, 1740
Also a house at 11 Rue Daguesseau (no longer standing), the Hôtel de Gesvres, 23 Rue Croix-des-Petits-Champs (no longer standing), and a house at 16 Rue Saint Sauveur, these latter three buildings being attributed to F. Debias-Aubry

(e) A house at 47 Rue de la Harpe – attributed to F. Debias-Aubry, 1735

(f) Hotel Thoynard, 9 Rue du Coq-Héron, attributed to F. Debias-Aubry, 1735

(g) Cotelle house, Rue Saint-André-des-Arts, 1737

(h) Petit Hôtel de Bouillon, 15 Quai Malaquais, 1745

Toro inspired the decoration of these houses, which display the scrolls and chimeras, and the medallions and vases of his engravings. Le Pas-Dubuisson was one of the good architects of the Régence, comparable with J.-M.-A. Hardouin and J.-B. Marteau, the friend of Jean Bérain.

A passion for baroque sumptuousness is apparent under the Régence, subsiding after 1730. At the home of the Comte de Toulouse, Grand Admiral of France, Vassé senior decorated the gilded gallery, where he enframed compositions painted in the previous century and distributed a profusion of nautical trophies. But by 1720 the most original protagonist of baroque tendencies was Oppenord. The Regent's architect, and friend of the collector Pierre Crozat junior, he was acquainted with the Venetian pastellist, Rosalba Carriera, and was the owner of two paintings by Watteau, who used to copy his sketches. His position is central to the artistic movement of the Régence and the evolution of rococo. His architectural designs were picturesque, rusticated and enlivened by rocks, stalactites and vermiculation. Lions crouch in deepening grottoes beneath balconies. In the Place des Victoires, griffins supported the balcony of the Hôtel de Saint-Albin (Pl. 19). The design for the Gaudion house in the Marais, which was probably only partly executed, shows several of the chimeras widely used in the decorative art of the Régence, but which had become rare on the façades of buildings. They still support with their jagged wings the balcony of No. 133 Rue Saint-Antoine. Bérain had already introduced the dragon into the decoration of Meudon, but classicism dismissed such weird and ugly monsters.

Dragons and chimeras, familiar to readers of Mmes d'Aulnoy and Leprince de Beaumont, were a part of the mythology of this restless age. Oppenord's fantasies have the scales of lizards, webbed paws, and the coarse and wrinkled skins of toads. The contortions of this distressing beast are redeemed by the grace of the nymphs and the joy of the seraphs, created by Borromini and observed by Oppenord at the Lateran. The artist plundered the entire repertoire of nature; and, like the great ornamentalists of his century, he suggested not only the motifs, but 'material effects' which sculptors excelled in translating into wood, stucco and stone. Old men's hair turned into seaweed and their beards into shells, as on the doors of rococo houses. A sea wind speeds a train of Nereids. A swan sings among the bass-viols and bagpipes. Cupids slay eagles and ride on goats and dolphins. The models for monumental sculpture include roses, palms, shells and the wings of bats. Of such were the caprices which chiefly inspired rocaille decoration.

The publisher of the three collections of Oppenord's engravings, Gabriel Huquier, wrote that the Regent 'was always astonished by his prolific production', but nothing has survived of his work in the prince's service, except the beautiful designs for the grand salon of the Palais-Royal, which Fiske Kimball has published. We do not know the house, built by him in the Quartier des Halles for the ennobled merchant, Pierre-Michel Couet; but the salon of the Hôtel d'Assy is still intact (Pl. 20), and the salon of the Château de la Grange, mutilated in the nineteenth century, is known by a design preserved in Stockholm.

Oppenord's fame and the official position which he occupied for some years have earned for him a number of unsubstantiated attributions. Although recent evidence has thrown little light on the work of the star artists, it has revealed that they had many satellites. Thus, the grand salon of the Hôtel d'Evreux (Elysée) was not decorated by

Oppenord, as has been said. The trophies of arms, certainly the finest of the Régence, were designed by Hardouin and carved by Lange (Pl. 29). The salon of the aides-de-camp probably belongs to the same programme of decoration, carried out in 1723. After 1730 Oppenord had outlived his popularity. 'This architect', wrote d'Argenville, 'was often the object of envy.' His style, steeped in Borrominian precedents, which he had passionately admired during his Italian years, found detractors among the new generation. In a letter to his compatriot N. Tessin (the younger), the Swedish architect Hårleman, friend of the classicist Chevotet, refers to 'the taste of M. Oppenord and that of M. Vassé who, in my opinion, is much to be preferred to the former'.

In the days of his celebrity, Oppenord had an admirer in Pierre de Vigny, whose reputation, obscure today, ought to be re-established. He was one of the best informed of Parisian architects on contemporary international developments. A pupil of Robert de Cotte, Vigny had visited Italy in 1720, and built the French embassy in Constantinople. He also knew England, where the Royal Society, on Fontenelle's recommendation, welcomed him to membership. His most important building seems to have been the hospital of Lille. A great lover of painting, he had very strong and independent views about the arts. He dared openly to express his admiration for gothic art and to extol the genius of Borromini: 'Our architects languish nowadays in a kind of slavery, which ties them to an exclusive subservience to the ancient monuments of the Greeks and Romans. They need a propitious genius to release them, like among others Borromini who showed the way in Italy.' Among his very many clients were the restaurateur Chenizot, Labarre de Carroy, Antoine Crozat Le Riche and the Duc de Luynes.

The Hôtel de Chenizot (Fig. 1, p. 3, Pl. 31), Rue Saint-Louise-en-l'Isle, was reconstructed on the foundations of a building of the previous century. The *corps de logis* facing the road dates from 1726. The alternation of smooth courses and vermiculated rustication, the two tall slabs ending in half-moons, the decoration of the door leaves, derive from designs by Oppenord of the same period. Beneath the balcony, dragons, strain their gaping jaws, recalling those of the Hôtel Saint-Albin, and still more those of the Roman fountains designed by Giovanni Fontana during the pontificate of Paul V Borghese, for whom the fabulous beast was the heraldic emblem. The 'auricular' cartouche above the pediment is of a type common in Italy and the south of France. More subtle, the radiating motif, which dominates the court, is at once shell, sheaf and peacock's tail. Work on the house must have been spread over several stages, but the metalwork of the stairs (Pl. 32) and of the two balconies are of the same vintage. The garden front, which seems to have been the most recent part, already reflected the forms adopted by Vigny around 1730. This was when he built for Antoine Crozat le Riche the popular Cour du Dragon, a large scheme planned for letting as dwellings and commercial premises, near the Marché Sainte-Marguerite and Saint-Germain-des-Prés. These buildings, traditionally, but wrongly, attributed to Cartaud, were destroyed in recent times. The picturesqueness of the shopping court, where two staircase towers oversailed for support on to squinches, used to be admired. Above the doorway, the appearance of the fabulous animal masking a sham œil-de-bœuf was in honour of Sainte-Marguerite, patroness of the scheme, and of Mme Crozat, née Legendre (Pl. 33).

Mention must be made of other little-known masters of Parisian rococo whom documentary evidence has revealed. J.-.B. Vautrain was the author of the Hôtel du Tillet, Rue des Francs Bourgeois (Fig. 14, p. 56), and the Vatard house, Rue de Cléry (Pls. 59 and 60), where he used here and there the same motifs: the basket-arch on consoles and the shield wrapped in the skin of a winged lion. At the Hôtel du Tillet, the balcony exaggerates the movement of the inward-curving doorway. One senses an architect troubled by building-line controls. But a bold and uninhibited designer sometimes turned the public highway regulations to his own advantage. At the Hôtel de Jaucourt (Pl. 43), Desmaisons and his master-mason Varin suspended a rotunda above a void. Unexpectedly the upper detailing of the building, as conceived by Desmaisons, has links with certain Viennese work of J. B. Fischer von Erlach. Other Parisian architects of the reign of Louis XV recognisable from their works are Victor-Thierry Dailly, Pierre François Godot, Martin Goupy senior, the Quirot family and H.-Q. Desbœufs, to whom the Paris of the period owed some excellent buildings. Some, who made their careers in the provinces, worked occasionally in Paris, showing less constraint in private jobs than in official architecture. In the house of the Trois-Chapelets, 27 Rue Saint-André-des-Arts (Fig. 22, p. 77), Claude-Louis Daviler is no less monumental, but freer than in the cathedral of Langres. The iron balustrade of the balcony assumes the contours of one of the bulging chests *en tombeau* of Cressent or Gaudraux.

Meissonier, Thomas Germain, Lajoue and Pineau senior were the principal creative influences guiding the development of rocaille taste in the middle years of the reign of Louis XV, i.e. between 1730 and 1750. All were associated with architectural work and shared certain characteristics in their inspiration, but Pineau senior, who collaborated with many architects in their decorative designs, is the one whose

12 J.-R. Cochois: Hôtel, 47 Rue Saint-André-des-Arts, 1740

47

manner is most frequently detectable in domestic buildings. Under Meissonier's influence, Pineau supposedly introduced the 'contrast', that is to say dissymmetry, which first appeared in his work about 1736 and at once became widespread in Paris. On window-heads, the ornamental keystones are elaborate; the distorted escutcheon is set askew and has a chicken's wing attached. Wings, shells, foliage and roses are the adornments of consoles, which curve inwards to about the same extent in elevation as in section. The straight line has disappeared from ironwork, and a continuous movement runs through the entire metal system, in which graceful motifs are incorporated: flowers in bloom and shells like ammonites set in the veins of red marble in certain Italian paving. Pineau's sanguines, light and sensitive, often carry captions explaining their intention. After his return from Russia in about 1730, we can follow him year by year until his death in 1754. Jean-François Blondel, Tannevot, Leroux and later Le Carpentier and Briseux each in turn enlisted his services. Among all the architects who employed him one of the more curious was Pierre Boscry. An admirer of Bernini, he built a freely interpreted copy of Sant'Andrea del Quirinale for the Seminary of the Irish. At the end of the century one could still see in the park of Neuilly-Plaisance 'a flight of steps ornamented with a baldacchino of M. Boscry's design, with carved pilasters surmounted by lions holding palms fixed to it'.

The fine hôtels d'Orrouer (Pls. 64–9) and de Feuquières (Pl. 72) were built by the contractor Charles Boscry, probably to the plans of his son Pierre, and decorated by Nicholas Pineau. But the most zealous champions of this designer were the grandsons of Jules Hardouin-Mansart, who both practised architecture with distinction, the elder in his capacity as a dutiful parishioner of Saint-Eustache, the younger, the Comte de Sagonne, among the incidents of an eventful life. Theirs was already an old friendship when, in 1743, Pineau assisted Mansart de Sagonne in the construction of Saint-Louis de Versailles. Nine years earlier Mansart had been responsible for a building in Paris, for the wealthy young ladies of the community of Saint-Chaumont (Fig. 8, p. 34), which would have seemed very frivolous without the mask of wisdom adorning the door. The façade ebbs and flows like one by Guarini. Before Charles-Nicolas Cochin had disapproved of 'these S-shaped contours which are so fashionable that they are now used for the plans of buildings', contemporaries thought highly of them. The art critic P. Estève dwells upon the contrasting play of curves in a house with an undulating front like this one; no segment of it must be out of sight: 'At the ends may be placed concave parts which, as if turning back upon themselves, converge at a fixed point and satisfy the general instinct which wants to know everything without effort.' This is what Mansart did. The arch-head ornamentation suggests Pineau's authorship, and the balcony, which bears his imprint everywhere. It is one of four or five decorative schemes by his hand which enhance the external architecture of a Paris building. In 1752, when work on the Claustrier house, at 56 Rue des Francs-Bourgeois (Pl. 80), brought together Mansart de Sagonne and his decorator for the last time, the flagging inspiration of rococo was near the end of its career.

Classical nostalgia

The grace of the rocaille style, its variety and the abundance of masterpieces which it produced compel our admiration. The noblemen and financial magnates of the reign of Louis XV had the spirit of magnificence. Priceless sculpture, mirrors, furniture and ornaments would not have filled so many homes without the unanimous support of a cultivated society for its artists' ideas. Writers have told us of the elegant decoration which surrounded them, while architects praised the 'choice taste' of works which have survived to fill us with wonder. Certainly both the major and the minor artists of rococo were in no doubt about the beauty of the style which flourished in their hands. From 1730, however, at the very time when the movement was at the peak of its influence, a number of theorists took up their pens to indict it.

After the final years of Louis XIV, the age of great undertakings seemed finished, and many people turned nostalgically towards a reign in which France, in her political supremacy, had followed an ideal of simple beauty. The publication of *L'Architecture française* by Jean Mariette, continued and completed by Jacques-François Blondel, assembled the best of what French monumental art had produced thanks to Perrault, the Mansart family and their more loyal disciples. If, by chance, a design too obviously seduced by rocaille taste appeared in the collection, Blondel would remove the offending features with fraternal tact. At a period of economic and intellectual competition with England, the book was no less significant for the nationalism of its title, seemingly a reply to Campbell's *Vitruvius Britannicus*. For the historians of the time, the passage of the years had been interspersed with a few brief moments of splendour, separated by longer periods of decadence. One had perhaps reluctantly to admit that, since Louis XIV's death, France, with its fops and fripperies, was passing through an era of decline comparable with those which succeeded the ages of Pericles, Augustus and the Medici. The France of the Great King had perhaps emulated, or even surpassed, the perfection of classical antiquity. Now, for the fashionable critics, she was dishonoured by the imitators of Borromini, who had broken the precepts of Roman classicism.

The Académie Royale continued to pontificate gravely about perfect proportions and the orders; but, to live, most of its members had to compromise between strict conformity and the tastes of their worldly clients. Montesquieu recognised the need for rules and deplored the whims of fashion which spoiled good architecture: 'Architects have often been obliged to raise, lower and widen doorways, because women's dresses required these changes; and the rules of the art have become enslaved to such caprice.' Voltaire, on the other hand, sympathetic to the fashionable tastes of his noble patrons, ridiculed the architecture of the pretentious. The year is 1733, and the writer, while out walking with the Cardinal de Polignac and the Marquis de Rothelin, meets an upstart who is about to build: 'We found a fellow surrounded by painters, architects, sculptors, would-be connoisseurs and sycophants:

> *"I've gold galore, and wit in ample share,*
> *My taste, dear sirs, is quite beyond compare . . .*
> *The cash is here, so listen, while I speak. . . ."*
> *At once the rabble crew comply with zest*
> *And rack their addled brains at his behest.*
> *A mason, in Vitruvian pretence,*
> *Draws him a plan of brash magnificence. . . .'*

From the publication of his first theoretical works, which occurred at the zenith of rocaille, Jacques-François Blondel refused to reproduce the works of the architects in fashion, as a protest against 'indiscreet richness', to which the public was only too well accustomed. Boffrand and Blondel were agreed on one point: the ornamentation of the day, which had first appeared in interior decoration, might have remained there to flourish without harm, but unhappily, like a parasitic plant, it had spread to façades. The attack launched against rocaille grew in violence in the writings of the engineer Frézier, in Soufflot's lectures and from the pens of several art critics. Amongst others, the Abbé Leblanc assailed the accumulation of unrelated ornaments: dragons, rocks, shells, grotesques and arabesques, Chinese figures and bats' wings.

The protestations against rocaille were heard in the cultivated circle of Mme de Pompadour. Her brother, M. de Vandières, better known by the name of Marigny, was destined for the post of Directeur des Bâtiments du Roi, and prepared for his responsibilities by a journey which has remained celebrated. Guided by Soufflot, the Abbé Leblanc, and Charles-Nicolas Cochin junior, Vandières visited Italy in 1750. After their return, Cochin and the Abbé Le blanc co-ordinated their onslaught. In an account published a little later, Cochin attributed so much importance to the journey that it has become traditional to link it with the origins of the classical revival in France. Cochin aimed his shafts especially at the decorative arts, which in his view impaired by their extravagances the orderly arrangement of buildings. In 1754 he wrote in his *Supplication aux orfèvres*:

> It is requested that the sculptors of apartments, when executing trophies, may be pleased to refrain from making scythes smaller than a table-clock, a hat or a tambourine bigger than a violincello, a man's head smaller than a rose, a bill-hook as large as a rake. And may we at least hope that, when things could be square, they will be good enough not to distort them by those S-contours which they seem to have learnt from calligraphers and which are so much in fashion that they are nowadays used in the planning of buildings.

The architecture of reason

In the enlightened Europe of 1750, speculative minds reflected upon the nature of architecture, the validity of traditional structures and the resistance and properties of materials. The scientific spirit sought to identify the laws of architectural composition, in the hope of founding beauty on reason. The notion of applying mathematical ratios to architecture, whether or not these are related to the proportions of the human body, is a dream which goes back to Greece, and permeates modern times from Brunelleschi to Valéry and Le Corbusier. During Louis XIV's reign Blondel had defended the value of mathematical proportions against Claude Perrault. Under Louis XV the architect Briseux rather surprises us by affirming that one of the most enterprising protagonists of rocaille used a geometrical basis: 'Mister Pineau has a perfect understanding of the finer points of sections. His mouldings, which he designs to his own taste, are almost always in harmonious relationship; if they deviate, it is by so little that the most practised eye cannot detect it.' When he published his scheme for the Hôtel d'Augny (Pl. 93), today the Mairie of the 9th arrondissement, Briseux indicated the modular scale. The Abbé Laugier, whose illuminating essays on architecture fascinated the generation of Louis XVI, took up the idea. The division of surfaces must be controlled by one unit of measurement, which will recur under variable numerators. With Alberti and Scamozzi, Laugier regulated the height of rooms in terms of their floor areas. He proposed that the elevation of a hôtel should be divided into nine parts: four for the ground floor, three for the first storey and two for the second.

As far back as the fifteenth century Alberti had thought of a building as an organism which, in one respect, derived its beauty from an exact adaptation to its purpose. For many theorists of the Age of Enlightenment – Cordemoy, Lodoli, Laugier – the external appearance of a building had to express its function. No subterfuge was admissible. A pediment must not crown a building unless it corresponds to the two sloping sides of a roof. Our generation has talked a great deal about functionalism, but Diderot defined it once and for all: 'A piece of architecture is beautiful when there is solidity and this can be seen, and when there is the commodity needed for its purpose and this, too, is apparent.'

The disciplined system of antiquity, from which twentieth-century functionalism escaped, required a theoretical justification. Laugier found this in Vitruvius, who considered the temple to be a transposition of the primitive hut, and the columns as the equivalent of the tree-trunks used to build it. From this he deduced that only the giant order should be used, i.e. extending over all the storeys of the building. Here he came into conflict with Jacques-François Blondel, who still taught that the

13 J.-R. Cochois: Plan of Hôtel de Marillac, Rue Sainte-Avoye (now demolished), 1747

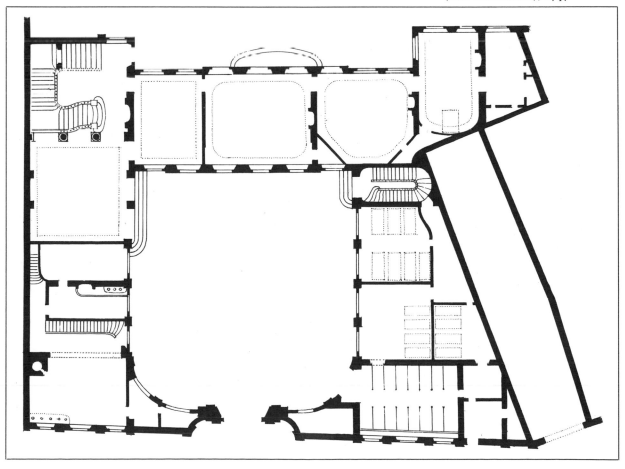

orders should be superposed in the manner of François Mansart in his masterpieces of Maisons and Blois. Laugier had little use for the arcade, insisting upon contrast and simple masses, and vigorously handled mouldings. Several passages, too little heeded by critics, deal with the private dwelling. Laugier is not speaking, he says, of 'those little bourgeois houses, where thrift rules all and one makes out as well as one can'. He is thinking of the hôtels and châteaux. Here, as everywhere, a single order should be planted on the base of the building, so that a strong and masculine entablature results. If there are no orders, the façade should be proportioned as if there were, the surface being evenly divided between openings and wall surface. Window-sills should be linked by a single band extending the whole width of the façade, and there should be few mouldings round windows, so as to avoid oversubtly proportioned enrichments imperceptible to the eye of the beholder. Few ornaments, too, but festoons, palms and chains of foliage, tastefully carved, may counteract the bareness of walls between storeys.

Laugier dwells less than Blondel on interior planning and comfort. He was mistrustful of draughts in suites of interconnecting rooms, but did not advocate the importation of stoves. He liked round rooms and alcoves, provided that their enframing pilasters conformed to the general arrangement of the room. For staircases he disapproved of circular flights, which were to prove a spreading fashion despite his strictures, and he liked the well to be lighted from the top. He exhibited a plan for Paris, opening up many new streets to display the monuments to better advantage. Along the streets, the middle classes and the poor were to be housed in apartment blocks. At the back these would have views of the gardens of the rich, who would occupy pavilions isolated in the middle. This, in any case, was a tendency that would characterise areas close to the boulevards under Louis XVI. Recent studies of Laugier have made it possible to detect echoes of his work in neoclassical theory, and to appreciate his influence on the monumental art of this phase. Undoubtedly the eighteenth century in Europe revealed a new approach to composition in plan and mass, which went far beyond the application of classical method and modular laws. But, in recommending the giant order, Laugier anticipated the desire for grandeur, which was soon to inspire French art after the Seven Years War. Blondel and the Italian Algarotti, articulate but discredited witnesses, watched the disintegration of a system deriving from the Renaissance, and which the reign of Louis XIV had raised to its perfection; and Sir William Chambers in England and Christian Weinlig in Germany offered some resistance to Laugier's opinions. But the Parisian architects of Louis XVI's time – Ledoux, Boullée, Girardin, Cherpitel – unhesitatingly preferred the principles of the daring amateur. To judge by their achievements, it appears that the critical attitude of the enlightened theorists of 1750 did not stifle artistic inspiration. By a few simple guide-lines and positive suggestions, Laugier stimulated the creative imagination which fashioned the ultimate masterpieces of the Ancien Régime.

The century of enlightenment, in which criticism was so active a force, still fixed its gaze upon the Graeco-Roman ideal, and it so happened that at that time classical archaeology was broadening the range of its investigations. The archaeological revival was an aspect of world discovery, which was such a general feature of the times. In Italy knowledge of antiquity had steadily advanced since Ciriaco d'Ancona and Mantegna. In France it was not new, and by the eighteenth century the movement had become international in scope. The field of discoveries now embraced Italy, Sicily, Dalmatia, Greece and even Syria. The distinctions between Greek, Etruscan and Egyptian were still ill-defined, but confusion between the first two is not yet completely dissipated. About 1725 the academies of Tuscany were extolling the Etruscan past and exhuming the griffins and sphinx, which found their way into architectural decoration around 1765. Scholars frequently conferred in Rome, and meetings, friendships and correspondence multiplied the contacts between Italians and their tramontane colleagues. The Comte de Caylus, who dominated French archaeology of the period, stayed only once in Italy, but journeyed as far as Troas and was familiar with the collections of Holland and England. A member of the Academy of Painting, his influence and protection extended to several artists, and he was one of the main French initiators of the neo-classical movement. Less reliable, but more enthusiastic, the Brandenburger Winckelmann guided European aesthetic thinking at the end of the century by his forceful writing.

The stimulus of the Continent had early engaged the British in archaeology, and Goethe admired their success in this branch of learning. Their taste for long voyages, pertinacity and cash were directed to the service of discovery. Lord Burlington and William Kent were in Rome in 1719. Robert Wood divulged the antiquities of Palmyra and Baalbeck. Stuart and Revett studied the buildings of Greece, Adam the ruins of Spalato. In Rome the British mingled with the Italians in their exploration of local sites. The boring of a well in the Campagna had uncovered Herculaneum in 1719, but the ruins of Pompeii were not identified until 1764. Today it seems that the influence shed on eighteenth-century art by the antiquities of these two towns has been somewhat overestimated. For a long time the King of Naples monopolised the secret of the excavations, but clandestine visits, hasty sketches and the pilfering of a few objects of practical evidence, mislaid perhaps in Piranesi's studio, had thrown light on certain mysteries. The official publication of the antiquities of Herculaneum was offered to the Abbé Barthélemy in 1755, and to Winckelmann three years later. Enlightened Europe placed ardent hopes in the rediscovery of Graeco-Roman civilisation. The prophets of doom had believed that they saw in the degenerate art of the Borrominians a relapse similar to what they called 'the darkness of Gothic times'; but the new dawn now breaking still bore memories of the Renaissance. The richer documentary sources of archaeology was able to provide architecture and decoration with the elements of a new harmony.

Artists now shared the enthusiasm of scholars. Raphaël Mengs and Gavin Hamilton, two painters established in Rome, were paving the way for Davidian classicism. The engravings of Piranesi, which played tricks with human scale and perspective, offered a grandiose and fantastic vision of the city of the Caesars. At the Palazzo Mancini, home of the French Academy, young artists eagerly supported the movement, and never had this institution, created by Colbert, more completely fulfilled the intentions of its founder. From 1760 to 1780 most of the former 'king's scholars' were to enjoy the favour of the French aristocracy. During their Italian years, under the eyes of Piranesi and the Abbé Barthélemy, the architects made measured drawings of the ancient monuments. Soufflot, Dumont and David Leroy revealed the Greek orders to the French: the Doric of Sunium and the Ionic of the Erechtheion, differing from their Roman imitations.

53

One man in particular commands attention, Charles-Louis Clérisseau, architect, painter of ruins and decorator of Parisian hôtels, who
had a worldwide influence on neo-classical evolution. A Prix-de-Rome
winner in 1746, he prolonged his stay in Rome by twenty years, and
was the friend of Winckelmann and Piranesi. He initiated the architects
Erdmannsdorf and Robert and James Adam in the study of ruins,
inspired the architectural creations of Chambers in London and of
Cameron in St Petersburg, and advised Catherine of Russia and Jefferson. In Rome relations were established between artists and the amateurs who were to become their patrons. Soufflot's journey in the company of the young Marquis de Vandières began the architect's career in
Paris. The Duc de Nivernais, French ambassador to the Papacy, commissioned Peyre the elder to plan his hôtel. For the Intendant Boutin,
'who devoured every antiquity', Barreau was to carry out one of the
first French decorative schemes in the Greek style. The Comte d'Orsay,
who travelled as far as Sicily, entrusted to Clodion the sculpture of a
burial chapel, in which Egyptian urns, obelisks and statues were ranged
beneath a dome copied from the Pantheon. Bergeret de Grancourt,
who accompanied Fragonard and his wife to Italy, was guided in
Rome and Naples by the architect Paris, who later worked for the same
financier's son on his villa at Le Roule. Parisian amateurs amassed
valuable collections of antiques. The financier Bouret owned the
'Etruscan pitcher', in which Caylus wished to be buried.

Palladianism

The prestige of the ancient world aroused fresh interest in its sixteenth-
century interpreters: Vignola, Michelangelo and Palladio. With
some of the students at the Palazzo Mancini admiration for the latter
equalled their respect for antiquity. De Wailly's inclinations were
evenly balanced between imperial Rome, the Renaissance and high
baroque. Le Geay's teaching and the Abbé Barthélémy's influence had
encouraged his archaeological pursuits. With his friends Peyre and
Moreau-Desproux, he made a detailed reconstruction of the baths of
Diocletian, in which Piranesi was interested. But he also measured and
drew the ceilings of the Gesù, decorated by Pozzo, and the baldacchino
of St Peter's. A little later he followed in the footsteps of the baroque
generations by decorating the Palazzo Spinola in Genoa, and the axial
chapel of Saint-Sulpice in Paris. In the decoration of Parisian hôtels,
he showed his interest in French Renaissance sculpture and in Jean
Goujon's canon of female forms. About the time when de Wailly was in
Rome, Victor Louis was making drawings in St Peter's, and his com-
panion Helin was recording the windows of the Palazzo Farnese, while
Poyet and Raymond concerned themselves with the buildings of Vignola
and Peruzzi. For many of their contemporaries, however, the architectural authority of the sixteenth century was epitomised in Palladio. The
master of Vicenza was admired for the simplicity of his masses and harmonious proportions. When he was in Italy, Goethe, too, admired the
architect's buildings at Vicenza and, as he was buying a new edition of
Palladio's great work at a bookseller's in Padua, five or six people
surrounded him in the shop and complimented him upon his acquisition: 'Taking me for an architect, they congratulated me for wishing to
study Palladio. In their estimation he merited a place far above Vitruvius, because he had a deeper understanding of antiquity and had
succeeded in adapting it to modern needs.' After the eclipse of baroque,

the Italian architect's designs remained a vital source of inspiration until the decline of the Napoleonic era.

In Paris, the example of the Palladian villa upset the traditional conception of the nobleman's residence, replacing the closed and secluded domain of the hôtel court by the detached, free-standing, pavilion. Yet France was not the first nation to experience a Palladian revival. In Venice, since 1720, the architects Preti, Calderari and Temanza had been nursing back to life the style and the glory of their compatriot. To the British, Palladian principles had been known since Inigo Jones brought them home with him in 1615. Eclipsed during Sir Christopher Wren's time, Palladianism had returned to favour during the second quarter of the eighteenth century by the contrivance of the Earl of Burlington and the architects Campbell, Paine and Isaac Ware. The ideal of the Whig aristocracy of George II's reign, Palladianism had led sooner than in France to an enthusiasm for antiquity. As early as 1730 certain English buildings show astonishing evidence of precocity. We need only mention the assembly-rooms at York by Lord Burlington and the hall of Holkham Hall (1730–35) by William Kent, in which the Ionic colonnade, the coffered soffit, the friezes of frets and wave scrolls, and the festoons and bucrania compose a grave and solemn harmony, which a Frenchman would think contemporary with Napoleon. With such examples before him, one can understand Horace Walpole's smile, when Parisians welcomed to their homes the 'Greek style', which they thought they had discovered. In 1764 he recorded a remark of the French ambassador, M. de Guerchy, to the Duchess of Bedford: 'Why, Madame, you have something Greek there without realising it.' But perhaps Walpole was exaggerating a little, when he wrote in 1766: 'Their apartments are bewildered by the mere suspicion of a Doric frieze.'

To note this priority on England's part is not to infer that it had any influence upon the formation of the Louis XVI style. In the third quarter of the century, French art critics expressed contradictory opinions about British architecture, from which no arguments can be drawn. The laudatory judgment of Pingeron was countered by the severe appraisal of the Abbé Leblanc, the friend of Marigny and Soufflot; but contacts and exchanges certainly took place between the two nations. In 1740, when the Borrominian Pierre de Vigny sought election to the Royal Society in London, he prudently asked his English colleagues to pardon the liberties which he might have taken with the general hospital of Lille. Landscape gardens, of English origin, became common in France after the mid-century. Sir William Chambers had known Mique and de Wailly at Blondel's lectures and was to be inspired by Antoine. He remained in touch with Marie-Joseph Peyre and David Leroy, and even invited Soufflot to London. Gondoin visited England and may have imitated the Admiralty colonnade at the Ecole de Chirurgie. An amateur as knowledgeable as the Prince de Ligne seems to have admitted that suggestions from England could have inspired the style of the time: 'I already disliked the woodwork and the irregular, contorted, designs of rocaille, before the English had brought us back the beautiful ancient forms from their journeys to Greece. . . .'

The influence of Robert Adam

But it was after 1780 when anglomania really appeared in France, affecting decorative taste, political ideas and dress. This was the time of the influence of Robert Adam, to whom is often attributed the return to favour of grotesques, so called because they decorated the imperial apartments buried like 'grottoes' beneath the Farnese vineyard on the Palatine hill. They are fanciful compositions, in which foliage is mingled with chimeras, sphinx, medallions, hydras, shields and bat's-wing fans. In fact, grotesques had always been represented in interior decoration, from Raphaël to the followers of Watteau, but archaeology had rediscovered the fountain-head. When Robert Adam was in Rome in 1754, he saw immediately and clearly how to exploit them in creating his distinctive style. But Clérisseau had been considering for several years the possibilities of fresh interpretation offered by these decorative forms. So Robert Adam, as certain fairly recently published passages from his letters to his brother James disclose, sought instruction from Clérisseau. Well knowing the kudos gained by Robert Wood for his publication on Palmyra, Adam dreamed of attaching his own name to a discovery of the same order. The antiquities of Dalmatia provided the answer. He was richer than Clérisseau and was able to pay for his services.

In 1757 the two men went to Spalato, Diocletian's Dalmatian capital, and 'took views and plans' of the ruins. When his lavish folio edition appeared in 1764, Adam acknowledged Clérisseau's part with guarded thanks, reserving to himself the principal role at this milestone in the progress of the classical revival. Installed in London in 1758, Robert Adam and his brothers shepherded into fashion a type of grotesque ornamentation based on antique paintings in Rome and the sigillated pottery of Arezzo, which enjoyed dazzling success. In England the vogue for this form of decoration lasted twenty years and declined after 1778, when the burdens of the American war turned English art towards less expensive modes, more restrained in taste. But the Adam style now spread to the Continent, where it influenced decorative art until the end of the Napoleonic era.

14   J.-B. Vautrain: Hôtel du Tillet, 31 Rue des Francs-Bourgeois, 1740

From about 1765, however, the *genre arabesque*, practised by disciples of Watteau, like Huet and Peyrotte, had been revived in France as a result of the archaeological movement, but in a manner far removed from the Adam style. For the salons of the Hôtels d'Hallwyl and d'Uzès (1766), Ledoux had designed foliage and chimeras which heralded a new development of the arabesque. In 1776, Clérisseau created for the grand salon of the Hôtel de la Reynière one of the finest examples in Paris of Roman grotesques. Executed by La Vallée-Poussin, it was sold in the nineteenth century and went to England, where it has recently been identified. Scenes from the *Iliad* are represented on oval medallions surrounded by foliage and vases, in a harmonious combination of mauve, sky blue and gold. The conception and colours already anticipate the Empire style. The elements of this scheme are preserved in the Victoria and Albert Museum, as are those of the Hôtel de Sérilly, which have similarities.

The transition of styles

Until 1770, while the public was still hesitating to relinquish the tastes of the rococo age, the new architecture was taking its first tentative steps and disclosing the themes, which it would develop in future years. It is always interesting to note, at each stage in the evolution of a style, the waning of the old forms and the emergence of the new, and every such evidence of the transition must be mentioned. Among dated examples of the dying Louis XV style are the Claustrier house, 56 Rue des Francs-Bourgeois (1752) (Pl. 80), the Pavillon de Hanovre (1757) (Pls. 106–7), and the oval staircase of the Palais-Royal (Pls. 99 and 100) and the apartments which it served (1755–60). The Claustrier house, built by Mansart de Sagonne, retained a serpentine balcony, but the arch keystones, where endive once grew, displayed fluting and nailheads. At the Pavillon de Hanovre everything was still rocaille: consoles, window joinery and pilasters (with their shafts adorned with acanthus) which Laugier considered dreadful. Designed by Chevotet, the building showed the Maréchal de Richelieu's attachment to the tastes of the past. The decoration of the Palais-Royal, the work of Contant d'Ivry, was published in the *Encyclopédie* in 1760. The stems of palms, condemned in Cochin's writing in 1754, frame the mirrors of the state bedroom (Pl. 101); but in the *grand salon*, with its rhythmic succession of columns, each door is surmounted by a beribboned vase. Surely as many omens for the future as survivals from the past! A few premonitory signs appeared in the pavilion built by Le Carpentier for the financier La Boissière. The flat-roofed ground floor offered unusual decoration. On the outside, on each of the square bas-reliefs above the openings, two or three figures were grouped as if on metopes, an arrangement later adopted by Brongniart and Boullée in several hôtels. But there is no certainty that the interior decoration, as it appears on engravings, corresponds to the original design, for the pavilion seems to have been remodelled about 1770 by Guillaume Couture, Le Carpentier's pupil and collaborator.

The transition of styles steadily proceeded in both architecture and the decorative arts. As early as 1753 the merchant Lazare Duvaux was selling chests-of-drawers 'à la grecque' to Mme de Pompadour. About 1756 a step taken by La Live de Jully, one of the amateurs who very deliberately guided the evolution of taste, marks an interesting stage. He invited the architect Barreau de Chefdeville, the bronze-worker Philippe Caffiéri and the clock-maker Julien Leroy to design the decoration and furniture of his study. The architecture has gone, but several items of the furnishings, a cabinet, the table and the clock, have been lately identified. The rather heavy construction of the first two imitates examples of Boulle, for these artists were reverting to the classicism of 1680. But the decoration uses elements which are new in choice and combination: frets, wave mouldings, rosettes, pineapples, and laurel leaves woven into slender festoons, which have been compared to well-ropes. This repertoire of ornament constituted what was soon called the 'Greek taste'. Cochin, Mariette and Grimm were unanimous in placing its popularity close to 1760. Caylus thought highly of it.

15 Martin Goupy: His own house, Rue des Prouvaires (no longer standing), 1740

58

The two decorators employed by La Live – Le Lorrain and Barreau – are still being discovered by researchers. A scheme by the former, dated 1754, has been noted by S. Eriksen at the *slott* of Akerö, 100 kilometres from Stockholm. Here there is no concession to rocaille, but an Ionic order framing niches and doors with classical cases. Le Lorrain had trained in Rome with Piranesi and Jardin, who was also one of the French precursors of neo-classicism in work carried out in Copenhagen. The hand of Barreau de Chefdeville has been recognised by M. F.-G. Pariset in some decorative designs for the Hôtel Boutin and the Intendance of Bordeaux. On plain backgrounds, friezes of frets and wave scrolls are distributed with the lavish emphasis which characterises their use on La Live de Jully's furniture. The style 'à la grecque' was not directly inspired by archaeological discoveries, but rather by the desire to emulate antiquity. In 1756 neither Leroy nor Revett had published their works on Greece, and almost all the ornamentation described under the arbitrary title of 'the Greek taste' was already found, in different combinations and contexts, among sixteenth-century architects.

In 1758 this conventional Hellenism clothed several private houses. The architect Moreau-Desproux, back from Rome in the preceding year, designed the Hôtel de Chavannes at the Porte du Temple. The plans disappeared in a fire at a notary's office, but we still have fine drawings of the boulevard elevation. Of modest proportions, it is five bays wide, the two at the ends, slightly projecting, being framed with giant pilasters, which convey an air of grandeur to the scheme as a whole. A dentilated pattern along the entablature, and a frieze of interlaces and olive foliage between the storeys, proclaim it a work of the 'Greek taste'. Laugier, while expressing the reservations that one would expect, appears to have detected in it signs of future grace:

> The architect who drew the plans for the house of M. de Chavannes at the Porte du Temple has shown the public that things can be done on a grand scale in a small space. If, instead of pilasters, he had put columns; if the dentils of the cornice were not of a zigzag type, and if the same ornamentation were not repeated on the plinth separating the storeys; if this plinth were removed, and if the band-mouldings of the windows above were connected with those below, this house would be cited as a model. Such as it is, it proves its author's merit and suggests a talent which will go far.

Another of the finest houses 'à la grecque' is No. 9 Rue du Faubourg-Poissonnière (Fig. 26, p. 85), described in a paper of 1759:

> M. Trouard, architect, has had built since his return from Rome in the Rue Poissonnière ['above the Boulevard', says another article] a fine house which, in its external decoration and formal details reveals the author's taste. . . . The staircase and formal arrangement of this house are worthy of note. The façade has a noble simplicity, adorned with two orders of windows, separated by a guilloche and surmounted by an elegant salient cornice of fine proportions.

Frets and wave scrolls were to remain the characteristic ornament of Parisian houses between 1755 and 1770. But, as early as 1764, La Live was regretting the consequences of his experiment: 'It was after the completion of this study that the taste for the Greek manner spread until it is now used absurdly in everything: crockery, jewels, fabrics, hairdressing and even shops, which almost all have signs "à la grecque".

All of which shows that ways will be found of making the best things ridiculous when they are abused.'

The transitory vogue for the Greek manner is evidence of a much deeper artistic crisis, the significance of which cannot be misunderstood. According to Fiske Kimball, the researches of La Live and his circle were without issue and neo-classical art did not appear in France before 1770, by which time English influence had brought it into prominence. In the history of the decorative arts and of furniture, however, a close study of the designs of Louis and Prieur for the court of Warsaw, and of the furniture of Pierre Garnier, J.-F. Oeben and Balthazar Lieutaud have made it possible to place the first stages of the Louis XVI style between 1760 and 1770. During this decade domestic architecture offered rare, but significant, evidence of inspiration drawn from antiquity and the Renaissance. M.-J. Peyre designed, for Mme Leprestre de Neubourg, a sort of Italian villa of austere appearance, with no decoration but a Tuscan peristyle and niches. About 1765 courtyards with Doric pillars, an interpretation of the Pompeiian atrium, appeared in the *folie* of the Intendant Boutin, a work of Barreau de Chefdeville, and at the Hôtel d'Hallwyl, one of the first creations of Ledoux (Pl. 120). In 1769, a Palladian arch, supported by two colonnettes, adorned the Hôtels de Saint-Florentin and Grimod de la Reynière, both neighbours of the Place Louis XV. It was again this feature, skilfully revived by Soufflot, which gave a monumental appearance to the hôtel of the Marquis de Marigny. Such conceptions heralded the flowering of the Louis XVI style.

In the view of contemporaries, rococo ornamentation spread from the inside to the outside of buildings. An inverse process was seen after 1760, when the architectural form imposed its own strict discipline upon the interior decoration. Classical order reassumed the place in apartments which it had occupied under Louis XIV. The semicircular arch succeeded the three-centred, the pilaster the palm-stem, and the acanthus the endive of rococo. Columns and pilasters framed stucco panels and carved wainscots. Designs now came into vogue for which the ornamentalist engravers supplied countless patterns. The *Iconologie* of Jean-Charles Delafosse, finished in 1768, remained loyal to motifs selected ten years earlier in the circle of La Live de Jully and Choiseul. To the fret and the wave, his repertoire added the laurel torus and the heads of rams and lions, leaving the cornucopia to La Londe, the bouquets of flowers to Ranson, and the vine to Cauvet and Petitot.

In the hands of these masters and those of their rivals, Forty, Prieur and Salembier, the Louis XVI style lightened imperceptibly and arrived at its incomparable charm. In decoration, which gave such delight to the age of sensibility, infinite variations were played on the theme of the lyre and the mask of Apollo, ribbons and rustic attributes, hearts and the quiver of Cupid. Twenty years before, at Bellevue, Mme de Pompadour had sprayed rose-water over her porcelain roses; and now, flowers, real, carved and painted, or brocaded into the silks of Philippe de la Salle surrounded Marie-Antoinette at Fontainebleau and Trianon. The enemies of rocaille had criticised the confusion which, in their eyes, reigned in its ornamentation. Henceforward the arrangement was clearer, and the elements represented conformed more closely to their models. As the sculptured objects became more distinct, they also projected further from their supporting wall, thus exemplifying, according to the aesthetic theories of Nordenfalk, a constant process in the life of styles.

Dreamland

In 1785 de Wailly was designing 'Etruscan' architecture for David, as a framework for *The Oath of the Horatii*, and Chénier was drafting the rhythms of *La Jeune Tarentine*. But, if the Graeco-Roman ideal inspired the major creations of French culture, domestic architecture and the arts of decoration and gardening were drawing heavily upon sources foreign to the neo-classical movement. From about 1780 the taste for disciplined perfection was opposed by an art of greater freedom and colour, of impulse, sentiment and imagination. The decadence of rococo was a response to the first stirrings of romanticism. The classical façades of Brongniart and Moreau no doubt had less appeal to the stroller on the boulevards than the fanciful creations inspired by the lure of the East and the Middle Ages. The hanging garden of the Hôtel Deshayes faced the establishment of the Chinese Baths; the kiosk of the Hôtel de Montmorency heralded the leafy shades of the Café Turc; not far away, the 'Vauxhall' of the Rue de Bondy displayed every style; behind its gothic front, the ceiling of a night-club in the form of a dungeon was supported by columns from Paestum. Higher up, a classical order and baroque caryatids framed the oval salon. The architect Michel Mellan, who had conceived this public dance hall and ran it himself, achieved an equal success with an amusement park, the Redoute chinoise, which he established on the Saint-Laurent fairground. A painter called Munich skilled in the arts of trompe l'œil, collaborated in Mellan's activities.

In the Italian tradition, painters like Munich, Sarrazin, Boquet, Nebel and Deleuze lavished the magic of theatrical illusion in *folies* and playhouses. Bedrooms and salons simulated the interiors of summer-houses or gardens in spring. In the Hôtel d'Argenson (Pl. 142), the mirrors arranged by de Wailly multiplied *ad infinitum* the reflections of the canephorae. His own hôtel, the chapel of the Virgin in Saint-Sulpice and the little boudoir of the Hôtel de Villette were among the creations of the same architect, which inspired this eulogy by his biographer: 'Who has not recognised in his works those dynamic flashes so familiar in Michelangelo, that brand of fire peculiar to Bernini and that characteristic intelligence of Vignola, so fertile in resource?'

A vogue for the conventionally exotic had mingled dragons and pagodas in the decoration of rocaille, and inspired Voltaire's *L'Orphelin de la Chine* and Favart's *Soliman II*. The Middle Ages, resuscitated by Benedictine scholars, now made its entry into painting. The mandarins and sultans were succeeded by troubadors and paladins. Ladies in the audience of a famous play fainted, when the Sire de Vergy had his wife served with the heart of her lover. On the initiative of the Directeur des Bâtiments, M. d'Angivillers, the best historical painters illustrated the great moments of French medieval history for the chapel of the Ecole Militaire; and, about 1785, there appeared in Paris the first houses in the gothic style.

In this period of tottering public finances, architects committed to engravings and drawings the grandiose dreams which reality prevented them from materialising, and this 'Architecture visionnaire' could provide the material for another book. In Rome, the Venetian master Piranesi anticipated Goya and Blake in the realm of hallucination and anguish, while a strange, funereal, mood inspired the engraved compositions of Jean-Charles Delafosse and Louis-Jean Desprez. In the tranquillity of his study, Boullée re-created, if unwittingly, the architecture of ancient Egypt.

In landscape gardens, copied from England, the reader of Richardson and Rousseau returned to the simplicity of nature, experienced a sense of primeval innocence and communed with eternity. Cottages, dungeons, pagodas and cenotaphs aroused in him a longing for distant lands and recollections of times past. In forlorn caverns echoed the lugubrious murmur of falling water.

We shall have to evoke at greater length the incongruous fairyland, in which the final years of the Ancien Régime were frittered away.

16   Fourcroy and other artists:
     Hôtel Jacques Samuel-Bernard,
     42 Rue du Bac, 1730–40

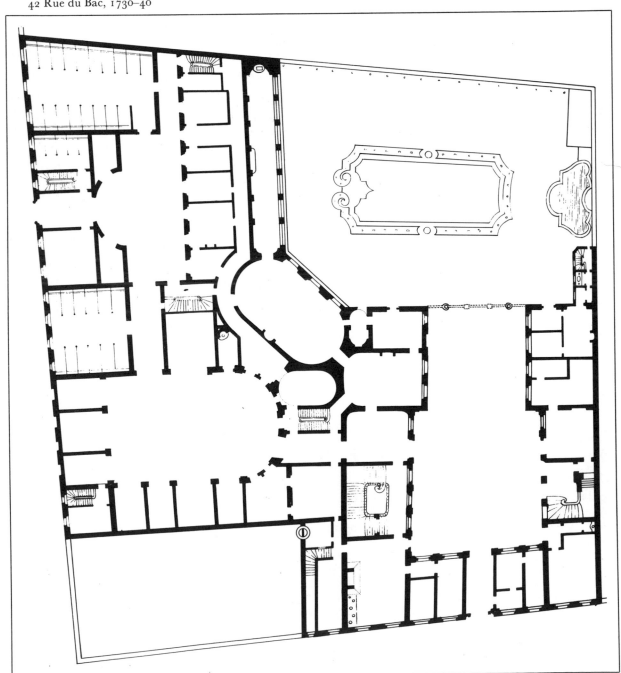

6 The middle-class home

'What makes Paris the most flourishing town in the world,' observed Voltaire, 'is not so much the number of magnificent hôtels in which opulence is displayed with some degree of ostentation, but the prodigious number of private houses where one lives in a comfort unknown to our parents and not yet attained by other nations.'

The apartment buildings, however, varied greatly in their importance and the quality of their architecture. The more modest were those in the central areas, where they rose on constricted sites previously occupied by houses with gothic gables. The most important were built by financing societies, whose properties extended over streets and even quarters.

The architectural conception of such buildings determined by economics and time-honoured custom, evolved slowly. The theorists concerned themselves little with the subject. One reason for this was to be found in the humble circumstances of their inhabitants. Jacques-François Blondel passes disdainfully over these 'buildings of little consequence' and this 'subaltern architecture'. He instances with distaste a merchant's house in the Rue des Mauvaises Paroles. But, between the time when the publisher Mariette had had the plans engraved and Blondel had commented upon them, the merchant had got himself ennobled and the shop had become an office. . . . The Graeco-Roman orders, in which alone resided the true excellence of architecture and the solicitude of the theorists chiefly lay, did not adorn these commonplace edifices. For want of columns and pilasters, the façades of the middle class eagerly welcomed rocaille, which the nobility reserved for interior decoration. As far back as 1738 Blondel had reprimanded the bad taste of such ornament, and after 1750 interest turned away from these dowdy structures, which did not seem worth engraving. Quickly skating past apartment houses in his talks to students, the professor cited favourably the bleak compositions of his friends Franque and Cartaud. However, he recorded his esteem for the architect Tiercelet, who had dealt with the subject in his *Architecture moderne*.

> The aim has been [wrote the author], to present in this collection many individual schemes and, among them, examples of those built every day in Paris for leasing to merchants. For houses of this type there is no need to use the orders. It is much more important to know how to dispose the parts of the building than to be acquainted with the proportion of columns. . . .

Tiercelet presented some twenty projects, many of which were adapted to confined or irregular sites (Pl. 21). In the eighteenth century the centre of Paris was rebuilt within its existing limits. The medieval houses were becoming ruinous, and the office of the Grands Voyers often ordered their demolition. Survey reports reveal that 'in order to effect an exchange', some redistribution of plots was occasionally attempted. More often new houses were built on narrow lots designated since time immemorial. The permanence of site boundaries is a striking feature of the topography of old cities. The Rues Saint-Martin and Saint-Denis still have houses of a single bay. Exiguous plots were counterbalanced by the number of storeys. Indeed, this town 'built in the air' stupefied Montesquieu's Persian visitor: 'The houses here are so high that one would swear that they are only inhabited by astrologers.' The apartments designed by Tiercelet had up to five storeys, disposed within the stipulated height of sixteen metres laid down in the by-laws in force since Louis XIV's reign.

There is no point in presenting an oversimplified classification of the building types which have come down to us, for the shape of sites and the way of life of their owners led to ever different solutions. Between the rented house of the Rue Saint-Martin and the nobleman's hôtel in the Faubourg Saint-Germain, the intermediate possibilities were unlimited. For the street frontage, the minimum provision implied sufficient width for a shop and an entrance to the building as a whole. The entrance passage received its feeble light from an oculus, pierced in the single leaf of the door and partly screened by a monogram or some other motif in wrought iron. In the Rues Chapon, de la Huchette and des Boulangers, some fine house doors of the Louis XV period survive. In the more felicitous examples, a house door or carriage entrance is placed between two shops, which gives a symmetrical design to the façade. The focus of interest was then likely to be the middle bay and its balcony, which provided one of the themes for poetic attention in rococo architecture. The other decorative elements were the carved keystones of windows and the banisters of stairs. Sometimes the recess of a well, used for washing carriages and 'horses' feet', would be decorated. One of the prettiest rocaille wells is to be seen in the court of No. 3 Rue des Lions. At 51 Rue Montmartre, the well is oddly located under a niche in the entrance passage. Other domestic needs were satisfied by water from Rungis and Belleville drawn at public fountains and brought to the upper floors by water-carriers.

At a time when the staircase was the sole means of access, the richest apartments (and often the darkest) were the lowest above the mezzanine (*entresol*). The first-floor apartment housed the owner or 'principal tenant', who took the whole house on lease and sublet the other storeys. The height of the ceilings and the rents grew progressively lower as one climbed to the top, so that the whole social hierarchy was gathered under the same roof. At the end of the century, the contrast between the squalid mezzanine and the rich apartment above it annoyed the moralists: 'While the architect has contrived to provide the first floors with ostentatious height, he has crushed the mezzanine. Once past the third floor, he has steadily reduced the air space until the seventh is as constricted as the mezzanine. Inhuman architects, you have adopted the mentality of the rich. . . .' Today, when the climb no longer entails any effort, the situation is reversed. The benefit of light, air and a view raises the price of the upper floors of blocks in which the different classes no longer mingle – a paradox of our time.

64

Plan of apartments

Certain houses which, on plan, had façades only five metres wide extended to a depth of thirty metres. The site was then divided between two or three *corps de logis*, separated by small courts and with passages underneath. Obviously, with so little space, one family would occupy two or three floors, thus following a very old Parisian custom. Tiercelet reproduces some plans of houses built by colleagues and improves them according to his lights. We can easily recognise in his 'distribution 29' the house erected at 151 *bis*, Rue Saint-Jacques by Claude-Nicolas Lepas-Dubuisson (Pl. 22). The façade, already monumental in character, has been widened by four bays, bringing up to nineteen metres the frontage of 'the site in question . . . on one of the finest and most frequented streets in Paris'. The handsome apartment on the first floor has two studies or, if one prefers it, salons on the street side, while one of the bedrooms and the dining-room enjoy the tranquillity of the court. The kitchen is on the ground floor in the region of the shop back-premises, which means that dishes have to be taken through the court and up the main staircase. That hardly seemed inconvenient in an age when the staff of the royal kitchens used to cover some hundreds of metres separating the Grand Commun and the Salon de la Guerre. Right up to the twentieth century, some of the fine houses of the Faubourg Saint-Germain remained unfit for letting as middle-class flats, because there were no kitchens in the best suites. Blondel particularly admired the commodious planning of the academician François Franque. The plan of the house built by the latter at the angle of the Rues de la Verrerie and du Renard conforms to the standards indicated by Tiercelet. In the principal apartment, however, a private staircase rises directly from the kitchen to the dining-room, a novel feature of domestic comfort; and each of the three dwellings is arranged between a main, and a secondary, staircase, common practice during the Régence.

In *Manon Lescaut*, the Chevalier des Grieux waits for the maid to come and open the front door of the apartment, while Manon hastily disposes of another lover by way of the little stairs 'which connected with the *cabinet*'. Thus was born the folklore of the back stairs. The only access for servants, tradesmen and visitors laden with cumbersome packages, this domestic alleyway, often sordid, but for generations essential to middle-class vanity, was to survive until the arrival of the refuse-chute. In Louis XV's time, it was still usual for the principal rooms to intercommunicate, but by the end of the century architects had learned how to give them independence.

Take, for example, the Richomme house, 12 Rue du Sentier, where a lobby serves the dining-room, salon, main bedroom and kitchen, which from now on becomes part of the apartment. The end rooms of an extensive suite, when such an arrangement existed, took the names of *cabinet* and *arrière-cabinet*. Two servants' bedrooms were generally provided in an apartment containing four principal rooms. The kitchen, connected to the first anteroom, might have service stairs. Privies were allowed one door in the apartment and another on the staircase. Rooms were wainscoted to breast height. Toiles de Jouy, and the wall-papers of Robert, Windsor, Réveillon, and Arthur and Grenard, introduced the pastoral motifs of J.-B. Huet and arabesque decoration into the houses of the Louis XVI period. Stoves were only provided in anterooms and dining-rooms, where they were accommodated in recesses. Reception-rooms continued to have fireplaces, their construction being improved about 1780 by Désarnaud, an architect from Lyon. Apart-

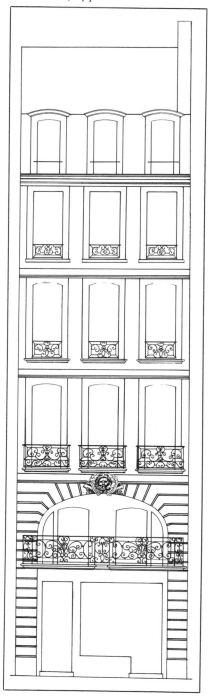

17 Pierre de Vigny: House of La Barre de Carroy, 42 Rue François Miron, 1742

ment buildings, when erected in pairs, benefited from the light of a larger court, divided into two by a low wall and with a common well. Typical and well-preserved examples of this arrangement can be seen in houses surrounding the Opéra-Comique and the Odéon.

Dwellings in large groups

'A town's beauty', wrote Leclerc du Brillet in 1738 in the *Traité de la police*, 'consists in the beauty of its streets, but the beauty of the buildings makes the excellence of the streets.' Middle-class property owners and religious communities built with a sense of working for the general harmony of the city. A uniform treatment was applied to groups of tenements built along a street, round a shopping court or a monastic close. The phenomenon of the modern city awakens our interest in the evolution of the collective dwelling and its standards of construction in the past. Some idea of this can be gained from the Rue de la Ferronnerie, built under Louis XIV for the chapter of Saint-Germain l'Auxerrois. The architect, Monnicault by name, erected over two levels of cellars a row of shops, surmounted by an *entresol* (mezzanine), two further storeys and a habitable penthouse. Originally each of the houses had a single occupant, before being let as flats. Between 1715 and 1730 the architect Thierry-Victor Dailly had occasion to build several groups of dwellings for his monastic clients. In the precincts of Saint-Germain-des-Prés, he succeeded in giving a monumental appearance to the houses of the Rue Childebert, with (on the ground floor) an alternating rhythm of shops and entrance doors, and (on the upper storeys) pilasters and pediments. This group was demolished to make way for the Boulevard Saint-Germain, but a fountain which ornamented the entrance to the street has been moved to the Place Monge. Two well-preserved schemes, however, deserve attention. From 99 to 105, Faubourg Saint-Denis, stands the terrace of fine houses of the Prêtres de la Mission. In the Place Baudoyer (Pl. 53), the Pourtour Saint-Gervais had kept its sober unity, marred at the corner of the Rue des Barres by the vanity of Maître Camuset, a notary, who disdained the general conception and chose an architect of his own.

Property developers often grouped houses about an internal court accessible to traffic and trading. In the Quartier Saint-Germain-des-Prés, the financier Antoine Crozat, and his wife, had opened the picturesque Cour du Dragon during Louis XV's reign. Later, certain apartment schemes were planned round an inner street, which sometimes had offshoots, to form what came to be called a 'square' or '*cité*'. Such was the group built for the Comte de Faudoas between the Rues Saint-Honoré and Bailleul (1780–82, archts. Mellan and Bergevin). Long known as the Cour d'Aligre (Fig. 49, p. 135), this passage was still open to traffic in 1910, and many years before our day had solved the problem of eliminating the narrow court, with its perpetual twilit gloom. Louis-Denis Le Camus drew inspiration from it in the plan for the Quartier Choiseul-Opéra-Comique, for which nine contractors shared the works. Ledoux, concerned for the well-being of the greatest number, was able to apply his social and aesthetic ideas to two 'units' of collective dwellings built for M. de Saisseval at La Grenouillère and for (the American) Hosten in the Rue Saint-Georges.

The architect's chief preoccupation was to replace, so far as possible, internal courts by open ones and to get light into them. In the plan for fifteen houses for Hosten, of which only four were built – but these at the height of the Revolution – the paths of an English garden wandered among the buildings. The scheme even reveals that the green space was to extend underneath one of them, past columns which already performed the function of the reinforced concrete pilotis of the present day. At the bottom of the Rue Saint-Denis a similar experiment was tried out in a group of 110 flats, which bore the name of 'Maison batave' (1792, archts. Sobre and Happe) (Pl. 177). Water from a sort of grotto supplied an illusion of freshness, while a winged figure of Mercury watched over the city's business from the top of the building. Elegant during the Directoire, this housing scheme, into which billowed the polluted air from the Halles, had become shabby by the time Balzac wrote about it. The novelist made it the home of Molyneux, a grotesque little capitalist and Birotteau's landlord,

> in one of the angles, on the sixth floor, for his health's sake, the air being only pure when seventy feet from the ground. Here the good landlord enjoyed the enchanting view of the mills of Montmartre, while pottering among the gutters, in which he grew flowers, notwithstanding the police regulations regarding the hanging gardens of modern Babylon. His flat comprised four rooms, excluding his precious privies on the floor above.

We have seen how favourable Louis XVI's reign had been to property speculation. In Paris, men like Lenoir, Caron, Ducret, Aubert and Prétrel had opened up entire streets.

Neo-classical façades

Since the period of the Greek taste, the elevations of tenements had an austere elegance, with an occasional order of pilasters, as at 1 Rue du Mail, 17 Boulevard du Temple and 4 Rue Caumartin (Pls. 146–7) (1780, archt. A. Aubert). To appear larger, the main entrance often incorporated beneath its arch a window or œil-de-bœuf of the mezzanine. On narrow façades, the architect deliberately emphasised the vertical features, by linking the windows of the two upper storeys with the same casing. Above the windows, recessed panels (for which the fashion spread, despite Blondel's condemnation) might accommodate bas-reliefs, symbolising the Arts, the Seasons or the Senses by depicting children playing with their mother. These would generally be mouldings bought from stucco-specialists like Feuillet, Chevalier, d'Hollande or Goutheinze, and examples can be found almost everywhere. Among the architects who excelled in the design of this building type were Beaudoin, Happe, Ducret, Bouchu, Rougevin, Porquet and Mullard. . . .

At the corner of the Rues de Bretagne and Vieille du Temple stands a very fine apartment block (Figs. 35 and 36, pp. 106 and 111), on which the series of the Five Senses, cast by d'Hollande, has been used twice (1777, archt. Blève). Nos. 1 Rue des Petits-Champs (1778, archt. Pasquier), 51 Rue Mazarine (1771, archt. Desmaisons), and 1–3 Rue de l'Odéon (1781, archt. Brûlé) are also interesting corner-houses. The building at 12 Rue du Tournon (Fig. 34, p. 101), erected to the plans of Neveu and, in the process, watched with interest by Soufflot, has been described as a masterpiece. An encased window and balcony, the only one of fifty-three to be decorated, is sufficient to attract attention and create a focal feature in the design. In major schemes, like the outer precinct of the Palais-Royal and that of the Halle au Blé (disappeared), the architects were not afraid of monotony. The elevations projected by Lenoir for the Rue d'Angivilliers, with their fifty bays of seven storeys, are astonishingly modern. The same uniformity characterises the seven buildings constructed in the Rue Saint-Honoré by Antoine, although the architect crowned them with an attic in the middle. As with the Adelphi, built on the Thames embankment by the brothers Adam, simple rented houses benefit from monumental treatment. When he visited Paris under the Directoire, the Prussian architect Gilly, an emulator of Bélanger and Ledoux, was struck by the uncompromising façades, and the aspects of the city which he recorded in his sketchbooks offered a curious preview of the present.

18 Contant d'Ivry: Hôtel de Thiers, 19 Place Vendôme (plan), 1747

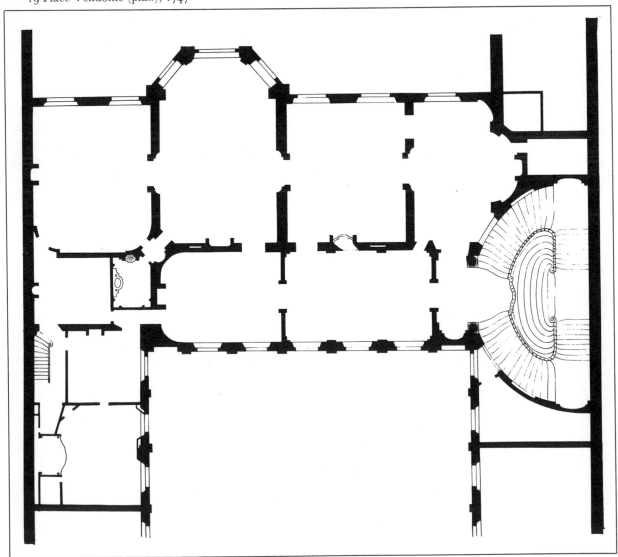

7 The nobleman's hôtel

Its evolution in the course of the century

The closing years of Louis XIV's reign and the Régence established the ultimate form in which the hôtel was disposed between court and garden. A phase in art and social evolution determined the character of these grand residences which shared a similar architectural inspiration and conception of prestige. The main door opened in the curve of a half-moon or 'round turret'. The arms of the owner were carved on the tympanum, like the stemma of Italian palazzi. The name of the hôtel would be inscribed, for everyone to see, on a slate tablet. 'Mme de Nesmond', wrote Saint-Simon, 'was the first woman of her position to have inscribed on her door: Hôtel de Nesmond. It caused laughter and scandal, but the notice remained and became the model and father of those which, in every shape and form, gradually inundated Paris.' Once past the main door, the architecture adhered to hierarchical principles. On both sides of the court of honour, occasionally on one side only, the front part of the site accommodated the house-yard, stables and coach-house. These secondary wings gave place to the residence itself, until the middle of the century generally crowned by a pediment. Two rooms deep, it was an impressive building, comprising two parallel suites of apartments, one open to the court; the other, provided with the more spacious frontage and contrived for the exclusive pleasure of the owner and his guests, looked out upon the garden.

At the Hôtel de Noailles, the end of the court was capped by a dome, like that proposed by Mansart in his 'grand design' for Versailles, so that the royal presence might be known from afar. Carriages could drive up to the entrance of the house, before withdrawing to the yard, which was connected to the court of honour by two openings to facilitate circulation. The visitor of quality exchanged the company of his servants for those of his host, passed through a succession of anterooms and arrived at the reception suite, which faced the French-style gardens. There was nothing aloof about such pomp, so long as the social obligations of the Ancien Régime expected a great lord to cater for the comings and goings of his family and dependants – officers, tutors, priests, secretaries, tenants and protégés – liveried and lodged in rooms of six to eight beds above a stable of thirty horses.

Later, when the Restauration had re-established the pattern of fashionable life in the Faubourg Saint-Germain, the great romantic writers found a relic of a vanished order. Since then, many hôtels of the

Régence and of Louis XV's reign have been destroyed to make way for the Boulevard Saint-Germain, but they have been recorded on engravings through the scrupulous editorship of Mariette and commented upon by Jacques-François Blondel, who gives their architects and, sometimes, their decorators. Like the two Mansarts, Robert de Cotte and Lassurance superposed the orders, the better to express the division of the building into several storeys. The giant pilasters of the Hôtel de Gournay were unique in reaching to the full height of the oval court, and reveal Boffrand's innovating brilliance, which heralded the monumental art of the end of the century. Where there were no columns, the court dress of French architecture, the elevations of Courtonne and Nicolas Dullin were divided in their width by a discreet rhythm of vertical bands of rustication. As at Versailles, sprays of trophies counteracted the bareness of trumeaux. The presence of an oval lobby, as in the Hôtel Matignon, might result in a three-sided salience in the middle of a façade. Decorative restraint and classical simplicity epitomised these designs.

It was elsewhere, in Lorraine and at Chantilly, that Boffrand and Jean Aubert exploited the bold planning and exuberant ornamentation which placed them in the European stream of baroque architecture. After the neo-classical reaction, the old nobility showed their loyalty to the forms adopted during the Régence, for these expressed the dignity of their rank. The main building of the Hôtel du Châtelet (Pls. 121–4) was distinguished by the giant order, a major architectural fashion, of which the Abbé Laugier had recently become the keenly supported protagonist. The shafts without fluting betrayed the admiration felt by the architect Cherpitel for the Roman frontispieces of Maderna and Galiléi. More familiar, the garden elevation was adorned with a three-sided fore-part in the tradition of the Régence (Pl. 124). In 1775 Horace Walpole described this house as one of the most handsome in Paris. The Hôtel of the Maréchal de Broglie, designed by Le Boussier, exhibited a completely military austerity on both the court and garden sides. It was typical of those 'hôtels with such flat façades, built about the time of Voltaire's death' in which Stendhal staged the meeting of Julien and Mlle de la Môle. A few warlike trophies, carved in low relief, were the sole decorative features. When he built the Hôtel d'Uzès (Pls. 115–19), the young Ledoux had to respect the traditional plan of ducal residences, for he was circumscribed by the foundations of an old building. Opting for the giant order, he did not follow his master Blondel who, at that time, resented the success of his enterprising pupils.

Master-architects as original as Boullée and Jean-Charles Delafosse continued to maintain the tradition of the classical hôtel between court and garden. In the court of the Hôtel Alexandre, 16 Rue de la Ville l'Evêque (Fig. 28, p. 88) Boullée repeated his design of 1764 for the Tessé *folie* at Chaville. The delicate peristyle, adorned with beribboned oculi, reveals a fashionable architect and no sign of the enormous buildings, which he created on paper after 1780.

While giving due credit to Delafosse, in his renowned capacity as an ornamentalist, for the Hôtels Titon and Goix, 58 and 60 Faubourg Poissonnière (Pl. 135), we can claim little novelty for the plans. At 58, however, one device shows his skill. The court, rounded in front like a horseshoe, widens at the back to make the *corps de logis* more spacious. In his engravings Delafosse shattered the traditional principles of design, subjecting the harmony of his masses to uncalculated hazards of equilibrium, and exacerbating the conflict of loads and bearing forces with

70

a temerity which suggested a 'tragic' disregard for structural realities (E. Kaufmann). But in the Rue du Faubourg Poissonnière the structural work reflects sound practice and, without the worry of an untried system, he was able to give free rein to his decorative imagination at a few selected points of the building. Here he applied some of the motifs which, in their combined effect, made his reputation as an ornamentalist: lions' snouts on the main entrance, laurel branches above the doors, and friezes of foliage between the storeys. In the entrance passage, two niches protect antique urns, the sides encircled with interlaces and laden with festoons sheltering Lilliputian figures, just as Delafosse had engraved them in his *Trophées*. Ledoux, Boullée and Delafosse were among the most original creative designers of this period, and their domestic buildings deserve the closest attention. Various rivals, to whom

19 Pierre Quirot le Jeune: His own house, Rue de la Jussienne, 1752

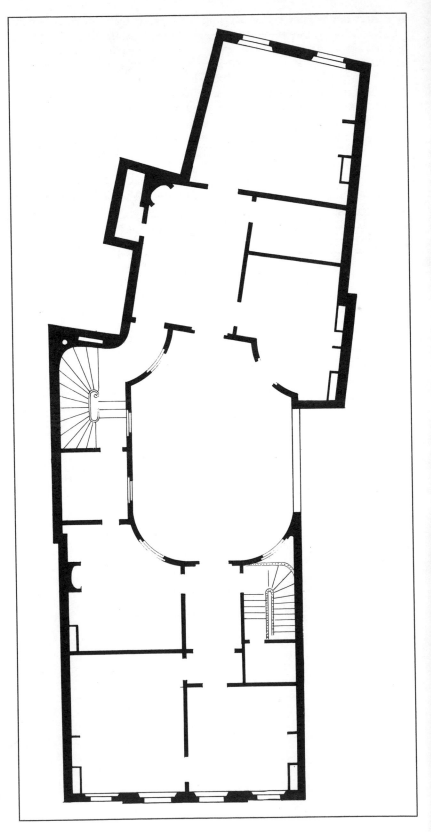

20   J.-R. Cochois: Plan of his house,
Rue du Bouloi (now
demolished), 1754

reference has been made in another work, found active employment in their wake.

In this field, too, we must guard against the arbitrary classification of buildings in terms of over-precisely defined prototypes. Creative imagination, financial resources, changes in living habits, the merits of the site and the accidents of orientation have inspired schemes too widely divergent to be classified systematically. All we can do is to follow the uncertain evolution of a few tendencies in the grouping of buildings, the place accorded to gardens and the arrangement of rooms. The Parisian hôtel long remained a closed and secret oasis, sometimes concealed in a complex of ordinary houses. Several writers have given the name 'hôtel on the street' to premises with a court preceded by a *corps de logis* of two rooms' depth which occasionally had shops, but always a carriage-entrance and a genteel apartment for rent above the entresol (mezzanine). Hôtels of this kind were built in Louis XV's reign, often on the foundations of an older structure, e.g. the Hôtels du Tillet (Fig. 14, p. 56) and Chenizot (Fig. 1, p. 3), the Julliennet house (once the Hôtel d'Andelot), or even No. 47 Rue Saint-André-des-Arts (Fig. 12, p. 47).

Under Louis XVI, the 'hôtel on the street' assumed the appearance of a Roman palazzo. In the case of the Hôtel Grimod de la Loube (disappeared; 1775–78, archt. Jaunez), the building's cubelike mass, rusticated quoins, doorway and inner court reproduced all the characteristics of Italian models. An Italian conception is also evoked by two fine houses built at Nos. 2 and 4 Rue de Tournon (1780, archt. Lemonnier, consultant, ?Bélisard). The Hôtel de Mercy-Argenteau (1778, archt. Perlin) followed the same precedents as those of the Hôtel de la Loube. The state apartments faced the avenue, and for the Austrian ambassador his hôtel was to prove a chilling reminder of Viennese palaces of the Freyung and the Herrengasse.

Great changes were at that time taking place in the conception and formal organisation of buildings. Their analysis is a delicate matter, but the tendencies which emerged were a variation, rather than a complete elimination, of those of baroque times. It no longer seemed necessary to design the elevation of a building in terms of a central element, predominant in height and mass. From 1750 pediments became rarer, as Laugier noted with satisfaction. They were sometimes replaced in hôtels by a simple acroterion surmounted by a coat of arms. The absence of any salient feature, and the repetition in sequence of a similar bay across the entire extent of a façade could be most effective, as the Procratie of Venice prove. This arrangement, which Louis handled triumphantly on the Palais-Royal, is found in hôtels after 1770, but was not the general rule, and certain variations might be applied to a giant order, even when extended over the whole front. The alternation of openings and pilasters obeyed a subtle cadence. At a time when the doctrine of harmonic proportions was returning to favour, monumental art clearly illustrated the relationship suggested in ancient philosophy, and instanced by Alberti, between musical successions and architectural rhythms. Usually the movement was only propagated in brief sequences, but if we go round a free-standing structure, like the Châteaux de Bénouville or des Boulayes (archts. Ledoux 1770, Girardin 1785), we see the gradual development of a rhythm enlivened by slight variations. In the Hôtel de Monaco (Pl. 145), Brogniart accentuated the two end bays, where he doubled the pilasters and enriched the decoration of window-casings. In other instances, the giant order embraces only a few bays in the middle: three at the Baron de Breteuil's house, and five at the Hôtel de Montholon, where the bareness of the end bays contrasts with those in the middle and enhances the latters' monumental effect. In several cases, the giant order was restricted to the end bays, an arrangement adopted by Moreau-Desproux at the Hôtel de Chavannes and copied by Bonnet de Boisguillaume at the town-house of the Marquise de Boufflers, where the handling of the colossal order represented composition in a major mode. The modesty of certain façades without columns, however, is at times more sympathetic.

21 J.-R. Cochois: The same house, street and garden elevation.

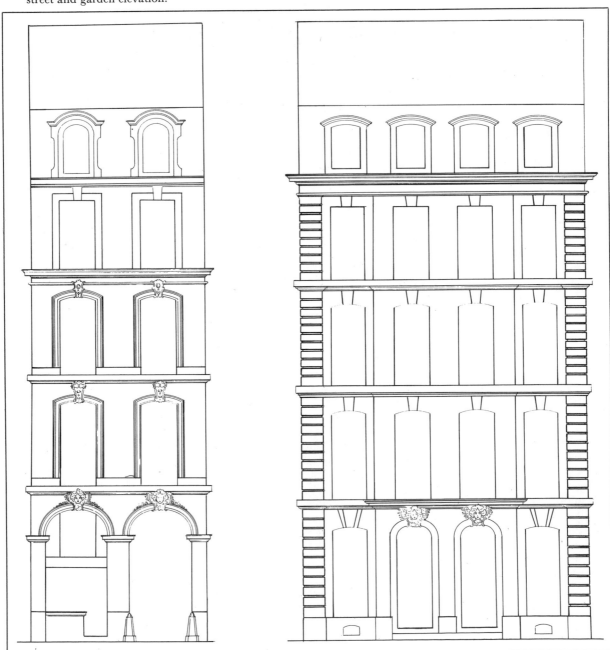

François Mansart's ideal of a hierarchy, gradually modulated between the central dominant and the lateral parts of a building, gave place to the contrasting of simple masses. The cube and the cylinder were uncompromisingly juxtaposed in schemes designed to be admired from the outside and from every angle. There were already signs in this architecture of the application of Cézanne's principle, which was to sow the seeds of cubism. The detached block of the Italian villa succeeded the secluded precinct of the hôtel court. It was a supreme irony that, at this moment when aristocratic society stood at the edge of the abyss applauding *Figaro*, it exposed itself to the full glare of the Third Estate. In the still semi-rural areas of La Grenouillière, the Champs-Elysées and along the Boulevards, a new harmony was developing between the architecture and its natural setting. In the Rue de Provence, Ledoux raised the Hôtel Thélusson (Pls. 159–63) in a pre-romantic garden studded with wild rocks. Laden with evocations of the Forum and of Hadrian's villa, but astonishingly close to our day in its bare-surfaced masses, this palace stood in the middle of a rural landscape. Its success was prodigious and all Paris enrolled to see it. During the Restauration the Hôtel Thélusson was bought by a tailor named Berchut, and subsequently demolished to provide space for the extension to the Rue d'Artois, today Rue Laffitte.

The only private palace which can compensate us for the loss of the Hôtel Thélusson is the Hôtel de Salm (Pls. 153–7), even if the fire of the Commune has obliterated the original decoration. A site as unstable as that of the Hôtel Thélusson obliged Pierre Rousseau to project the main *corps de logis* on a raft from a central point of support. This architect had no mind for commonplace solutions and, as is suggested by a curious caricature by Vincent, dated from Rome and entitled 'Rousseau cogitating', the companions of his student years sensed this. In the Rue de Lille, a classical triumphal arch was inserted between two colonnades; and, as at the Palais-Royal and the Hôtel de la Vrillière (Pl. 127), the passer-by looked straight into a home of the privileged classes. Two bas-reliefs evoke a Roman *suovetaurilia* and the Triumph of Titus. In the court, a little Ionic order allied to a giant Corinthian suffice to adorn the peristyle. When the scaffolding was dismantled, the harmony of the elevation facing the Seine and its rotunda amazed Jefferson:

> I have fallen in love [he wrote to Mme de Tessé], not with a woman, but with a house! . . . In Paris I was struck by the Hôtel de Salm and went daily to the Tuileries. The chairwoman, indifferent to my passion, never had the delicacy to put a chair for me in the direction of the object of my admiration. And so, sitting on the parapet with my head turned, I used to leave with a stiff neck.

Like the Hôtel de Thélusson, the Hôtel de Salm affords reliable proof of the architectural mastery attained in France on the eve of the Revolution.

A balance was established in the Hôtels de Salm and Thélusson between the central rotunda and the cubic mass of lateral buildings. Newton's contemporaries liked the round form, which was applied to boudoirs, *grands salons* and Italian-style staircases, i.e. lighted from the top. Occasionally the house itself was round, like the one which Trou (known as Henry) built at the foot of Montmartre for the Fermier-Général Vassal de Saint-Hubert. Carried on a 'crown' of Grecian pillars, it was a sort of 'tholos', comparable with Ledoux's toll-houses of Reuilly and La Villette. Notwithstanding Fiske Kimball's view, it is incorrect to say that round rooms in France were a belated imitation of England. They are found under Louis XIV and XV, especially in pavilions like those of L'Aurore at Sceaux, Trianon and Le Butard (Gabriel) and Gennevilliers (Servandoni), nor had France waited for English examples before expressing the mass of such rooms on the outside of buildings.

Moreau and Goupy were designing rounded projections about 1770, that is to say before Adam's publications, in which examples are shown. Moreover they could turn to models offered during previous reigns by Boffrand and Cartaud. The theme of the rotunda, much relished in Louis XVI's reign, reappears in the châteaux of Combreux, Surville, Le Menil-Riant and elsewhere. Sometimes, two might enliven the extremities of the *corps de logis*, like those which Bergeret junior tacked on to the former Beaujon *folie*, built by Girardin in the manner of a Dutch farm. As far back as 1733 we saw the young Desmaisons building for Mme de Jaucourt, at the corner of the Rues La Vrillière and Croix-des-Petits-Champs, a strange building with rounded protuberances carried on squinches over the void (Pl. 43). This overhanging structure looks to us like a last manifestation of the medieval bartisan and Blondel speaks in this context of a 'house in the form of a tower'. If the neo-classical age abandoned the audacities of the old stonemasons, the architect André Aubert was still able to erect a tower at the entrance to the Rue Caumartin. Given an extra storey in the nineteenth century, it has lost the female figures of its balcony, savagely mutilated to provide space for signs. But it bears continued witness to the geometrical taste of the time. The austerity of its architecture was, in addition, mitigated by the delights of an Anglo-Chinese garden on top.

We can see, in an apartment building at 136 Rue Amelot, one of the circular courts, condemned by certain theorists, which appear frequently on the survey map of 1810. Bélanger built several, but the most remarkable example was provided for the Hôtel de Saint-Priest by the architect and archaeologist Jean-Arnaud Raymond. The containing wall of this grandiose amphitheatre was recessed at three points by three high niches, and the plan imitated the frigidarium of large Roman baths.

Such forms were based on Roman monuments, as archaeology thought fit to interpret them. But certain enterprising designers, already influenced by romantic sympathies, sometimes also copied from these monuments the changes wrought by the passage of time. At the entrance of the Hôtel Thélusson, a 'great gaping mouth with nothing to say', a monumental arch rested on piers which were only a quarter of the normal height, bearing the same relationship to classical triumphal arches as a basset to a greyhound. Ledoux had been attracted by the engravings of Piranesi and Barbault, in which the arches of the Circus Maximus and the 'Golden house of Nero' are shown embedded in accumulated earth and ruins up to the springing line of their imposts. A scheme by Ledoux for the Hôtel de Montesquiou d'Artagnan develops the same theme. Boullée, in his turn, was to put forward models of what he called 'buried architecture'.

Graeco-Roman ornaments were used in profusion on façades. The Etruscan sphinx appeared from 1765 on banisters and on the acroterion of entrance-doors. Emperors' busts and gorgons' heads were placed in round niches. Bands of bas-reliefs ran along attics and round rotundas. Clodion modelled some of these friezes: the triumph of Galathea on the Hôtel de Sainte-Foix, children's games for the home of Mlle de Bourbon

22 Claude-Louis Daviler: Simonnet
house, 27 Rue Saint-André-des-
Arts, 1754

23 Ironwork designs which corroborate attribution of several houses to J.-R. Cochois:

(a) Cochois house, 29 Faubourg Saint-Martin, 1740

(b) Claude Aubry house, 1732

(c) 47 Rue Saint-André-des-Arts, 1740

(d) Central balcony, 47 Rue Saint-André-des-Arts, 1740

(e) Aulard house, Impasse des Trois Visages, from an old photograph as are: a house, 11 Rue de la Ferronnerie and Nourry house, 115 Rue Saint-Honoré (the latter two attributed to Cochois)

(f) Nourry house, first floor

Condé. On the entrance of the Hôtel de Salm, the preparations for a sacrifice, carved by Roland, recalled a Roman *suovetaurilia*. At Mlle Guimard's house, Ledoux called in Félix Lecomte to celebrate the triumph of Terpsichore, and Raymond proposed to represent, in front of Mme Vigée-Lebrun's studio, a group of her pupils at work. Most of these friezes have been dismantled, destroyed or replaced by plaster casts. The procession of children of the Pavillon Gouthière is probably one of the last to remain in its original position.

The covered entrance

We must now consider the interior space of the hôtel, both in its organisation and in its convenience for living.

In Louis XIV's reign a flight of steps was usually placed before the main building. This looked impressive, but exposed the visitor to the weather when he descended from his carriage. The exacting Blondel condemned the misuse of pediments on private houses, but recognised their value in deflecting rain-water from both sides of the steps. Sumptuously dressed for a winter ball, ladies wanted to arrive under cover, and this was a consideration which had not been ignored by Louis XIV's contemporaries. A covered carriage-way extending through the building was needed, as Le Pautre had contrived for the Hôtel de Beauvais, Cottard in the Hôtel de Biseuil and Hardouin-Mansart in the Hôtel de Lorges. In 1705 the Swedish architect Tessin submitted to Louis XIV a scheme for completing the Louvre, which provided for carriages to arrive under a peristyle. The King examined the model in the company of the Resident, Cronström: 'His Majesty asked for some clarification regarding the galleries. I said that . . . those below would serve for the entrances and staircases, for carriages, for the guards when they attended H.M. on horseback and the weather was foul, and to enable people in the courts to proceed under cover. . . .'

It seems, therefore, that in northern countries it was normal to provide for arrival under cover. Boffrand had noticed this in Germany and planned for it at the palace of Lunéville. In Louis XVI's day Le Camus thought it essential in big houses. After 1760 we find it at the Hôtel de la Mark and at the Marquis de Gallifet's, in a hôtel in which the reception suite was on the ground floor. In the Chaussée d'Antin, on ground confined by the Rue Basse du Rempart and in a zone saturated by underground water from the so-called 'Grange Batelière', architects willingly sacrificed the ground floor for the benefit of a *piano nobile*. In these houses, which bear a closer resemblance to Italian palazzi than to hôtels in the French tradition, carriages passed under the *piano nobile*, sometimes in a gyratory movement, as in the Hôtel Thélusson and in (the architect) de Wailly's house. Visitors ascended the height of the ground floor, to be welcomed on a landing serving the reception-rooms around it.

In the Middle Ages and the Renaissance our ancestors were not afraid of the cold. A few Parisian houses of the sixteenth century and Henri IV's reign have preserved their staircases open to the courtyard. For a long time nostalgia for Italy affected architects and persuaded them to design open entrance-halls, which enabled the cold to penetrate the house. During the Régence, the Hôtels de Noailles and d'Humières were arranged like this. But Blondel gives us to understand that, at the Hôtel Biron, the Duchesse du Maine had to glaze the open bays of a hall, originally designed to be exposed to the fresh air. The ground floors were very cold in winter. In the Palais-Royal and the Hôtel de

Noailles, we find them almost entirely reserved for pages, gentlemen in waiting and servants. Their proximity to the gardens, however, made them suitable for accommodating summer-rooms. Some houses had 'summer salons', where stucco ornaments, fountains and trellises created the same fresh, country atmosphere as in the *sala terrena* of Italian residences. In the period of Louis XIII and Louis XIV, the Queen Mothers Marie de Médicis and Anne of Austria had their own summer apartments on the ground floor of the Louvre.

The halls and first anterooms were not panelled with wood. Their decoration was carved in stone, and the module of their columns had to be the same as on the façade. The Hôtels de Matignon, de Roquelaure and de Lassay have retained these handsome features. According to Le Camus, a first anteroom contained, in a large cupboard, the footmen's hats and overcoats and, in another, the candlesticks; while one or the other might hold, during the daytime, the folding bed of the servant on night duty. Through a second anteroom the visitor came to the staircase.

Staircases

For at least four centuries, from the unknown master of Chambord to Charles Garnier, the principal staircase of a palace offered exceptional opportunities to the architect's invention and the craftsman's skill. The staircase was above all the place of reception and splendour. Louis XIV would often welcome his guests from the top of a grand stairway. There, his glory might prevent him from stepping down towards the visitor, but his words of welcome were always timely and often impressed the court by their aptitude. When the great Condé returned to Versailles after his victory at Seneffe, he asked Louis XIV to excuse his gout-ridden bearing: 'Cousin,' replied the King, 'when, like you, one is laden with laurels, walking is bound to be hard.' Such was the privileged purpose of a grand staircase at the time when the Escalier des Ambassadeurs, one of the most splendid which ever existed in France, was built at Versailles. It disappeared with the coming of Louis XV to provide space for the bedroom and private accommodation of Madame Adélaïde, for by then convenience had ousted pomp. Every great house, however, had its staircase of honour, while in other parts of the dwelling humbler stairs would be allotted to servants and the lower orders. When Mme de Sévigné installed herself in the Hôtel Carnavalet, in the district which was to give her 'fine air', she was delighted to find close to her room 'a fairly adequate little private staircase; it will also be the morning stairs for my servants, my workpeople and my creditors'.

A tradition, nowadays disputed, attributed to Mme de Rambouillet the idea of placing the staircase of honour in the angle formed by the main building and one of the court wings, on the right if possible, where the visitor would instinctively turn. Placed there, it ensured communication between the service wing and the *grand appartement* without interfering with the suite of rooms. As a rule, it was also the only space occupying the full height of the building. For one going up or down, it offered constantly changing views, which enabled the decorator to contrive surprises.

The commonest plan was that of the staircase '*à la française*', in which two or three straight flights hugged the walls of a rectangular well, round a central void or 'hollow newel'. According to Boffrand and Blondel, the stairs must be on the right when going up. The first flights must rest on a string wall, with an œil-de-bœuf to light the way down to the cellar. The string wall was occasionally replaced by an ingeniously constructed cloister vault, like that of the Hôtel Matignon. Higher up, at each succeeding storey, the resistance of the stair-head beam absorbed the load of steps and strings. Among the staircases 'in the French style' of old Paris, the one at 6 Place Saint-Sulpice by Servandoni is one of the most impressive in scale and in the boldness of its construction (Pl. 96). Designed with equal success by the same architect, the staircase of the Hôtel d'Auvergne has unhappily disappeared (Pl. 95). Innumerable other examples of this type were installed, and they were not unknown in neighbouring countries, including Britain. But Orientals apparently liked the continuous-ascent type better, represented by the *scala regia* of the Vatican. When the architect Pierre de Vigny built the French embassy in Constantinople, he designed straight staircases

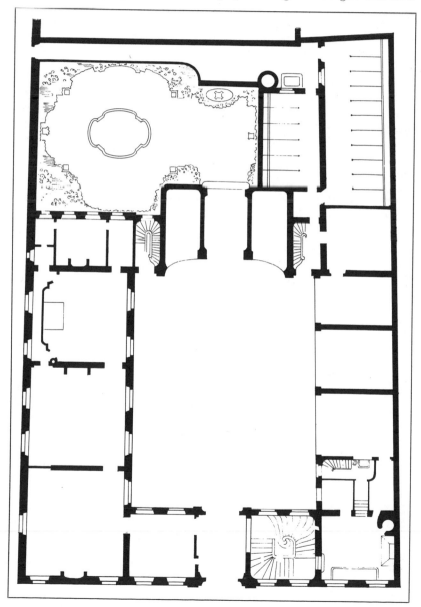

24 Mouret: Hôtel d'Estiaux, 1 Rue de Lille (plan), 1754

in preference to 'escaliers à la française', to avoid disconcerting the Turks.

The staircase of the Hôtel Dodun (Pls. 13–15), Rue de Richelieu, was one of the most agreeable of the Régence. The beauty of their decorative sculpture distinguished the Louis XV staircases of the Hôtels de la Grange and d'Ecquevilly (Pl. 63) in the Marais. That of the Hôtel de la Vrillière (Pls. 129–30), already neo-classical, is mentioned in an almanac of the time as 'of the latest taste', an appreciation justified by its magnificence, its banisters, and its ceiling painted in trompe-l'œil. In the Hôtel de Saint-Priest, for which the architect was certainly Jacques-Denis Antoine, the principal staircase is decorated by female statues representing the Arts (Pl. 131). This is a masterpiece by the artist who designed the staircase of the Palacio de Alba y Berwick in Madrid and that of the Hôtel des Monnaies, one of the most majestic of the century.

The classical tradition of the century of Louis XIV was perpetuated in other original creations. In 1770, when Monseigneur de Beaumont had the old archbishop's palace, by Notre-Dame, rehabilitated, the architect Desmaisons built a staircase of honour which attracted contemporaries by its elegance. This was an open stairway comprising three parallel flights: the one in the middle, supported on string walls, extended to mid-storey, where the stairs divided. From there the two upper flights, carried on flying strings, gave access to the apartments. On the inner face of the well, an Ionic order, statues in niches, and a soffit with coffers and rosettes contributed to an imposing scheme of decoration. Desmaisons considered the staircase to be one of his best works and had engravings made of it in 1780. If the neo-classical period was to proliferate circular stairs, in spite of Laugier's strictures, the era of rococo had been addicted to elliptical and basket-handle staircases. These respective forms had been used by Contant d'Ivry in the Palais-Royal (Pls. 99–100) and the Hôtel de Thiers, Place Vendôme (Pl. 98). We shall refer to them again for the beauty of their decoration.

Court ceremonial and private life

The eighteenth century was the first in which the form, size and decoration of rooms were differentiated according to their function. Until then, the living-rooms and state apartments in palaces were called without distinction *salles* and *salons*. Before the eighteenth century, sovereigns and great lords did not separate their official and private lives. Henri IV received the Spanish ambassador, while playing leap-frog with his children, and the Queen was brought to bed in public. At Versailles, the apartment of a princess might be divided into two by a passage, along which filed foreign tourists. Almost continuously on show, Louis XIV submitted until the end of his days to an etiquette which he himself had imposed. But the shy and secretive Louis XV must have endured reluctantly the constant comings and goings which disturbed the peace of his palace. When he had to pose for Quentin La Tour, the King led him to the furthest part of the suite 'to be less disturbed', an action which drew this response from the bumptious pastellist: 'I did not realise, Sire, that you were not master in your own house.'

Yet it was in Louis XV's reign that a distinction was created between official life and time devoted to family, friends, study and repose. Thus Blondel divided the dwellings of persons of quality into three categories of rooms: the formal or state apartment; the apartment for company, dedicated to intimate conversation, so dear to the century of the *philosophes*; and that of 'commodity', reserved for personal life and convenience. In practice, the distinction was not always apparent. The company-rooms took turn and turn about with those for formal occasions, which were often distributed between two storeys of the hôtel. In Louis XV's time, the prominent middle section of the garden façade was favoured for the state suite: on the ground floor, the *grand salon*, on the floor above the state bedroom.

Grands salons

The planning of a *grand salon* posed delicate problems, for its height had to be proportioned to its superficial area, necessarily greater than that of the adjoining anterooms. The architect might crown the room with a calotte or shallow dome, contained within the height of the floor above. This was the course adopted by Boffrand at the Hôtel d'Argenton, where Coypel decorated the cupola. If, like the Palais-Bourbon, the building consisted of only a ground floor, the dome was incorporated in the roof frame. Under Louis XV, *grands salons* in the Italian manner, i.e. occupying the height of two storeys, were rare in Parisian houses. Oppenord designed one at the Palais-Royal, as part of a decorative scheme today disappeared, which was to the Régence what Versailles is to Louis XIV style. This salon, located at the right angle formed by a suite of rooms and the Galerie d'Enée, was projected on consoles over the Rue de Richelieu. At the lower level, between Ionic pilasters, a relic of the 'grand taste', oval medallions at mid-height adorned the panelling, an arrangement which Oppenord was to repeat a little later at the Château de la Grange-du-Milieu. Above the chimney-piece was placed a mirror framed with figures *en espagnolette*, common with Oppenord; and this, with a corresponding mirror at the end of the Galerie d'Enée, combined to give the illusion of an endless vista. At the higher level of the salon there was a balcony, capable of holding an orchestra. Statues placed in niches alternated with trophies, and terms supported the archivolts of windows, through which the light streamed down into the room below. At night, a chandelier and clusters of candles, held by tritons and naiads, shed their brilliance upon the green Campagna, clouded brocatel and violet Breccia, marbles which, with crimson tapestries, formed the background for selected masterpieces of the Venetian school.

This type of room, with its high dome or lantern, was sometimes called a *salon à l'impériale*. The one contrived by Boffrand in the Hôtel de Canillac, Rue des Francs-Bourgeois, was circular in shape and cleverly supported on the corbelling of a squinch. In the Hôtel de Jeaucourt, Rue de la Vrillière, two squinches, executed by Varin to the designs of Desmaisons, carried the fore-part of an oval salon, which has unhappily lost its decoration of 'Chinese-Tartar figures'. The baroque period made frequent use of the ellipse in architecture, and it may be worth recalling that Kepler had attributed this figure to the orbit of heavenly bodies. France is indebted to Le Vau for *grands salons* of oval form, e.g. those of Raincy and Vaux, the latter being a target for the admiration of the *précieuse* Mlle de Scudéry. A music party, painted by Lancret, has an oval salon for background, which strongly recalls that of Montmorency (Pl. 166), built by Cartaut for Pierre Crozat at the beginning of the eighteenth century. The Hôtel Biron has preserved

25 House in the Greek taste, 12 Rue de la Lune (house of the Sœurs de la Charité, now Ecole d'Electronique), about 1760

two large oval *cabinets*, from which the panelling, probably designed by Jean Aubert, was removed in the nineteenth century, but restored quite recently to its original setting, thanks to the vigilance of a few experts and generous financial support. The Louis XV panelling of the elliptical *grand salon*, decorated for Jacques-Samuel Bernard, and auctioned in the 1880s, is today in the museum of Jerusalem.

The two finest oval salons of the Louis XV period remain those of the Palais Soubise (Plas. 85–7), where they are placed one above the other in a pavilion built by Boffrand for the Prince Hercule-Mériadec and his young wife. On the ground floor, in the Prince's salon, stucco panaches, on which Jean-Baptiste II Lemoyne and Lambert-Sigisbert Adam modelled allegorical compositions, surmount wainscots which have just been restored to their original 'flax-grey' (with faint reflections of green). On the floor above, the oval salon of the Princess is the most beautiful room of a house in which an incomparably happy coalition of the decorative arts was accomplished under Boffrand's direction. Between the arches, Natoire painted on the panaches eight scenes from the story of Psyche, who personified the soul and love. On the ceiling, against a sky-blue background, delicate filigree tracery recalls Rouen porcelain. In his day Boffrand enjoyed international status, and his work at the Palais Soubise invites comparison with other elliptical salons scattered throughout Europe.

At Stupinigi, in Piedmont, the *salone* occupies the entire height of the building, with balconies at first-floor level, linked by a passage running behind the columns and embracing the room. At Frain (Vranov), in Moravia, the oval hall, in which the ancestors of the Counts of Althan are honoured, occupies one of the buildings fantastically silhouetted on a cliff-top overlooking the wooded valley of the Taya. Ferocious statues of bygone lords form a solemn ring about the walls, while above them on the domed ceiling floats a fresco vision of the deification of the House of Althan. Near Munich, in the pavilion of Amalienburg, the mirror-heads carry cartouches filled with a profusion of motifs: cornucopias, harps, violoncellos, and kettledrums played by cupids. Along a serpentine cornice, roses, vine leaves and pitchers of water mingle with gulls and herons. In this masterpiece of Cuvilliès, the rococo deploys all the exuberance encouraged by the use of stucco and scagliola, materials more tractable than the wood of Parisian panelling. And yet, in the salon of the Princesse de Soubise, the absence of any sharp division between walls and ceiling, the illusion of open sky through the rays of gilded filigree, and the interplay of mirrors surrounding the room result in an enlargement of space, which is the secret of baroque art.

The ellipse continued in favour after rococo. At the Hôtel Thélusson, Ledoux's masterpiece, the harmoniously projecting curve of an oval *grand salon* was the central feature of the façade (Pl. 159). None the less, the neo-classical period, more or less consciously dominated by the Newtonian theory of gravitation, preferred the perfect figure of the circle. If that agreeable theorist, Le Camus de Mézières, held oval rooms to be the more voluptuous, round ones seemed to him gayer; and he himself had put round and oval dance halls side by side at the Colysée, a place of public entertainment built to his plans in the groves of the Champs-Elysées. In the Hôtel Delahaye and in the salon of the Princesse de Bourbon-Condé, an order of Ionic pilasters ringed the room. In the pavilion of the Comte de Lauraguais at the Hôtel de Brancas (Pl. 171), Bélanger alternated the columns with niches containing deep sofas. There, as in the Hôtel d'Orléans, the entablature carried a campana thronged with cupids. At Beaujon's house at Issy, at the Hôtel de Salm, and at the home of Mme Thélusson, there was a double dome, the first calotte being pierced in the middle to reveal another, on which might be painted a fleecy sky, the heavenly train of Olympus or the topmost branches of a forest. In some instances, light from invisible windows entered through the central oculus; and an orchestra hidden behind the circular balustrade could be heard without being seen.

In a dependent pavilion of the Palais Bourbon, Callet painted Venus, Adonis and nymphs on the compartments of the lower dome, the open centre of which could be closed by a mobile 'lid', hoisted upward by a system of brass tapes, while mirrors all round the room rose out of the floor to mask the windows:

> The upper part of this ceiling is removed by mechanical means and fitted into the groups of clouds which pass behind the circular gallery, the top of which serves as a platform for the musicians, whom one does not see, but whose sweet strains strike the organ of hearing agreeably. At the same instant and by the same means, the windows disappear and are replaced by mirrors which occupy their full height. The salon is then lit by a soft and agreeable light which it receives through the ceiling. The harmony between these mirrors and those opposite to them multiplies to infinity the grandeur of the room and its decoration.

In the round rooms of Bagatelle, and of the Hôtels de Tamnay, Beaumarchais and Thélusson, the dome was hemispherical and decorated with coffers, following the example of the Pantheon of Rome.

Salons de compagnie

Less formal were the *salons de compagnie*, where people met in the after-

26 L.-F. Trouard: His house in the Greek taste, 9 Rue du Faubourg Poissonnière, 1758

noon for conversation, gaming or music. For these rooms, symmetrically placed dummy doors were not recommended, because they discouraged guests from sitting close to them, for fear they should open. The furniture would include sofas, corner-cupboards, console-tables, a desk and a harpsichord by Ruckers, perhaps decorated by Audran or Gravelot. The inner face of the façade and the cross-walls were panelled. A wall opposite windows might be embellished with mirrors or tapestry, and the seat-coverings and curtains could be varied according to the season. Door-curtains, much in favour during the Régence, went out of fashion at the end of Louis XV's reign. The chimney-piece usually occupied a cross-wall, so that the company could form a circle round it without the cold draught caused by a line of doors extending throughout the suite. The principal ornament of the room, the chimney-piece had to be in view of the entrance, so that its mirror would enable the mistress of the house to recognise new arrivals before rising to greet them. However, it could with advantage be placed to face the windows, so that the light would fall on the book of a fireside reader; for reading aloud was one of the pastimes of these ladies 'who in the twilight of their beauty opened their minds upon a brilliant dawn'. A man of letters was generally 'minister of these little realms', whose lively atmosphere is adequately depicted in J.-Fr. de Troy's picture *A reading from Molière*.

Eating-rooms

The eating (or dining) room, which had formerly been only an anteroom, made its appearance in the eighteenth century, but was still only a big-house luxury. The plans of apartments of Louise XVI's time continue to describe it as 'anteroom serving as eating-room'. Under Louis XV, it was recommended that this anteroom should be kept somewhat apart from the other reception-rooms, for 'the humidity, and the smell of fruit and meat at all seasons of the year are communicated too easily to the adjoining rooms, tarnishing furniture, gilding and bronzes . . .'. Moreover, if the rooms were included in a suite, the company could not enjoy the vista, when the servants were engaged in laying or clearing the table in the closed dining-room. An engraving has survived of a dining-room – described as salon – which appears to have been decorated about 1720, in a suite of summer-rooms (which no longer exists) of the Palais Soubise. A feature was the fountain, placed between statues of Ceres and Bacchus, who provide the good things of the earth. Fountains were a source of much inspiration to designers. Dolphins and fish played among the water-plants round the conch. The water *buffets* of classical gardens thus found their way into the house and brought freshness to summer-rooms. The Slodtz family were known for their skill in cutting basins from marble and moulding the lead for them.

A Louis XV fountain can be admired in the anteroom of the Col de Cygne at Fontainebleau, and Nicolas Pineau's drawings have made us familiar with some very beautiful examples, which adorned the dining-rooms of the Receveur-Général Boutin and the Prince Isenghien. In the house of the Fermier-Général Le Normand d'Etioles, Madame de Pompadour's husband, a nymph accompanied by a duck and a spaniel surmounted the shell. The two Louis XVI fountains, designed by Cherpitel for the hemicycle which terminates the dining-room of the Hôtel du Châtelet (Pl. 124), surpass in elegance those of the Hôtel de Courcelles and Neveu house, 12 Rue de Tournon. After a dinner at the financier's (Jean-Joseph de la Borde), Horace Walpole described ironically to the

Countess of Suffolk the dining-room of a large Parisian house, in which the ostentation of his hosts was only equalled by the ill-demeanour of the servants: 'If ever you should meet a person of taste to guide you, your dining-room will be adorned with large hunting scenes in gilded frames of every colour and, to crown one of them, you will put a pointer flushing a partridge, which will take wing on the panelling a little further along.'

By the middle of the century, the dining-rooms of palaces had become sumptuous. That of the Palais-Royal, says a contemporary description 'is ornamented with an architecture in stucco which vies with marble in its freshness and brilliance'. In the home of the Duc de Nivernais, landscapes painted by Hubert Robert lured the diner's gaze to far horizons of the imagination. In the Hôtel Thélusson, a 'festival to Bacchus' and a 'festival to Flora', compositions 'analogous to the usage of the room', had been painted behind stucco columns imitating the breaching of Aleppo. At the Hôtel d'Aumont, in the Place Louis XV, in a scheme reassembled in our day in the Hôtel de la Trémoille, bacchic symbolism discreetly sketched into the decoration accompanies female statues carrying cornucopias. In the Rue de l'Arcade, in a 'little house', where the Prince de Soubise, vanquished commander of Rossbach, spent his remaining days in the society of charming companions, musicians could be hidden in the heights of an invisible gallery.

27   L.-F. Trouard: Banisters in the same house, 1758

State bedrooms

The eighteenth century remained faithful to state bedrooms, organised on the classic model of Louis XIV's room at Versailles. Towards the end of the Ancien Régime, however, they existed mainly to satisfy the demands of etiquette and were rarely slept in. The bed faced the windows, or the wall separating them (if the room had only two). Framed by columns, it was divided from the rest of the room by a railing. In the enclosure so defined, the walls were covered with tapestry, which could be renewed from season to season; but the summer hangings, and the winter ones also, had to match the colours of the panelling which embellished the rest of the room. The Régence occasionally permitted wood in its natural colour, but soon the taste for light and gaiety brought into fashion white picked out with gold, a combination which still flourished in a few state bedrooms of Louis XVI's reign. But white is tiring to the eyes and was often replaced by pastel shades of green, jonquil, lilac and delicate blue. Pale yellow was the rage about 1740, often combined with a sky-blue bed and blue curtains. At the end of the century, green was held to be the colour most favourable to rest. The bed might be placed in a recess, a relic of the old-fashioned alcove, which obliged servants to pull it out to make it more conveniently. Underneath the draperies of the recess were doors leading to the *petit appartement*. By this means, at his levée, the great man withdrew from the gaze of strangers admitted to the state apartments. Safe from prying eyes, he passed into a small study to dictate letters, breakfast and talk to his family, and give his steward the orders for the day.

The Palais-Royal had two fine state bedrooms. The Regent's had

28   L.-E. Boullée: Hôtel Alexandre,
      16 Rue de la Ville l'Evêque,
      1763

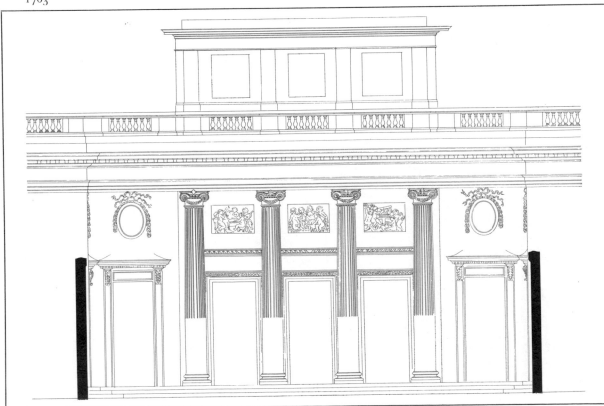

been designed by Oppenord in 1716. The author of *Curiosités de Paris* describes it in these terms:

> Next one passes into the bedroom of M. le Régent, which has been enlarged and improved recently. The ornamental sculpture which decorates it, the mirrors and the elegant disposition of the alcove make this room entirely charming. The alcove, which contains a splendid bed, is supported by two guilded columns of the composite order and enclosed by a balustrade of the same taste. The beauty of the chimney-piece matches all the rest.

We know from the Regent's inventory that the hangings were crimson damask. Forty years later, Contant d'Ivry tried to emulate the beauty of this room in one of the last suites of the Louis XV style, created in the same palace for the Regent's grandson (Pl. 101). The *Encyclopédie* published an engraving of this state bedroom and contrasted the beauty of its Corinthian columns with the already outmoded caprices of rocaille. Under Boffrand's direction, two state bedrooms were decorated at the Palais Soubise, for the occasion of the marriage of the Prince Hercule-Mériadec and a nineteen-year-old widow named Sophie de Courcillon. From the Prince's alcove a secret staircase climbed to that of the Princess. The carved and painted allegories in the husband's room depicted Hymen, Military Glory, Truth and Wealth; and, in the wife's, Cupid, the Graces, and Minerva, goddess of wisdom. Boucher, Jean Restout and Trémollières shared in the painting of these mythological compositions.

The Hôtel de Luynes, destroyed to make way for the Boulevard Saint-Germain, contained a state bedroom installed by Moreau-Desproux at the time of the vogue for antiquity. The furniture, the bed and the back of the room were covered with brocaded satin. The columns of the alcove and the panelling, ornamented with smoking incense-burners, were reassembled in the Louvre a few years ago (Pl. 126). The room has retained its white background and gilding, which contemporaries considered magnificent. In less elaborate rooms, the alcove might simply be framed with pilasters, as in the Baronne d'Espagnac's house, with sculptured doors, as in the Hôtel de Tessé, or with panelling on which allegories of sleep and silence might be painted.

Galleries

Galleries were already common in the seventeenth century, and the best painters had vied with each other to adorn them. But, while these masters enjoyed ever increasing admiration, the arrangement of their compositions and the decorative sculpture which framed them often seemed out of date to the contemporaries of rocaille. At the Palais-Royal, the Galerie d'Enée, built by Mansart and painted by Charles-Antoine Coypel, was given an exuberant chimney-piece in 1716 designed by Oppenord. Three years later, Mollet applied the taste of the Régence to the high gallery of the Hôtel de Bullion, where Vouet had illustrated the *Odyssey*. In the Hôtel de Toulouse (today the Banque de France), Robert de Cotte was at that time ornamenting the gallery which François Mansart had built many years before for the Duc de la Vrillière (Pl. 25). The room, forty metres long, ended on a 'squinch', overhanging the Rue Neuve-des-Bons-Enfants. In compartments defined on the ceiling, François Périer had painted Apollo vanquishing Night, the Hours, Juno commanding Aeolus to unleash the winds against the

Trojans, and Neptune and Thetis. Opposite the windows were deep recesses, which Robert de Cotte replaced by mirrors to make the room lighter. The Comte de Toulouse had completed the collection of Italian and French pictures, which had adorned the walls since the Duc de la Vrillière's time. Vassé senior surrounded these compositions with fretted borders, and decorated the doors and corresponding chimney-piece at opposite ends of the room. Above the door, according to a description, Diana and her nymphs appeared agreeably surprised by the beauty and magnificence of the setting. As became the house of the Grand Admiral of France, the decoration borrowed its principal symbols from the sea. A ship's prow escorted by Tritons and Winds surmounted the mantel of the chimney-piece. Net, shell, turtle and crab attended Amphitrite on a bas-relief. Stripped of its paintings and ravaged by time, the gallery was restored in 1875. It has in part preserved the orna-mentation of Vassé senior and recovered its gilding, which amateurs of the past would have preferred less uniform.

More subtle in its splendour, the gallery of the Hôtel de Villars was built and fitted out by Leroux in 1732, i.e. at the happiest phase of rocaille (Pl. 71). A profusion of mirrors, placed opposite the windows and even on the wall between them, vastly magnified the size of the room and, as at Versailles, reflected the garden and made the walls seem transparent. Bernard and Pineau carved a sort of filigree pattern for the frames of the looking-glasses, supplied by the *miroitier* Garnier. Turpin gilded the bronzes of Leraistre. Baron Pichon's collection con-tained the commemorative inscription discovered in the foundations of the gallery. The panelling is today shared between the two English 'châteaux' of Waddesdon and Mentmore. As at the Luxembourg and the Hôtel de Toulouse, the only chimney-piece had a purely decora-tive purpose, being too small to provide heat for such vast rooms, which were used nevertheless for dancing at winter receptions.

The middle of the century and the transition from rocaille to the Pompadour style offer no examples of galleries as fine as these, at least among the hôtels of the capital. But an admirable gallery in the Parisian manner was constructed at that time in the château de la Grange, residence of the celebrated Maréchal de Saxe at the time of his retire-ment. On the ground floor, this example of a *sala terrena* is entirely decorated with the stucco-work of the famous Monsiau (known as Chevallier), and helps us to imagine what the (long gone) *salons frais* may have been like at Fontainebleau and Trianon. In the Hôtel de Toulouse, a fairly unobtrusive rhythm of composite pilasters alternated with the pictures and mirrors; at La Grange, the architectural order dominates, the sculptured decoration being confined to a few handsome military trophies. A similar course was followed with the two galleries in the Palais-Royal designed by Henri Piètre, 'architect in ordinary' to the Duc de Chartres.

The eighteenth century had already played havoc with Richelieu's apartments. In the Cardinal's lifetime, the 'Galerie des Hommes illustres' had been dedicated to twenty-five characters from French history, painted in broad outline by Philippe de Champaigne and Simon Vouet. Another gallery, in which Richelieu displayed his own collec-tions, extended from it. After his death, all this part of the palace was little by little transformed by successive generations, and the impressive galleries gave place to small suites, pleasantly situated on the main courts of the palace. The old gallery of 'Illustrious Men' had lost two-thirds of its original length and measured about sixteen metres at the time of its transformation by Piètre. The architect introduced Doric pilasters with delicately incised shafts. Opposite the middle window, a niche held a statue of Flora, surrounded with foliated decoration which extended in festoons across the springing line of the ceiling and garlanded the oval medallions placed upon the trumeaux. The gallery opened into another called the Salle de Gombaud, a name recalling a well-known pastoral poem illustrated in tapestry hung in this room during the Régence. Piètre was called in to refashion the decoration of the Salle for a mid-Lent ball given for Marie-Antoinette on 26 February 1778, and three designs for it are known, including the one (now in the Musée Carnavalet) which had been the particular choice of the Duc de Chartres. On a stylobate adorned with festoons rises a colonnade of Ionic pilasters framing depressed arches. The work, hurriedly undertaken, was completed on the stipulated day. The Queen arrived half an hour after midnight with Madame Elisabeth and the Comte d'Artois and left at five o'clock. In spite of her passion for gambling, which had been the despair of the court in Vienna, we are told that she refrained that night from chancing her luck at faro.

Presentation of works of art

The splendour of their furnishings was in itself an invitation to display the finest art collections in such galleries. Nanteuil engraved a portrait of Mazarin, sitting at the entrance to the gallery which today accommodates the exhibitions of the Bibliothèque Nationale. The view discloses the antique statues and Italian pictures, which make the dying Cardinal say: 'All this I must leave behind.' In the first years of the eighteenth century, Oppenord designed for Girardon, a great collector of antiques, the decoration of a gallery which we know from an engraving. In it we can detect echoes of Roman 'antiquaria' and of the museum of sculpture by Scamozzi adjoining the Sansovino library of Venice. A pretty series of watercolours, perhaps painted by François Boucher's wife, introduces us to the simple gallery of Jean de Jullienne, administrator of the Gobelins and devoted friend of Watteau. Between mirrors and ranges of bookshelves surmounted by Chinese vases, a wonderful collection of pictures was grouped in serried ranks against a background of bold, flower-patterned, brocade. It was much the same at Blondel de Gagny's, the Place Royale collector, and in many other houses.

At a time of encyclopaedic curiosity, collections combined the masterpieces of man with the products of nature. A few years ago an exhibition entitled 'Le cabinet de l'amateur' re-created the picturesque confusion of marquetry pictures, jade, 'anamorphoses', bronzes, genealogical specimens, stuffed armadillos, elephants laden with obelisks, and those 'spy-glasses to frighten people' which the good Chrysale talked about. We know from drawings (signed Courtonne) about the natural history gallery of the financier Bonnier de la Mosson where stuffed quadrupeds clambered over the tops of display cases. For the Duc de Picquiny's scientific *cabinet*, Lajoue painted eleven door-heads, illustrating the arts and sciences, which were engraved by Cochin and often copied. A scheme designed by Henri Piètre, and perhaps supervised by Louis, shows us what the public gallery for the bronzes of the House of Orléans would have been, if financial disaster had not forced the Duc de Chartres to sell his collection. From this we can appreciate the arrangement usual for art collections at the end of the century. Pedestals and brackets carried busts, antique and Renaissance bronzes, and small reproductions of royal statues. A number of these works are drawn with enough precision to be identifiable, and we easily recognise a collection of small sculptures, many of which figure in Richelieu's inventory and had not left the Palais-Royal since his day.

Amateurs well understood which subjects could properly be displayed together (e.g. the *Borghese Gladiator* paired with the *Discobolos, Sleeping Ariadne* with the *Dying Gaul*, etc.). They liked to arrange small and medium-sized bronzes on low commodes, alternating with *médailliers*, of the type made by Charles-André Boulle, whose furniture continued to enjoy admiration throughout the century. In the galleries of the Prince de Condé and the financier Beaujon, bronzes, vases and busts must have been presented in this way in symmetrical groups.

Rooms devoted to art collections, which did not follow the elongated form of a gallery, were known as *grands cabinets*. In the case of most collectors, light from the windows cast the shadow of the visitor on the pictures and made the varnish reflect. In the 1750s, a public exhibition of the King's pictures had drawn attention to this failing, and amateurs were aware of the advantage of rooms lighted from above. This method, which dispensed with the need for windows, provided a more extensive surface for exhibiting pictures. It was also acknowledged that glazed openings in the ceiling of libraries and print-rooms diffused a light more favourable than any other to concentration and study. But this type of lighting is difficult to achieve in our climate, where rust causes joints to spring and, consequently, leaks. In the church of St Merry,

29 J.-J. Lanoue de La Couperie
    (Architect) Jacques Lucotte
    (Ironsmith): Banisters of the
    Hôtel de l'Hôpital, Boulevard
    du Temple (demolished), 1762

the architect Richard had installed horizontal glazing in the three oculi through which light streamed down into the Communion chapel. But, to keep rooms damp-proof, most architects preferred to rely on high windows pierced in the vertical elements of an attic or lantern. At Versailles, François d'Orbay chose this system for the Escalier des Ambassadeurs, which Gabriel destroyed. Oppenord, at the Palais-Royal, lit the *grand salon d'angle* and several other exhibition-rooms by lanterns. Such two-level rooms were difficult to design for buildings in which they had not been foreseen at the start of construction, for they entailed the sacrifice of space on the upper floors. About 1785, when the Direction des Bâtiments was carefully preparing the public presentation of the royal collections in the Grande Galerie of the Louvre, a commission visited various buildings in Paris for which this method of lighting had been chosen, and found glazed lantern-lights at the house of the Président de Saint-Fargeau and in a shop of the Rue Saint-Denis. At the Elysée, the Beaujon gallery was lit from above, as was that of the Prince de Soubise in his little house of the Rue de l'Arcade. The auctioneer Paillet, who held his sales at the former Hôtel de Bullion, had adopted the system. His colleague Lebrun, husband of the celebrated portrait-painter Elisabeth Vigée, copied it in his handsome premises of the Rue de Cléry. One of the members of the commission was Jean-Arnaud Raymond, the architect and friend of Lebrun, who was also completing a monumental gallery in the dealer's private hôtel. The experiments made at this time later enabled Raymond himself and Percier to design the glazed ceiling of the Grande Galerie of the Louvre.

Chapels

There were few great houses without their own chapel. We find two in the Hôtel de Noailles, a large complex of buildings transformed several times in the course of a century. We know that the Hôtel d'Armenonville contained a chapel decorated by Cartaut and that Servandoni built one at the Hôtel de la Live. In that of the Hôtel Matignon, the sculptor Robillon (probably the man who decorated the château of Queluz in Portugal) disposed cherubs and the rays of an aureole about the dove of the Holy Ghost.

The Hôtel Biron had its chapel at first in the basement, a rather unhappily chosen location, and then under the main staircase, which was not much better. 'Chapels,' wrote Blondel, 'must be well away from all mundane activities; they are too often put close to dining-rooms and anterooms accommodating servants.' For this reason, the Duchesse de Mazarin, when she had the former Hôtel d'Etampes transformed, wisely decided to put the chapel in a separate building. Mme de Seissac did the same at the Hôtel de Clermont. A directive of the Cardinal de Noailles, dated 24 April 1709, regulated the conduct of services in domestic chapels.

In 1739 the chapel of the Hôtel de Choiseul-Gouffier was refurbished and blessed by the Abbé Le Bœuf, the famous historian of the diocese. Six years later, Mgr de Ventimille authorised the ladies of Choiseul to have the three masses of the night of Christmas said in their hôtel, 'seeing that their infirmities prevent them from going to church'. In 1775 the marriage of Mlle de Bourbonne and the Comte d'Avaux was celebrated in the chapel of the Hôtel d'Havré. Usually a chapel of modest size was fitted up in a small *cabinet* directly above the court,

as had been the custom since the Middle Ages. The Duchess de Saint-
Simon, wife of the diarist, had an oratory of this kind made as an extension to a little *cabinet*, which enabled that pious lady to keep an eye on
her servants' comings and goings in the court of the hôtel. As the Saint-
Simons were tenants of the La Force family, they had to demolish
these factitious appendages on the expiration of their lease. Tiny
oratories might be contrived in wall-cupboards, and often had no
other purpose than to justify a symmetrically placed door. 'The practices
regarding the siting of chapels,' wrote Briseux, 'vary with the diocese.
In some, it is permissible to include it in the *corps de logis* and even in
a wardrobe, provided that this is not in a bedroom. . . .' The oratory
of the cardinals of Rohan, concealed in the 'cabinet of monkeys' (Pls.
90–1), is fairly unexpected. There was also one in the 'grand Chinese
cabinet' of the Duc de Richelieu, a far from edifying character, but
who always respected religious matters, despite his associations with the
philosophes.

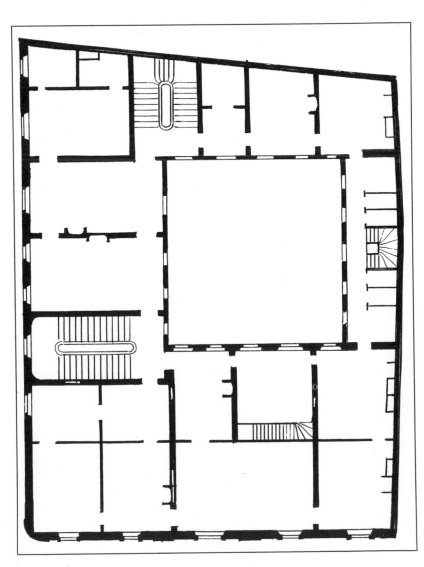

30 F. Franque: de Crillon house,
    Rue du Renard (plan), 1768

8 *Pavilions and* folies

In every age Parisians have longed to be rid of the tumult and dust of the city during the summer months. The still rural areas of the *grands boulevards* and, further out, the suburban villages were dotted with villas and gardens; and, on these properties simple or elegant, life was free from the rigours of etiquette and the ceremonial of the great hôtels. Louis XIV had early escaped, with a small circle of favoured courtiers, to Marly and Trianon from the suffocating protocol of Versailles, and by the end of the reign and the coming of the Régence the Princes d'Orléans and de Condé had copied the monarch's example. The Duchesse d'Orléans, the Regent's wife, had two 'pavilions' at Bagnolet, while in the fields where the Hôtel des Invalides already stood the first Palais Bourbon was built for another princess of royal blood. It was not a hôtel, but simply a ground floor with a terrace roof in the Italian manner and nothing to suggest the frigid appearance which the building owes to Napoleon. On the Seine side the horizontals of the façade harmonised with the riverscape, and were later to act as a restraining influence on the monumental scheme for the *place* created by Louis XV and Gabriel. Close by the Palais Bourbon, the Marquis de Lassay built a smaller, but very elegant, dwelling. The pavilions and *folies*, which were to appear on the periphery of Paris in the course of the century, were the natural heirs of these Parisian Trianons.

If some of these houses had not survived to our day, and if engravings and the indiscretions of family records had not disclosed others, the mass of literary allusions would have sufficed to evoke their memory. The Régence still called these retreats by the old name of *folies*,* a reference to the dense foliage which hid them from curious passers-by. They were equally well known by the names of their owners. Near the Faubourg Saint-Antoine, the *folies* Cornu and Regnault went back to the Middle Ages. The origins of the Folie Méricourt are more uncertain, but it is clear that the term *folies* had nothing to do with the foolish ostentation of the rich or the dissipations of noble lords, who were supposed to have used them for surreptitious love-affairs. The confusion arose later. The Baronne d'Oberkirch visited the home of the Receveur-Général Boutin and, after duly admiring the extravagant whimsies of the financier, concluded in these terms: 'He has called his

* Although the English word 'folly' in the architectural sense, stems from the same root, its meaning is very different from the French *folie*.

garden "Tivoli", but the popular name is the Boutin Folly. Folly is the right word; he has spent or buried there several millions.' But the name generally given to these dwellings by the eighteenth century was 'little houses', not because they were small, but from a play on words deriving from popular humour. The idea of *folie* was obviously associated with madness, and at that time lunatics were confined in the Hôpital des Petites Maisons or Little Houses – not the first instance, perhaps, nor the last, of a Parisian pun.

Fashion favoured different *faubourgs* and villages in turn. Bercy and Bagnolet were in vogue under the Régence and until the middle of the century. The brothers Paris, who had so dexterously liquidated Law's system before diverting their interests to the slave traffic in Angola, built a whopping pavilion at Bercy, which earned the name of 'Pâté-Paris'. A valuation of the house, in 1739 noted still-life paintings by Oudry in the dining-room, and mythological subjects in the *grand salon* by Coypel. Considering 'its standing, situation and proximity to Paris', it estimated the property to be worth 120,000 livres and the annual rental at 4,000. In the Rue de Montreuil, the Folie Titon was decorated by Lafosse, Jouvenet and Boulogne senior, and it was in this house surrounded by gardens that Réveillon installed his manufactory of wall-paper and, from it, that the first balloons took to the air. In the Rue de la Roquette and the middle of the century, the Comte de Clermont succeeded Réaumur, and replaced the inventor's laboratories with a theatre. Chaillot, the scene of the Abbé Prévost's lovers, was a traditional resort and remained so. Auteuil, dear to Boileau, was inhabited by Quentin La Tour, the financier La Popelinière and Mme Helvetius. The popularity of this district declined after the death

31 S.-N. Lenoir-le-Romain: Hôtel Rigoley de Juvigny-Giambonne, Rue de Bondy (now Rue René Boulanger, demolished), 1776

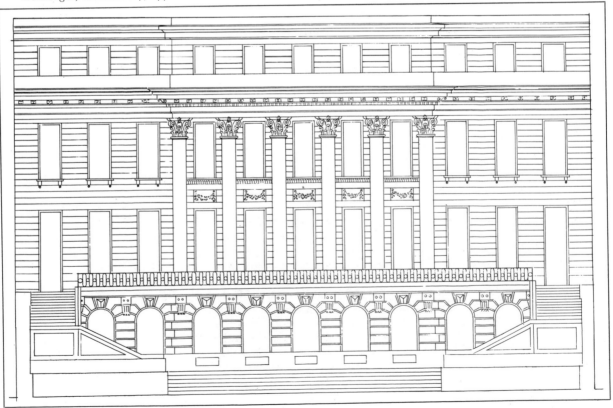

of Mme de Pompadour, when Louis XV abandoned La Muette, so that he might no longer see the leaves of Bellevue which the Marquise had so much loved. The extension of the *faubourgs* of Paris had established many 'little houses' at La Ville l'Evêque and Les Porcherons, i.e. between the Madeleine and the Rue Saint-Lazare. The Quartier Montparnasse, Le Roule and Monceau, Montmartre and Neuilly witnessed the building of the last *folies* of the Ancien Régime.

Legend and truth

Charles Pinot-Duclos wrote:

> Mme d'Albi charged me with finding her a little house. . . . They have become so common and so public that some parts of the suburbs are entirely given over to them. . . . It is true that since they have ceased to be secret, they have ceased to be indecorous; but they have also ceased to be necessary. Today, for many people, a little house is simply a false front, a place where, in order to appear to be pursuing pleasure, they go to be a little more bored in secret than they would be by simply staying at home.

We must therefore repudiate the tradition which saw nothing but rustic love-nests in these suburban haunts.

And yet the same legend clung to certain Parisian *folies* and Venetian *ritrovi* of the time. The mezzanines of the San Marco quarter were the setting for the nobility's supper parties between their departure from the theatre and return to distant palaces; and Magny, the forgotten author of *Spectacles Nocturnes*, tells us about the *ritrovi* of Paris:

> There is not a man of quality at Cithcropolis who, two or three times a week, does not gather his select little party of friends for a little supper in a little house. . . . With dishes more exquisite than lavish, and sparkling champagne served by the most gracious of hands, until all dissolves in fun and frolic, surely this is the only pleasure in life?

Whoever needs proof of the habitual luxury of such little suppers may turn to the inventory drawn up after the death of the Maréchal de Soubise. Ageing in the cellars of his *folie* lay 'nine thousand bottles of wine, both red and white, and liqueurs'.

By way of an example, let us try to recapitulate the *folies* of a very gay character, notorious in the amorous chronicles of the eighteenth century, the Maréchal-Duc de Richelieu. According to the Marquis d'Argenson, Richelieu gave a grand supper on 21 November 1740 at a 'little house' which he owned beyond the Vaugirard toll-gate. On the panelling were carvings of subjects taken from the mythology of love. 'A fine start to the supper was the sight of the old Duchesse de Brancas, eager to examine these figures, putting on her spectacles and, tight-lipped, coldly peering at them, while M. de Richelieu, candle in hand, explained them to her.' Eleven years later, an architect's survey report takes us to Les Porcherons, into a house belonging to the heirs of a M. Péricard, except for the chimney-pieces, panelling and other decorations placed there by the tenant, M. le Duc de Richelieu. Carriage and bridle entrances from the Rue de Clichy lead into a forecourt planted with trees. From thence we must continue into a second court to find a two-storey pavilion, its five bays aligned with a long terrace.

97

On the ground floor are a reception-room, a dining-room and a *cabinet*; and, on the floor above, a salon, an anteroom and a bedroom. There are wall-papers from China in ornamental borders, and we know from other evidence the Maréchal's predilection for Asiatic art. The floor and walls of the bathroom are tiled with Dutch faience. There are also 'different paintings representing various subjects. . . .' The vagueness of the terminology and the clerk's erasures fail to conceal a certain embarrassment. Urgently needed repairs were the reason for the visit. The west front was liable to collapse, but the architect P.-H. de Saint-Martin was ready to rebuild it to an agreeable design attached to the report and the Maréchal's signed authority.

The Duke had two masterpieces of sculpture transported from one to the other of his *folies*. These were the 'Esclaves' of Michelangelo, which belonged to the Richelieu family until they were transferred to the Louvre. Was it to Vaugirard or Les Porcherons that the amateurs Mayran and Bachaumont went to admire them, accompanied by the sculptor Falconet? In a flattering letter, dated September 1749, Bachaumont expressed his gratitude to the fortunate owner.

In the same year Richelieu bought the sporting estate of Gennevilliers, where he had an ice-house dug, and built a little round temple. Louis XV went to hunt there one summer's day and, with Mme de Pompadour, dined in the ice-house, where a play was performed.

Richelieu was as inconsistent a patron of the arts as he was inconstant as a lover. He began a job with one architect and finished it with another. Dullin, N. d'Orbay, Saint-Martin and Servandoni strove in turn to satisfy his whims. A long and loyal friendship, however, seems to have linked the Duke and Chevotet, for in 1740 he witnessed the architect's marriage contract and, seventeen years later, invited him to refurbish the former Hôtel d'Antin. It was here that Chevotet built in the garden the celebrated Pavillon de Hanovre (Pls. 106–7), which Voltaire called the fairies' pavilion. Only the façade has survived, now re-erected in the Parc de Sceaux, but the various projects by Chevotet have come down to us, and several accounts give us glimpses of the splendour of the decoration carried out by Eisen and Brunetti.

Architecture of the pavilions

Richelieu's pavilion had perhaps to yield pride of place to a luxurious villa at Les Porcherons, built a few years earlier for the Fermier-Général de la Boixière. In a garden, also designed by Chevotet, Le Carpentier built a pavilion in the Italian manner, which exemplified to perfection the plan elaborated by architects of the House of Orléans in the days of the Régence for pavilions at Bagnolet. The rectilinear suite, beloved of the past, was renounced for a concentration of rooms, favouring constant communication from one part of an apartment to another. Le Carpentier offered varied room-shapes: an oval and a circular salon, and octagonal bedrooms and dining-rooms. Light entered through lanterns. Caryatids and nymphs, placed in niches, ringed the salons. About 1770 a pupil of Le Carpentier seems to have transformed several of the pavilion's rooms, mingling echoes of rocaille with the first stirrings of neo-classicism.

The pavilions of La Boixière and Croix-Fontaine, works of the same architect, inspired Jean-François de Bastide to write an attractive novel with no less a title than *La Petite Maison*. The plot is woven round the Marquis de Trémicour and the youthful Mélite in a pavilion so elegant

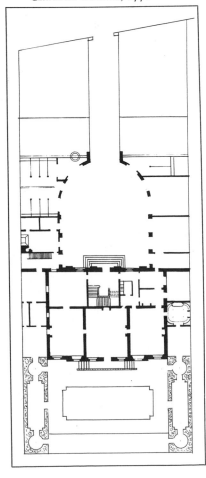

32 Cellerier: Plan of an Hôtel Chaussée-d'Antin, 1776

'that Le Carpentier could have imagined nothing more ingenious'. Bedrooms, boudoirs and salons are round and octagonal. The floors are of cedar wood; the consoles, laden with porcelain, are of grey-blue marble. In a boudoir, artificial trees are reflected in mirrors veiled with gauze, so that one imagines oneself in the middle of a quincunx bathed in a mysterious light. Walls and hangings are sulphur-coloured, soft green and lilac. Thanks to a process discovered by the varnisher Dandrillon, the paint of panelling exhales the perfume of violets, roses and lilies of the valley. Musicians, concealed in a passage encircling a room, are heard through a partition of mirrors, a fashion emanating from Germany. Both La Popelinière and M. de Monville had a private orchestra attached to their opulent persons.

The author of *La Petite Maison* names the fashionable artists who collaborated in the decorative scheme. A little bath suite is enlivened with arabesques by Huet and Peyrotte, mythological subjects by Boucher, flowers by Bachelier and stucco work by Clérissy. The ceilings

33 Brongniart: Pavillon de Valence – Timbrune, Rue de la Chaussée-d'Antin, demolished, 1776–7

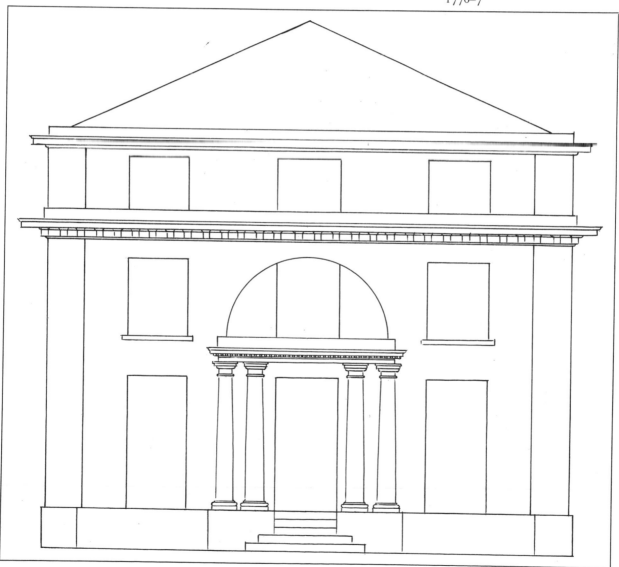

are by Pierre and Hallé. At the end of her wonderstruck visit, Mélite surrenders to the passion of the Marquis. Few periods have combined with such delicate perception the allurements of art and love.

Since the Florentine A. F. Doni, writing in 1550, no author had offered the fashionable world such an agreeable work as Bastide's on the art of adorning a place in the country. By the middle of the century, 'little houses' had become so luxurious that the Abbé Coyer suggested to the government that a tax should be levied on these secondary residences. The police records which have made it possible to identify them are no proof that they were the objects of surveillance, but they probably indicate the hypocritical interest of certain commissioners in what might be going on inside them.

While the Louis XVI period saw the realisation of the most prodigal *folies* imaginable to eighteenth-century epicureanism, the neo-classical ideal clothed their exteriors in an austere architecture far removed from their frivolous purpose. The models were often chosen from Palladio and his Venetian followers, who had adapted the forms of antique temples to the frontispieces of their villas. Thus the temple-house reappeared, like the *folie* of the Prince de Soubise in the Rue de l'Arcade, the Courman house, and the Chevalier de Beauregard's *folie* at Chaillot (Pl. 150). They prove, wrote the moralist Dulaure, 'the modesty of the god which inhabits them'. The Carré de Beaudouin pavilion at Ménilmontant, better (if wrongly) known as Folie Favart, reproduced the lines, if not the proportions, of the Villa Ragona at Ghizzola; which survives only as an engraving in the second book of Palladio. The actual design has not come to light, but a deed authenticated by a notary shows us that, at the time when the pavilion had just been built, the architect Moreau-Desproux was a creditor of the owner, Nicolas Carré de Beaudouin, to the tune of 3,000 livres. In 1782, in the temple of Hymen, erected in the Place de Grève on the occasion of the birth of the Dauphin, Moreau-Desproux was to show once again his admiration for Palladio. His colleague Chevalier de Beauregard stuck to the temple form for his villa at Chaillot. But the device, copied from the house of the gods, could seem too pompous in the country, and Palladio himself contrived to add a measure of charm by framing the central temple with two galleries or 'barchesse'. The two low wings bordering the court, which Cellerier provided for the Prince de Soubise, may be an echo of this.

Buildings of this type attracted the most original plans of the century. In the traditional hôtel, the main body of the house comprised two parallel sets of rooms, one orientated towards the court, the other to the garden. The rectilinear layout was replaced in pavilions by a compact disposition, weak in vistas, but more convenient, and adapted to easy communications between the various rooms of a suite. Pleasure was found in varying the geometrical figures of rooms. The rectangle, sometimes ending in a hemicycle, accompanied the octagon, the circle, the semicircle and the oval (which remained in favour after the baroque age). Curves and truncated angles met tangentially. Irregularities of the site were countered by hinged joints. The architects, with a skill admired by their contemporaries, fitted all these forms smoothly together, leaving the smallest possible areas of dead surface, in which cupboards, sideboards, alcoves and niches were accommodated. In pavilions and hôtels of compact plan, the rooms often encircled a central space, occupied by a staircase or some form of stateroom, lighted from the top by the glazed oculus of a dome.

Classical and pre-romantic gardens

The novelists of the century have described the mysterious gardens of *folies*. We know the two plans by Chevotet for those of the Pavillons de Hanovre and de la Boissière. Perhaps they lack the spaciousness of the designs by the same architect for the '*parcs*' of Orsay and Champlatreux, but they bear witness to the continuing tradition of Le Nôtre. In the reign of Louis XV, Desgots, Leclerc, La Chapelle and La Guêpière had maintained the principle of symmetry characteristic of the classicism of the master, while introducing the arabesques of rococo into the patterns of flower-beds. The eclecticism which marked the artistic crisis of the mid-century years was to lead to a few experiments in Italian gardening. Long before Fragonard drew the cypresses of the Villa d'Este, Montesquieu and the Président de Brosse had expressed their admiration for the Borromean Isles. The Italian grove planted by the gardener Crosnier for the Receveur-Général Boutin earned for the property the name of Tivoli, which was also given to two other gardens of the neighbourhood during the Empire: 'It is a ravishing place for enjoyment', wrote a lady visitor. 'There are surprises at every step; grottoes, shrubberies, statues and a charming pavilion furnished with princely splendour. One must be a king or a financier to create such visions. M. Boutin often holds exquisite suppers here, which are no less sumptuous than the setting.'

34 Neveu: His own house, 12 Rue de Tournon, 1776

A delight in picturesque walks, which was to give birth to Bagatelle and the Folie Sainte-James (Pls. 172–3), was a novelist's theme before it inspired garden designers. The fashion began to spread about 1760, at the time when J.-J. Rousseau described the Elysée of M. de Wolmar in the *Nouvelle Héloïse*. Fifteen years later, Carmontelle undertook for the Duc de Chartres the improvement of Monceau, of which a few traces still survive in the present '*parc*'. Here, while the theorist combined the lingering magic of baroque with a foretaste of romantic sensibility, the artist contrived a multiplicity of surprises and exotic features.

Carmontelle would have been greatly offended at the suggestion that he had wanted an English garden at Monceau, for he himself disclaimed it and the French at this time spoke only of 'picturesque' or 'landscape' gardens. In his own words, Carmontelle had offered for the contemplation of perceptive minds a garden uniting 'all times and all places'. Very different from classical gardens, the entire effect of which could be grasped at a single glance, the picturesque garden guided the visitor along unpremeditated paths, disclosing in succession a variety of 'tableaux'. Little buildings or *fabriques* signposted the walk unpredictably: at Monceau, a ruined castle, a farm, a dilapidated temple of Mars, a Dutch windmill and a Tartar tent. One of the attractions was a Chinese swing, named after the game of 'tilting at the ring', in which a turn-table, moved by men placed underground, was sheltered from the sun by three pagodas. 'Two iron branches', Thiéry tells us, 'support dragons on which the gentlemen ride astride; while, on two other branches, reclining Chinamen hold in one hand a cushion, on which the ladies sit.' The Parc Monceau has preserved, covered in ivy, the pyramid copied from the Roman tomb of Cestius. The columns surrounding the oval pool or 'naumachia' came from Saint-Denis and belonged to the uncompleted chapel of the Valois. A white marble temple was removed by Louis-Philippe to the island of the Pont de Neuilly.

The neighbourhood of the Bois de Boulogne held a special attraction for the fashionable world, because it was close to both Paris and Versailles. The Bois was no more than a fragment of the forest of Rouvray, which in the past had drawn the court of Philippe le Bel for the pleasures of hunting. La Muette, where Gabriel had rebuilt a house for Louis XV, has preserved the memory of the royal pack of hounds (= *la meute*) in its name. At Auteuil, the salons of the Marquise de Boufflers and Mme Helvetius welcomed all the distinguished minds of the age. All Paris came every year to hear the offices of Holy Week at the abbey of Longchamp, until Mgr de Beaumont was obliged to forbid this very secular pilgrimage. From Auteuil to Neuilly a succession of properties encircled the Bois, which still preserved a country look. Some of the landscapes of Moreau the Elder and Bruandet reveals the charm of these rural places, where later the gardeners of the Second Empire were to tame nature all too successfully. Built under Louis XVI by the same architect, Bélanger, the Folie Sainte-James (Pls. 172–3) and Bagatelle (Pl. 174) are rich in the cherished memories of Parisians. Bélanger was a child of the Rue Sainte-Antoine, full of wit and invention, who became the intimate of princes and the lover of the prettiest stars of the stage. Far from the beaten track of the school of Ange Gabriel, he drew upon the buildings of Robert Adam and the compositions of Piranesi as the sources of a personal manner which heralded the Directoire style. A journey to England in his student days made him realise the coming success of landscape gardens with the French aristocracy.

This led to his choice as the regular architect of the Comte d'Artois, whose English tastes he was able to satisfy.

A wager with the Queen had set the Prince to work on Bagatelle, where the house was built in sixty-three days and the garden planted in ten years. The even more fabulous creation of his neighbour, Baudard de Sainte-James, brought ruin to the financier, its owner. Bélanger therefore designed two 'picturesque' gardens in which a pre-romantic sensibility found tangible expression. Kiosks, pagodas, pyramids and castles beckoned the visitor to distant climes and vanished civilisations. Dairies and cottages invited the innocent pleasures of rural life and simplicity of heart. In a setting which was a blend of nature and artifice, the soul, cleansed and purified, rediscovered the serenity of an earthly paradise and responded to the presence of the Creator: 'Who has not thought of growing better? Who has not voiced anthems of gratitude and love, and risen to the planes of eternity in such privileged retreats?' (Lezay-Marnézia.) In these, the final, creations of the Ancien Régime, Bélanger exploited all the resources of enchantment and the treasury of dreams. At Bagatelle, a Scottish gardener, Blaikie, supervised the planting. A stream was crossed by a 'rock bridge', a 'bridge of love' and a 'Palladian bridge'. On an island stood the tomb of the King of Hearts, and on its banks rose a Swiss châlet, a Paladins' tower, a Chinese tent, an antique grave and a philosopher's abode. The marvel of the Folie Sainte-James was its subterranean maze, where only a faint light penetrated and the thunder of a waterfall echoed. A grotto was hewn out between rocks transported to Neuilly from Fontainebleau, a laborious operation which did not pass unnoticed by the King.

9 Artists' and writers' houses

By 1795, with the fading of the revolutionary years, Parisian society was already back, in the view of a particularly astute observer, in the reign of Louis XVI. The accident of birth, the advantages of wealth and the less common gift of ability brought three types of people into contact in the fashionable world, putting artists on the same footing as the gentry and the rich. 'Talent, wit, charm, and renown in the arts drew flattering attention. In fact, a taste for pleasure usually obscured all lines of separation; and society resembled a grand ball where everybody rubbed shoulders, and went where he chose with the sole aim of spending a few agreeable hours. . . .' An actress, a scholar, a painter and sometimes even a writer could flaunt the train of a great magnate without offending anyone. Lavish building went with lavish gaming, splendid collections and sumptuous equipages. Each exploited the advantages of his position to acquire a palace: a Beaumarchais exported rifles, a ballerina ruined her noble lovers, while a fashionable architect obtained substantial discounts from contractors when building his own house.

Probably for this reason, a few architects' houses appear among the most elegant of the century: those of J.-P. Varin, Rue de Seine (Pl. 58); Quirot (le Jeune), Rue de la Jussienne (Pl. 92 and Fig. 19, p. 71); and P. Rousseau in Montmartre. The monumental house of the Troîs Chapelets, 27 Rue Saint-André-des-Arts (Fig. 22, p. 77), was built for the widow of Nicolas Simonnet of the Academy of Architecture. In the Louis XVI period the house of Ch. de Wailly, Rue de la Pépinière, displayed both the imagination and the financial success of its owner. It was conceived as the centre-piece of an impressive group of three dwellings, which included the home of the sculptor Pajou, a friend of the architect, and its fellow which was not finished. At de Wailly's, carriages entered under cover between columns copied from Paestum, and set down their passengers at the foot of an immense circular stair-case, lighted from the top. Above a ground floor reserved for the service quarters, the *piano nobile* was hardly less magnificent than the *grand salon* created by Wailly in Genoa in the palazzo of the Marquese Spinola. The apartments on this floor were disposed between a winter garden and a terrace. A belvedere surmounted the house, to which Pajou also applied his high talents. The sculptor, who completed Jean Goujon's fountain by the addition of three nymphs, had assimilated the manner of the sixteenth-century masters, dear to de Wailly. A large-scale replica of the Three Graces by Germain Pilon, then at the Célestins, adorned a fountain at the bottom of the stairs, the circular well being decorated with plaster casts of Goujon's nymphs. Such was the admiration of contemporaries for these figures celebrated by Diderot, that other reproductions were to be found at the Hôtel de Gallifet and in the residence of Legrand and Molinos, architects in partnership at 6 Rue Saint-Florentin. The plan of Pajou's house reveals a three-horse carriage and a safe for silver, which scarcely suggest poverty. Of more modest appearance, the home and studio of Clodion occupied a choice position in the Chaussée d'Antin.

Among the more commodiously lodged painters of the century, the first who comes to mind is Largillière, for whom the ennobled lawyers of the Marais came to sit at his house (with its carriage-entrance) in the Rue Sainte-Avoye. A large and handsome still-life, with which the painter ornamented his staircase, has recently been identified in the Parisian art trade. In the Place Dauphine, Audran and Oudry together decorated the studio of the miniaturist J.-B. Massé. Oudry's part included the painting of 'an oval "corbeille" and, on the plinth, four birds of China and eight monkeys artfully clothed, representing comical actions'. In the Rue de la Pelleterie, Boucher exploited the magic of trompe-l'œil in the salon of Desmarteau, one of the engravers who had spread the painter's fame by publicising his creations. The whole interior of the room simulated a garden enlivened by various creatures. Swans swam upon a pond with herons wading. A stream was covered with ducks, escorted by ibis and parrots. The doors imitated fountains where cupids played amid seaweed, dolphins and shells. Desmarteau's son later transported this scheme to his house of Le Cloître Saint-Merry. It now belongs to the Groult collection.

Antoine Callet, a regular portrait-painter to Louis XVI and one of the decorators most in demand during his reign, had his own *folie* in the Rue du Montparnasse (Pl. 140). But it may have been beyond his means, for we find him urgently imploring Mme de Thélusson's steward to pay him sums owing for the decoration of several salons in the celebrated mansion of the Chaussée d'Antin. Callet, however, was able to complete his house. Less fortunate than Louis XVI's painter, the master-ciseleur Gouthière was ruined by his apartment speculation and *folie* in the Faubourg Saint-Martin (Fig. 37, p. 114).

In the middle 1780s Madame Vigée-Lebrun used to hold one of the most frequented of literary and fashionable salons at her house in the Rue de Cléry. Mmes de Sabran and de Rougé, the Maréchal de Noailles, Vaudreuil, the witty Prince de Ligne and the gluttonous Grimod de la Reynière, Rivarol, Marmontel and La Harpe gathered round the young artist, drawn by her hospitality and charm, and enthralled by her brilliant reputation. Her husband, J.-B. Pierre Lebrun, a great connoisseur as well as an able business man, had wit enough to shine at these receptions, but usually neglected his wife and applied the money which she earned to purposes which Mme Lebrun was happy to forgive. Their house was a former hôtel of the Chevaliers de Lubert, but the suite where she received her guests was very confined. There were not enough chairs for the throng of visitors, many of whom had to sit on the carpet – and the Maréchal de Noailles, who was fat, had difficulty in getting up.

For his part, Lebrun expanded his business interests every year, buying in Italy and Holland an ever increasing number of works of art, which he sold to amateurs in Paris. He himself had amassed valuable collections 'for his own enjoyment and that of his wife, who added to the charm of her person the most enchanting wit and the greatest talent for painting'. As the garden of the Hôtel de Lubert was very large and extended as far as the Rue du Gros-Chenet (combined with the Rue du Sentier in 1849), Lebrun was keen to build on it. His aim was twofold. On the Rue de Cléry side, he transformed the court of the Hôtel de Lubert into a spacious and well-lighted room, where he used to preside at the sales which were so eagerly attended.

At the other end of the grounds, towards the Rue du Gros-Chenet, he built an elegant residence where his collections were exhibited. Lebrun entrusted the programme to an architect friend, J.-A. Raymond from Toulouse, whose recent election to the Royal Academy had now installed in Paris. The building today is unrecognisable, but the design has come down to us (Pl. 152). On the *piano nobile*, a joint anteroom connected the suites of husband and wife. The principal rooms affected the round, oval and octagonal forms, popular in the fine houses of the period. On the floor above, the art gallery was twenty-eight metres long by twelve in height. It was terminated on one side by an apse preceded by columns in antis, an arrangement used in antiquity and dear to the Scotsman Robert Adam. According to Lebrun's inventory, low marquetry chests carried a few medium-sized bronze reproductions of celebrated antique sculptures: *The wounded Gaul*, *Laocoön* and *Ariadne sleeping*. The apse contained a plaster cast of the Apollo del Belvedere.

35 Blève: Apartment house, Rue Vieille du Temple and Rue de Bretagne – plan of first floor, 1776–7

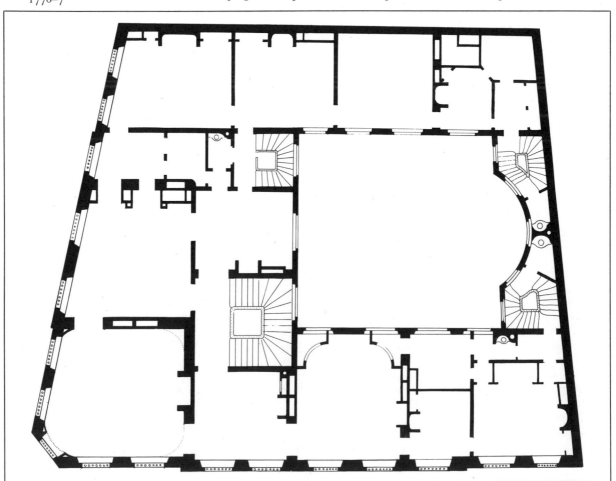

The great amateur's pictures were displayed symmetrically on the upper part of the walls. Higher still, the coving of the ceiling was decorated with arabesques in grisaille and the daylight streamed into the gallery through a glazed lantern.

The suites of rooms looked on to a circular court, a masterly piece of design by Raymond (Fig. 48, p. 133). At the level of the first floor were niches sheltering statues; while above, a long bas-relief in the antique manner followed the inward curve of the façade. Two of the surviving drawings show the successive stages of the scheme. On the first, the bas-relief displays a group of girls drawing and painting – a delicate compliment to Mme Lebrun who conducted classes for students. But the idea was not retained, and Foucou, the sculptor, depicted Apollo surrounded by Muses and Genii. Behind this decorative setting stretched the garden of the Hôtel de Lubert and its great trees which Mme Lebrun saw from her oval bedroom. If the gallery recalled certain other Parisian rooms, like the dining-room of the painter Callet or the gallery of the Folie Soubise, the proportions and the impeccable design of the court made an exquisite composition, in which Raymond may well have equalled the master whom he regarded as the greatest of all, Palladio. The programme was finished in 1787, the year in which Mme Lebrun exhibited at the Salon of the Louvre the celebrated portrait of Marie-Antoinette and her children.

Raymond, who had directed the work as a disinterested friend, is not mentioned in Mme Vigée-Lebrun's memoirs. She would probably have preferred the plans of Brongniart, whose wife and daughter Ziguette were her friends. Compromised by the Queen's favour and Mme du Barry's friendship, Mme Lebrun emigrated in 1790 and spent twelve years abroad. On the day of her return to the Rue du Gros-Chenet, the staircase was filled with flowers, but some of the contractors' bills had not been settled: 'M. Lebrun', she wrote, 'had reserved this job for me, to my great disappointment.'

Other gifted women have spoken in their recollections of the houses where they lived. Mme de Genlis, who was responsible for the education of the Princesses d'Orléans, was lodged in the convent of Bellechasse with her pupils:

> In my bedroom I had a large alcove, only half of which was occupied by my bed, and from here there was a passage opening into the princesses' room next to mine, and from which I was only separated by a glass door with no silvering or curtain, so that I could see from my bed what they were up to. . . . One of the rooms of the suite contained in cupboards my collection of natural history.

Elsewhere Mme de Genlis speaks of the 'charming pavilion' which she occupied at Bellechasse and claimed to have planned. No doubt she had expressed certain wishes to the worthy architect Poyet, whom the Duc de Chartres had commissioned with this little building, before entrusting him with bigger things (Pl. 141).

Some writers found particular solutions to their architectural dreams. 'Tired of seeing our regimented dwellings and uninspired gardens', wrote Beaumarchais, 'I built a house which gets mentioned, but I am no artist, inde irae.' The story of this building is as paradoxical as the career of its owner. Beaumarchais had his home built in 1790, perhaps with stone from the Bastille in process of demolition, and on the threshold of the Faubourg Saint-Antoine, from which the revolutionary movement erupted. The author had refused to acquire the Hôtel de Monville (Pl. 139), close to the Madeleine, where Boullée had provided the ultimate refinements of comfort for an eccentric client. He had friends in Bélanger and, probably, de Wailly, who may have introduced to him the young and brilliant Paul Lemoine, his collaborator on the Théâtre Français. Certainly Lemoine made himself known to Beaumarchais and persuaded him to accept his design. The deep exedra opposite the garden recalled Bramante's at the Vatican, the Villa Giulia and more recent examples by J.-A. Raymond at the Hôtel de Saint-Priest and at the Lebruns' mansion. The plan of the interior provided for secluded nooks, from one of which the writer of comedies, who had become suspicious, could keep an undetected eye on his abode. Before inviting Hubert Robert to decorate the panelling of the salon, Beaumarchais informed himself about his prices and paid him the compliment which follows:

Paris, this 24th May 1790.
This morning, Sir, I saw M. Le Moine, who told me he had just left you. He taught me nothing on your account; like him, I knew your value. Your ingenious mind is as free as your art and enlivens a great talent. Your designs for decoration, Sir, are such that I should be honoured to compose myself, were I as good a poet as you are an excellent painter. Of every kind of painting, yours is the one which charms me most, whether because it is better fitted to my taste for the picturesqueness of nature, or because the salons which I have seen decorated by you seem to resemble more closely the walk outside. . . .

Bélanger had devised this walk for Beaumarchais, so that it emerged opposite the Bastille by an underground passage. A temple of Bacchus, a monument to the ancestral deities of Voltaire and other features were scattered at random beside the paths. How easy to think of the moonlit garden and the intrigues of *La Folle Journée* and of the pavilion where Fanchette slipped 'an orange and two biscuits' to Chérubin! A modest inscription excuses the bizarre pretensions of the owner: 'This little garden was planted in the first year of liberty.'

10 Comfort and decoration

The concern for comfort, which is such a conspicuous characteristic of our own age, developed very slowly through the years. As long ago as 1630, the Marquise de Rambouillet took precautions against the cold which amazed her companions of the Précieuses, but the wine continued to freeze in the glass of Louis XIV as he sat at his sumptuous table. The process of evolution, however, passed through an important phase in the eighteenth century, when the desire for physical well-being became apparent in the home and its furnishing, being closely related to developments in the decorative arts. The criticism and defence of comfort, even if it was not yet described by this term, were at the centre of a much wider debate deriving from the value and vanity of luxury. In writings inspired by this conflict of ethics, decoration and comfort were generally linked in the same apologia or censure.

The interest of this controversy lies in the way in which it enables us to throw light on the real meaning of rococo, as understood in the very broad sense of decorative refinement and of escape into an imaginary world. It helps us to unravel the kinship of the style with the psychology of those circles of society which saw it spread and encouraged its success. Louis XIV's attitude towards the nobility undermined their moral standing. Often supplanted by the middle class in government appointments, they watched their political role decline. Summoned to the court, they were ruined by their efforts to cut a brilliant figure. Domesticated by the monarchy and deprived of its favours, they loosened their connections with country life, were represented on their properties by disloyal agents and saw their resources dwindle. While English noblemen built their finest houses in the shires, the French 'quality' lavished less upon their châteaux than their town-houses, where henceforth their concern was greater for personal welfare than for outward display.

Thus the upper classes abdicated a part of their function in society and accepted the aims of the bourgeoisie. Montesquieu noted that their interests had ceased to be identified with those of the state. They also underwent an experience common among privileged groups, who find compensation for the loss of high authority in a dream-world existence and fashionable frivolities. Among the evils which tormented them, as the Marquis de Mirabeau and Sébastien Mercier pointed out, was boredom; but the attractions of art were an appropriate diversion and calculated to beguile the vaguely restless spirit. The Régence has points in common with the exciting period in Venetian art which coincided with the decline of the republic's maritime domination, when a traditional preoccupation with religion and the glories of the city gave way before a tide of sensibility, to the delight of a small number of enthusiastic amateurs. Imagination, music, melancholy, love and silence invaded the world of Giorgione, to create a perfect distraction for the leisured aristocracy from disquiet and foreboding.

This was also the situation with the contemporaries of Watteau, who offers so many subtle affinities with Giorgione. Around him, the decorative arts combined to promote the same escapism. The imaginary fauna of the arabesque, the craft of illusion in painting and its flights of rustic fancy, and the tortuosities and exuberant vegetation of rococo ornament conspired to carry the heart and mind away to a land of dreams. The decorative setting in which society spent its days reacted upon its way of life. The moralists deplored the weakening effect of excessive refinement upon character, and the prejudice of the old Romans is reflected in their disapproval: 'The man whose furniture and jewels are guilloched', wrote the Marquis de Mirabeau, 'will inevitably be guilloched in mind and body also. The man with flax-grey and rose-coloured paint wears this livery in his dressing-gown, in the cut of his clothes, and in his attitude.' We share the feeling of these contemporary observers that the whole framework of life, its music, clothes, exquisite manners and philosophical postures, were tarred with the same brush. From this there emerge the features of someone whom we may call the rococo man, 'guilloched in mind' and evidenced of a culture which spread through European society in the eighteenth century.

In a letter to his friend Thieriot, Voltaire speaks of *entresols* 'lacquered, gilded, faced with porcelain where it is pleasant to philosophise', and at the Hôtel du Temple, amid Oppenord panelling and Audran's arab-esques, in the Chinese *grand cabinet* of the Duc de Richelieu and at Suzanne de Livry's house, the young author acquired a taste for art and luxury. He took pleasure in enumerating the refinements in the apart-ment of his *Mondain*:

> *Here Poussin's classic skill, the sensuous grace*
> *Of sweet Corregio have befitting place,*
> *Festooned and bordered in rich gilded frames.*
> *The sculptured figure Bouchardon proclaims;*
> *To Germain's hand the silver we can trace,*
> *And tapestries from Gobelins match the art*
> *Of painters' colour in their every part,*
> *While twenty times such objects meet the gaze*
> *On walls where brilliant sconce and mirror blaze.*

At this time, when he deliberately placed the man of the world in a setting to his own taste, Voltaire had already become the competent amateur whose rooms at Cirey, designed by a Parisian decorator, are described for us by Mme de Graffigny:

> There is little tapestry, but much panelling, on which are framed some charming pictures; there are mirrors, admirable lacquered corner pieces, porcelain, caskets, a clock supported on a curiously shaped grotesque, endless things of this kind, costly and choice. . . . From there one passes into the little gallery, which is scarcely more than thirty or forty feet long. Between its windows are two very handsome small statues, on lacquered pedestals: one of the Farnese Venus, the other of Hercules. . . .

It was the type of apartment which discreetly accommodates both work and leisure, of sufficiently modest size for the convenience of daily existence, and ornamented with delightful taste. A lady of quality in Dancourt's play *Les Agioteurs* is presented adapting for herself just such an *entresol* and taking advice from a friend about the display of her china. The Baron de Thiers, who lived in the Place Vendôme in the hôtel built by his father in Louis XIV's time, had a little *entresol* decorated by the architect Varin, which he preferred to his large suite. Provided with a bathroom, lit by windows on the *place* side, and adorned with a collection of celebrated pictures, it offered, wrote Blondel, 'a favourite place for the master of the house to retire to'. It was very much in this spirit, characteristic of the time, that Louis XV subdivided Versailles to protect his personal life in an inner sequence of rooms, with a secluded *cabinet* and all those pretty 'rat holes' which are among the renowned features of the palace.

36 Blève: The same: elevation on the Rue de Bretagne, 1776–7

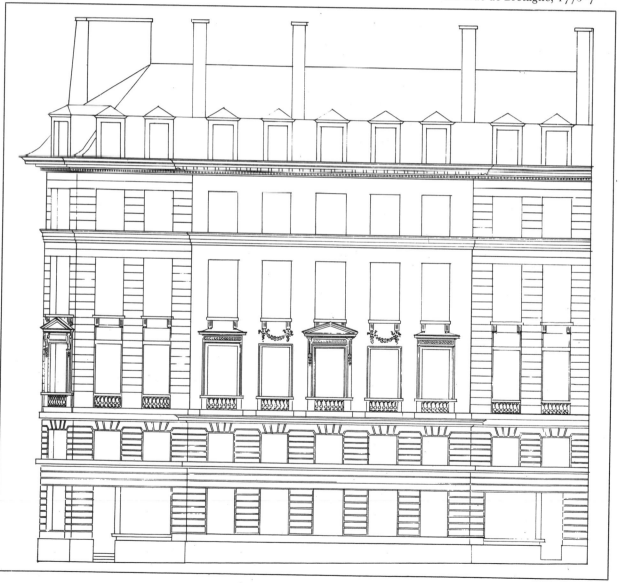

For a lady in frail health, whose husband spared nothing to please her, Blondel created a little suite, which he described at length in his course of lectures. Antechambers, closets and dressing-rooms were skilfully disposed about her bedroom. When she rose, the lady passed into a little room to which saleswomen from the fashion trade, who might arrive during her protracted toilet, had direct access. The circular shape given to the end of the room allowed for the provision of wardrobes to hold her dresses and informal wear. This inward curvature of the walls, which the strict theorist proscribed for state apartments, was acceptable 'in small rooms intended for the pleasure and accommodation of an attractive woman whose grace and charm should be apparent from the arrangement of the rooms which she chooses for her regular abode'. One *cabinet* of this little suite was called *méridienne* (=siesta) 'because, placed in a recess, was an ottoman, a kind of day-bed, where it is quite common to sleep in the afternoon in hot weather, or where one can rest undisturbed in case of slight indisposition'. Muslin curtains covered the only window of the room, in which too much light might have been harmful to repose. Some consideration was paid to chamber-maids. Between the bed recess and the passage behind it, a mirror mounted on a mobile frame could be hoisted to the floor above by a ratchet device and counterweights. When lowered, it illuminated the passage; when raised, it allowed the bed to be made without dragging it into the middle of the bedroom. Chimney-pieces were provided in the anterooms to make service easier. The walls were painted with flowers and arabesques, but the high price of such decoration 'is no occasion for astonishing an amateur with eyes enlightened by taste, who takes pleasure in adorning the retreat of a cherished spouse'.

While Blondel was describing in the style of a man of 'sensibility' the attentions of a model husband, Diderot was denouncing 'this luxury which, allied to loose morals, turn our apartments into little retreats'. The supercilious Marquis de Mirabeau went further:

> Have you a palace? Then it must contain a winter suite, another for summer, and one for baths, plus *entresols, cabinets,* closets, boudoirs, book rooms, privies, communicating doors, secret staircases, etc. . . . Lights are needed for all this and the confused architect . . . abandons Vitruvius and takes Daedalus for his master. He hands over his labyrinth to the decorator, who seeks out the nooks and crannies, screens the chimney-piece, hides the doors, alcoves the bed, and deforms the panelling. Lacquer and mirrors do the rest.

These luxurious retreats, denounced by the moralists, were the indispensable setting for amorous intrigues in the gossip and romances of the period. Under the transparent disguise of Oriental fiction, which Montesquieu made fashionable, an account appeared in Holland of the *entresols* of Choisy at the time when Louis XV was living there with the Duchesse de Châteauroux:

> Among other things to be admired there was a little apartment contrived above Cha-Séphi's, with which it communicated by a private staircase. This was the favourite's suite: the delicacy of the sculpture, the gold and the blue, the fastidious furniture and the many fine mirrors, skilfully placed, enhanced the simplicity and gave it a strikingly alluring air. In a word, here was art entirely exploited in the service of comfort, good taste and gallantry.

In *Angola*, the Chevalier de la Morlière introduces us to two lovers in a fashionable apartment:

> 'Why', said the Marquis, 'you have there a superbly ornamented chimney-piece, and these cabinets from China, are they from the Rue du Roule? I am mad about that man. Everything he sells is priceless and so unusual. . . .' 'Yes,' said the Countess, 'it's been quite well chosen.' 'Indeed,' continued the Marquis, 'your taste in all this is divine. Look at these grotesque figures. What remarkable workmanship! This one, in particular, which is so like your booby of a husband – two peas in a pod! . . .' They then proceed into a room furnished with a day-bed, covered with rose and silver damask.

The art trade and the craftsmen

The man of the Rue de Roule? A commercial announcement states that 'the Sieur Bazin, Rue du Roule, obtains crystal and porcelain from foreign countries, ornamented with gold, silver and bronze gilded with ormolu'. It was to him and his neighbour Vigier that the modish amateurs of La Morlière and Dancourt used to go treasure-hunting. In Watteau's day, the art trade was conducted on the Pont Notre-Dame. Haberdashery, jewellery and the sale of pictures were handled by the same dealers. In the Gersaint shop, a lady seems to be choosing a jewel in front of a dressing-case and a mirror, while other visitors have eyes only for the paintings. A little later, frame-makers and traders in ceramics, furniture and pictures congregated between the Rue Saint-Honoré and the Seine. As fashionable Paris extended westward, they were drawn towards the Faubourg which they have now made famous. In Louis XV's reign, pictures were bought in the Rue Saint-Honoré at Poirier, '*à la Couronne d'Or*'; and at Hébert, '*vis à vis le Grand Conseil*'. Pierre Le Brun was at the '*Roi des Indes*' before moving to the Rue de l'Arbre Sec, '*vis à vis la Rue Bailleul*', perhaps underneath the rococo balcony of the Eynaud house. Round about 1740 Pingat was still restoring pictures on the Pont Notre-Dame, at the '*Armes d'Espagne*'. But one also went to his colleagues on the Quai de la Mégisserie, Boileau and Denis Budlet, especially if one was hard up, for their neighbour Collins of Brussels, who restored the King's pictures and those of the Duc d'Orléans, had the reputation of being dear. Frames, called at that time *bordures*, might be carved by Michel Lange, sculptor to the Duc d'Orléans, but in Louis XV's time they could be procured from the Maurisan family, Ph. Cayeux, Charny and Launay. . . . Somewhat later, Guibert became the brother-in-law of Claude-Joseph Vernet and framed his seascapes, working as well at Versailles and the Trianons. Glomy bequeathed his name to those passe-partout frames edged with gilded netting or painted in wash, which encased drawings and prints. Rémy and Machard dispersed celebrated collections at auctions. Paillet had his sale-room in the Rue Platrière at the former Hôtel de Bullion, while in the Rue de Cléry, as we have already seen, that of J.-B. Pierre Lebrun was built on a monumental scale and was also used for concerts.

With the *Journal du Garde-meubles* and the *Comptes de la Maison du Roi*, the *Livre-Journal* of Lasare Duvaux is one of the best-known documents on the eighteenth-century art trade. Duvaux enjoyed the custom of Mme de Pompadour, and furnished the Château d'Asnières for the Marquis d'Argenson, and the former Hôtel de Roquelaure and the Château de Champlâtreux for the Président Môlé. He purveyed 'furniture, panelling, frames, door-heads, and screens of India paper, China paper and woven paper'. He would lend furniture to amateurs and leave them to decide whether it suited their rooms. In August 1758, when the Maréchal de Richelieu and his architect Chevotet were equipping the Pavillon de Hanovre, Duvaux delivered 'a chest in old pagoda lacquer, ornamented in bronze gilded with ormolu, and an Italian Griotte marble top'; the cost of transport was six livres. Perhaps the piece did not give satisfaction, for the Maréchal, although an admirer of old lacquer, soon returned it to the supplier.

Privacy

With an aristocracy haunted by its concern to escape the critical eyes of its servants, the taste for comfort went with a liking for seclusion and privacy, and the master class bore the full brunt of the author's irony, when he spoke of 'lackeys, that cursed species, who in those days spent their time in spying on their masters'. For his part, Blondel – a man of the middle class – constantly reminded architects not to interrupt a sequence of rooms by lobbies, where servants habitually gathered. There were domestics, however, in the original sense of the word, i.e. household dependants, who were often linked to those whom they served by the strongest of bonds. The Baron de Besenval, whose anger had offended an old servant, would rather have given up his hôtel than have seen him go. A Lenten sermon by the Abbé Laugier, often mentioned on these pages as a perceptive critic of architecture, reminded their lordships of the court of their duties towards their retainers. The records of probate registries, where wills were deposited, reflect the generosity of bequests to servants in a world in which the social antagonisms of the nineteenth century had not yet weakened the links of dependence or solidarity forged in the feudal Middle Ages.

The ingenious devices introduced into the house were an expression of a twofold anxiety: to alleviate the drudgery of servants, but also to avoid their presence as far as possible by multiplying the means of serving oneself with the least effort. This period thought up the dumb-waiter, mounted on casters and equipped with a vast number of drawers and handles. The *athénienne*, brought into fashion by the publisher Eberts in 1773, enabled the mistress of the house to make tea on the tripod of the Delphic oracle. Within the height of a *piano nobile*, the comparatively

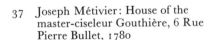

37 Joseph Métivier: House of the master-ciseleur Gouthière, 6 Rue Pierre Bullet, 1780

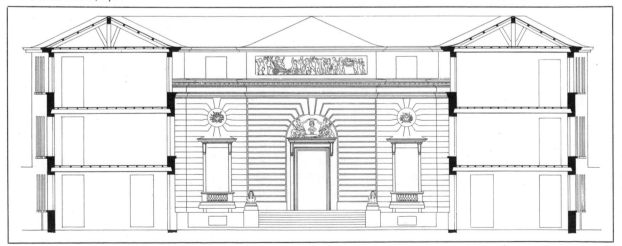

low private rooms were surmounted by an *entresol*, from which the servants only came down at the summons of a bell. The latter, an invention of the previous century, was in wide use during the Régence. In 1721, in an isolated hôtel on the still deserted outskirts of the Faubourg Saint-Germain, the Papal Nuncio pulled the rope of his bell, alarmed at what he thought to be a burglary. In the *Liaisons Dangereuses*, Valmont tells of his nocturnal invasion of the apartment of Cécile Volanges: 'She threw herself towards the bell cord, but my agility restrained her arm.' When Mme de Genlis, a victim of her own absent-mindedness, arrived at the home of Voltaire and his niece before the stipulated time: 'The servants seemed utterly taken aback; there were frantic sounds of summoning bells, of hurried comings and goings and of doors suddenly slammed and opened.' Louis XV, mistrustful and secretive, had bells installed in all his houses. At Choisy, the ring of a bell was the signal for the already laid 'flying table' to rise from the basement with which came four attendant serving tables bearing what had earlier been ordered in writing.

In Louis XIV's reign, Mazarin and the Marquis de Vilayer had introduced in Paris the chair-hoist, ancestor of the lift, and the King had one made at Versailles for one of his daughters, Mlle de Sens. One evening the contraption broke down and left the Princess incarcerated until the wall could be pierced to let her out. This accident did not discourage the Condé family from having a lift at Chantilly and another at the Luxembourg, which served all floors. Louis XV had a chair-hoist constructed for Mme de Châteauroux by Arnoult, the machinist of the Menus Plaisirs. The author of the *Mémoires secrets pour servir à l'histoire de la Perse* refers to the King's favourite as Rétima: 'It was for her that machines were invented convenient and proper for transporting her from one place to another at times and circumstances which her lover considered to deserve great attention.'

For a long time the taste for magical spectacles had kept the minds of stage 'machinists' on the alert. Loriot, Guérin, Arnoult and Tranoy were among the cleverest of a century in which Servandoni, de Wailly and P.-A. Paris designed scenery for the Opéra. In the salon of the Hôtel de Monville, a single cord instantaneously closed all the oculi of the lantern. Brass chains drawn over pulleys and cogs raised mirrors from the floor and spirited away false ceilings. In the *Erreurs instructives*, Jonval describes a bed 'worthy of Archimedes and Loriot' which alternately rose and fell on powerful springs. In the Hôtel Thélusson, a mirror installed by Reynard disappeared by opening a window between two salons. In the house of the Conseiller Chavannes, the architect Moreau designed shutters concealed in the thickness of the walls which were lowered in the imposts of the arched window-bays. Louis was soon to copy the idea for the Intendance at Besançon, where the window-openings can be entirely masked by shutters running in slideways on either side.

Warmth

A hinged chimney-piece panel provided discreet communication between the two adjoining hôtels of the Maréchal de Richelieu and a lady of his acquaintance, and – not surprisingly – became the talking-point of the century. Another equally ingenious contrivance was passed over in silence, no doubt because it operated in the fireplace of a man of spotless reputation. In the presbytery of Saint-Eustache, a rotating stove,

115

38   H. Piètre: Salon of the Hôtel
d'Orléans, Rue de la Chaussée
d'Antin, about 1780

designed by Jean Mansart de Jouy warmed in turn the bedroom and the study of the highly respectable Abbé Secousse. The battle against the cold made good progress in the course of the century. Little fireplaces, devised for Versailles by Lassurance and Pierre Lepautre to warm the royal apartments, found wider application during the Régence.

Laugier advocated double windows. Sometime chaplain to the court of Lorraine, he had unhappy memories of the iron stoves which heated the great rooms of King Stanislas and were used in Paris under the name of Nancy stoves. Their warmth, he declared, singed the head and left the feet cold. The second half of the century preferred stoves in faience. Placed in recesses, they did not open into the room to be heated, but into an anteroom or some adjacent corner, where they could be tended out of sight. Neo-classical art gave to the flue the form of a column, and to the furnace that of a Roman altar, when it did not make it the pedestal of a statue copied from the antique. A Diana, perched like this in the gallery of the Elysée, was given the features of the late Marquise de Pompadour, who thus continued to live in her old home in disguise. A good way of heating apartments was to encase the flues from the kitchen in the walls, for the stoves were extremely hot. Indeed, when Mme du Barry and Ledoux received Louis XV at the Pavillon de Louveciennes, four of the cooks fainted. Ledoux was never to become familiar with the fan-type ventilator, to which he makes a characteristically vague reference in 1805, but the use of the piped heating system spread. For M. Chabannes, Moreau-Desproux had installed in 1758 'a stove of a new kind, fixed solidly on the ground floor. It carries the heat through great pipes to the storeys above and heats the whole pavilion. Vent-holes ensure the circulation of air. No stove is visible in the house.'

Under the instructions of Ledoux, the heating system of the Hôtel Thélusson was constructed by Bartolini, the contractor who had similarly equipped the Elysée. Marentin also supplied stoves in the 'antique' manner, some of which are still carrying statues in the dining-room of the Château des Boulayes. Fine examples are preserved, too, in the Hôtel de Besenval and in the Palais Abbatial de Royaumont. Franklin did research into the improvement of stoves, while the architect Désarnaud, who had built in the cold valleys of the Vivarais, introduced into Paris a system of 'economical and salubrious fireplaces' with a reputation which still endured under the Consulate. Many other inventions were submitted to the Académie d'Architecture during the century. Sound-insulation, for example, was not an unknown luxury. It was applied in Mme de Pompadour's suite, where flock and cotton waste were placed between the flooring-joists. Certain internal walls of the Palais Bourbon are still packed with hay.

All these contributions to comfort were to be found in rooms of Louis XVI's time.

Bedrooms

Bedrooms, Le Camus tells us, should be papered in green, which is most favourable to rest, and the children's wing cannot be too gay. The closed alcove was no longer in fashion, but the bed was still placed in a recess, which might be framed with pilasters, as in the Baronne d'Espagnac's house, or with carved doors, as in the Hôtel de Tessé (Metropolitan Museum, New York), or by painted panels on which Silence watches while Morpheus sleeps, as at Mme de Kinsky's. The curtains might be held in place by a loop and move underneath a pelmet, or be bunched in the Italian way, as with Mme de Brunoy. A bed in the Polish manner (in memory of Marie Leszczinska), sheltering beneath the panaches of a canopy, would be draped with lampas or nankeen. A watercolour by Henri Piètre shows us the bed of the Duc d'Orléans, covered with sulphur and lilac silk. At Bagatelle, the bedroom of the Comte d'Artois, Grand Master of the Artillery, imitated the interior of a tent, with lances supporting the curtains of the bed and cannons serving as firedogs (Pl. 175). Here there appeared for the first time the decorative variations with which Percier later soothed the repose of warriors Bonaparte and Moreau.

When the bedroom of a lady of fashion was not round, or oval like that of Mme Vigée-Lebrun, one of these forms was given to the adjoining boudoir. Very low and sometimes very small, this room would be surmounted by an *entresol*, from which the maid would descend by an internal staircase at the call of her mistress. A recess, placed opposite the chimney piece, might contain an ottoman, a kind of sofa curved to the shape of the room. The boudoir of the Hôtel Perrotin de Barmond, 102 Rue Vieille-du-Temple, and those of the Hôtel de Breteuil, one circular and the other elliptical, may be quoted as fine examples (Musée Carnavalet). In the Hôtel Goix, 60 Rue du Faubourg-Poissonnière, an oval boudoir has come down to us intact (Pl. 136). Surrounded by mirrors, set slightly back in recesses, it is crowned by a bold three-row cornice of pearls, acanthus leaves and pods. Jean-Charles Delafosse, who made sixty drawings for this hôtel, had drawn on his recollections of the decorative designs of Antoine Le Pautre and his emulators during the ministry of Mazarin.

39 E. Fr Legrand: Hôtel de Gallifet (today the Italian Embassy), 73 Rue de Grenelle – garden front, 1784

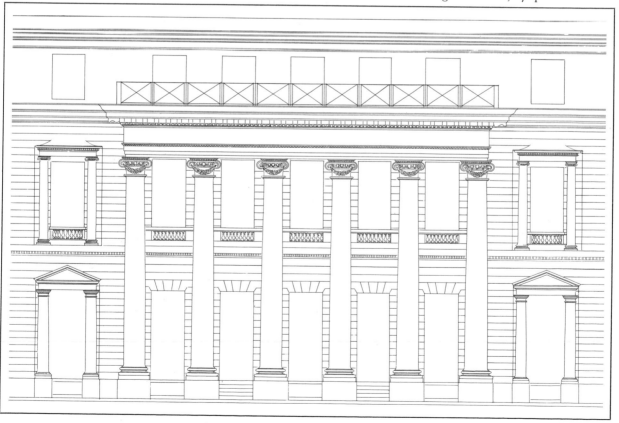

Sanitary installations

Sanitary installations were already in wide use and greatly improved. A bath 'suite' was indispensable to the comfort of a 'little house' or of a fashionable mezzanine. The bathroom was connected to a boiler-house, containing the cold-water tank and a large copper 'cumulus' placed over a wood stove. These two vessels were raised a few feet above floor level, so that the water, passing through lead pipes, reached the taps of the bath by gravitational pressure. An architectural treatise of 1738 describes a bidet, supplied with hot or cold water according to the season.

Patte's *Cours d'architecture* proposes a room with two baths, probably similar to the one provided by Le Carpentier in the Hôtel de Montmorency. A service closet and privies complete the bath suite. The author does not speak of a flush, but the specifications provided for a pan in faience with a valve, and a cistern with a tap. The room was ventilated by a pipe three inches wide, which came down from the ceiling. A handle opened the valve, which closed again automatically by the effect of a lead weight. In other cases, the valve was opened by lifting the flap-seat. The absence of a trap could lead to accidents, as a news item in the *Journal de Paris* reveals. In an apartment of the Left Bank, a man-servant had dropped his watch through the valve opening of an upper floor. He took a lighted torch to look for it in the cesspit, and caused a serious explosion. In the late eighteenth century decorators adorned bathrooms with an elegance which would astonish our age, but was still in fashion when Corot painted the lake of Nemi and its banks in the bathroom of his friends the Robert family. Like miniature Roman thermae, the bathroom of Mlle Dervieux was octagonal and ornamented with polychrome arabesques, the figures standing out in white against a pale blue stucco background. In the middle a round white marble basin served as a bath. The room was open on one side to a

40 Fr Soufflot le Romain : Hôtel de Montholon, 21 Boulevard Montmartre, 1785

120

musicians' gallery, so that the fair creature, captivated by their playing, could splash in time with the music'.

In the Baron de Besenval's hôtel, Rue de Grenelle, the bath suite occupied the basement. Vases, a naiad and large bas-reliefs by Clodion adorned a Doric hypogeum contrived by Brongniart, but so cold, the story goes, that one could not bath in it without risking a fatal attack of pneumonia. There was more comfort in the home of the Prince de Soubise, where the elliptical bathroom was lighted by a dome. The white veined stucco wall was ringed by a frieze in low relief, white also, but on a background of Campan green. The radiating slabs of the paved floor combined white veined marble with Italian Griotte. Loyal to the tastes of his youth, the Prince hung paintings by Boucher on the mirrors. 'The bath-room curtains', wrote Le Camus, 'will be whiter than snow. But Diana sometimes runs through forests and her skin may be affected by the heat of the sun. In such a case, curtains with a blue background might be more successful.'

Panelling and carved ornamentation

Mural decoration offered particular opportunities to eighteenth-century artists. The craft, which already flourished in the Fontainebleau of Henri II, had spread even to the middle-class house by the time that Argan was hiding his cash in the panelling of his alcove. In the eighteenth-century panelling had become indispensable to the well-being of the French, when they lived abroad. M. de Fontenay had Pineau to design the interior woodwork for his house in Dresden. J.-J. Rousseau was constrained to admire the wainscoting of M. Dupin in the Hôtel Lambert, but railed against M. de Montaigu, the ambassador of France in Venice, for having panelled marble and stucco walls, which might

41 J.-A. Raymond: House of Mme Vigée-Lebrun, circular court, 8 Rue du Sentier (demolished), 1785

well have been enlivened by the work of a rival of Zelotti or Ricci. Panelling was an item of trade and export. It justified an extra charge to a new tenant and led to surreptitious dismantling operations. An advertisement of 1784 describes a set of panels painted by Watteau (cf. Pls. 9 and 10), which still fetched their price on the Paris market among

42   P. Rousseau: His house, 25 Rue de La Rochefoucauld.

122

connoisseurs. King Augustus III of Poland had ordered wainscoting from Paris for his portrait gallery, his bedroom and his throne-room. Executed by the joiner Jadot, it underwent official valuation in the former Noviciate of the Jesuits before its departure for Warsaw.

In Louis XV's reign, the abundance and beauty of Parisian panelling, the chosen field of rocaille, were a source of admiration. Towards the end of the nineteenth century, it was frequently stripped, and nowadays is as difficult to identify as the names of the designers, which only appear incidentally in the documents of public records. The humble careers of these sculptors in wood, almost all of them academicians of Saint-Luc, deserve none the less to be studied. Their chisels patterned the panels, pilasters, door-frames and wall-linings on which the joiner, on the architect's instructions, blocked out the sections to be carved. The projection left for the moulding had to be large enough to prevent the artist's tool from exposing the tongue-and-groove joints, a mischance which could entail expensive valuations and actions for damage. In the Hôtels de Brancas and d'Orrouer, the stripping of some of the woodwork has revealed the designs for the panels and their carving, accurately drawn on the wall, just as the burning of the Campo Santo at Pisa in 1944 disclosed the patterns under the frescoes.

In 1723 Jules-Michel Hardouin submitted the design for the trophies carved by Michel Lange in the *grand salon* of the Elysée. They are comparable in beauty with those of the goldsmith Ladoireau in the Galerie des Glaces, and can be attributed to Oppenord. Louis-Jacques Herpin appears to have carved a set of panels for the Palais Soubise, of which he published engravings (Pl. 24). He can be traced to the Louvre, to Marly and to the Hôtels de Matignon, Carignan, Belle-Isle and Ormesson. In the interests of speed, the ornamentalist-sculptors preferred to work as a team. Taupin, Le Goupil and Dugoulon are known from the accounts of Versailles and Notre-Dame. In 1720 Gabriel senior invited them to decorate, in the Place Vendôme, the *grands appartements* of the Regent's mistress, La Parabère, while Dominique Simony, who had worked under Mansart, took charge of the *entresols*. A very discreet survey report takes us into the favourite's dressing-room, in which Chinese porcelain was displayed on consoles, as in the little gallery at Versailles and in the homes of the characters in Dancourt's plays. The decoration of the hôtel of La Parabère has been wrongly linked with Boffrand's influence, but undoubtedly takes its place among the masterpieces of rocaille. Almost all the decoration of the Hôtel de Roquelaure-Molé is the joint work of Pierre Juliance and Pierre Fournier. It has been possible to recognise work by Louis Dupain, Philippe Varin, Alexandre Jouasse, Martin-Jacques Stanguier and some others, who were employed in Louis XV's reign in the hôtels and palaces of Paris.

During the Régence, a profusion of sculptured ornaments decorated the upper panelling, i.e. in the space between the dado and the cornice. Trophies of battle, hunting and the sea filled Vassé's panels in the Hôtel de Toulouse and those of Lange in the Elysée, similar to those carved by Nicolas Pineau at the same period in Peter the Great's study. The Hôtel de la Trémoille, Boulevard Delessert, has preserved the woodwork of the former Hôtel Bonnier in the Place des Victoires, for which a drawing initialled by Oppenord survives in America. Narrow panels, showing allegorical figures of Fame brandishing trumpets underneath the pendant borders familiar to painters of arabesques, alternate with wide ones bearing trophies of the chase: clumps of shrubs hung with quivers, horns, game-bags and huntsmen's spears, while hounds sniff the scent of dead hares. Confronted with works of this kind, Boffrand was later to exclaim: 'This decoration is overloaded with ornament. Make it more restful.' Oppenord showed more restraint in the corner salon of the Palais-Royal and at la Grange du Milieu, where oval frames are placed between two bare spaces halfway up the panels. But in its highest expression rocaille preferred in such contexts an unpretentious trophy or one of those rosaces so fashionable in the Louis XV style as interpreted by Chevotet, Gabriel and Jacques Verberckt. Above and below the panel, in spaces cut out in the form of a heart, a bat's wing, a flower basket or a 'Chinese plant' seemed to have broken away from the cross-bow arch framing the composition.

About 1730 Nicolas Pineau returned from Russia, where he had clearly admired the baroque designs of Rastrelli. Some of the mirror-heads engraved from his drawings for the new edition of Daviler in 1738 were directly copied from the Italian architect. The text informs us that they were carved in a Parisian hôtel, which we recognise as the Hôtel d'Orrouer, where Pineau and his studio had been responsible for the magnificent decoration from 1732 (Pls. 67–8). Thanks to the discovery of his drawings in an attic at Angoulême towards the end of the last century, he is one of the ornamentalists of the period of whom we are least ignorant. We have already met him in the Hôtel de Villars (Pl. 71) with the ladies of Saint-Chaumond and in the Hôtel de Marsilly (Pls. 77 and 79). The supposition that he worked at the Palais Soubise cannot be lightly dismissed, although the jealous authority of Boffrand would have reduced him to the role of a brilliant executant. His production was enormous and contemporaries regarded him highly. His drawings for the bedroom of the Comte de Middelbourg bear under the shells and close to the mouldings the names of the practitioners who were to share in carrying out the job: 'Mr Laforest, Mr Germain, Mr Balthazar, Mr Berger.' Pineau gave a fresh orientation to the art of sculptured panelling, when around 1736 he brought into fashion the dissymmetrical and picturesque style of Meissonier. To mention only what survives in Paris, the salon of 26 Rue Cambon is one of the most beautiful examples of this manner (Pl. 70). Blondel, who condemned rocaille, after having been one of its masters, was obliged to agree that 'MM. Pineau, Lange and Verbeck have contributed in rendering our dwellings worthy of the admiration of unprejudiced nations'.

In its natural state the Dutch oak, which was used for lining walls, made rooms dark. For this reason, domestic interior designers left this so-called panelling *à la capucine* to monasteries and churches, and primed the wood with a light-coloured paint. The master-painters' technique is known from manuscript recipes, like that of Nicolas Pineau, and from different treatises published in the course of the century. The process of size-colouring or *chipolin* entailed five operations. First, the natural wood was treated (by means of a brush of wild-boar bristle) with a boiling mixture prepared as follows:

> Take three cloves of garlic and a handful of wormwood leaves, which you will boil in three tankards of water, reducing the quantity to a quart: pass the juice through muslin and mix it with a tankard of good and strong parchment glue: add to it half a handful of salt and a wine-glass of vinegar: bring the lot to a boil over the fire.

The second operation was preparatory, the application of seven to nine coats of Bougival white, carefully polished with dogskin. The third consisted in smoothing down this preparatory surface with pumice. The fourth was a matter of rectification, by the use of irons which brought back into relief the carving dulled by the density of the white undercoat. Finally, the artist applied the colour chosen according to the vagaries of fashion and the tastes of the client. Pale yellow was the rage about 1735, described in specifications and artists' accounts as 'little' yellow, 'fine' jonquil, sulphur, straw and lemon. These hues were obtained from a basic vegetable pigment, the yellow lake of Troyes, more or less adulterated by white and ochre of Berry. The delicate jonquil was the choice of the Duchess d'Alincourt for her *entresol* of the Rue Saint-Honoré, straw for Mme Trudaine in the Marais, and sulphur of Jacques Samuel Bernard for his hôtel of the Rue du Bac. A sample of this shade was taken a short while ago from the *grand salon* at 26 Rue Cambon.

Recognised harmonies grew up between the pale yellow of the woodwork and the colour given to hangings. In 1740 it was blue, and later lilac, which complemented yellow in the colour charts. In 1739, Mme du Châtelet's bedroom at Cirey, decorated in the latest fashion, was

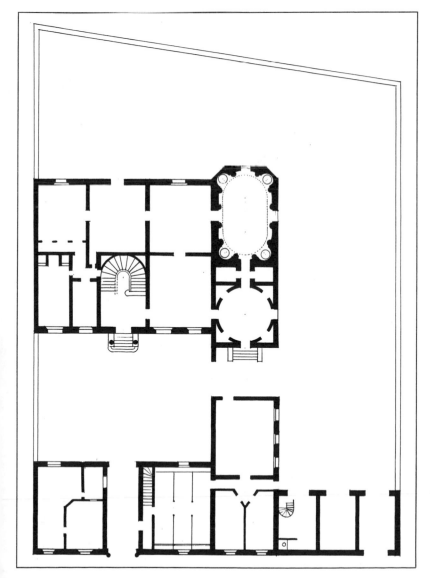

43   Hôtel de Botterel-Quintin,
44 Rue des Petites-Écuries
(plan), 1785

125

44 Hôtel de Botterel-Quintin,
The dining-room

'panelled and painted in light yellow, with pale blue borders; a recess in similar manner, framed with charming India papers. The bed is in blue moire and everything is matched, yellow and blue, down to the dog's basket: the wood of the arm-chair, table, corner pieces, writing-desk'. In the bath suite, a dressing-closet had panelling 'painted willow-green, light, gay, divine'. Flax-grey, water-green, rose and turquoise were the chosen range of Louis XV's subjects. The carved ornamentation of the woodwork might be emphasised by using a lighter or darker colour. About 1742, if we may believe the Duc de Luynes, the fashion was to apply green as a contrast to a white background. The Château de Villarceaux still has a salon painted in the original water-green shade. Two salons at Champlâtreux are respectively rose and turquoise

45 J. Méthivier: His own house,
     Boulevard Saint-Denis, 1789

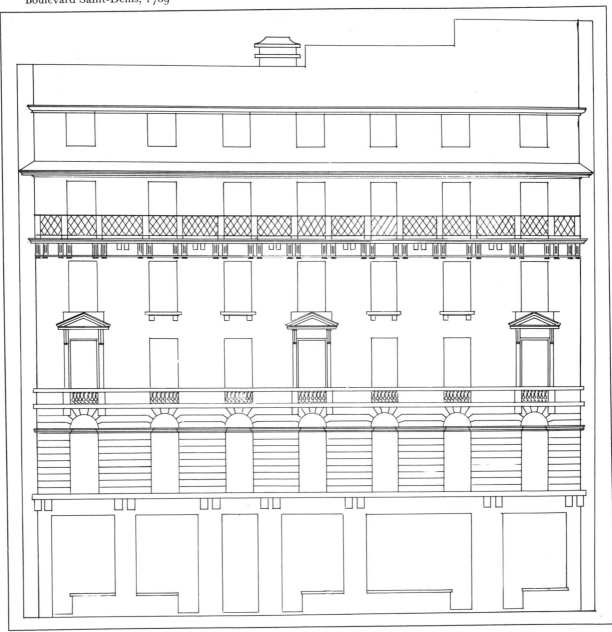

128

and both are set off with white. Le Camus de Mézières, writing in Louis XVI's reign, advised green for bedrooms: 'It assumes the nature of foliage. Sleep seems to find in it a soothing sweetness. Green is favourable because of its uniformity and its constant hue is suited to repose.' We have encountered symphonies in blue and gold at Mme Vigée-Lebrun's, blue and yellow in the suite of Mme de Genlis at the Palais-Royal, yellow and lilac in the hôtels of Mme de Montesson and the Duc d'Orléans in the Chaussée d'Antin. Around 1785 puce and vermilion made a discreet appearance to enliven the yellow sienna background of sham marble. Since 1720, however, the commonest combination, at any rate in state apartments, was white and gold. The conventional use of gold leaf flattered the vanity of the new rich and ruined the nobility, for the brilliance of the gilded panelling on a white base was rapidly tarnished by the smoke from chandeliers, destructive emanations from food, and insecticidal preparations.

Decoration in relief during the Louis XVI period

Neo-classicism restored to the Graeco-Roman orders the position which they had occupied in apartments under Louis XIV. The repetition of similar motifs, such as capitals, modillions, ovoli and scrolls, soon led to casting them in moulds, to save time and money. Thenceforward the craft of the stucco-worker gradually eliminated that of the wood-carver. Stylobates, entablatures and pilasters framed stucco panels moulded in low relief, on which was deployed the rich vocabulary of arabesque ornament. A strict symmetry seems to have suddenly restrained the exuberance of chimeras among the hydras, swags and roundels. Identical elements are found in several houses. The Hôtels de Gallifet and de Jarnac, and the residence at No. 10 Rue de la Chaise thus retain the same arabesque panels.

The same series of the five senses, represented by children playing, was often used for suites of rooms, placed over doors or on the exterior above windows. It belonged to the stucco-craftsman D'Hollande, who had taken out a patent to foil imitators. The Monsiau family (known as Chevalier) had a stucco works and shop on the Boulevard de la Chaussée d'Antin. In the Rue Saint-Nicolas, at the corner of the Rue du Faubourg Saint-Martin, a block of dwellings, like those we have today in the Quartier Montparnasse, lodged a number of skilled craftsmen. Here Goutheinze sold 'works in alabaster and stucco, like shafts of columns, vases, incense-burners, etc. . . .' The stucco-workers Métivier and Feuillet ornamented the hôtels of Ledoux; Cauvet was employed by Brongniart, while the antique-minded Dugourc was Bélanger's brother-in-law. All these ornamentalists succeeded in counteracting rigid classical discipline by a voluptuous grace, for which Clodion and Pajou, anticipating Prud'hon, set the pattern.

Printed fabrics and wallpapers

Stucco and alabaster were inexpensive substitutes, commoner than marble among noblemen who could no longer afford to live splendidly. As early as Louis XIV's reign, the need to maintain appearances had taught decorators to simulate costly materials, and by 1780 the painters Sauvage, Gébelin, Boileau and Julien de Parme were using the method of grisaille to imitate objects in low relief. An overdoor in grey monochrome by Sauvage cost sixty francs. After economising in marble, industry turned its inventive genius to alternatives to painting. Waxed fabrics, flock-paper, wall-paper and *toiles de Jouy* extended the illusion of luxury to the lesser rooms of wealthy houses before bringing a measure of gaiety to the average home. Mechanised methods were applied to the printing of wall-papers in the workshops of Robert, Réveillon, Arthur and Grenard, and the India-paper manufactory of Oberkampf. By this means the pastoral subjects of J.-B. Huet, the grotesque motifs of Rousseau and La Vallée-Poussin, and topical scenes like the balloon ascents of the Montgolfier brothers acquired wide popularity. In the Hôtel Thélusson, Robert used for Madame's bedroom a mat white paper with a bold design of trees and castellated towers, a paper imitating Delft tiles in a closet, and elsewhere a flowered silk paper with a crimson background, with green and buff in cupboards.

Decorative painting

Apartments enlivened by gilding and delicate colours were also the setting for compositions of decorative painting, which would be placed over doors and mirrors, on pendentives and above chimney-pieces. Painters specialised in particular subjects. Desportes and Oudry were renowned for their hounds and game. Watteau invented the rustic idyll and lovers' conversation pieces, fields exploited also by Lancret, Pater and more obscure practitioners, such as Octavien and Bonaventure de Bar. The breaking of seals on the property of André Tramblin, sometime professor at the Académie de Saint-Luc, disclosed in his studio 'twenty-four pictures, copies of Lancret and Wataut, and canvases of forty'. His son, Charles-André, continued in the same line, which was also exploited by Quillard in Portugal and Norblin de la Gourdaine in Poland. A disciple of Bérain and pupil of Audran, Watteau excelled in the arabesque applied to woodwork, the panels of doors and ceilings. We have preserved the 'Cajoler' and 'Bacchus', which Watteau placed under light barrel arches for a boudoir in the Hôtel Poulpry, now the 'Maison des X'.

The salon painted by Lancret for the Hôtel de Boullongne, 23 Place Vendôme, was dispersed at a sale in 1896, but the Musée des Arts Décoratifs has picked up certain elements, notably *La Pèlerine*, the *Dame au parasol* and the *Turc amoureux*. In the *Cabinet des Singes* (monkeys) of the Hôtel de Rohan (Pls. 90 and 91), the grimacing animals take part in the rustic games of humans: blind-man's buff, leap-frog, stilts, etc. This scheme is the work of Christophe Huet, helped by his collaborators Dutour and Crépin, one of whom painted the animals and the other the landscapes. Roland de la Porte excelled in still life, and Blain de Fontenay continued Monnoyer's tradition of flower pictures. In the oval salon of the Hôtel de Jaucourt, 1 Rue de la Vrillière, an imitator of Huet and Peyrotte depicted Chinese Tartars. As far back as the reign of Louis XIV, the presence of the Jesuits in Pekin and diplomatic contacts between France and Siam had initiated a vogue for Asiatic art.

In the *Loves of Psyche and Cupid*, La Fontaine alludes to the decoration inspired by China which surrounded the King in his Trianon of porcelain. Watteau, who re-created all the styles which were dear to his contemporaries, painted the goddess Thvo-Chung and Chinese slaves and musicians in the Château de la Muette. Some curious verses by Jean Fréron, Voltaire's enemy, warmly salute the originality of the Chinese taste, while the ships arriving at Nantes distributed materials and ceramics all over France. They also brought old lacquer, which the cabinet-makers, from Charles-André Boulle to Guillaume Bennemann brilliantly exploited. In a few instances lacquer-ware was mounted in panelling. A fine and rare example survives in the Niarchos collection. However, most of the items of mural decoration with Chinese themes, which have been preserved, are copies by Parisian 'japanners', like Neuchâteau, Ch.-A. Tramblin, Samousseau or the celebrated Martin family. The great Hôtel du Maine, and the Hôtels du Tillet, Duret, and de Clermont d'Amboise had salons decorated in this way. The Musée Carnavalet has some panels which were carved and japanned for the Maréchal de Richelieu, whom Voltaire criticised for bad taste. A disdainful reference by Germain Brice to the Chinese decoration of the Thévenin house in the Rue Sainte-Anne, and some passages in which Blondel censures those 'ornaments from Peking' are proof of the cold attitude of the classicists towards Oriental fashions.

Illusionism

Throughout the century, decorative art deliberately cultivated the artifices of pretence. The same artists designed the stage settings of operas, firework displays, the court ballets, and the decoration of châteaux and hôtels. Two hundred years earlier, Palladio, Vittoria and Veronese had introduced into villas and palaces the devices of perspective, combining architecture, sculpture and painting in the same space for the purposes of music and dancing. The middle years of the eighteenth century acclaimed the talent of Gaetano Brunetti and his son, who had practised trompe-l'œil in England, following the examples of Sir James Thornhill and Verrio. They transformed the chapel of the Enfants Trouvés into the stable of Bethlehem and painted false columns in the church of Sainte-Marguerite de Charonne. The staircases of Bellevue, the Petit-Luxembourg and the Hôtel Soubise have disappeared, but that of the Hôtel de Luynes has been partly saved by its removal to the Musée Carnavalet. Between the columns and arches painted by the Brunetti family were deployed what Blondel called 'gallant subjects': flute and lute players, a flower-seller offering flowers to a lady of quality, two women with a child whom they are amusing with a bird. These characters were perhaps painted by a 'figuriste' like Eisen or Soldini, whose frequent collaboration with

46 E. Damesme: Brasserie Weel, Rue Richer – a Greco-Gothic building, (demolished) 1793

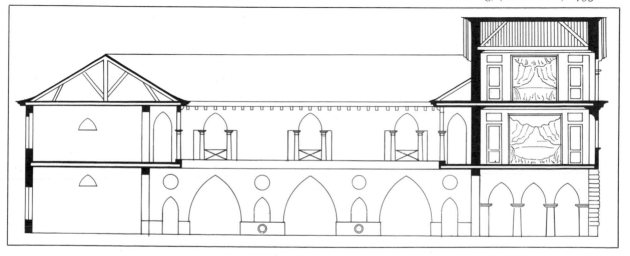

131

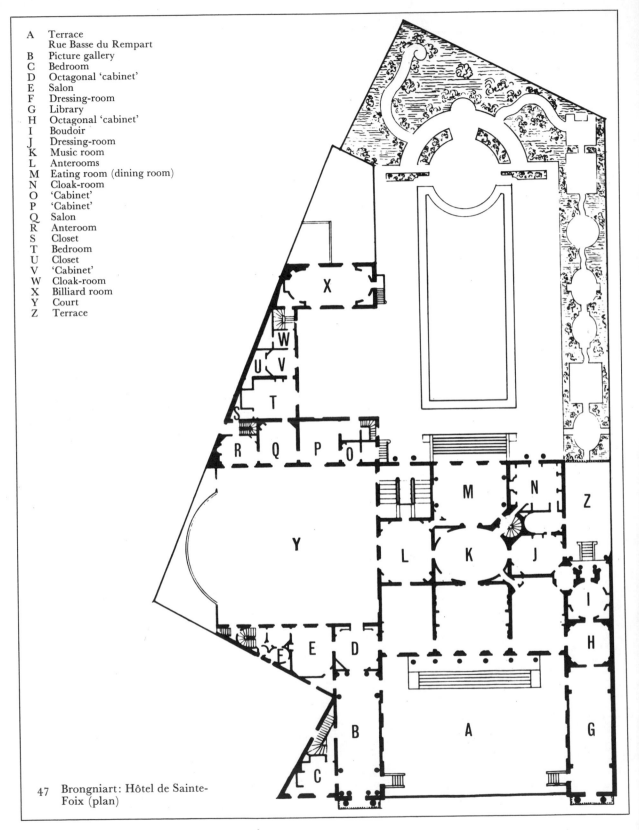

A   Terrace
      Rue Basse du Rempart
B   Picture gallery
C   Bedroom
D   Octagonal 'cabinet'
E   Salon
F   Dressing-room
G   Library
H   Octagonal 'cabinet'
I   Boudoir
J   Dressing-room
K   Music room
L   Anterooms
M   Eating room (dining room)
N   Cloak-room
O   'Cabinet'
P   'Cabinet'
Q   Salon
R   Anteroom
S   Closet
T   Bedroom
U   Closet
V   'Cabinet'
W   Cloak-room
X   Billiard room
Y   Court
Z   Terrace

47   Brongniart: Hôtel de Sainte-
      Foix (plan)

132

Brunetti father and son recalls, if distantly, the relationship between Mengozzi-Colonna and Tiepolo.

A journalist tells us about another scheme of decoration which has disappeared:

> M. Brunetti has applied his talents to the staircase of the hôtel of M. le Maréchal de Richelieu, Rue Neuve Saint-Augustin. He has painted a piece of Corinthian architecture of singular richness and magnificence. Felicitously contrived optical illusions offer scope to the ideas of connoisseurs. M. Soldini has placed in the intercolumniations figures lit by reflection, which are most effective. On what appears to be open sky, the young artist has painted Fame holding in one hand a trumpet and seeming to rise out of the palace on her way to distribute laurels.

Perspectives painted by De Machy deepen the well of the staircase of the Palais-Royal, which has come down to us almost intact, with its banisters forged by Corbin and Caffieri's cupids. The staircase of

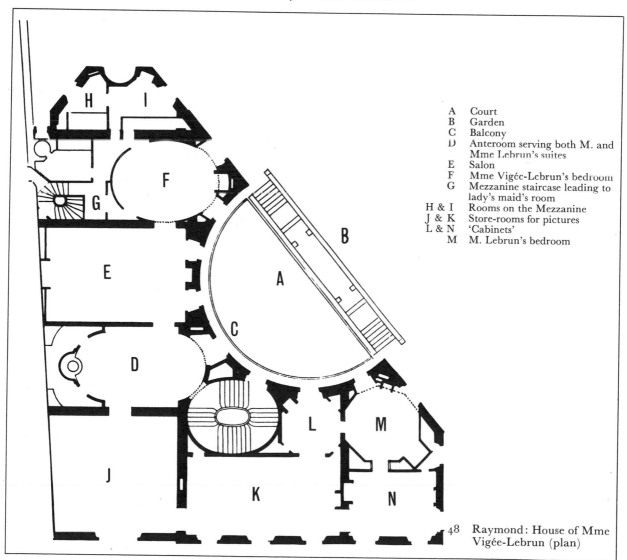

A   Court
B   Garden
C   Balcony
D   Anteroom serving both M. and Mme Lebrun's suites
E   Salon
F   Mme Vigée-Lebrun's bedroom
G   Mezzanine staircase leading to lady's maid's room
H & I   Rooms on the Mezzanine
J & K   Store-rooms for pictures
L & N   'Cabinets'
M   M. Lebrun's bedroom

48   Raymond: House of Mme Vigée-Lebrun (plan)

the Hôtel de Thiers (Pl. 98), also the work of Contant d'Ivry, has unfortunately lost its paintings by the Italian Piètre, who decorated the Opéra. In the town hall of Nancy, a staircase in which frescoes continue the sequence of columns and interlaces of the balustrade give us some idea of the possibilities of such decoration.

Decorative painting and the magic of trompe-l'œil were exploited, as we have seen, in many artists' homes. In 1760 the lawyer of an architect involved in litigation with Mlle Deschamps described the decoration carried out in the actress's dining-room: 'The most admirable features are groups of figures and birds and clumps of shrubs in relief.' At about the same period an advertisement informs us that 'Belleville, glass painter, excels in branches and garlands, on facing mirrors, which produces the effect of a bower of blooms'. The taste for decorative illusion was to outlive the rococo age and to achieve its ultimate refinements in the reign of Louis XVI. Drawing-rooms simulated the interiors of summer-houses, and dining-rooms presented the appearance of arbours. Putti carried off bedroom curtains into the heavens. Despite their fragility, some of these schemes of decoration still exist. The round salon of the Pavillon de Madame at Montreuil and the dining-room of the 'hamlet' of Chantilly both represent the inside of a grove, with the sky apparent through the topmost branches. Writers like Bastide, Vivant-Denon and Cailhava used such settings for their romantic plots. Indeed, the imagination of novelists had no difficulty in competing with the inspiration of artists.

In imitation of Italy, decorators had long used trompe-l'œil on the exterior of houses, to lengthen the vista of a court or garden. Although most of these works have disappeared, with their lath and plaster backing, engravings enable us to appreciate the architecture and trellis-work painted by Jacques Rousseau in several hôtels in Louis XIV's day. The young Pierre Dullin, nominated for the Académie de Rome, preferred to stay in Paris, where the Duc de Richelieu invited him to depict, in the court of his Place Royale house, a sun-dial surrounded by allegories of time. In 1766 the view from the Hôtel d'Hallwyl was improved by a colonnade painted on the wall of the Carmelite nuns, on the far side of the adjoining street. Ledoux had thus embraced the public highway in his design. In Louis XVI's reign, the painter Munich, who was the recognised decorator of public dance halls or 'Vauxhalls', depicted the buildings of a medieval village in the *folie* of the Trésorier Chartraire de Montigny. Ingenious compositions could also be seen at the Fermier-Général Kolly's residence and in the Hôtel de Tamnay, where cypresses painted on walls created the illusion of an Italian garden.

Mythological painting

According to Paul Valéry, the fantasies of trompe-l'œil have no place in pure art, and certainly such facile stratagems do not belong to historical painting, which contemporary opinion put at the top of the hierarchy of subjects. Painters like the Coypel dynasty and François Lemoine had attempted an unequal struggle with Rubens and the great Italians. In the Hôtel d'Argenton, Rue des Bons Enfants, Antoine Coypel painted a ceiling which Charles-Antoine Coypel later described in a tribute to his father, and which the Marquise d'Huxelles compared with those of Raphaël in the Farnesina: 'A rare thing to be seen is Mme d'Argenton's house, in which Coypel has painted the triumph of

Cupid over the Gods comparable with the banquet of Raphaël.' And yet, by the middle of the century, the Comte de Caylus and the Abbé Laugier were sorrowfully noting the eclipse of historical painting in interior decoration, where it had enjoyed such brilliant success in the time of Vouet and Le Brun. The taste for white ceilings, and the wide application of panelling and mirrors had driven it out of rooms, which it was reputed to darken. By the insistence of architects, it was now confined to 'perching' over doors, where the space, limited by a rocaille frame, allowed for only two or three performers in some minor episode. Boucher, Carle Van Loo and Tremolières showed their skill in such work. After 1750, however, a return to the 'grand taste' of Louis XIV's reign revived the custom of entrusting walls and ceilings to the talents of the best painters, and some of these compositions survived the disaster of the nineteenth century. The management of the Crédit Foncier, Rue des Capucines, has preserved a ceiling by Louis Le Lorrain: *Cupid taking captive the three Graces.* The same artist decorated the Hôtel d'Harcourt and the *folie* of the financier La Boixière. Before they were placed in position, some of these pieces, painted on canvas, were shown at the salon of the Louvre, where Diderot saw them and passed judgment: 'Zephyr and Flora, ceiling subject. These are two figures linked by festoons on a blue background. The Zephyr seems to me to have lightness. The Flora is a mute figure, which has nothing to say to me.' He was speaking of a ceiling by Vien, which has never since left the Hôtel de Hollande.

The apotheosis of Psyche, the subject of a Boucher tapestry, was the inspiration of J.-B. Pierre, *premier peintre* of Louis XV, for a ceiling of the Palais Royal. From Raphaël to the end of the eighteenth century, the theme of Psyche was one of those which had most appeal to men of classical inclinations. It gave the artist an opportunity for the prolifera-

49 Bergevin and Mellan: Cour d'Aligre, Rue Bailleul, 1782

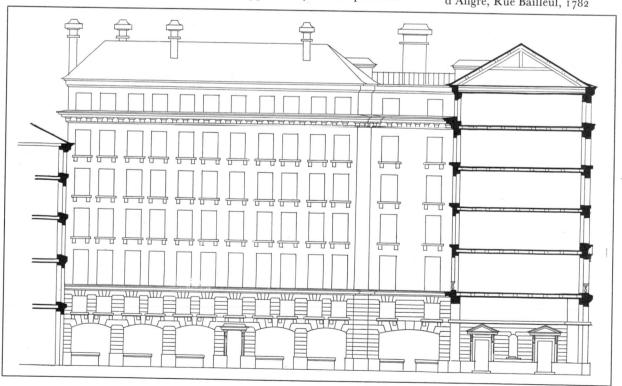

135

tion of golden-haired nudes in the medallions of a cove or the panaches of a rocaille salon. But this allegory of the passions and torments of the soul is also one of the most touching of pagan myths awakening in our minds and hearts the most sympathetic response, so much so indeed that the early Christians adapted it to their own purposes. Natoire painted the story of Psyche in the oval salon of the Princesse de Soubise (Pls. 85–7), as Michel Corneille senior had done in the Hôtel de Hollande and Lebrun for the Bishop of Langres. According to the legend told by Apuleius, Psyche was so beautiful that she was loved by Cupid himself. Natoire shows her carried away by an eagle and welcomed by nymphs at the entrance of Cupid's palace. The god, however, only comes to her in the dead of night and forbids her for the time being to know his name or see his face. Psyche shows her sisters the presents of her mysterious husband and, further on and by their jealous advice, she lights her lamp over Cupid as he sleeps and, by allowing a drop of hot oil to fall on him, wakes him up. Psyche implores his pardon and is subjected to trials ordered by Venus and Ceres. After these tribulations, the final episode painted by Natoire leads us with Psyche into the palace of Jupiter, where the marriage feast is to be celebrated. The Christian symbolism of the fall, atonement and forgiveness is apparent beneath the veil of pagan allegory.

Gods, nymphs and heroes haunted domestic decoration, as though they had come to share in the daily life and the annals of an aristocracy

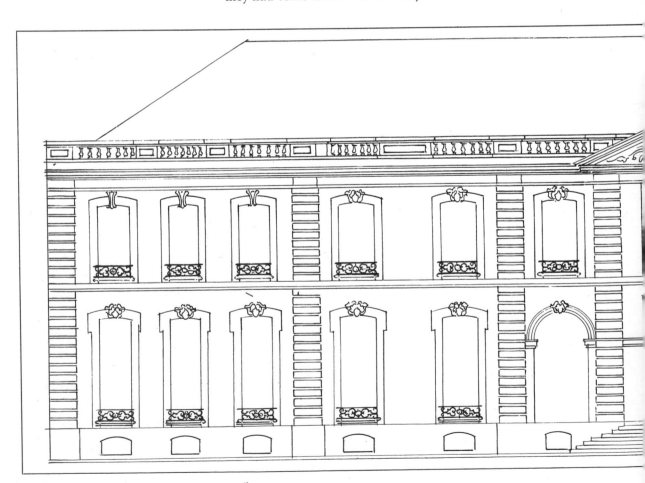

still versed in mythology and fable. Neither tapestry, nor painting ceased to depict the *Iliad*, the *Aeneid*, *Gerusalemme Liberata* or *Orlando Furioso*. The arts of a Christian society, turned sceptic, but remaining at once polite and warlike, fully exploited the themes long since propounded by Ariosto at the court of Ferrara: 'Ladies, knights, arms and love.' At the end of Louis XV's reign we detected the first vestiges of romanticism, when a sentimental generation widened still further the field in which classical art had until then found inspiration, adding to the repertoire of decorative art the picturesqueness of nature, children's games and the lure of distant lands. Sensitive and humane, the masters of the period had the gift of stirring emotions and, as one of them tells us, ranged over 'the immense circle of human affections'.

50 Jean Courtonne: Hôtel de Noirmoutiers, 138 Rue de Grenelle, 1723

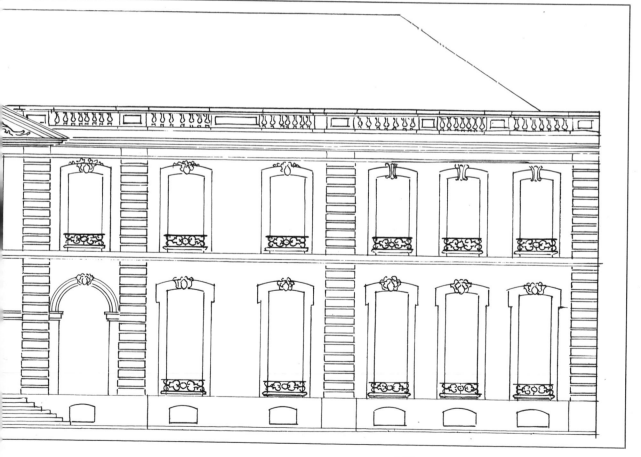

Illustrations

N. DESÈGRE

1   Hôtel Pujol, 5 Rue Béranger, 1715: *œil-de-bœuf* from
     inside. One can see part of the Hôtel de Polisy,
     built by Sébastien Buirette.

N. DESÈGRE
2   Hôtel Pujol: the garden front.
3   Hôtel Pujol: *œil-de-bœuf*.
4   Hôtel Pujol: doorway.

N. DESÈGRE

5   Hôtel Pujol: detail of doorway.

P.-A. DELAMAIR
6   Design for Hôtel Soubise, 60 Rue des Francs-
    Bourgeois, 1705 (Munich Library).
7   Elevation of the Hôtel de Rohan – on the courtyard,
    87 Rue Vieille-du-Temple, 1704 (Munich Library).

CLAUDE III AUDRAN
8 Ceiling of the Hôtel de Flesselles, Rue de Sévigné
   (now in the Musée des Arts décoratifs in Paris).

A. WATTEAU
9– Decorative panels from the
10 Hôtel de Poulpry, Rue de
Poitiers.

P. FR. GODOT
11   Eynaud house, Rue de l'Arbre-Sec, 1717.

J.-B. BULLET DE CHAMBLAIN
12   Hôtel Dodun, 21 Rue de Richelieu: front door.

J.-B. BULLET DE CHAMBLAIN
13   Hôtel Dodun: the staircase.

J.-B. BULLET DE CHAMBLAIN
14 Hôtel Dodun: design for the staircase (Stockholm
    Museum).

J.-B. BULLET DE CHAMBLAIN
15 Hôtel Dodun: bas-relief of children on the staircase.
16 Hôtel Dodun: design for the front elevation
(Stockholm Museum).

OPPENORD
17– Sketches for decorations (Stockholm
18 Museum).
19 Engraving of a detail of the courtyard of the
    Hôtel de Saint-Albin, Place des Victoires – after
    1723 – demolished 1785.

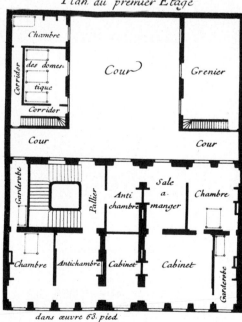

Plan du premier Etage

dans œuvre 63. pied

OPPENORD

20 Engraving of the salon of the Hôtel de Chavaudon,
   Rue des Francs-Bourgeois.

TIERCELET

21 Plan of a town house, after Tiercelet, 1738.

C.-N. LEPAS DUBUISSON
22 House, 151 Rue Saint-Jacques, 1721.
23 Hôtel, 120 Rue du Bac, 1713–15: carving by Louis
Dupain.

L. HERPIN (decorator)
24 Design for a dining-room for the Hôtel Soubise.

R. DE COTTE (architect), VASSÉ SR. (decorator)

25 Gallery of the Hôtel de la Vrillière, now the
    Banque de France.

R. DE COTTE (architect), VASSÉ SR. (decorator)
26 Engraving of the Gallery of the Hôtel de la
    Vrillière.
COURTONNE
27 Hôtel de Noirmoutiers, 138 Rue de Grenelle, built
    by Courtonne in 1722: detail of the decoration – the
    hen with the golden eggs.

ARCHITECT UNKNOWN
28   Wall decoration in the Hôtel de Boullongne,
      Place Vendôme, painted by Nicolas Lancret.

JULES-MICHEL HARDOUIN (architect), MICHEL LANGE
(sculptor)
   29   Trophy in the Grand Salon of the Elysée, 1722.

SULPICE GAUBIER (and another architect)
30   Hôtel de Choiseul, Rue Saint-Romain.

PIERRE DE VIGNY

31 Front door of the Hôtel de Chenizot, 51 Rue
Saint-Louis-en-l'Ile, 1726.

PIERRE DE VIGNY
32   Hôtel de Chenizot: banister of the staircase by
     Nicolas Viennot.

PIERRE DE VIGNY

33 Fabulous beast above the doorway of the Cour du
    Dragon (now in the Musée du Louvre).

DENIS QUIROT THE ELDER (architect)
34   Hôtel de Bersan, 110 Rue Vieille du-Temple, 1731:
      banister of the staircase, by Fr Lesquillier.

DENIS QUIROT THE ELDER (architect)
35– Hôtel de Bersan: details of the banister of the
36 staircase.

DENIS QUIROT THE ELDER (architect)
37 Hôtel de Bersan: the front door, carved by
Fouquier and Stangué.
LOUIS FOURCROY (architect), VARIN (sculptor)
38 The front door of the Hôtel Jacques Samuel
Bernard, 46 Rue du Bac, 1730.

ARCHITECT UNKNOWN
39 Front door of the Hôtel Langlois de La Fortelle,
    Rue des Francs-Bourgeois.

façade sur le jardin

CH. BERNARD
40 Hôtel, Cul-de-sac de Ménars,
1732: design.
41 Rondet house, 35 Rue de la
Harpe, 1730.

ALAXANDRE JOUASSE (sculptor)
42   Front door of the Hôtel de Mortemart, 14 Rue
      Saint-Guillaume, 1731

P. DESMAISONS

43   Hôtel de Jaucourt, 2 Rue de la Vrillière, 1733.

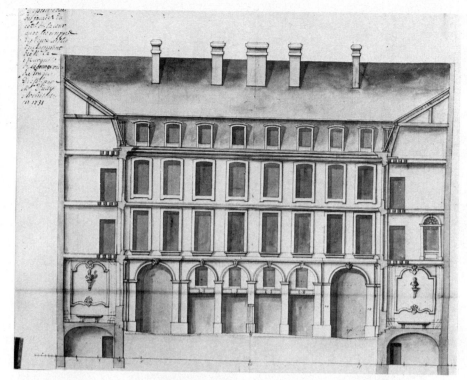

THIERRY-VICTOR DAILLY

44– Designs for the Hôtel Lelièvre de la Grange,
45 4 and 6 Rue de Braque, 1737.

MARTIN GOUPY
46   Robillard house, 15 Rue Montorgueil, 1729.
47   Dubuisson house, 29 Rue de la Parcheminerie, 1736.

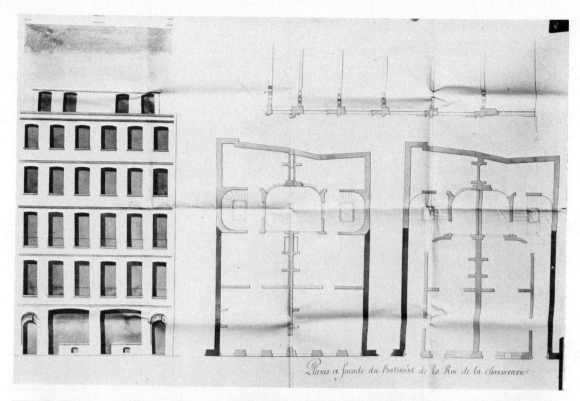

Plans et façade du Bâtiment de la Rue de la chanvrerie

ARCHITECT UNKNOWN
48 Design for a pair of houses, Rue de la Chanvrerie.
Attributed to H.-Q. DESBEUFS
49 Dalençon-Dorville apartment house, 70 Rue des
     Gravilliers, 1737.

H.-Q. DESBEUFS
  50 Bonin apartment house, 17 Rue Sainte-Croix-
      de-la-Bretonnerie, 1734.
  51 Moreau de Saint-Just apartment house, Rue de la
      Monnaie, 1745.

JACQUES V GABRIEL (?)
52   Camuset house, 14 Rue François Miron, 1737.

JACQUES VINAGE
53 Houses in the Place Baudoyer (4 to 12 Rue
François Miron), 1734.

FR DEBIAS-AUBRY

54   Hôtel de Bouillon, 17 Quai Malaquais, 1740 – now
the Ecole des Beaux-Arts.

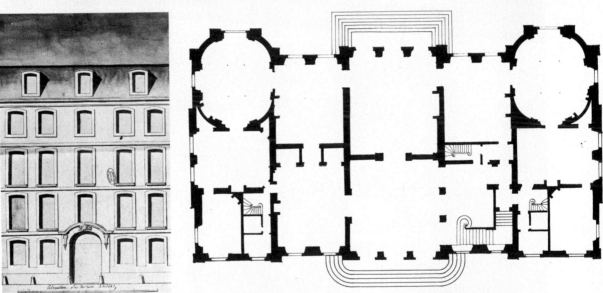

FR DEBIAS-AUBRY
55 Cotelle house, Rue Saint-André-des-Arts, 1737.
LOUIS JOUBERT
56 Design for the elevation of 7 Rue Maître Albert, 1741.
JEAN AUBERT
57 Plan of Hôtel Peyrenc de Moras.

PIERRE JEAN VARIN
58   His house, 57 Rue de Seine, 1740.

J.-B. VAUTRAIN

59 Belon-Vatard house, Rues Poissonnière and de Cléry,
1740.

J.-B. VAUTRAIN
60   Detail of the Belon-Vatard house.

J.-B.-A. BEAUSIRE
61   Hôtel d'Ecquevilly ou du Grand Veneur, 60 Rue
      de Turenne, 1734: banister of the staircase by
      Lebrun and Daguinot.

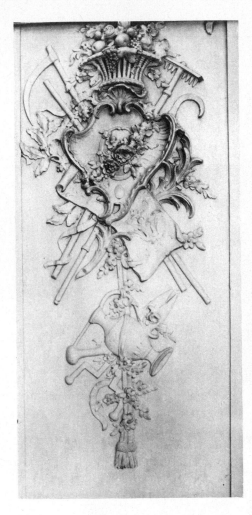

J.-B.-A. BEAUSIRE
62 Hôtel d'Ecquevilly ou du
    Grand Veneur: trophy of
    gardening implements.
63 Hôtel d'Ecquevilly ou du
    Grand Veneur: blazon under
    the staircase.

CHARLES AND PIERRE BOSCRY
64   Hôtel d'Orrouer, 87 Rue de Grenelle, 1731: the
      garden front.

CHARLES AND PIERRE BOSCRY
65   Hôtel d'Orrouer: doorway, present state.

CHARLES AND PIERRE BOSCRY
66 Hôtel d'Orrouer: design for the doorway.

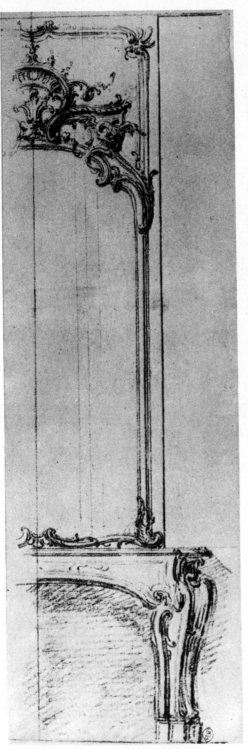

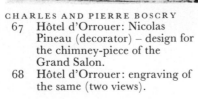

CHARLES AND PIERRE BOSCRY

67   Hôtel d'Orrouer: Nicolas
     Pineau (decorator) – design for
     the chimney-piece of the
     Grand Salon.
68   Hôtel d'Orrouer: engraving of
     the same (two views).

NICOLAS PINEAU (decorator)
69   Hôtel d'Orrouer: relief above the chimney-piece,
        present state.

MICHEL TANNEVOT
70   His house, 26 Rue Cambon: panelling by Nicolas
     Pineau (decorator).

Autre Décoration interieure de la Gallerie de l'Hôtel de Villars
prise sur sa largeur

Echelle de 1 2 3 4 5 6 *Pieds*

Partie du Plan de la *Gallerie sur sa largeur*

J.-B. LEROUX (architect), N. PINEAU (decorator)
71   Engraving of the gallery of the Hôtel de Villars,
     116 Rue de Grenelle, demolished.

CHARLES AND PIERRE BOSCRY
72 Hôtel de Feuquières, 58 Rue de Varenne, 1736:
design for the façade.
N. PINEAU (decorator)
73 Sketch for the decoration of the same façade.

CL. BONNOT (architect), N. PINEAU (decorator)
74   Hôtel de Marcilly, 18 Rue du Cherche-Midi, 1738:
      the courtyard façade.

CL. BONNOT (architect), N. PINEAU (decorator)
75   Hôtel de Marcilly: details of the banister on the
       staircase.

C. L. BONNOT (architect), N. PINEAU (decorator)

76 Hôtel de Marcilly: details of the banister on the staircase.

77 Hôtel de Marcilly: design by N. Pineau for the staircase.

78 Hôtel de Marcilly: details of the banister on the
     staircase.
79 Hôtel de Marcilly: design by N. Pineau for the
     staircase.

J. HARDOUIN MANSART DE SAGONNE (architect),
N. PINEAU (decorator)
80   Claustrier house, 56 Rue des Francs-Bourgeois, 1752.

JEAN AUBERT and J.-B. LEROUX (architects)

81 Designs for *portes cochères* of the Palais Bourbon and the Hôtel Mazarin (demolished).

JEAN HARDOUIN MANSART DE JOUY
82   Engraving of designs for a chimney-piece.

ARCHITECT UNKNOWN
83   Hôtel de Luteaux, 27 Rue Lhomond, 1736: the
     garden front.

PIERRE DE VIGNY
84   De la Barre de Carroy house, 42 Rue François
     Miron, 1742.

BOFFRAND
85   Hôtel Soubise: the oval salon, 1734.

BOFFRAND
86– Hôtel Soubise: the oval salon,
87 1734. Paintings by Natoire.

BOFFRAND
88   Salon at the Arsenal decorated by the architect
      Dauphin.

BOFFRAND
89   Salon at the Arsenal decorated by the architect
       Dauphin. Detail.

SAINT MARTIN (architect), LANGE (sculptor)
90 Paintings by Huet, Dutour and Crépin, in the
    salon des singes, Hôtel de Rohan, 81 Rue Vieille-
    du-Temple.

SAINT MARTIN
91   Paintings by Huet, Dutour and Crépin, in the
salon des singes, Hôtel de Rohan, 81 Rue Vieille-
du-Temple.

QUIROT LE JEUNE
92   His house, 2 Rue de la Jussienne, 1752.

CH. E. BRISEUX

93 Hôtel d'Augny, Rue Drouot, 1752: engraving of
the garden front.

94 Engraving of a design for a salon.

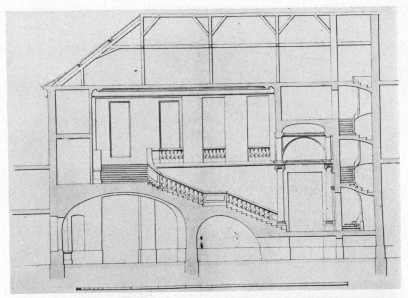

SERVANDONI
95 Design for the staircase for the Hôtel d'Auvergne,
    Rue l'Université, 1740.
96 Staircase of his house, Place Saint-Sulpice, 1757.

CONTANT D'IVRY

97 House of Choiseul-Gouffier,
Rue Etienne Marcel, 1738:
carving by Casimir Duhamel.

98 Staircase of the Hôtel de
Thiers, 19 Place Vendôme,
1747.

CONTANT D'IVRY
99 Staircase of the Palais-Royal, about 1765.

CONTANT D'IVRY
100 Staircase of the Palais-Royal.

Elevation du côté du Lit de Parade.

CONTANT D'IVRY
101   State bedroom of the Palais-Royal.

CONTANT D'IVRY
102   Palais-Royal façade.

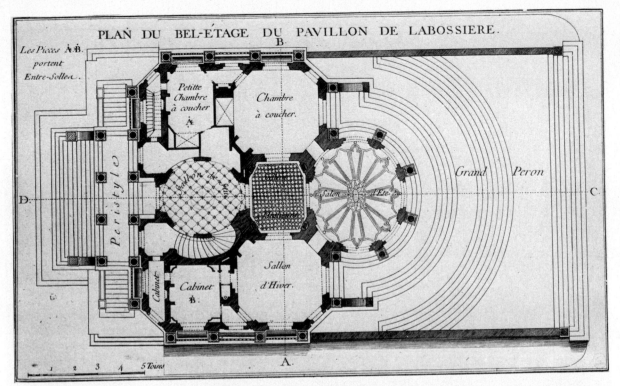

PLAN DU BEL-ETAGE DU PAVILLON DE LABOSSIERE.

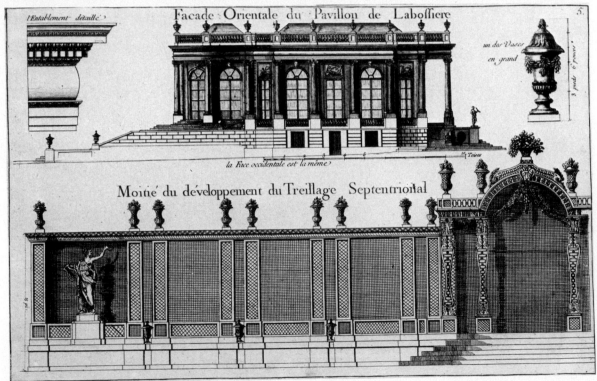

Façade Orientale du Pavillon de Labossiere

Moitié du développement du Treillage Septentrional

ANTOINE-MATHIEU LE CARPENTIER and
GUILLAUME COUTURE LE JEUNE

103– Pavillon de la Boissière, Rue de Clichy, 1751–70:
104 engravings of the plan and the façade.

SAINT-MARTIN
105 Design for restoration of house of the Maréchal de
     Richelieu à Clichy.
CHEVOTET
106 Pavillon de Hanovre, 1757: design. (Destailleur coll.)

L.-F. TROUARD
111 His house, 9 Rue du Faubourg
Poissonnière, 1758.
112 His house: detail of the
banister.

PIERRE-LOUIS MOREAU-DESPROUX

113   Design for Hôtel de Chabanne, Boulevard du
        Temple, 1758.

Face Sur la Cour de l'hotel Duzès Du troisieme Projet

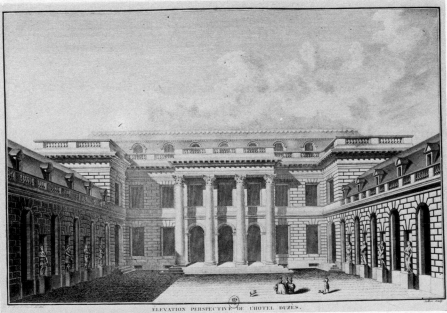

ELEVATION PERSPECTIVE DE L'HOTEL DUZES.

CHERPITEL
114 Design for the Hôtel d'Uzès. (Rejected).

LEDOUX
115 Hôtel d'Uzès, Rue Montmartre, 1767–69:
     engraving of the courtyard façade.

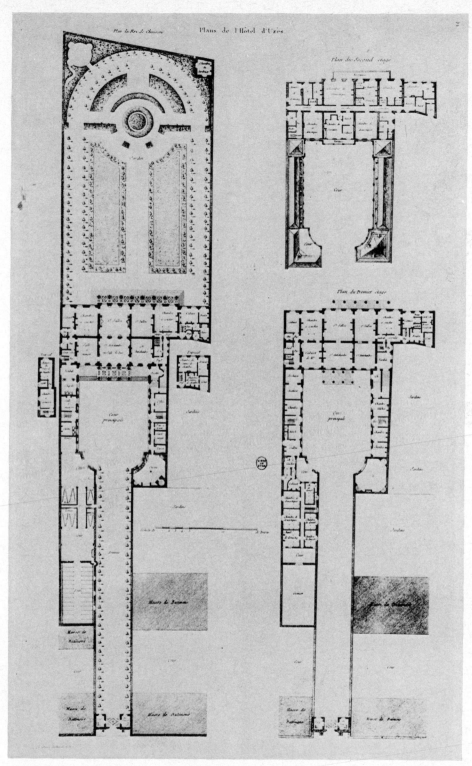

LEDOUX
116 Hôtel d'Uzès: engraving of the plan.

LEDOUX
117– Hôtel d'Uzès: decorative panels in the salon
118   ('Europe', 'America') carved by Boiston.

ROUSSET
119   Hôtel d'Uzès: design for the salon. (Rejected).

Elevation de l'Hôtel de Halwil, sur la Rue Michel le Comte.

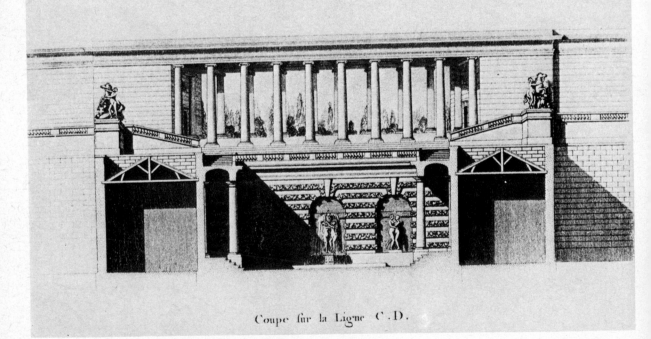

Coupe sur la Ligne C.D.

LEDOUX
120 Design for Hôtel d'Hallwyl, Rue Michel-le-Comte,
1766.

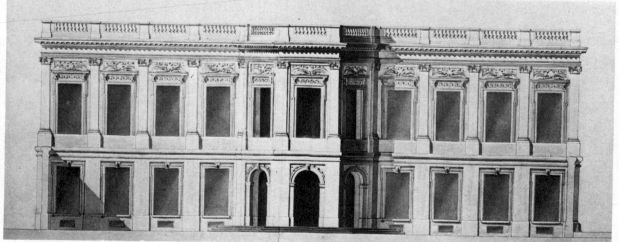

CHERPITEL
121   Courtyard of the Hôtel du Châtelet, 127 Rue de
       Grenelle.
122   Design for the Hôtel d'Harcourt, Rue l'Université.

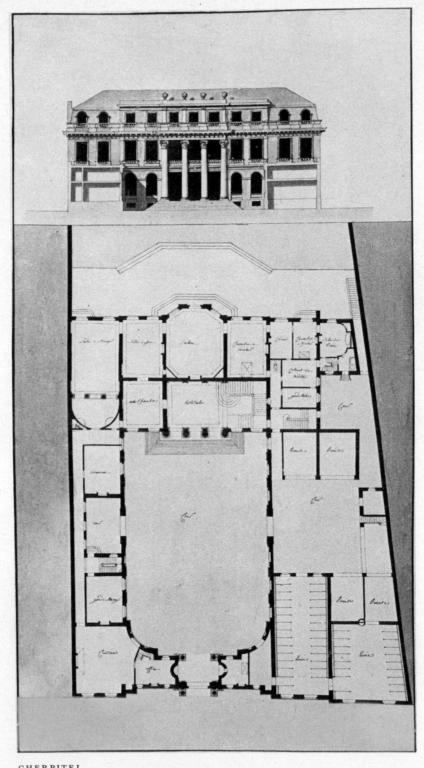

CHERPITEL

123 Design for the Hôtel du Châtelet – elevation of the
     courtyard façade and plan (British Museum).

CHERPITEL
124 Architect's sketch of garden front of the Hôtel du
     Châtelet (British Museum).
125 Dining-room in the Hôtel du Châtelet.

MOREAU-DESPROUX
126 Room from the Hôtel de Luynes, now in the Musée
du Louvre.

CHALGRIN
127 Hôtel de La Vrillière, Rue
     Saint-Florentin: drawing by
     Sir William Chambers.
128 Hôtel de La Vrillière:
     sculpture by Gois in the
     courtyard.

CHALGRIN
129 Hôtel de La Vrillière: view of
     the staircase.
130 Hôtel de La Vrillière: details
     of the banisters.

JACQUES-DENIS ANTOINE
131 Hôtel Brochet de Saint Prest, 28 Rue des Saints-
Pères, 1774: detail of the staircase.

JEAN-CHARLES DELAFOSSE

132 Engraving of a decorative vase.

133 Hôtel Delbarre, 58 Rue du
     Faubourg Poissonnière:
     decorative vase, 1774.

JEAN-CHARLES DELAFOSSE
134   Hôtel Delbarre, details of the staircase.

JEAN-CHARLES DELAFOSSE
135 Hôtel Goix, 60 Rue du Faubourg Poissonnière: the
    garden front.

JEAN-CHARLES DELAFOSSE
136 Hôtel Goix: detail of the oval boudoir.
137 Maquette of a stove.

BOULLÉE
138   Hôtel de Brunoy – façade on the Champs-Elyseés:
         engraving.

MAISON DE M.ʳ DE MONVILLE
COTE DU JARDIN.

Nᵒ. 56.

Durand del.

Janinet sculp.

BOULLÉE
139 House of M. de Monville: engraving.

face sur la Cour

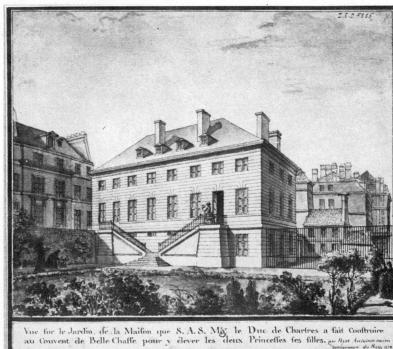

Vue sur le Jardin, de la Maison que S. A. S. Mgr. le Duc de Chartres a fait Construire au Couvent de Belle-Chasse pour y élever les deux Princesses ses filles. par Poyet Architecte ancien pensionnaire du Roy, 1778

BERNARD POYET

140   Design for the house of the painter Callet, Quartier Montparnasse, 1775.

141   Watercolour of the house of the Princesses d'Orléans at Bellechasse, 1778.

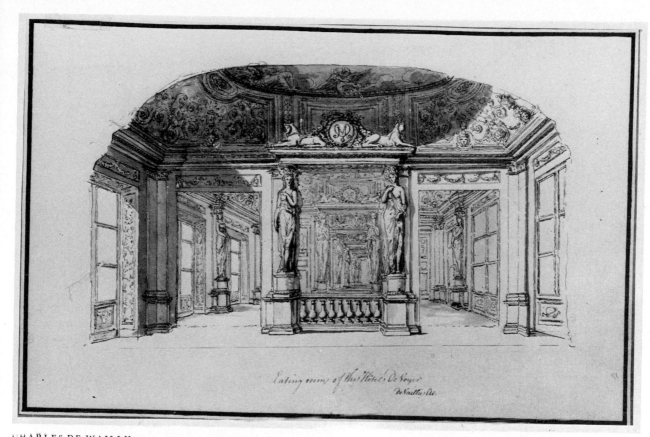

Eating room of the Hôtel De Voyer
deVailly As.

CHARLES DE WAILLY
142   Hôtel d'Argenson, Rue des Bons-Enfants: sketch by
      Sir William Chambers of the dining-room.

BRONGNIART
143 Hôtel de Sainte-Foix, Rue Basse du Rempart:
     engraving.

BRONGNIART
144   Hôtel de Bourbon-Condé, 12 Rue Monsieur, 1785.

BRONGNIART
145 Decoration of the Hôtel de Monaco (Musée
      Carnavalet).

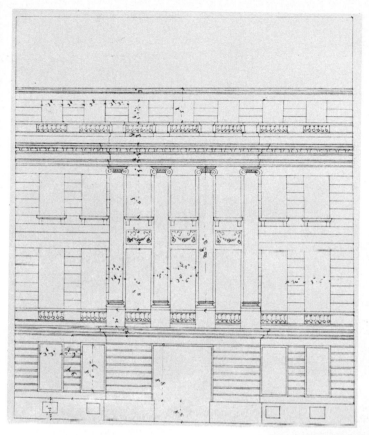

ANDRÉ AUBERT
146 House, 4 Rue Caumartin:
    design for the façade.
147 House, 4 Rue Caumartin:
    the façade today.

ANDRÉ AUBERT
148   Hôtel Deshays and Hôtel d'Aumont, Rue
      Caumartin: engraving.

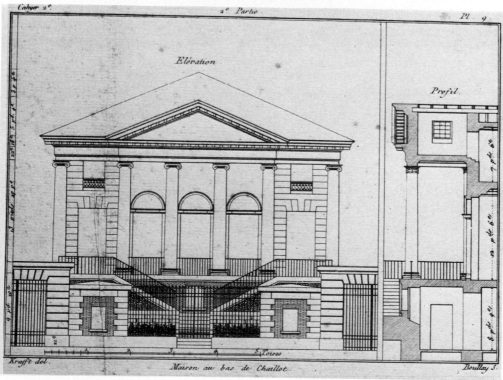

PAINTER UNKNOWN
149 Oval ceiling in the Hôtel Vassal de Saint-Hubert,
Rue Montmartre.
CHEVALIER DE BEAUREGARD
150 His house at Chaillot.

Salle à manger exécutée en zinc à l'Hôtel Soubise, par Cellerier Architecte.

CELLERIER
151   Summer dining-room in the house of the Maréchal
       de Soubise, Rue de l'Arcade, 1786.

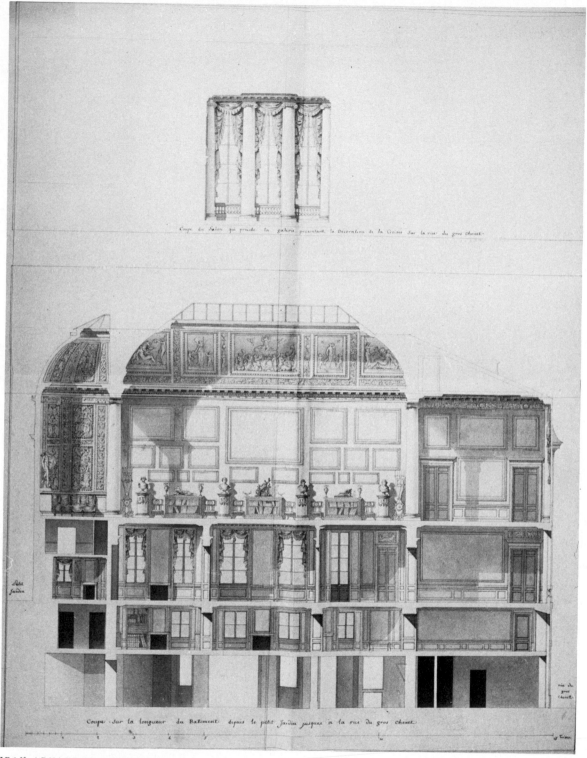

Coupe du Salon qui prende la galerie presentant la Décoration de la Croisée Sur la rue du gros chenet.

Coupe Sur la longueur du Batiment depuis le petit Jardin jusquer à la rue du gros chenet.

Petit Jardin

rue du gros chenet.

JEAN-ARNAUD RAYMOND
152   Design for the house of Mme Vigée Lebrun,
        8 Rue du Sentier, 1785.

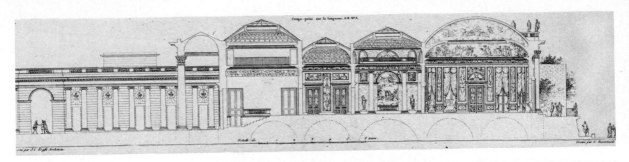

PIERRE ROUSSEAU
153– Hôtel de Salm, 1785.
155

PIERRE ROUSSEAU
156– Hôtel de Salm, 1785.
157

Attributed to LEDOUX
158 Design for decoration for the Hôtel d'Hallwyl, 1766.
LEDOUX
159 Hôtel Thélusson, Rue de Provence, 1782: general
      view.

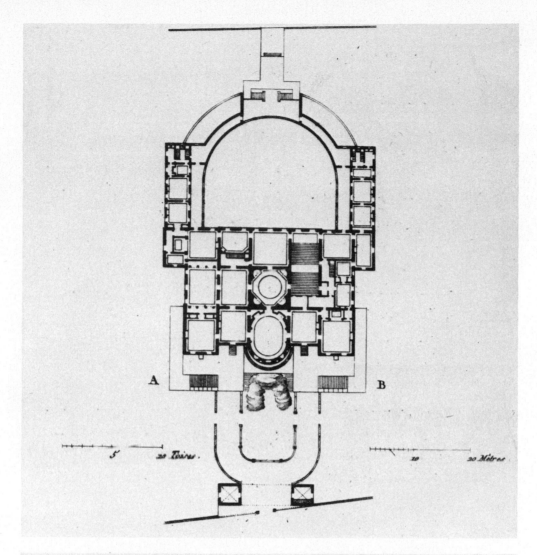

LEDOUX
160 Hôtel Thélusson: plan.
LEDOUX
161 Hôtel Thélusson: elevation.

coupe génerale.

antichambre.   Sallon de musique.   Sallon.

LEDOUX
162   Hôtel Thélusson: two sections.

LEDOUX or JALLIERS
163   Hôtel Thélusson: detail of a door.

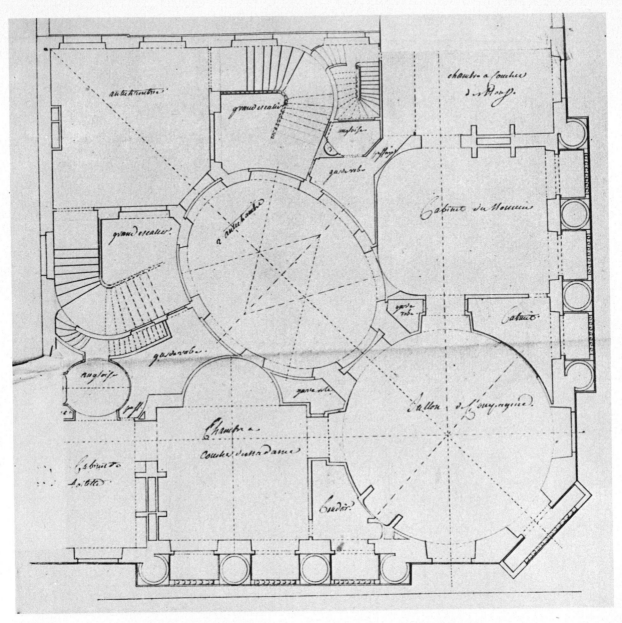

LEDOUX

164 Hôtel de Montmorency, 1770: plan, original
design.

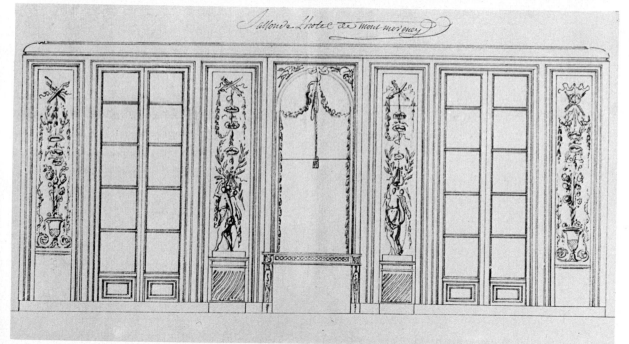

LEDOUX
165 Hôtel de Montmorency: elevation, original design.
166 Hôtel de Montmorency: decoration of the salon,
      original design.

Second antichambre
de l'hotel de montmorency

LEDOUX
167   Hôtel de Montmorency: section, original design.

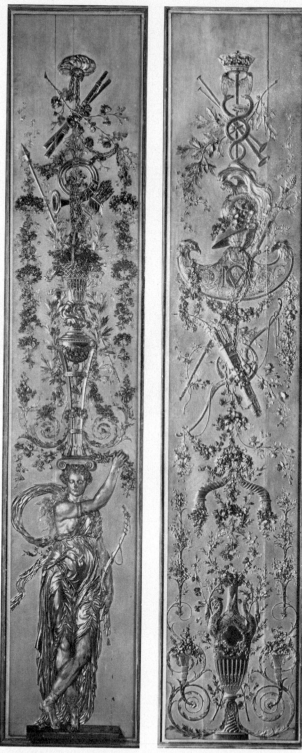

168 Hôtel de Montmorency: two panels from the salon,
    carved by Méthivier, now in the Boston Museum.

Vuë du côté de la Maison

LEMOINE LE ROMAIN
169   Hôtel Beaumarchais at Porte Saint-Antoine, 1790.

BÉLANGER
170   House of Mlle Dervieux, Rue de la Victoire: the
      dining-room, 1788.

BÉLANGER
171 Pavilion of the Hôtel de Brancas, Rue Taitbout, 1771.
172 Designs for the garden of the folie Sainte-James.

BÉLANGER
173 Designs for the garden of the folie Sainte-James,
       after 1777.

Élévation de Bagatelle du côté de la Cour D'honneur

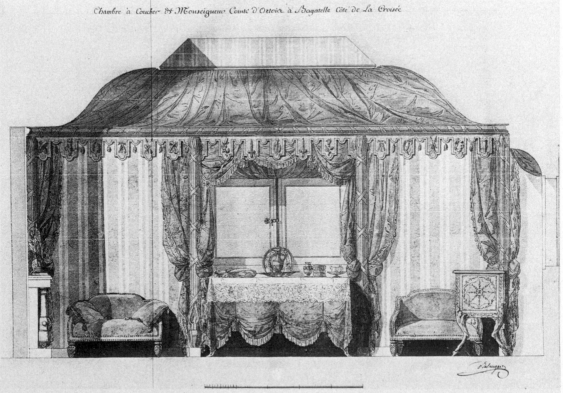

Chambre à Coucher de Monseigneur Comte D'Ortois à Bagatelle Côté de La Croisée

BÉLANGER
174   Bagatelle: design for the elevation, 1777.
175   Bagatelle: bedroom of the Comte d'Artois.

BÉLANGER
176   House in the Rue Joubert, 1785.

HAPPE and SOBRE
177   Cour Batave, 60 Rue Saint-Denis: design 1792.

Register of Architects

ADHENET Thomas
'Expert-bourgeois' from 1726. Rue du Bac in 1740, then Cul-de-sac de la Rue du Coq.
Houses Rue Baillet, 1730; Rue du Renard, 1732; Rue Saint-Denis.
Doc.: Arch. Nat. Z 1F 417, 423.

d'ALBARET
Architect at the Monnaie (Mint).
Publ.: *Différents projets relatifs au climat et à la manière la plus convenable de bâtir dans les pays chauds et en particulier dans les Indes orientales.* Engravings by C. R. G. Poolleau, 1776.

ALOUIS François
Died 1779.
Honorary inspector of the City works.
Rue de la Mortellerie.

ANDRÉ Jean-Baptiste
'Expert-bourgeois' from 1773 to 1792, architect to the Order of Malta and the Prince de Conti. Rue de Grenelle. Hôtel de Conti.
Château de l'Isle-Adam, completed in 1783.
Publ.: *Second cahier des Jardins pittoresques de Le Rouge, d'après des croquis pris en Angleterre.*

ANGO
'Expert-bourgeois' from 1772 to 1792.
Quai de l'Ecole.

ANTOINE Jacques-Denis
Paris, 6 August 1733 – Paris, 24 August 1801.
Academician, 1776.
Project for church at Charny, near Meaux, 1766 (Arch. Nat. Z 1J 903; Z 1J 1236). Main entrance of the Maison Huquier fils, prints publisher, Rue Saint-Jacques, opposite the Mathurins, 1760s. Project for the Théâtre Français (Mercure, 1770). Hôtel des Monnaies, 1771–77; drawings: B.N. Est. Va 625 fol., 6 volumes and Ve 90 pet. in fol. Hôtel Brochet de Saint-Prest, 28 Rue des Saints-Pères, today Ecole des Ponts et Chaussées, 1773 (building authorisation, Arch. Nat. Z 1F); account for fees due to Antoine – 8,000 livres, in Arch. Nat. T 27, Papers of the Abbé Bouville, *Etat de l'actif et du passé de M. Brochet de Saint-Prest*, p. 4). Tenements 229 to 235 Rue Saint-Honoré, 1774 (building authorisation, Arch. Nat. Z 1F 494, p. 13). Project for Saint-Nicolas du Chardonnet. Communion chapel and ambulatory of Saint-Nicolas-des-Champs, in collaboration with Boulland. Château de Mussy-l'Evêque, near Langres, before 1777. Château de Herces, near Houdan (cf. E. de Ganay, *L'Amour de l'art*, 1937, vol. I, p. 23, and *Ile de France*, 1930, vol. IV, p. 30), drawings of *fabriques* in the park, later than the château: Arch. Nat. N. III, Eure-et-Loir, 27. Completion of Palacio Alba y Berwick in Madrid, begun by Guilbert and continued by Ventura Rodriguez: grand staircase with top lighting, 1778. Transformation of Hôtel de Chavaudon, 1 Rue Bonaparte, 1779. Project for Hospice La Rochefoucauld, 1776. Château du Buisson (Eure), 1782; drawings in library of Ecole des Beaux-Arts. Transformation of Hôtel de Maillebois, Rue de Grenelle, 1783; and of Hôtel Bertier de Sauvigny, 11 Rue Béranger (Arch. de la Seine, série DE). Hôtel de Jaucourt, 45 Rue de Varenne (main entrance engraved). Hôtel de Mirabeau, Rue de Sèvres. Staircase, waiting-hall and record office of Palais de Justice; model in Musée Carnavalet, 1782–85. Façade of town hall, Cambrai, in collaboration with Jardin, finished 1785. Inner entrance of the Charité, Rue Jacob. Chapel of the Visitation, Nancy, today boys' school, 1785. Work at Saint-Germain near Corbeil, at Marville-les-Bois, at Le Rosay, Balagny, Bures, Croissy. House for the Earl of Findlater, near London. Project for a palace for the Prince de Salm at Kirn, near Kreuz nach: B.N. Est. Hd 207. Other projects according to the architect's papers: (Bibliothèque Nationale): Vauxhall at Fontainebleau; barracks of Moulins; assembly hall of the clergy at the Grands Augustins, Paris; Château de Verneuil (sur Indre?). Châteaux of Soulangé in Anjou; of Lorez; Morangis; Saint-Germain near Corbeil; Hérouville near Dourdan; Sénozan near Mâcon; Binanville; and de Rosny-Sully. Work at the Château de Rosny-Sully, Fleury, near Longjumeau; work at the Château de Sainte-Geneviève-des-Bois – a handsome half-moon-shaped building survives, but J. Cellerier also worked in this village.

Houses: Faubourg Poissonnière; Rues des Saints-Pères and de Verneuil. House at Châteaudun.

MS.: Letters from Italy, Library of the Institut de France. *Bibl.*: Pahin de la Blancherie, *Journal de la République des Lettres et des Arts*, 1777, pp. 29, 30, 58. L.H. vol. IV, pp. 247, 260. J. Duportal, *Le Figaro artistique*, February 1925. A. Lorion, *BFSHP*, 1961' M. Gallet, *Bulletin du Musée Carnavalet*, June 1963.

ANTOINE Antoine (brother of Jacques-Denis)
'Expert-bourgeois' from 1776 to 1792. Rue Saint-Benoît, near Rue Jacob.

ARCHANGÉ Jean-Louis
Born at Orsay 11 May 1750.
Pupil of Régemortes and Chevotet.
Château de Balizy, for the Chevalier de Chabrillan, 1784: project Arch. Nat. Z 1J 1313. Tenements in the Quartier Louvois. Château de Rochefort-en-Yvelines, for the Prince de Rohan-Rochefort, 1787 (demolished, but engraved). Theatre at Le Havre, 1789 (plan, section and elevation drawn by Friedrich Gilly, in the library of the Technische Hochschule, Berlin).

ARMAND
Family of building contractors and architects, represented about 1770 by Claude-Germain and after 1780 by Nicolas Armand.
House at 32 Faubourg Saint-Denis, 1767. Hôtel at the corner of the Rue Saint-Honoré and the Place du Palais-Royal (site of the Louvre department store), 1770. Buildings in Rue d'Amboise, 1782. House in Rue Chabannais.
Ref.: Arch. Nat. 940, 1050, 1083, 1093. *Almanach Dauphin* (Maçons), 1774.

ARNOULD Thomas
'Expert-entrepreneur' from 1738. Rue Condé in 1750.
Project for the Ecole de Chirurgie (about 1770).

AUBERT Jean
Died 1741.
Academician 1720; member of the Société des Arts et des Sciences, about 1730–35.
Completion of Palais Bourbon, and of Hôtel de Lassay, Rue de Lille, 1724. Decoration of the '*château*' and grand stables of Chantilly (1719–35). Hôtel Peyrenc de Moras (Musée Rodin), 77 Rue Varenne, 1719. Officers' accommodation in same hôtel, acquired by the Duchesse du Maine (contracts approved by Maître Laideguives junior, 13 March, 12 August and 13 October 1737). Château abbatial de Châalis, 1736. Work at Saint-Maur.
Bibl.: G. Macon, *Les arts dans la maison de Condé*, 1903.
Fiske Kimball, *Le style Louis XV*, Paris, 1950. Fr Souchal, 'Jean Aubert', in the *Revue de l'art*, 1970.

AUBERT
Family of building contractors and architects:

AUBERT Denis
Contractor. Tenement building, Rue d'Anjou, 1780. Work for the Marquise de Gensas, Rue Saint-Honoré.

AUBERT André
Architect, son of the above, 'expert-entrepreneur' from 1785 to 1792. Architect of state properties in 1792. Rue de la Madeleine in 1790.
Tenement, 28 Rue Buffaut, 1778. Hôtel Delahaye, 1 Rue Caumartin, 1781–82. Hôtel d'Aumont, 2 Rue Caumartin, 1781. Hôtel de Girardin, Rue Neuve du Luxembourg (Cambon), 1782. Tenements at 4, 6, 7 and 9, 21, 23, 33 Rue Caumartin. Maison Leblanc de Verneuil, Chaussée d'Antin, 1785. Hôtel Randon de Pommery, Rue Basse du Rempart, 1785. Hôtel d'Imméçourt, Rue Boudereau, before 1786. Maison Tourtille-Saugrain, corner of Rues de Provence and Taitbout, 1786–87. Hôtel de Mme de Mortainville, Rue Trudon, 1787. Hôtels Lepelletier d'Aunay and de Beauharnais, Rue des Mathurins. Hôtel for Mr Latine? An Englishman, same street. Tenement, 136 Rue Amelot. (?) Hôtel Pinsot, Rue Saint-Georges.

AUBERT Charles
Architect. Hôtel de Saisseval, Quai d'Orsay and Rue de Lille, 1784–85; façade (on Seine side) engraved by Le Campion. Maison Lanchère at Chaillot. House at 6 Place du Palais Bourbon. Institution Lemoyne d'Essoyes, Rue de Berry, 1798. Maison Varin in the Champs-Elysées, 1797.

Ref.: *NAAF*, 2 série, vol. VI. Arch. Nat. AB XIX, 213 Z 1j 1023, 1024, 1032, 1039, 1045, 1061, 1074, 1084, 1085, 1093, 1123, 1137, 1141, 1159, 1163, 1194, 1200, 1216. *Almanach des arts de l'an XII*. Watin. Thiéry. Krafft. Société du VIIIe arrondissement.

AUBRY Claude
Died before 1742.
Bibl.: *BSHP*, 1906.

AUBRY Jean
Work for the Marquise de Breteuil, Rue de Paradis (58 Rue des Francs-Bourgeois) in 1738. Arch. Nat. Z 1j 680.

AUMONT Jean
Maître-général de la Chambre Royale des Bâtiments, Ponts et Chaussées (Buildings, Bridges and Highways) of France.
Rue Quincampoix in 1730.

d'AVANDA François
Died before 8 October 1789.
Pupil of Chevotet at the Academy, 1739–45.
Ref.: *PVARA*, vols. V–VI.

BABUTY DESGODETZ François-Antoine
'Expert-entrepreneur' from 1744. Rue Bertinpoirée.

BACCARIT Claude
Architect of the Hôtel-Dieu, 1776. Father of the sculptor Louis-Antoine Baccarit.
Château de Buzancy for Guillaume Tavernier de Boullongne, 1755.

Decoration of choir of Saint-Germain l'Auxerrois, 1756.
Bibl.: Thierry. Laugier. *L'Avant-coureur*, 1760. Jean Stern, *Bélanger*, vol. I, 1930, pp. 220–2.

BARBE Ursin
Mentioned in 1772.

BARBIER François
Pupil at the Academy 1764–65.
Garden of the Hôtel de la Rochefoucauld, Rue des Petits-Augustins. Transformation of the Archbishop's palace, Cambrai, 1773. Tenement building Lhermite, Rue de l'Egout, Chaussée d'Antin (Rue des Mathurins), 1777–78. Country house for M. de Monville in the désert de Retz: drawings in Museum of Stockholm. Garden of the Hôtel de Thélusson, to the designs of Ledoux.
Bibl.: E. de Ganay, *GBA*, May–June 1955.
Ref.: Arch. Nat. Z 1j 967, 1035, 1059.

BARBIER DE BLIGNIERES Louis
'Expert-bourgeois' from 1730. Rue Pavée Saint-André-des-Arts (Séguier) in 1740.
Maison de Saint-Albin, Rues de la Corderie and du Marché aux Poirés, 1742. House in Rue des Quatre-Vents. House at 25 Rue Saint-André-des-Arts. Maison Roland du Vieuxpont, Rue des Cordeliers. School of Medicine, Rue de la Bûcherie (contract approved by Maître Chomel, August 1744).

BARRÉ Jean Benoît Vincent
Pupil of the Abbé Camus in 1753. 27 Rue Poissonnière in 1790.
Hôtel Grimod de la Reynière, Rue Bonne Morue (Boissy d'Anglas), 1767: drawing by architect Kamsetzer in the library of Cracow. Château du Marais at Saint Chéron (Seine-et-Oise) for the Lemaître family, about 1770. Château de Montgeoffroy at Mazé (Maine-et-Loire) for the Contades family, 1772–76(?). East front of the Château de Lude, for the Marquis de la Vieuville, 1785. Refurbishing of Château d'Hénonville, near Beauvais. Barré house, at north corner of Rues du Faubourg Poissonnière and d'Enghien, 1787–88. Schemes, carried out by Barnabé Guimard, for the Place Royale and church of Saint-Jacques-de-Coudenberg, Brussels, 1774–79. Suites in the Château d'Hénonville, near Beauvais; round temple in the park of Méréville.
Bibl.: L. Réau, *BSHAF*, 1937. Alexis Donnet, *Description des environs de Paris*, 1810, p. 229. A. Soulange-Bodin, *Châteaux du Maine*. P. Lavedan, *Histoire de l'urbanisme*, vol. II, p. 323; *Congrès archéologique*, 1961, pp. 179–84. Thirion, *Les financiers d'autrefois*. O. Choppin de Janvry, in *L'Œil*, 1970. Jean de Cayeux in *BSHAF*, 1968.

BARREAU DE CHEFDEVILLE François-Dominique
Paris 1725–65.
Pupil of Leroux. Grand Prix, 1749.

Redesigned interior for the Intendance de Bordeaux. Refurbishing of Hôtel Boutin, Clichy. Maison Boutin, Rue Portefoin. Decoration of *cabinet* of La Live de Jully (about 1756). Eglise Saint-Nicolas de Nérac (L. et G.). Scheme for transforming the Palais Bourbon, approved by the Prince de Condé in 1765, construction (with Goupy) authorised 10 January 1765 (B.N. Est.).
Bibl.: F. G. Pariset, 'Barreau de Chefdeville', in *BSHAF*, 1963. Arch. Nat. Minutier, XCII, 663.

BAUDOUIN or BEAUDOUIN
Delacroix tenement, corner of Rues de l'Echiquier and Saint-Denis, 1787. Tenements at corner of Rues de Varenne and Hillerin-Bertin, 1786. Hôtel du Sr Queul, Rue Martel, 1789. Tenements in Rue Fossés du Temple, 1791. Tenement, Passage Tracy, 1791–92.
Ref.: Arch. Nat. Y 9705. Z 1j 1191, 1215, 1222.

BAZIN
Mentioned in 1780.

BEAUSIRE
Family of architects:

BEAUSIRE Jean, 1651–1743
Academician 1719. Master of the City Buildings.

BEAUSIRE Jean Baptiste-Augustin, known as BEAUSIRE LE FILS. 1693 November 1764.
Academician, 1732. Master of the City Buildings. Transformation of Hôtel de Beauvais, Rue François Miron, 1730. Fontaine de la Reine, Rue Saint-Denis, 1732. Fontaine du Vertbois (fragments placed in the Square Saint-Julien-le-Pauvre). Hôtel d'Ecquevilly, 60 Rue de Turenne (contract 'between Blégny, for Hennequin, and Pierre-Jean Varin' approved, 19 October 1734). Château d'Avron, near Villemomble, 1735. Communion chapel at Saint-Paul (plans 1740). Fêtes de la Ville de Paris: capture of Menin, 4 June 1744; capture of Ypres, 27 June 1744; return of the King, 15 November 1744; birth of the children of the Dauphin and of Marie-Josèphe de Saxe, 19 July 1746, 26 August 1750, etc. . . . Engravings of decorations in Thévenard, Poilly, Hérissey, etc. . . . 'Fêtes' of February 1745.

BEAUSIRE Jérôme, known as BEAUSIRE LE JEUNE
Died in San Domingo, July 1761. Academician, 1740. Controller of Powders and Saltpetres of the Department of Paris.
Maison Gourdon, Rue des Cordeliers (contract approved by Maître Alléaume, 24 March 1735). Houses, Rues des Lions and du Vertbois, 1745. Decoration of Beauvais cathedral.

Ref.: Arch. Nat. H (*Procès-verbaux du Bureau de la Ville*), N II, Seine 109; N III, Seine 540, 712, 740, 785, 883, 1022, 1051; Z 1j 614, 654, 655, 657, 667, 669, 687, 693, 736, 740, 756.
Bibl.: The genealogy given by D. Labarre de Raillicourt in *BSHAF*, 1958, p. 87, needs correction in accordance

with the *PVARA*, Les minutes de l'étude LXXIX and the card-index of LaBorde. M. Gallet, 'l'hôtel d'Ecquevilly', in the *Album of the Festival du Marais*, 1967, p. 90.

BEAUVILLAIN Claude-Jacques-Charles
Practising in 1785.

BÉLANGER François-Joseph
Paris, 12 April 1744–1 May 1818.
Pupil of the Academy, 1764–65. Intendant des Bâtiments de Monsieur, architect to the Menus Plaisirs.
Works: Embellishments for the Prince de Chimay at the Porte Saint-Honoré, 1771. Pavilion of the Comte de Lauraguais in the garden of the Hôtel de Brancas, 1 Rue Taitbout. Works for the Prince de Ligne: in the gardens of Belœil, 1771; in the former Hôtel d'Epinay, Brussels, 1772; in the gardens of Baudour, 1775; project for a hall for the Italians between the Rues Boucherat and des Filles-du-Calvaire, in collaboration with Jalliers, 1772. Proposed hôtel in the Chaussée d'Antin for Sophie Arnould, 1773. Hôtel des écuries d'Artois, Rue de la Pompe (today Rue Carnot), Versailles. Catafalque of the King of Sardinia, 1773. Decorative scheme for Louis XV's funeral, 1774. Three views of the coronation ceremony of Louis XVI, 1774. Supposed stage design for Alceste (library of the Opéra). Pavilion of Bagatelle, 21 September–26 November 1777. Proposed hôtel for M. de Sainte-Foix, 1777 (B.N. Est. Va 285, III). Works at Maisons for the Comte d'Artois: summer dining-room, gaming-room, and refurbishing of little château; farm, *prévôté*, and pheasantry of Le Vésinet, and church of Mesnil-le-Roi, 1777–84. Proposed gallery for Lord Shelburne in London, 1779. Proposed reconstruction of Saint-Germain and restoration of Doric steps of the château. Designs for a palace for the Comte d'Artois and of a residential quarter, called 'La Nouvelle Londres', in the former nurseries of Le Roule. Artois stables, Faubourg Saint-Honoré and Rue Neuve de Berry, 1778–88. Works at the Temple: apartment of the Comte de Crussol; salon, dining-room and billiard-room of the Comte d'Artois, after 1777. Works at Fontainebleau: maison du Premier Ecuyer de Mgr, Rue de France; stables of the Comtesse d'Artois (1785); Bélanger's house, Rue des Bois. Tennis court for the Sr Charrier, 37 Boulevard du Temple (project 1780). House at Sèvres; maison d'Artois and stables, Vincennes, 1778–80. Works at the hôtel and stables of the Comtesse d'Artois, Rues de Lille and des Saints-Pères. Schemes for linking the Louvre with the Tuileries, and an opera-house at the Carrousel, 1781. Works for M. de Sainte-James: pavilion, temple and natural history room at Neuilly, after 1777. Apartment at 12 Place Vendôme. Works at Château de Mont-Saint-Père. Work for the Marquis de Coislin at Brimborion. Decoration of the Hôtel de Mazarin, Quai Malaquais. Work for M. de Laborde at Méréville: hall, large dining-room and small salon in stucco, billiard-room, winter and summer *grands salons*; *fabriques* in park: three bridges, temple, dairy (today in the park of Jeurre), mill, columna-rostrata, etc. Decoration for Mlle Dervieux, Rue Chantereine (de la Victoire): 'arabesque' dining-room, boudoir, bath suite, garden *fabriques*. House, Rue Neuve des Capucins (No. 20, formerly 18). House, Rue Royale Montmartre

(Pigalle), 1787. Designs for hôtels for the Maréchale de Mirepoix and Mme de Neukerque, house for Adeline Colombe, Rue Royale (10 Rue Pigalle). Hôtel de Lau, Rue Notre-Dame-des-Champs, 1788. Hôtel de Puységur, Chaussée d'Antin and Rue des Capucins (Joubert). Hôtel de Weymerange, Rue des Mathurins and Rue de la Ferme. Chapelle des Irlandais, Rue du Cheval Vert. Fire-pumps, Chaillot and Le Gros Caillou. Maison La Balue at Pantin. Houses in the precinct of the Carmelites of Beauvais. Park of Le Thillay for M. de Weymerange. Park of Suisnes for M. de Bougainville. Works at Buzancy for M. Augeard. Thierry garden at Ville d'Avray. Three houses, Rue Saint-Georges, 1788 (maisons Girardot, Grand and Brontin, 1805). '*Ferme d'agrément*' for M. de Castellane, Neuilly, 1790. Versfère-Arcelöf garden (Krafft, p. 48). Maison Talleyrand, Allée des Veuves (Avenue Montaigne), 1791. Bélanger house at Santeny, 1810. Vigier baths, Pont Royal. Restoration of the Hôtel Dervieux for Mlle Lange. Abattoir de Rochechouart, 1808. Dome of the Halle au Blé, 1808–13. Celebration of the return of the Bourbons, 3 May 1814. New (state) seals of France. Translation of remains of Louis XVI and Marie-Antoinette to Saint-Denis, 21 January 1815. Funeral ceremonials in Notre-Dame, 21 January 1816 and 1817. Decoration of Notre-Dame for the marriage of the Duc de Berry, 17 June 1816.
Original drawings: B.N. Est. Ha 58 to 58 f.
Attributions rejected: Maison Raibaut, 20 Rue Joubert. Château des Boulayes, Tournan (S. & M.).
Publ.: *Construction d'une halle aux vins*, Paris, 1808.
Bibl.: Jean Stern, *A l'ombre de Sophie Arnould, François-Joseph Bélanger, architecte des Menus Plaisirs, premier architecte du Comte d'Artois*, 1930. Kerstin M. Gjesdahl, 'La Folie Saint-James', in *Information d'histoire de l'art*, 1962.

BELHOMME Maurice
'Expert-entrepreneur.' Rue au Maire.
Practised about 1724–40.

BELLANGER Guillaume
In practice in 1763.
Tenements round the Halle au Blé.

BELISARD Claude Billard de
Academician 1776. Architect to the Prince de Condé.
24 Rue Platrière in 1790.
Transformation of the Palais Bourbon, 1765–88 (Cl. M. Goupy and P. L. Lemonnier, contractors, 1765–74; Gingaud de Buffeix in 1788). Building of the *petits appartements* of the Hôtel de Lassay 1771–79, and trellis-work pavilion housing the group by Pigalle: *Love and Friendship*. Elevations of the Place du Palais Bourbon, 1776. Theatre and 'Pavillon d'Oronthée', Chantilly. Hôtel Cassini, 32 Rue de Babylone, 1768–71: album of designs in the Ed. de Goncourt collection.
Bibl.: G. Macon, *Les arts dans la maison Condé*.
Ref.: Arch. Nat. T 1603: inventory after death. Catalogue of Goncourt sale, 15–16 February 1897. Lot no. 373.

BELLICARD Jérôme-Charles
Paris, 23 February 1726–28 February 1786.

Grand Prix, 1747. Known chiefly for his work as an archaeologist and engraver. 'Controller' of châteaux of Compiègne and Fontainebleau.
Hôtel of the Marquise de Matharel, Rue Notre-Dame-des-Champs, 1758–59.
Publ.: Observations sur les antiquités d'Herculanum (in collaboration with Cochin le Jeune), 1754.
In the series of Portes cochères of Le Cannu, pl. 1 is signed 'Bellicart inv.' It appears to have been designed for the Hôtel de Laval, Rue Coquillère.
Ref.: Arch. Nat. Z 1j 855.

BELLU
Former pupil of the Académie Royale.
Salon des Antiques in the Ducal Palace of Dijon, about 1785.

BENOIST Louis
Died 25 October 1734. 'Expert-entrepreneur' in 1716. Academician, 1728.
House, Rue Saint-Denis, south corner of the Rue Grenéta. Maison Henri, Rue des Petits-Champs.
Benoist's part in the work carried out at the Hôtel Gouffier de Thoix, Rue de Varenne, is difficult to account for. When the *expertise finale* took place, he represented the contractors' interests, while his colleague J.-F. Raymond seems to have been charged with those of the Marquis even before construction began.
Ref.: Arch. Nat. Z 1j 527, 548.

BENOÎT DE FORTIER
Family of architects, of whom François Benoît de Fortier was practising in 1770.

BERGEVIN Louis-Catherine
Rue Barouillère (near Rue de Sèvres) in 1792.
Group of tenements for the Comte de Faudoas, Rue Bailleul, 1781. House for M. Charpentier, *commis des finances*, Rue Meslée, 1784. Maison Bergevin, 51 Rue de Seine.
Ref.: Arch. Nat. Z 1j 1068, 1080, 1126.

BERNARD Charles
Died 30 October 1751. Rue Le Regrattier.
Hôtel de Monaco, Rue Cadet, 1722 (cf. *VP*, 1920, p. 62). House for the Comte de Trénoux, Rue d'Antin, 1726. Maison Rondet, 35 Rue de la Harpe, 1730. Hôtels, Cul-de-sac de Ménars (contract approved by Maître Bourron, 1732). Maison de Rambuteau, Rue de l'Arbre-Sec (contract approved by Maître Hargenvilliers, 7 July 1724). Work at Hôtel de Parabère, Place Vendôme, 1732. Maison Clément, Rue des Deux-Portes, 1739.
Ref.: Arch. Nat. Z 1j 435, 553, 573. M. Rambaud, *Doc.* 1, pp. 18 and 415.

BILLAUDEL Jean-René
1733–86. 2e Prix de l'Académie, 1754. Academician 1774.

BILLAUDEL Charles-Jacques
Died 1762. Academician 1729. 'Contrôleur des Bâtiments du Roi.'

BIMONT
Family of contractors and architects.

A Bimont was inspector of the Ecole Militaire in 1771.
A female Bimont took part in 'l'offrande des femmes artistes à la Constituante' on 21 September 1789.

BLANCHARD Jean-Luc
'Expert-bourgeois' from 1758. Still active in 1792.
Rue du Four Saint-Honoré, then Rue Française (Marie Stuart), then Rue Royale Saint-Antoine (Birague).
Apartment of Mlle Deschamps, Rue Saint-Nicaise, before 1760.
Bibl.: Carsillier.

BLAVET Jacques
Died 1763. Rue du Petit-Bourbon and at Bourg-la-Reine.
Hôtel d'Argenson, Faubourg Saint-Honoré, 1758. Maison Sue, Rue de l'Arbre-Sec, 1758. Maison Thomas, Avenue de Saint-Cloud, Versailles, 1758. House, Rue d'Enfer, 'opposite the dining-hall of the Luxembourg'.
Ref.: Arch. Nat. Z 1j 839, 843; *La Feuille nécessaire, L'Avant-coureur*, 1761, p. 824.

BLÈVE Jean-Louis
Architect 'expert-bourgeois' from 1766 to 1792. 'Architecte des Bâtiments civils' in 1798. Rue des Ecouffes in 1790. Inspecteur des Bâtiments Civils in 1798.
Tripe-shop of the Ile des Cygnes, 1766. Hôtel de la Saule at Le Petit Bercy, 1768. Hôtel de Persan, Rue des Fossés du Temple, 1771. Grand Hôtel de Persan, 5 Rue Bonaparte, after 1771. Petit Hôtel de Persan, between court and garden, 9 Rue Bonaparte. Tenements for Doublet de Persan, 7 and 9 Rue Bonaparte, after 1771. Tenements for the Sr Pierre Guérard, at the corner of the Rues Vieille du Temple and de Bretagne, 1777. Cavaignac tenements, Rue Trainée-Saint-Eustache, 1790. Salle du Tribunat at the Palais-Royal, 1801. Work for the Corps Législatif at the Palais Bourbon.
Ref.: Arch. Nat. Z 1j 925, 948, 994, 1044, 1048, 1054, 1088, 1179, 1214, 1215. F 4 1248.

BLONDEL
Family of architects (no known relationship with François Blondel (1618–86):

BLONDEL François or Jean-François, 1663–1756. Academician.
Choir of Saint-Jean-en-Grève (contract for joinery approved by Maître Cadot, 28 December 1719). Choir and chapel of the Virgin at Saint-Sauveur (contract for marble-work, étude xxx, 14 July 1728).
Presbytery of Saint-Merry, 1732 (completed by P.-L. Richard). Tenements for Maillard de Balore, 61 Quai de la Tournelle, 1731; for Guillier de Hauteville, Rue de Condé 1733; for the Président Hénault, Rue Saint-Honoré, opposite the Jacobins, 1740. House at Le Grand Charonne (engraved). Hôtel de Rouillé, Rue des Poulies (id.), decorated by Nicolas Pineau. Maison Blondel, 8 Rue du Croissant. Fountain in the Park of Hôtel des Gardes du Corps, Jouy-en-Josas. Palais des

Consuls, Rouen, 1734–39. Hôtel des Gardes du Corps, Versailles, 1752; cf. Arch. Nat. Z ij 810.
Work in Switzerland: Hôtel Gédéon Mallet, Place Saint-Pierre, Geneva. Cramer house, Cologny. Lullin house, Genthold (restored in 1954).
The decoration for the marriage of Mlle Bernard de Rieux with the Marquis de Mirepoix was engraved by Blondel.

BLONDEL Jacques-François

Born Rouen 1705, died Paris 1774.
Academician. Professor at the Academy 1756–74.
Orangery near Florence. Gardens of the Marquis de Saint-R***, 'on the Brittany road, 21 leagues from Paris'. Hôtel Petit de Marivat, Place Dauphine, Besançon. Decoration of the Porte Saint-Martin, 7 September 1745 (Blondel, *Cours d'architecture*, vol. II, p. 280, and drawings of de Swart in the Musée Carnavalet). Stage design, painted by Labbé and Tremblin, at the Grands Jésuites (*Mémoires de Trévoux*, September 1748). Project and foundations for an opera-house, in the gardens of the Hôtel Carignan, Rue de Grenelle (Blondel, *Architecture française*, vol. III, p. 15). Decoration of the gallery of the Hôtel de Choiseul, Rue de Richelieu (former Hôtel Crozat. Blondel, *Cours d'architecture*, vol. I, p. 109, note K). Transformation of the Blondel house, Rue du Croissant. Main entrance of the archbishop's palace, Cambrai (*Cours d'architecture*, vol. III, pl. XXVI).
Works at Strasbourg: general plans, *aubette* and screen for the cathedral. Works at Metz: Place d'Armes, 1764–65 (partly defaced), portal of the cathedral (destroyed), Rue d'Estrées, Place Saint-Etienne. Proposals for the decoration of the choir of the cathedral of Châlons-sur-Marne.

Publ.: *De la distribution des maisons de Plaisance et de la décoration des edifices en général*, 2 vols: 1737, vol. I, *Les Maisons de plaisance* (dedicated to the Prévôt des Marchands Turgot); 1738, vol. II, *La Décoration des edifices*. *Discours sur la manière d'étudier l'architecture et les arts qui sont relatifs à celui de Bâtir*, 1747. Various articles on architecture in *L'Encyclopédie*, 1751–65. *L'Architecture française, ou recueil de plans, d'élévations, coupes et profils* . . ., 4 vols, Paris, 1752–56. *Discours sur la nécessité de l'étude de l'architecture*, Paris, 1754, *Discours sur la nécessité de joindre à l'étude de l'architecture celle des sciences et des arts qui lui sont relatifs*, 1771. *Cours d'architecture civile*, 4 vols., Paris, 1771–73. *L'Homme du monde éclairé par les arts*, published by J.-F. de Bastide, Amsterdam, Paris, 1774. Recueil contenant la description du Château de Blois, relevé par ordre de M. le Marquis de Marigny en 1760, Paris, Bibl. de l'Institut, MS. 1.046.
Bibl.: Diderot, Préface de *L'Encyclopédie*, 1751. François Franque, 'Eloge de J.-F. Blondel, in *Journal des Beaux-Arts et des Sciences*, March 1774, pp. 559–70. *Le Nécrologe des hommes célèbres*, 1775, pp. 225–36. P. Patte, biography of Blondel in vol. V of the *Cours d'architecture civile*. A.-N. Dézallier d'Argenville, *Vies des fameux architectes*, 1785. Auguste Prost, *Jacques-François Blondel et son œuvre*, Metz, 1860. *PVARA*. Jeanne Lejeaux, 'Jean-François Blondel 1683–1756', in *L'Architecture*, 1927, pp. 395–400; 'Un architecte français, Jacques-François Blondel', in *Revue de l'art ancien et moderne*, 1927, vol. II, pp. 223–34, 271–85; 'Jacques-François Blondel, Professeur d'Architecture', in *L'Architecture*, 1927, pp. 23–7. François Georges Pariset, 'La Grille du chœur de la cathédrale de Strasbourg', in *Archives Alsaciennes*, 1927, pp. 171–6. Jeanne Lejeaux, *La Place d'Armes de Metz*, Strasbourg, 1927; 'L'œuvre gravé des Blondel', in *Estampes*, 1928, pp. 106–14, 145–53. Robin Middleton, 'Jacques-François Blondel and the *Cours d'architecture*', in *Journal of the Society of Architectural Historians of Great Britain*, 1959, pp. 140 et seq. E. Kaufmann, 'The Contribution of Jacques-François Blondel to Mariette's *Architecture Française*', in *Art Bulletin*, 1949. M. Gallet, 'Blondel', in *Encyclopaedia Universalis*, Paris, 1968.

BOFFRAND Germain

Born Nantes 7 May 1667, died Paris 18 March 1754.
Academician, 1709. Inspector-general des Ponts et Chaussées, 1732.
Preliminary studies for the Place Vendôme, in collaboration with Jules Hardouin-Mansart. Hôtel Le Brun, 49 Rue du Cardinal Lemoine, 1697. Work at the Hôtel de Mesme, Rue Sainte-Avoie. Hôtel d'Argenton, later Chancellerie d'Orléans, 19 Rue des Bons-Enfants. Hôtel de Canillac, Rue des Francs-Bourgeois, 1707. Restoration of the Hôtel de Mayenne, 21 Rue Saint-Antoine, 1709. Hôtel du Petit Luxembourg, Rue de Vaugirard, 1709. Hôtel de Montaran, Rue des Francs-Bourgeois. Hôtel Amelot, 1 Rue Saint-Dominique, 1712. Work at the Hôtel de Broglie, Rue Saint-Dominique, near Bellechasse, 1712 (contract of 23 April, Arch. Nat. T 89 1). Hôtel Melchior de Blair, Rue Vivienne. Main entrance of the Hôtel de Villars, 116 Rue de Grenelle, 1712. Hôtel de Torcy, 80 Rue de Lille, 1713. Hôtel de Seignelay, 78 Rue de Lille. 'Bâtiment du Mail' at the Arsenal, 1714–25. Hôtel de Duras, Faubourg Saint-Honoré, 1718. Boffrand houses, Rue de Braque and Rue Hérold. Work at the Hôtel de Broglie, Rue Saint-Dominique (contract approved by Maître Le Prévost, 12 April 1729). Hôtel de Vendôme, Rue de Varenne (contract approved by Maître Gaillard, 14 August 1720). Oval pavilion and apartments of the Hôtel Soubise, about 1733–37. Châteaux de Saint-Ouen, de Béarn (at Saint-Cloud), de Cramayel and de Bossette.
Work at the Salpêtrière. Well for the Hospice de Bicêtre, 1733–35. Gallery at the Hôtel de Ville. Work on the 'Grand Chambre' and on the Hôtel de la Première Présidence. Hospital of the Enfants-Trouvés, Parvis Notre-Dame.
Second order of the main entrance of the Merci, Rue des Archives. Chapel of the Saint-Esprit. Portal of the cloister of Notre-Dame. De Noailles chapel at Notre-Dame. Proposed Communion chapel at Saint-Merry.
Bridges of Sens and Montereau. Arsenal, Lyon. Porte Saint-Jean at Melun.
Pavillon de Bouchefort, near Brussels, 1705 (not completed). Palais Ducal, Nancy, 1717 (work suspended in 1720, but recommenced by Em. Héré to fresh plans). Hôtel de Craon, Nancy. Palace of Lunéville, 1703–23. Châteaux de la Malgrange and de Haroué. Abbaye d'Autrey.
Designs for residences for the house of Schönborn (Study for Würzburg; Kunstbibliothek, Berlin).
Publ.: 'Description de ce qui a été pratiqué pour fondre en bronze d'un seul jet la figure équestre de Louis XIV

élevée par la Ville de Paris', in *Livre d'architecture*, 1745. *Œuvres d'architecture de M. Boffrand*, 1754.

Bibl.: Patte, *Abrégé de la vie de Boffrand*, 1754. L. Battifol, 'La construction de l'Arsenal et Germain Boffrand', in *Revue de l'art ancien et moderne*, 1931, vols. I and II. P. Lavedan, 'Le Pavillon de Bouchefort', in *Les Mélanges van Puyvelde*, 1949. Fiske Kimball, *The Creation of the Rococo*, 1943 (and subsequent paperback); French version published in 1950, under the title of *Le Style Louis XV*. J.-P. Babelon, *Histoire et description des bâtiments des archives Nationales*, 1969. F. Souchal, *Aspects du mouvement artistique en Lorraine au temps de Léopold, Ecole du Louvre*, 1950. Jörg Garms, *Studien zu Boffrand*, Vienna, 1962, typescript. Jörg Garms, 'L'Aménagement du Parvis Notre-Dame', in *Art de France*, 1964. J. Garms, 'Germain Boffrand et l'Eglise de la Merci', in *BSHAF*, 1964. J. Garms, 'Les Projets de Mansart et de Boffrand pour le Palais Ducal de Nancy', in *Bulletin monumental*, 1967.

BONAMY Sylvain-Edme
Pupil of the Academy in 1764. Practising in 1776.
Ref.: Arch. Nat. Z 1j 1005.

BONNEAU (BONNOT)
Family of building contractors and architects, active in the middle of the eighteenth century.

> BONNEAU Claude
> BONNEAU André-François
> BONNEAU Jean-Baptiste

A Bonnot, a member of a family of contractors active in Louis XV's reign, was architect of the Hôtel-Dieu in 1779.

BONNET DE BOISGUILLAUME
Family of architects:

BONNET DE BOISGUILLAUME Claude
House for a Mr Biet, lawyer, at Saint-Leu-Taverny, called 'La Chaumette', 1771. House for Maître Lepot d'Auteuil, notary, Rue Saint-Honoré, 1776.

BONNET DE BOISGUILLAUME Pierre-Alexis
Pupil of Blondel. 2e Grand Prix, 1774. Rue Hautefeuille in 1771, Rue Basse, Porte-St-Denis in 1779. Inspecteur-Général des Bâtiments Civils in 1798.
Hôtel de Boufflers, Boulevard des Italiens (site of the Crédit Lyonnais), 1779–82, two versions of the scheme in the Arch. Nat. A fragment of the interior decoration, published by Rouyer and Darcel, *L'Art architectural*, vol. II. Design for the Théâtre Italien, 1777 engraved. *Fabriques* in the Jardin Boufflers at Auteuil, site of the Villa Montmorency.
The Academy of Architecture retained the following projects by Bonnet: temple to the glory of the Bourbons; porte de ville de guerre, terraced stairs.

Ref.: Arch. Nat. Minutier XCVIII, 631. Z 1j 953, 1005, 1051; F 17 1265 10. Mémoires secrets, 10 June 1777.

BOSCRY Charles
Contractor.

BOSCRY Pierre
Son of the above. Died 1 March 1781. Architect. Candidate for the Academy in 1742, 1755, 1756, 1758. Rue Cassette in 1743, Rue d'Enfer in 1767.

The activities of father and son are difficult to distinguish between 1726 and 1740.
Maison Bernard, Rue de la Huchette, 1714. Construction of Hôtel d'Avaray, under the direction of Le Roux, 1721. Work at the Incurables, 1724. Maison Catherinet, Rue Mazarine, 1728. Main entrance of the Marché Bucy, 1726. Main entrance of Hôtel de Montauban, Rue de l'Université (engraved). Buildings and chapel of the Collège des Lombards, Rue des Carmes, 1738. Château de Neuilly-Plaisance, and *fabriques* in the park, after 1735. Hôtel d'Orrouer, 87 Rue de Grenelle, 1732. Hôtel de Marguerite Grivel d'Orrouer, Comtesse de Feuquières, 58 Rue de Varenne, 1736. Hôtel du Prat, 60 Rue de Varenne, extensions 1732–50. Design for the Hôtel de Broglie, 19 Place Vendôme.
Ref.: Arch. Nat. T 188, Z 1F 422, Z 1j 513, 546, 572, 597, 605, 610, 628, 705, 758.
Bibl.: Portefeuille de Bachaumont. Blondel, *Architecture français*, III, p. 29, 90; *Cours d'architecture*, vol. III, p. 368. *Almanach d'Hébert*. La France littéraire de l'Abbé Delaporte. *Dictionnaire de Hurtaut et Magny*. Argenville. Dulaure. Françoise de Catheu, in *BSHAF*, 1950. M. Gallet, 'The Hôtel d'Orrouer in Paris', in *Apollo*, February 1968.

BOUCHU Paul-Antoine
Born at Lyon. 2e Grand Prix 1755. 'Expert-bourgeois' from 1773 to 1792. Rue Sainte-Avoye, close to Geoffroy Langevin, in 1792.
Tenements of the Rue Feydeau, opened in 1780 in the grounds of the Marquis de Verneuil. Monument commemorating Mortagne, 1786.
Ref.: Arch. Nat. Z 1j 1086, 1125. Mémoires secrets, 31 December 1785.

BOUILLETTE DE CHAMBLY François
'Expert-entrepreneur.' Active 1760–70. Rue Saint-Martin, opposite the Fontaine Maubué.

BOULLAND Jean-Baptiste
Born at Troyes, 1739, died in Paris, 1813. Pupil of Moreau-Desproux in 1762. Architect to the chapter of Notre-Dame, 1773. 'Expert-bourgeois' from 1774 to 1792. Rue la Feuillade.
Choir of Saint-Nicolas-des-Champs (with Antoine), 1775. Abbaye de Jarcy (S. & M.), 1780; B.N. Est. Va 237 and 242.
Ref.: Arch. Nat. Z 1j 1086.

BOULLÉE
Family of architects:

BOULLÉE Louis-Claude
Commissioner-General of Roads, 1732. 'Expert-bourgeois', 1742.

Maison Le Cour de Lanty, Rue Saint-Honoré (contract approved by Maître de Savigny, 1732). Maison du Collège d'Autun, Rue Saint-André-des-Arts (contracts approved by Maître Mouette in 1733 and 1735). Maison Caumartin, Rue Sainte-Catherine (de Sévigné), 1733. Maison Lallier, Rue des Postes. Carriage entrance of the Hôtel de Boisboudran, at the Temple, design prepared in collaboration with J. Pinard, 1744.
Ref.: Arch. Nat. Z 1j 639, 649, 656, 668, 743.

BOULLÉE Etienne-Louis
Born in Paris 12 February 1728, died 6 February 1799. Son and pupil of the above, pupil also of P. E. Lebon de Lejay and of Blondel. Academician 1762. 'Intendant des Bâtiments' of the Comte d'Artois 1775.
Design for the Hôtel des Monnaies, 1762 (engraved). Design for the Palais Bourbon, 1765. Salon de l'Hôtel de Tourolles, Rue Charlot. Maison Beaujon, Rue Dauphin. Château of the Comte de Tessé at Chaville: plans, section and elevations, dated 27 November 1764; plan of the property engraved by Le Rouge. Hôtel Racine de Monville, Rue de la Ville-l'Evêque, after 1764. Hôtel Alexandre (Suchet, during the Empire), 16 Rue de la Ville-l'Evêque; façades engraved by Roger, after 1762. Boullée house, Rue Royale, 1777. Pavillon Beaujon at Issy, before 1778. Projected hôtel for Beaujon at Fontainebleau. Hôtel de Thun, Chaussée d'Antin, about 1771-74. Hôtel de Pernon, Chaussée d'Antin. 'Numerous projects for foreign courts', cf. Rondelet, 'Notice sur Durand'. Hôtel de Brunoy, completed 1779. Works at the Hôtel du Temple, after 1775, for the Comtesse d'Artois, Rue de Bourbon (Lille) and Rue des Saints-Pères. Design for the main entrance of the Charité, Rue Jacob, included anonymously in the work of Lequeu, B.N. Est. Ha 80a, sheet 48 and engraved by Taraval. Château de Chauvry at Montmorency, property of Mme de la Massais. Château du Perreux at Nogent-sur-Marne. Work at the prison of the Grande Force, Rue du Roi de Sicile. The Bourse, Rue Vivienne. Redesign of the Treasury in the Hôtel Mazarin, Rue Neuve-des-Petits-Champs. Drawings, collected under the title 'Architecture de Boullée', bequeathed by his nephew Bénard to the Bibliothèque Nationale.

Bibl.: Villar, 'Notice sur Boullée', in *Mémoires de l'Institut*, vol. III, Histoire 43, an IX. L.H. vols. IV and V. Emile Kaufmann, 'Three Revolutionary Architects – Boullée, Ledoux and Lequeu', in *Transactions of the American Philosophical Society*, Philadelphia, 1952, vol. XLII, p. 3. Helen Rosenau, *The Ideal City*, London, 1959; *Boullée's Treatise on Architecture*, London, 1952. 'Boullée and Ledoux as Town-planners', in *GBA*, March 1964. Hélène Leclerc, 'E.-L. Boullée et la competition pour une nouvelle salle d'opéra, 1781', in *Revue d'histoire du théâtre*, 1965. J.-M. Pérouse de Montclos, *Boullée*, 1969; Robin Middleton, in *Architectural Design*, July 1970.

BOURDET Barthélémy
Bureau des Tapissiers, Rue Saint-Martin, 1740. Maison Bourdet, Rue du Haut-Pavé.
Ref.: Arch. Nat. Z 1j 711.

BOURGEOIS
Family of architects:

BOURGEOIS Pierre
Deputy 'Syndic des experts' in 1769. Rue de la Harpe.

BOURGEOIS Louis-Denis
'Juré honoraire' in 1769. Rue de la Colombe.

BOURGEOIS Louis-Sylvain
Rue de la Colombe in 1769.

BOURGEOIS (le Frère Nicolas)
Practised about 1710-30. Work in Rouen: *Pont tournant des Tuileries*.

BOURLA Jean-Bruno-Joseph
Practising in 1784. 'Architecte des Domaines' in 1795.

BRAY Pierre
Died before 1770. Architect, 'expert-bourgeois' from 1747. Rue des Fontaines-du-Temple in 1760.
Houses, Rue des Fontaines-du-Temple, opposite the Madelonettes; and Rue Vieille-du-Temple, 1754.
References: Arch. Nat. Z 1F 460, fol. 103; 461, fol. 8. Z 1j 775.

BRÉBION Maximilien
1716-96. Grand Prix, 1740.
In charge of work at Sainte-Geneviève after Soufflot's death. Access staircase to the *salon carré* of the Louvre, 1782. Marché Sainte-Catherine, 1785. Restoration of the Observatory, 1786. Design for the Opéra (Arch. Nat. O 1 629).

BRETEZ Louis
Died 1738. Architect, perspectivist. Rue Saint-Martin, in front of the Fontaine Maubué, in 1706; Rue des Mathurins in 1736.
Publ.: La perspective pratique de l'architecture, 1706.
Bibl.: M. Gallet, 'Un document sur le Plan Turgot', in *BSHP*, 1966.

BRICE LE CHAUVE
See LE CHAUVE

BRISEUX Charles-Etienne
Died 23 September 1754.
Hôtel de la Ferté (later Gaignat), Rue de Richelieu, 1738. House for the Prince d'Isenghien at Suresnes. Hôtel d'Augny, Rue Grange-Batelière (Mairie of the IXe arrondissement), 1748-52. Abbaye de Saint-Just-en-Chaussée. Project for the Prieuré Saint-Jean-de-Latran. Designs for the Château de la Londe in Normandy and for Government House at Arras.
Publ.: L'art de bâtir les maisons de campagne, 2 vols. 4to, 1743. Traité du beau essentiel dans les arts, appliqué particulièrement à l'architecture, followed by a Traité des proportions harmoniques, 1 vol. 8vo, 1752.
Bibl.: L. Deshairs, *Nicolas et Dominique Pineau*.
References: Arch. Nat. Z 1F 452, fol. 114v. Z 1j 675, 803.

BRODONT Séraphin
Mentioned in 1760.

BRONGNIART Alexandre-Théodore
Born Paris 15 February 1739, died Paris 6 June 1813.
Studied under Boullée and Blondel. Academician 1781.
Theatre at Caen, about 1765. Hôtel de Montesson, Chaussée d'Antin, February 1770–May 1771; elevation of
garden front in Musée Carnavalet, and another (confirm-
ing the identity of the first) in the Archives Nationales.
Hôtel of the Duc d'Orléans, 17 Rue de Provence, altered
by Henri Piètre. Hôtel Taillepied de Bondi, Rue de Richelieu and Boulevard Montmartre, 1771; elevation in the
Musée Carnavalet (document of 4 August 1769 defining
building lines). Hôtel built for Radix de Sainte-Foix (bare
ownership to Jacques-Louis-Guillaume Bouret de Vézelay),
Rue Basse du Rempart; plan (before C.-J. Happe's alterations), Arch. Nat. Z 1j 1171; elevation, B.N. Est. Coll.
Destailleur No. 688: 1775. Hôtel de la Massais, Boulevard
de la Chaussée d'Antin and Rue de Choiseul, 1776–78.
Hôtel de Mlle Carotte, Chaussée d'Antin, begun late
1776; sketch in Arch. Nat. Z 1j 1010. Hôtel de Courcelles,
94 Faubourg Saint-Honoré, 1776. Hôtel de Mlle Dervieux,
Rue Chantereine. Houses in Rue Neuve des Mathurins,
between the Rue de l'Arcade and Rue de la Ferme, one
built for M. Grisard de Baudry, after 1776. Hôtel de
Monaco, 59 Rue Saint-Dominique, completed July 1777;
drawings in Arch. Nat. Z 1j 1036 and Musée Carnavalet.
Parc de Maupertuis, near Coulommiers, about 1780.
Capuchin Monastery d'Antin (church of Saint-Louis
d'Antin and Lycée Condorcet). Hôtel de Mlle de Bourbon-
Condé, 12 Rue Monsieur, two versions of project dated
June 1780 in Arch. Nat. Z 1j and minutes de l'étude,
XCII, 822; estimate in archives of Chantilly. Brongniart
house, 49 Boulevard des Invalides (project in Arch. Nat. Z 1j
1076). Hôtel de Montesquiou, 20 Rue Monsieur. Chamblin
house, Rue Masseran. Hôtel Damas d'Anlezy, at the south
corner of the Rue de Babylone and the Boulevard. Pavilion
of the Archives of Saint-Lazare, Rue de Babylone (project in Arch. Nat. N III, Seine 811. Château de Trilbardou
(S. & M.), after 1783. Château du Teil, near Sens. Work at
the Hôtel de Montmorin, Boulevard des Invalides and Rue
Oudinot, 1789. Hôtel Masserano, 11 Rue Masseran, 1787.
Work at the Ecole Militaire: riding school, finished 1785;
observatory, mess-hall, pavilions and railings enclosing
the south side of the Cour Royale. Church at Romainville,
1785. Théâtre des Arts, 1791, built for Lomel, later Théâtre
Louvois et du Vaudeville. Works at Bordeaux, 1793:
theatre, Bacalan mill, decorative setting for a civic festival
at the cathedral on 10 December; quays and various buildings at La Réole. Work for Mme de Montesson at the mill
of Romainville, 1797. Apartments for Mme Cabarrus,
formerly Tallien, 1802 (Allée des Veuves or Rue de Babylone). Concert hall of the Rue de Cléry. M. de Roger's
gardens. Gardens of 200 *arpents* and *fabriques* for M. de
Sivry at Villemomble. Decoration for the 'Table des
Saisons', carried out at Sèvres. Plan of the cemetery of Le
Mont-Louis (Père La Chaise), 1804. The Bourse, begun in
1807, completed by Eloi La Barre.
Bibl.: J. Silvestre de Sacy, *A. T. Brongniart*, 1940.

BRUANT François
Academician 1706.
Hôtel de Belle-Isle, Rue de Bourbon and Quai d'Orsay,
site of the Caisse des Dépôts et Consignations (contracts
approved by Maître Meunier in April 1722).
Bibl.: L.H. vol. III, pp. 173–4.

BRULÉ Jean-Baptiste
Rue de Paon, at the Petit Hôtel de Tours in 1781.
Tenements, 1 Rue de l'Odéon, 1781.
Ref.: Arch. Nat. Z 1j 110. Y 1100. Y 9507.

BUCAILLE-DUMONT Louis
Mentioned before 1780.

BUIRETTE Sébastien
Died 13 February 1759. 'Ingénieur des villes de guerre.'
Candidate for the Academy from 1720 to 1742. Rue de
Richelieu.
Inspection of works at the Château de Champs, 1703–6.
Work for the Duc de Bouillon, Quai Malaquais, 1735–39;
for M. du Pradel, Rue Bourg-l'Abbé, 1722. Maison
Antoine Dehem, Rue Danielle Casanova (contract ap-
proved by Maître Capet, 1725). Maison Poirier, Rue
Thévenot (Réaumur) (contract approved by Maître
Gachier, 1725). Hôtel Fargès de Polisy, Rue de Vendôme
(2 Rue Béranger) (contract approved by Maître Perret,
20 June 1727).
Ref.: Arch. Nat. Z 1j 533, 552, 559, 576, 590, 597, 599,
600, 614, 659, 664, 686; Minutier, XXXI, 165: Inventory
after Buirette's death, dated 1 March 1759 (D. Wildenstein,
Documents inédits sur les artistes du XVIIIe siècle).

BULLET (Jean-Baptiste BULLET de CHAMBLAIN)
1656–1726. Academician 1699.
Work in collaboration with his father, Pierre Bullet, on
Saint-Thomas d'Aquin, Saint-Germain-des-Prés, and at
La Rochelle. Designs for portals for Saint-Roch, Saint-
Sulpice and the Oratoire. Château de Champs, 1703–6.
Hôtel Dodun, 21 Rue de Richelieu, after 1715. (?) Château
de Bry-sur-Marne.
Bibl.: Runar Strandberg, 'Jean-Baptiste Bullet de Chamb-
lain, architecte du roi', in *BSHAF*, 1963, pp. 195–225.
'Les dessins d'architecture de P. Bullet pour la Place
Vendôme et l'Hôtel Reich de Pennautier d'Evreux', in
GBA, February 1965. 'Le Château de Champs', *GBA*,
February 1963.

BURON
Family of architects:
  BURON Jacques
  'Expert-entrepreneur' from 1766 to 1792. 9 Rue Culture
  Saint-Catherine (Sévigné) in 1792.
  Maison Buron, 17 Rue Sainte-Croix de la Bretonnerie.

  BURON Jacques-François
  Transformation of the choir of Sens cathedral, 1765.
  Hospice des Petits-Ménages, 1785; façade engraved by
  Michelinot. Towers of the church of Chessy. Much
  architectural work in Burgundy on religious buildings.
  Façade of the church of Cruzy (Yonne), begun by
  Ledoux.

CALLET Charles-François
Born Paris, 10 March 1755, died about 1835. Pupil of Bélisard. Inspector 'des travaux du Palais' in 1780.
Posthumous publ.: Notice historique sur la vie de quelques architectes du XVIᵉ siècle, Paris, 1842.

CAPRON
'Expert-entrepreneur' from 1780 to 1792. 24 Rue de Charonne in 1792. Surveyor to the fabric of Saint-Sulpice.

CAQUÉ
Family of building contractors:

CAQUÉ Pierre
Died 3 July 1767.
Corbin house, Rue Saint-Martin and Rue de Venise, 1727. Zilgens house (for commanding officer of Swiss Guard), Rues Montmartre and du Croissant, 1755. (?) House at 13 Rue Tiquetonne (perhaps in consultation with Oppenord). Portal and choir of the Oratoire (for which the same architect had submitted drawings), 1745. House, Rue Montorgueil. Many houses in the quarter of the Halles. Maison Micault D'Harvelay, Rues Saint-Gilles and Saint-Pierre au Marais, 1767.

CAQUÉ fils, (?) Guillaume-François
'Expert-entrepreneur' in 1760. Rue du Four Saint-Eustache.

CARON
Choir of the church of Saint-Romain de Sèvres, 1769–78. Marché Sainte-Catherine, to the plans of M. Brébion, 1783. Tenements lining the Rues de Jarente, Necker, d'Ormesson. Fontaine Necker, Impasse de la Poissonnerie.
Ref.: Arch. Nat. G 9 101. Z 1j 1022.

CARTAUD Jean-Sylvain
Born Paris 1675, died 15 February 1758. Academician 1742. Architect to the Duc d'Orléans.
Portal of the Barnabites in the Cité, 1703, moved to the church of the Blancs-Manteaux and altered. Hôtel Pierre Crozat, 93 Rue de Richelieu, 1704. Houses, Rue de la Planche, 1705. Château de Montmorency, 1708. Work at the Palais-Royal, 1715–45 (service buildings on the Rue des Bons-Enfants). Maison Guillot, Rue des Mauvaises-Paroles, 1723. Hôtel de Janvry, 47 Rue de Varenne, 1732–33. High altar of Rouen cathedral, 1736. Portal and first bays of the nave of the Petits-Pères (Notre-Dame des Victoires), 1738. Maison des Orfèvres, Rues des Orfèvres, Jean Lantier and des Lavandières, 1740. Château d'Argenson, Neuilly, 1741. Maison Hurel, Rue Saint-Martin, 1744. High altar of Evreux cathedral. Chapelle d'Argenson, at the Madelonnettes du Faubourg Saint-Antoine. Church-wardens' pews in Saint-Roch and Saint-Eustache. Château de Bournonville, near La Ferté-Milon. Château de Chantelou. Presbytery of Saint-Etienne-du-Mont. Chapel of the Hôtel d'Armenonville.
Bibl.: Mariette-Chevotet-Blondel, *Architecture française,* 1727. Blondel, *Architecture français* and *Cours d'architecture, passim.* Bachaumont, Portefeuille de l'Arsenal, fol. 579. Brice, *Description de Paris,* 9th edition, 1752, vol. I, p. 378; vol. IV, p. 27. Pigagnol, 1769. vol. I, p. 451; vol. III, pp.

104, 152, 179; vol. IV, p. 483; vol. V, p. 521. D'Argenville, *Voyage pittoresque,* pp. 26, 147, 161, 164, 258. Arch. Nat. Z 1j 627, 629, 674.

CATHALA
2ᵉ Prix in 1782. Architect in charge of the demolition of the Bastille.

CAULLE Martin
Architect, 'expert-bourgeois' in 1705. Near the Ancienne Estrapade in 1712.
Maison Pérelle, Rue de la Huchette (contract approved by Maître Beaudouin, 20 May 1738).

CAUVET Gilles-Paul
Born at Aix-en-Provence 17 April 1731, died Paris 15 November 1788. Academician of Saint-Luc in 1762. Sculptor to Monsieur in 1774. Celebrated ornamentalist, who also practised as an architect.
Hôtel de Kinski, 57 Rue Saint-Dominique. Design for the Palais de Justice, Aix, 1786. Decorative works in the Hôtels de Nivernais, 10 Rue de Tournon; de Mailly-Nesle, Quai Voltaire; de Noailles; and the gallery of the Hôtel de Mazarin, 78 Rue de Varenne.
Publ.: Recueil d'ornements à l'usage des jeunes artistes qui se destinent à la décoration des bâtiments, engraved by J. de Roy, Paris, 1777.
Bibl.: A. de Champeaux, *l'Art 39,* 1885, vol. II, pp. 133–6; and 1874, vol. VII, p. 174. L. Deshairs, *Dessins originaux des maîtres décorateurs du XVIIIᵉ siècle.*
Ref.: NAAF, 1885, vol. VI, pp. 913–15.

CELLERIER Jacques
Born at Dijon 11 November 1742, died 26 March 1814. 'Ingénieur de la généralité de Paris'. Chairman of the committee for the 'dépenses de la Commune' in 1791. Deputy to the management of the Opéra in 1794. Member of the Council for Civic Buildings in 1812. Rue Vivienne in 1777.
Hôtel de Verrière, Rue Verte Saint-Honoré, 1774. Hôtel, 21 Rue de la Chaussée d'Antin, 1775–79. Tenements and Hôtel du Mme d'Epinay (Louise Tardieu d'Esclavelles, separated wife of Denis de la Live), 5 Rue de la Chaussée d'Antin, 1776–77. Transformation of the *café turc* into the *café chinois,* 1777. Maison du Duc de Laval, Boulevard Montparnasse, begun in 1777. Hôtel de la Maréchale de Nicolaï, Rue Louis le Grand and Boulevard de la Chaussée d'Antin, 1779. Hôtel de Montigny, Rue de Provence, 1778–82. Works at the veterinary school of Alfort, chemistry laboratory, pharmacy, forge and large dissection room, before 1786. House of the Prince de Soubise, Rue de l'Arcade, 1787–88 (Hôtel de Soyecourt, 1789). Church of Sainte-Geneviève-des-Bois. Transformation of the Théâtre de l'Ambigu, Boulevard du Temple. Stables of the Hôtel de l'Infantado, Rue Saint-Florentin, 1786. Triumphal arch of the Champ de Mars for the celebration of the Fédération, 1790. Hearse for transporting Voltaire's ashes to the Panthéon; drawing in the Musée Carnavalet. Théâtre des Variétés, 1808. Transformation of the Hôtel de Rohan, allocated to the State Press, Rue

Vieille-du-Temple. Restoration of Saint-Denis. Design for the fountain of the Bastille, 1810. Theatre of Dijon, 1810.

Tenements, Boulevard Montmartre, 1787–88.

Bibl.: Eloge de Cellerier par Bélanger, Library of the Institute, fonds Duplessis, 2384 8vo.

Ref.: Arch. Nat. Minutier XCII, 786, 807, 814. H 2135. Z 1j 980, 996, 1002, 1007, 1011, 1023, 1032, 1041, 1088, 1161, 1184, 1200, 1238. Mémoires secrets, 1 March 1777; 26 February 1777; 31 August 1782.

CHABOÜILLÉ Médéric-Joseph = CHABOÜILLÉ DE LA MAISON NEUVE

Born about 1742. Pupil of the Academy in 1769. 'Expert-entrepreneur' from 1774 to 1792. Rue Saint-Victor, opposite the Rue du Bon-Puits, in 1792. Tenements, Rue Faubourg-Saint-Honoré and Rue des Saussaies, 1783.

Ref.: Arch. Nat. Z 1j 1009.

CHALGRIN Jean-François-Thérèse

Born in Paris 1739, died 21 January 1811.

Pupil of Servandoni, Boullée and Moreau. Grand Prix in 1758. Academician in 1770. 'Intendant des Bâtiments' of the Comte d'Artois in 1779. Member of the Institute in 1809.

Hôtel de Saint-Florentin, 2 Rue Saint-Florentin, 1767; the elevations, apart from the main entrance, are by Gabriel – projets de Chalgrin: B.N. Est. Ha 50, and Arch. Nat. H 2161 2. Chapelle du Saint-Esprit, 30 Rue Lhomond, 1768. Gallery for the marriage of the Dauphin 1770 (Blondel, *Cours d'architecture*, vol. II, p. 273; engraving by F. M. A. Boizot and drawing by Nigelli after Chalgrin, reproduced in Egger, *Architektonische Handzeichnungen*, pl. 53). Saint-Philippe-du-Roule, 1772–84. Model for the church of Saint-Sauveur, noted in the Tuileries in 1783, at the Académie Royale in 1792, and in the Polytechnique in the nineteenth century, today disappeared. Collège de France, 1780; project B.N. Est. Ha 48. Work at Saint-Sulpice: north tower; organ-case, 1776; baptismal chapel; joinery of the doors under the peristyle, 1780–88. Hôtel de Mme de Balbi, Rues de Fleurus and Madame. Hôtel de Langeac, Rue de Berry and Champs-Elysées; shown as formerly, after storey added, B.N. Est. Va 280, in Howard C. Rice, *l'Hôtel de Langeac*, 1947. Façade and salon of the Château de Surville, near Montereau (Ganay, *Ile de France*, 1938, vol I, p. 3). Pavillon de la Comtesse de Provence, Avenue de Paris at Versailles; plan, Arch. Nat. R 2 522. Pheasantry of Brunoy. Hôtel des Ecuries d'Artois, Versailles; project, Arch. Nat. R 4 333. Table for the Duchesse de Mazarin, 1785. Staircase of the Luxembourg, 1795. Reconstruction of the Odéon, 1807 and after. Arc de Triomphe de l'Etoile, completed by Huyot, Goust and Blouet to their designs.

Publ.: *Plan topographique de l'église Saint-Philippe. Livre d'architecture contenant plusieurs temples et leurs détails. Description de l'arc de triomphe de l'Etoile*, 1810.

Bibl.: Viel, *Notice sur Chalgrin*.

CHAPOTET Jean-Louis

Born 1755, practising in 1780.

CHARPENTIER Jean

Chapel, *cabinet*, and garden of the Hôtel de Noailles, Rue Saint-Honoré, 1740. Vicariat de Saint-Roch, Rue Neuve Saint-Roch, 1750–52. House, Rue Saint-Honoré, opposite the Oratoire. Mill in the Park of Maintenon. '16 master suites in the Château of Champs.' Charpentier house, Rues Traversine and Clos-Gorgeau, 1755.

Ref.: Blondel, *L'Architecture française*, vol. III, p. 130. Arch. Nat. Z 1j 815.

Note: Jean CHARPENTIER is probably unconnected with

CHARPENTIER Antoine

Mentioned in 1743 (cf. *BSHP*, 1906).

CHARPENTIER Nicolas

Practising before 1773, and living Rue Lévêque.

CHATEAU Jean-François

'Expert' in 1761–69. Rue des Mauvais-Garçons.

CHÂTELAIN Isidore

'Expert-entrepreneur.' Rue Chapon in 1730.

CHAULOT Claude

Pitoy house, Rue des Bourdonnais. Main entrance (former) of the Charité (attributed also to Robert de Cotte), 1731. Gobert house, Rues de la Vieille Draperie and de la Juiverie, 1740.

Publ.: Engraving of the Charité, published by Chéreau.

CHAUSSARD Jean-Baptiste

Born at Tonnerre 4 September 1729, died in Paris 26 June 1818. Pupil of Contant d'Ivry and Chevotet, whose daughter, Anne-Michel he married. Candidate for the Academy in 1770. 'Architecte du roi' in the administration of the Château de la Muette. Partner of Moreau-Desproux after 1787. Rue de la Monnaie at this period; Rue de Grenelle Saint-Honoré in 1792.

Work at the Hôtel Matignon, 57 Rue de Varenne. Château de l'Ermitage, near Condé-sur-Escaut, for the Prince de Croy, 1754–67; plan of the property engraved by Le Rouge. Tomb of the Maréchal de Belle-Isle in Notre-Dame de Vernon, 1766. Garden of the Duc de Croy, Rue du Regard. Belvedere of the Duc de Croy on the plateau of Châtillon, 1764; site of the 'Tour Biret'. Hôtel de Meulan, Rue de Clichy. Chaussard, Augeard and Dumanoir tenements, Rue Saint-Fiacre and Boulevard Poissonnière, 1776. Maison Bonhomme at Clignancourt, 1780. Parc de Sarcelles, about 1788. Theatre and dependent buildings of the Folie Sainte-James: large aviaries, open-air room, hot-house, natural history room (today chapel) – see Krafft.

Bibl.: R. Dauvergne, *Les résidences du Mal de Croy* (1718–84), Paris, 1950.

Ref.: Arch. Nat. O 1 1913 1; Z 1j 922, 1052, 1181; H 2132 1.

CHAUVEAU Rene-Bonaventure

'Expert-entrepreneur.' Rue Saint-Martin, then Rue Galande.

A CHAUVEAU was an associate of the Académie de Saint-Luc in 1775.

CHELAUNEZ Léonard
Practising in 1780.

CHÉON
Family of architects and *vérificateurs*, among whom were Pierre, and Félix who decorated the Hôtel d'Espagnac, Rue d'Anjou, in 1788.
Ref.: Arch. Nat. F 7 4673; Z 1j 1187.

CHERPITEL Mathurin
Born in Paris, Rue de Bourgogne; died in the same house, 13 November 1809. Grand Prix in 1758. Academician in 1776. Assistant professor at the Academy. Professor at the Ecole Nationale d'Architecture in the year IX.
Scheme for the Hôtel d'Uzès, 1766 (Chartrier d'Uzès). Scheme for the Palais Bourbon, 1766 (cf. *BSHAF*, 1962, p. 80). House, Rue Saint-Honoré; drawing, B.N. Est. Va 232 d. Reconstruction project for the Hôtel d'Harcourt, Rue de Lille; Musée Carnavalet. Hôtel du Châtelet, 127 Rue de Grenelle, 1770. Hôtel de Rochechouart, 110 Rue de Grenelle, 1776; engraving from Cherpitel's perspective view. Work at the Hôtel d'Andlau, Faubourg Saint-Honoré. Tenements, known as 'Hôtel des Arts', Rues du Faubourg Saint-Martin and Saint-Nicolas, 1778–81. Project for work (including portal) at the church of Saint-Barthélémy dans la Cité; B.N. Est. Va 69. Church of the Gros-Caillou, 1775–90; B.N. Est. Va 68. Hôtel Necker, Chaussée d'Antin, completed in April 1777; design for panelling in Musée Carnavalet, B.N. Est. 143 C.
Publ.: *Recueil de Trophées*, Paris, Vve Chéreau, n.d.
Bibl.: Note at the top of Cherpitel sale catalogue, January 1810.
Ref.: Arch. Nat. Z 1j 967, 988, 1015, 1047, 1074.

CHEVALIER de BEAUREGARD Jean-François
Pupil of the Academy in 1771. Rome scholar in 1772.
Main staircase and suites in the Hôtel Pimodan (Hôtel de Lauzun), 17 Quai d'Anjou, 1780. Tenements, Rue de la Ville-l'Evêque and Rue d'Astorg, 1786. Courmont house, Rue de Surène, 1789. Chevalier house at Chaillot, 1781–82, engraved by Krafft, Gaîte and Prieur.
Ref.: Arch. Nat. Z 1j 1074, 1097, 1109, 1147. Krafft.

CHEVENY de la CHAPELLE
Family of architects and landscape-architects:

CHEVENY de la CHAPELLE Joseph-Joachim
Living Boulevard de la Chaussée d'Antin in 1790. Tenements, Rue des Saussaies and de l'Ancien Marché, 1773; Rue de la Ville-l'Evêque; Rues Montmartre and Grange-Batelière; Boulevard de la Chaussée d'Antin. Hôtel d'Aligre, Rue d'Anjou.
Bibl.: *La Feuille nécessaire*, 1759. *L'Avant-coureur*, 1761, p. 589.

CHEVOTET Jean-Michel
Born in Paris 1698, died 4 December 1772. Grand Prix 1722. Academician 1732.
Library of the Pères de Nazareth (drawings, Arch. Nat. N III Seine; verso of one shows main entrance; a copy probably by Harleman (after Chevotet) in library of the Ecole des Beaux-Arts, Paris), about 1724. Maison Testard du Lys, Rue Saint-Martin, opposite the Rue aux Ours, 1740. Transformation of the Hôtel de Montigny, Rue Saint-Honoré. Châteaux of Petit-Bourg, 1754; and Champlâtreux, 1751 (plan of the park in the collection of the Duc de Noailles). Church of Epinay-Champlatreux. Chapel of the Château d'Arnouville, about 1750–55 (for the latter, see Argenville, *Voyage pittoresque*). Work at the Hôtel de Croÿ, Rue du Regard. Gardens of Belœil. Garden of the Folie Laboissière, Rue de Clichy (cf. note on Le Carpentier in the Nécrologe). Parc d'Orsay, 1755–62 (plan, Arch. Nat. Z 1j 870). Transformation of the Hôtel d'Antin, Rue Saint-Augustin; and the Pavillon de Hanovre (moved in 1933 to the Parc de Sceaux), 1757–60 (drawings of buildings and garden, B.N. Est., collection Destailleur). Several of the buildings of Jean Fauvel de Villiers were erected to the designs of Chevotet. After 1760, Chevotet's work becomes confused with that of his son-in-law, J.-B. Chaussard. E. de Ganay ('Les jardins à la française au XVIIIe siècle', in *Les jardins de France*) attributes, without reliable evidence, the gardens of Thoiry and Beaumont-sur-Vingeanne to Chevotet.
Drawings by Chevotet for *L'Architecture française* by Jean Mariette (about 1722, library of the Ecole des Beaux-Arts, Paris, and Musée Carnavalet); also for the *Description de Versailles* by Monicart and the description of the Invalides by Péreau. Design for the Palais Bourbon, 1765.
Ref.: Catalogue of the Chevotet sale, by Basan, 18 March 1772.

CHIRIEIX Gabriel
Died 28 January 1751.
Ref.: BSHP, 1916. *NAAF*, 1885, vol. XI, p. 132.

CLARET Nicolas
Mentioned in 1777.

CLAUDE (Dominican friar)
Portal of church of Saint-Thomas d'Aquin, 1735–40. Church of the Carmes-Billettes, 1754.

CLAVAREAU
Family of architects, among whom:

CLAVAREAU Nicolas-Marie
Born Paris 1756, died Arras 10 February 1816. Work at the Hôpital Saint-Louis and at the Hôtel-Dieu.

CLÉRISSEAU Charles-Louis
Born in Paris, 28 August 1721, died at Auteuil, 19 January 1820. Grand Prix, 1746. Member of the Royal Academy of Painting, 1769. Member of the Academy of Rouen 1810. Decoration of the Café de la Villa Albani, Rome. Cell for Father le Sueur, in the manner of an antique ruin, at La Trinité des Monts. Project for the Château Borély, Marseille, August 1767. Decoration of the Hôtel Bouret, Rue Grange-Batelière, before 1777. Decoration of the Hôtel de la Reynière, Rue Boissy d'Anglas, 1777; drawings in the library of Cracow, parts in the Victoria and Albert Museum. Project for a Roman villa for Catherine of Russia, 1776. Palace for the Governor of Metz, today Palais de Justice, 1776–89. Projected triumphal arch for St Petersburg.

Publ.: *Antiquités de la France*, 1778, text by Legrand, 1804.
Bibl.: Jeanne Lejeaux, 'Ch.-L. Clérisseau, architecte et peintre de ruines', in *RAAM*, 1928. Louis Réau, *BSHAF*, 1938. Th. J. McCormick, *Charles Louis Clérisseau, a bibliography*, the American Association of Architectural Bibliographers, May 1950. J. Fleming, 'The Journey to Spalato', in *Architectural Review*, 1958, vol. II. Th. J. McCormick, 'A Ruin Room by Clérisseau', in *The Connoisseur*, 1962, vol. IV. B. Lossky, *Mélanges Lavedan*, 1954. E. Croft-Murray, *Apollo*, November 1963. Th. J. McCormick, 'An unknown collection of drawings by Ch.-L. Clérisseau', in *Journal of the (American) Society of Architectural Historians*, 1963. Clérisseau Exhibition, Edinburgh, report in *Ill. London News*, 1963, vol. I, p. 237.

COCHOIS Jacques-Richard
Died 15 April 1761. Rue Sainte-Apolline.
Maison Roux, 'à la Grosse Tête', Rue Montmartre (contract approved by Maître Delafosse, 21 April 1728). Maison Aulard, at the corner of the Rues Thibaut-aux-Dés and des-Trois-Visages, 1733. Maison Claude Aubry, Rue Saint-Denis, at the north corner of the Rue Grenéta, 1732. Cochois houses, Rue Saint-Louis-en-l'Ile, 1734; Rue du Faubourg Saint-Martin, 1734; Rue du Bouloi, 1754. Hôtel Cochois, intended for rent, 47 Rue Saint-André-des-Arts, 1740. Project for the Hôtel de Marillac, Rue Sainte-Avoie, 1741. House, Rue d'Enfer, 1743. Thomas house, Place de l'Estrapade, 1740. Douet house, Rue de Gaillon, 1740. Attributions: Nourry house, 115 Rue Saint-Honoré; house at 11 Rue de la Ferronnerie (before 1739).
Ref.: Arch. Nat. Y. Z 1F 438, fol. 120; V°, fol. 461. Z 1j 622, 624, 625, 631, 635, 652, 654, 655, 708, 727, 738. Minutier, LXVI, année 1738. M. Rambaud, *Doc.* I, pp. 420, 425.
The house at 115 Rue Saint-Honoré is designed in the manner of J.-R. Cochois.

COLIGNON Louis-Marie
Died in 1794. Gentleman. Rue du Four Saint-Eustache.
Property owner, Rue de Bailleul and in Montmartre.
House in Rue d'Argenteuil, 1762. Hôtel de la Vaupalière, Faubourg Saint-Honoré and Champs-Elysées, 1768. Hôtel de Traverse, Rue Notre-Dame-des-Champs, 1776.
Ref.: Arch. Nat. Z 1j 920, 999, 1070, 1110. Z 2 2460.

COLLET Jean-Baptiste
Proposals for an opera-house in 1784 (see *VP* IX, p. 137), and for a Place Louis XVI to be built on the site of the Bastille.
May be the same as a *contrôleur* at Blois and Chambord, who worked with Soufflot on the Château de Ménars.

COLLIN Charles
Building contractor (and architect).
Maison Lebrun de Saint-Vallery, Rue des Boulangers, 1730. Maison Gerblot, Rue Jean-Robert (des Gravilliers), 1740.
Ref.: Arch. Nat. Z 1j 611.

COLLOMBAT
Architect-decorator, author of a series of drawings pre-served at the Ecole des Beaux-Arts, among them a design for an alcove for the Président de Veyset.

COLSON F.-G.
Director of Buildings to the Duc de Bouillon.

COLSON J.-J.
Born 1749.

CONTANT D'IVRY Pierre
Born at Ivry 1698, died in Paris 1 October 1777. Academician 1728. Hôtel de Gouvernet, Rue du Coq Héron (contract approved by Maître Tannevot, 21 June 1725). Transformation of the Hôtel de Maurepas, 75 Rue de Grenelle, 1730. Hôtel Blondel de Gagny, Rue d'Anjou (ceiling engraved for *L'Architecture* by Daviler, publ. Mariette-Blondel, 1738). Choiseul-Gouffier tenements, Rues Pagevin and des Vieux-Augustins (Etienne Marcel and Hérold), 1737; project, Arch. Nat. T 153 23. Stables of the Château de Bissy, near Vernon, for the Marquis de Belle-Ile, 1741–42. Maison Bunnétat, Rue des Mathurins, near the Hôtel de Cluny, completed in 1746. Work at the Hôtel de Soubise. Belvedere in the Parc de Saint-Cloud. Château de Garges (see B.N. Est. Va 346, V). Transformation of the Hôtel Crozat de Tugny, 17 Place Vendôme (part of Hôtel Ritz) (contract and plans approved by Maître Du Tartre, 21 May 1744; plaster model of staircase; wrought-iron balustrade by Brochois). Transformation of the Hôtel Crozat de Thiers, Place Vendôme (headquarters of Crédit Foncier), 1744–47; projects, Arch. Nat. T 188 1; general plan, Z 1j 798; drawings in a Dutch collection. Abbaye de Panthemont, 108 Rue de Grenelle (today a Protestant church and Ministry of Ex-Servicemen), 1747–56. Grand Bureau des Tabacs, Rue Saint-Nicaise, 1750. Château and gardens of Arnouville-lez-Gonesse (see notes on Chevotet). Abbaye Saint-Vaast d'Arras monastic buildings and church (today cathedral), after 1754. Transformation of the Hôtel Blouin, 31 Faubourg Saint-Honoré, for M. Michel, about 1754. Church of Saint-Vannon de Condé-sur-Escaut (drawing by Taraval, after Contant, J. Wilhelm collection). Design for portal for Saint-Eustache (John Harris collection, London). Hôtel 'du gouvernement', Lille. Transformation of the Palais-Royal, 1756–70: hall, staircase of honour, Valois wing; schemes of decoration and furnishing published in *L'Encyclopédie*. Work at Saint-Cloud, 1762. Scheme for the Madeleine, 1764; abandoned in 1777 (drawings, Arch. Nat. N III, Seine 100. Soapstone model by Mérault in the Musée Carnavalet.
Publ.: *Œuvres d'architecture*, 1758 and 1765.
Bibl.: Lunsing-Scheurler, in *BSHAF*, 1920. M. Petzet, *Soufflots Sainte-Geneviève und der französische Kirchenbau des XVIII. Jahrhunderts*, 1961, pp. 91, 122 and *passim*. Robin Middleton, in *Journal of the Warburg and Courtauld Institutes*. M. Gallet, in *Bulletin du Musée Carnavalet*, 1965. J.-P. Babelon in *Revue de l'Art*, 1970.

CONVERS
Family of architects:

CONVERS Pierre

Architect to the Princesse de Conti.

Chapel and conventual buildings of the ladies of Saint-Chaumont, Faubourg Saint-Denis, 1782; watercolour in the Musée Carnavalet; engravings by Gaite, le Campion and Guyot.

CONVERS Claude-Pierre

Appears in the *Almanach des artistes* of 1776.

Church of Saint-Louis-du-Louvre, to the designs of Thomas Germain. Hôtel de Bérulle, 15 Rue de Grenelle, 1774. Houses in the Quartier Saint-Sulpice.

Ref.: VP, 13 January 1906, p. 16. Arch. Nat. Minutier, XCI, 1107. Z 1F 494, fol. 10 – building authorisation for the main entrance of the Hôtel de Bérulle, 1774.

CORBEILLER

Mentioned in 1785.

COTTE Robert de

Born in Paris 1656, died 15 July 1735.
'Premier architecte du Roi', 1708.

Houses by Robert de Cotte, 366–370 Rue Saint-Honoré, 1719; Rue de Lille, Rue du Bac and Quai d'Orsay, 1723, 1726. House, 82 Rue Neuve-des-Petits-Champs. Hôtels de Lude, Rue Saint-Dominique; Legendre d'Armini, Rue des Capucines (transformed by Rousset for the Meulan family in 1745); de Bourbon, Rue Neuve-des-Petits-Champs; Le Juge, Rue des Archives; de Bonrepos, Rue de Grenelle; d'Estrées, 78 Rue de Grenelle, 1713 (Embassy of the USSR); de Conti, Rue de Lille (adapted after 1719 for the Duchess du Maine by A.-C. Mollet). Transformation of the Hotel de la Vrillière (Banque de France), 1713–19. Abbaye de Saint-Denis, after 1700 (Maison de la Légion d'Honneur). Chapel of the Abbaye aux Bois. Chapelle des Chartreux. Main entrance of the Charité, 1732. Chapel of the Virgin, Notre-Dame-de-Passy. Portal of Saint-Roch, built after 1719 by J.-R. de Cotte. Water-tower of the Palais-Royal, 1719. Building of the Samaritaine, 1711–15. Royal library, Rue de Richelieu; wing of the Department of Manuscripts, and left wing of the court of honour (reconstructed at the end of the nineteenth century by J.-L. Pascal).

Place Bellecour, Hôtel des Concerts and public granaries in Lyon. Work at the Châteaux de Thouars and de Chantelou. Hôtel de Grammont, Besançon. Bishop's palace, Châlons-sur-Marne. Bishop's palace, Verdun, 1724–54. Hôtel du Grand-Doyen and Palais Rohan, Strasbourg, 1731–41. Ancien Château de Saverne. Churches of la Toussaint at Rennes, Saint-Jean and Saint-Etienne at Dijon, Saint-Charles at Sedan, and Saint-Alpin at Châlons-sur-Marne. Saint Sever barracks, Rouen. Tomb of Henri de Lorraine, Comte d'Harcourt at Royaumont (engraved). Hôtel Thurn-und-Taxis, Frankfurt-am-Main. Designs for Schlösser at Bonn, Poppelsdorf, Schleissheim, and Seelovitz (Moravia); the Vénerie in Turin, and for the Furies in the royal palace in Madrid.

Bibl.: Pierre-Marcel Lévi, *Inventaire des papiers de Robert de Cotte*, 1906. Jeanne Lejeaux, 'Robert de Cotte et la direction de l'Académie d'Architecture', in *BSHAF*, 1927.

Fiske Kimball, *Le style Louis XV*, 1950. L.H. vol. III, 1950. Bertrand Jestaz, *Le voyage d'Italie de R. de Cotte*, 1966. Daniel Ludmann, *Projets de R. de Cotte pour le palais épiscopal de Strasbourg*, *BSHAF*, 1968.

COUPART DE LA TOUCHE

Died about 1780. 'Expert-entrepreneur' from 1756. Rue Saint-Pierre, Montmartre, in 1760; Rue Notre-Dame-des-Victoires in 1773. Not the same as M. de la Touche, designer of the *grande galerie* of the Château de la Grange-du-Milieu, begun for the Maréchal de Saxe, completed for M. Raymond, about 1758.

Bibl.: D'Argenville, *Voyage . . .*, and *Feuille nécessaire*, 1759, p. 10.

COURTONNE
Family of architects:

COURTONNE Jean

1671–1739. Academician, 1728. Professor, 1730.

Additional floor to the Hôtel de Sillery, Quai Malaquais, 1712. Extension of the Hôtel de Vendôme, Rue d'Enfer (Ecole des Mines), 1715; see notes on Le Blond. Hôtel de Montmorency, later Matignon, 57 Rue de Varenne, begun 1721, completed 1723, under the direction of Mazin. Hôtel de Noirmoutier, 138–140 Rue de Grenelle, 1722.

Publ.: *Traité de perspective, avec des remarques sur l'architecture, suivi de quelques édifices considérables mis en perspective par l'auteur*, 1725.

COURTONNE Jean-Baptiste

Accessit, 1738. Architecte du Prince de Conti.

Work at the Hôtel du Temple and at l'Ile-Adam. Main entrance-doors of the Hôtel du Tillet, 31 Rue des Francs-Bourgeois, 1740. Château de Villarceaux, 1758.

A third COURTONNE was also a pupil of the Académie Royale.

Bibl.: L. H. Labande, 'L'Hôtel de Matignon à Paris', in *GBA*, 1935. Fontegrive (René de La Coste-Messelière), Un architecte parisien au XVIIIe siècle, in *L'architecte des collectivités publiques*, 1959 (unpublished notes on the decoration of the Hôtel Matignon). M. Rambaud, *Doc.* I.

COUSTILLIER Pierre-Gilles

Pupil of the Academy 1730–31. Draughtsman, 'garde-des-plans des bâtiments du roi'.

Maison Coustillier, Rue Daguesseau, 1753. Maison Pinard, Faubourg Saint-Martin, 1755.

Ref.: Arch. Nat. Z 1F 460. Z 1j 820 (drawing).

COUSTOU Charles-Pierre

Born in Paris 28 January 1721, died 22 January 1797. Son of the sculptor Guillaume (Ier) Coustou. Rome Scholar. Academician 1762. Side-altars of Saint-Roch. Work at the Château de la Muette.

COUTOULY Victor

2e Prix de Rome, 1773. Inspector of buildings to the Comte d'Artois.

COUTURE the Elder, Joseph-Abel
Contrôleur of the royal estates. Treasurer of the Sèvres factory. Rue de Savoie, 1777–90.
Tenements for the Dames Sainte-Elisabeth, Rue du Temple, 1776; engraving in the *Revue générale de l'architecture de César Daly*, 25e année, 1874; 4th series, vol. I, pl. 53 (vol. XXXI of the general collection). Neo-gothic design for the staircase of the Sainte-Chapelle – Musée Carnavalet.
Publ.: *Recueil de vases analogues aux cinq ordres d'architecture.*

COUTURE the Younger, Guillaume-Martin
Born at Rouen 1732, died 27 December 1799. Pupil of Le Carpentier. Academician 1773.
Hôtels de Saxe, Faubourg Saint-Honoré, and de Coislin, Place Louis XV. Pavillon de Coislin, Bellevue. Maison de M. Lenormand. Extensions to the pavilion of La Boissière, Clichy (according to the *Almanach Dauphin*, 1774). Roodloft of Rouen cathedral, 1773–77. Reconstruction scheme for the Palais de Justice de Paris, 1776: prisoners' gallery and court record offices, 1778. Work at the Madeleine, 1777–90. Reconstruction scheme for the Hôtel de Ville, Saint-Omer, 1786. Caen barracks, 1786–89.
Ref.: 'Notes on Couture le Jeune' by Soreau, in the *Magasin encyclopédique Millin*, 6e 1800, vol. III, pp. 505–11.

CRESSOT Denis-Edme-Antoine
Rue des Tournelles. Practising in 1790.
Works for the Marquis de Croissanville, 1790.

CUDEVILLE
Family of building contractors and architects:

CUDEVILLE Nicolas-François

CUDEVILLE Michel-Etienne
Maisons Michault, Rue Git-le-Cœur, 1717; Gaudart, Rue Vieille-du-Temple; Moulon, Rue de Bucy, 1730; Doremus, Rue du Mail. Bureau des Lingères, 1734 (the door has been re-erected in the Square des Innocents). Work for the Marquis de Marsay, Rue Michelle-Comte, 1731. House, Carrefour Saint-Benoît, 1729. N.-F. and M.-E. Cudeville often built to the plans of J. Mansart de Jouy.

Ref.: Arch. Nat. Z 1j 621, 651, 685, 700.

DAILLY Victor-Thierry
Collabeau house, Rue de Cléry, 1718. Dailly house, Rue Meslay, 1722. Buildings in the precinct of Saint-Germain-des-Prés, 1716: portal, commercial buildings and dwellings in the Rue Childebert; fountain, rebuilt in the Square Monge (see Banister Fletcher, *A History of Architecture on the Comparative Method*, 17th edition, 1961, p. 804 J, and original design in Mireille Rambaud, *Documents du Minutier central des notaires . . .* 1964, vol. I, pl. IV). First project for the Cour du Dragon, 50 Rue de Rennes, 1725. Buildings for the Carmelites of the Rue de Vaugirard. Grand Hôtel de Verrue, 37 Rue du Cherche-Midi, designed in 1719, built in 1735; main entrance re-erected in the Parc de Jeurre. Petit Hôtel de Verrue, 1 Rue du Regard. Hôtel du Gué, 3 Rue du Regard, demolished in 1907; staircase

balustrade in Musée Carnavalet. Hôtels de Rottenbourg and de Beaune, 5 and 7 Rue du Regard. Building for rental of the Prieuré Saint-Martin-des-Champs 1729. Hôtels Le Lièvre de la Grange, 4 and 6 Rue de Braque (contract approved by Maître Guérin, 7 May 1731; sculptures by Michel de Lissy and Jean Bourguignon; panelling of the *grand salon* reassembled in the Château de Nerville). Work at the Hôtel Crozat de Tugny (Hôtel Ritz) and at the Hôtel Crozat de Thiers (Crédit Foncier), 17 and 19 Place Vendôme; for Mme Le Gendre, Place des Victoires, 1728; and for Jacques de la Vallette at la Planche, near Bercy, 1740. Work at Saint-Bénigne Abbey, Dijon.
Ref.: Arch. Nat. E 1158 B (the copies of Dailly's designs are the work of Brice Le Chauve); S 3730; N III, Seine 69, 285, 464, 300, 302. Z 1F 433, fol. 26, V°; Z 1j 533, 539, 601, 602, 641, 646, 654, 655, 688, 689.
Bibl.: Pigagnol, *Description de Paris*, édit. de 1742, vol. VII, p. 87, inscription commémorative de la Rue Childebert par Dom Mabillon (Victore Theodorico d'Ailly, totius operis architecto, anno Domini MDCCXV, die 11 mensis Aprilis). Catalogue of the Salon of 1738, No. 123. Gaston Schéfer, 'L'Hôtel des conseils de guerre', in *VP*, 1907. J.-P. Derel in *BSHAF*, 1956, pp. 151–65. Hélène Verlet and R.-A. Weigert, in *MFSHP*, 1958, p. 34 and pl. XVII. Monique Hébert, *L'Hôtel de Beaune*, preface by L. Hautecœur, 1958. M. Rambaud, *Documents du Minutier . . . loc. cit.* M. Gallet, in *GBA*, March 1966.

DAMESME Emmanuel-Aimé
Born at Magny-en-Vexin 1767, died Paris 1822.
Maison Leduc, Rue Montparnasse, 1788. Château de Sillery (S. & O.). Houses, Rue Richer, 1795. Theatre of the Société Olympique, Rue Chantereine. Gardens of the Duchesse de Raguse at Viry-Chatillon. Theatre and prison, Brussels, 1817–19.

DAMOIS
Carpentier tenements, Rue de l'Université, near the Palais Bourbon, 1779.
Ref.: Arch. Nat. Z 1j 1050.

DAMUN Jean
Son-in-law of Jean-François Blondel. 'Contrôleur des magasins de la Ville.' Candidate for the Academy, 1756 and 1758. Rue Pastourelle in 1775.
Decorative settings for the city's festivities; fireworks for the second marriage of the Dauphin, engraved by J.-F. Blondel. Stage sets for the Prince de Conti at l'Ile-Adam. Design for the Théâtre Français (wrongly attributed to Damesme). Maison Mathieu, Rue Bergère, 1756–57. Maison Salles, same street. Hôtel de Beaupréau, Rue Croix-des-Petits-Champs (contract approved by Maître Matha, 19 July 1757).
Publ.: *Nouveau théâtre tracé sur les principes des Grecs et des Romains*, 1772; prospectus analysed in Patte, *Essai sur l'architecture théâtrale.*

DANJAN
Family of architects:

DANJAN Pierre-Paul
'Expert-bourgeois' from 1738.

DANJAN Pierre-Alexandre
'Expert-bourgeois' from 1751. Rue du Fouarre.
Priory of Longjumeau, 1762. Hôtel de la Trémoille, Rue Sainte-Avoye, 1745–47. Library of the Abbaye Saint-Victor, about 1780.
A Pierre-Victor Danjan, who may not be the same as Pierre-Alexandre, was imprisoned in the Bastille, with his servant, for Jansenism.

DARNAUDIN Charles-François
Born Versailles 1741, died Versailles 1805. Grand Prix 1763. 'Inspecteur des Bâtiments du Roi', 1778. Academician 1791.
Civic hospital of Versailles, 1775–89. Garde-meubles, 1780–83. Hôtel de Séran, Versailles, 1787. Church of Ville d'Avray; project, Arch. Nat. Z 10 221. Restoration of the Bassin de Neptune.
Bibl.: A. Louvet, *L'Architecture*, June 1935, p. 17.

DAUBANTON
Pupil of the Academy 1755–58. Mentioned in the *Almanach historique*, 1776. Architect and engraver of architecture. Collaborated in the 'cours de Blondel', and in its continuation by Patte.

DAUFRESNE
Family of architects:

DAUFRESNE Antoine
Died 1731.
Daufresne house, Rue Sainte-Apolline, 1713–26.

DAUFRESNE Gilles
Maison Diot, Rue des Gravilliers, 1735. Maison d'Héricourt, Rue au Maire, 1753.

Ref.: Arch. Nat. Z 1j 583, 664, 807. H 2127.

DAUPHIN Antoine-Nicolas
'Expert-bourgeois' from 1740. Rue de la Montagne Sainte-Geneviève in 1748.
Maison Boucher d'Orceval, Rue de l'Arbre Sec, 1744.
Ref.: Arch. Nat. Z 1j 745.

DAUVERGNE
'Expert-bourgeois' from 1790 to 1792. Rue des Sept-Voies, at the Collège de Reims in 1789.

DAVID
'Expert-entrepreneur' in 1715. Rue Neuve-Saint-Roch.

DAVILER Claude-Louis
Died 14 September 1764. Grand Prix 1730. Quai Bourbon in 1764.
Work at Auxerre: abbeys of Saint-Julien and Saint-Martin, bishop's palace. At Sens: abbeys of Saint-Pierre-le-Vif and Sainte-Colombe, general hospital, archbishop's palace, chapels in the chancel of the cathedral. At Langres: seminary, portal and towers of the cathedral. Châteaux de Noslon, de Ragennes and de Talmay. Abbaye de Molosme.

Churches of Moulins, near Noyers; and Andryès; of les Sièges, Vermenton and Bellechaume. Simonnet tenements, 27 Rue Saint-André-des-Arts, 1748 (Arch. Nat. Z 1F 451, fol. 94v. Daviler lived in this house in 1758–60: cf. 'Eaux et Forêts', in *Almanach Royal*, 1759, p. 242). Daviler probably built the house of the English Benedictines (today Schola cantorum), 269 Rue Saint-Jacques.
Bibl.: Jules Guiffrey, *Scellés et inventaires d'artistes*, 1885, vol. II, pp. 335–37. Bauchal, *Dictionnaire des architectes français*, 1887, p. 154. L. Hautecœur, *L'Architecture en Bourgogne*.

DEBAY Louis-François
'Expert-entrepreneur.' Rue de la Chaise.

DEBIAS-AUBRY François
'Expert-bourgeois.'
Hôtel du Président Duret, Rue Sainte-Dominique (ministère de la Guerre), 1714–20. (?) Hospital of Chaumes-en-Brie, 1719. Hôtel Desmares, 78 Rue de Varenne (ministère de l'Agriculture), 1720–24. Hôtel de Thianges, Rue Taranne, 1729. Hôtel Durey d'Armancourt, Rue de Vendôme. Hôtel Turgot, Rue Portefoin, 1733–35. Maison Desboullets, Rue Saint-Honoré and Rue de la Tonnellerie, 1727. Houses: Aubry, Rue Saint-Martin and de Venise, 1729; Aubry, Rue Saint-Victor and des Fossés Saint-Victor, 1729; Marois, Rues de Turenne and du Parc-Royal (Saint-Louis and Saint-François); Maison Delorne, Porte Saint-Denis; project, Arch. Nat. H 2138 (2), 1731. Cotelle, Rue Saint-André-des-Arts and des Grands-Augustins, 1739. Hotel Thoynard de Vougy, 5 Rue du Coq-Héron (Caisse d'Epargne), 1735. Grand Hôtel de Bouillon, 17 Quai Malaquais (on the foundations of a building by François Mansart – today Ecole des Beaux-Arts), 1740. Enlargement of the Hôtel de Gouvernet, Rue du Coq-Héron, 1742. Petit Hôtel de Bouillon, Quai Malaquais, 1745. Fontaine d'Arnouville. Attributions: Hôtel de Gesvres, 27 Rue-des-Petits-Champs (destroyed); house, 11 Rue Daguesseau (destroyed); and façade of 16 Rue Saint-Sauveur. No. 9 Rue de Montmorency may also be his.
Ref.: Archives de la Seine, DE 1. Arch. Nat. Z 1F 427, Y 9505, Z 1j 567, 568, 569, 570, 587, 595, 597, 604, 623, 628, 631, 645, 647, 650, 651, 655, 672, 674, 675, 678, 682, 693, 700, 723, 753, 801, etc. . . . Catalogue of the Aubry sale, by Basan, 9 February 1773.

DEBESSE Claude-Guillaume
'Expert.' Rue du Chantre in 1773.
Bibl.: Mémoires de Georges Wille, *passim*.

DE BOURGE
Family of architects:

DE BOURGE Antoine-Joseph
Grand Prix in 1761. Academician 1785.

DE COURTILLER
3e Prix 1731.
An architect of this name was working on improvements to the Parc de Cassan, near l'Isle-Adam, about 1775: Pavillon chinois.
Bibl.: Ganay, *GBA*, May–June 1955.

DELACROIX Pierre-Philémon
'Expert-entrepreneur' in 1727. Lived near the Porte Saint-Denis.

DELAFAYE
Practising in 1776. Rue Montmartre.
Ref.: Arch. Nat. Z ij 1006.

DELAFOND Pierre
Pupil of the Academy 1726–35. Practising in 1748.
Ref.: PVARA, EJ.

DELAFOSSE Jean-Charles
Born in Paris 1734, died in Paris 1791. Sculptor, pupil of J.-B. Poulet; architect and ornamentalist-engraver. Professor at the Académie de Saint-Luc, and at the Académie de Bordeaux.
Proposed abattoir on the Ile des Cygnes. Hôtel Delbarre, later Titon, 58 Faubourg Poissonnière, 1776–83. Hôtel Delbarre, later Goix, 60 Faubourg Poissonnière, same dates. Houses at Pantin, and in Paris, Rue Saint-Apolline, 1780. Barracks of Bonne-Nouvelle and of the Halle à la Marée, 1790.
Publ.: Nouvelle iconologie historique, Paris, 1768, republished by Daumont, Paris, n.d., and Guérinet, Paris, n.d. Dutch version by Jan de Witt Jansz (*Algemeen Kunstenaars Handboek . . . goinvonteerd . . . dor J. Ch. de la Fosse*, Amsterdam, n.d.). *Traité des cinq ordres*, n.d.
Bibl.: Prévost de Saint-Lucien, 'Quartier du Louvre', in *Le Provincial*, 1787, p. 93. Geneviève Levallet-Hang, *GBA*, 1927. Emil Kaufmann, *Architecture in the Age of Reason*, 1955, pp. 154–59. M. Gallet, *GBA*, March 1963.

DELAGAISSE
Sometime pupil of the Academy, practising in 1781.

DELAMAIR
Family of architects:

DELAMAIR Antoine
Died before 1719.

DELAMAIR Pierre-Alexis
1676–1745.
Houses: Brayer, Rue de Grenelle Saint-Honoré (before 1713); Copin, Rue Montmartre; Boulle de Chomot, Quai des Théatins. Works in connection with Delamair houses, Rues Montorgueil, Saint-Honoré, de la Sourdière, Montmartre, Saint-Benoît, de Harlay and Sainte-Avoye.
Hôtels de Cominges; de Pompadour, 142 Rue de Grenelle; de Rohan-Soubise, 60 Rue des Francs-Bourgeois; and de Rohan-Strasbourg, 87 Rue Vieille-du-Temple, 1704–9.
Châteaux de Buzancy in Soissonnais, de Mirebeau in Comté, de Maisonneuve in Brie, du Plessis-Neuchel in Gâtinais, de Bruel in Sologne and de Fontaine-le-Comte in Picardie. Projects for the Châteaux de Dangeau in Beauce, Cherperine in Maine and Manne in Provence (plan of the park in Munich library). General proposals for improvements to Paris.

Ref.: Arch. Nat. Y 10 975. Z ij 472, 733.
Bibl.: Ch.-V. Langlois, *Les anciens hôtels de Clisson, de Guise et de Rohan-Soubise au Marais*, 1922. J.-P. Babelon, *Historique et description . . .*
Delamair manuscripts and drawings: Arsenal, Nos. 2.912 and 3.054; Munich, 540.

DELAMOTTE
Died March 1731. 'Intendant des Bâtiments du Roi.'

DELAPOISE
Concerned with the demolition of the Bastille.
Maison Lepaute, Rue Saint-Thomas du Louvre, 1787.

DELARBRE Louis
Living Rue Montholon in 1792. Architect and building contractor; erected several buildings for Ledoux (including Maison Hosten) and imitated the master's style in his own works.
Tenements, Rue de Marivaux, west side, near the corner of the Rue Grétry, 1782. Tenements, 10 and 12 Rue de l'Odéon, 9 and 11 Rue de Condé, 1790.

DELARUE Jean-Baptiste
Died 1743. Academician 1723.

DELCOURT Nicolas-François
'Expert' in 1750.
Maison Bouillerot, Rue du Colombier (Jacob), 1748.
Ref.: Arch. Nat. Z ij 768.

DELESPINE
Family of architects:

DELESPINE Pierre-Nicolas
1661–1719
Houses: Rue Galande; Rue de la Mortellerie; 50, 90 and 92 Rue de Richelieu (disappeared); 21 and 23 Rue Saint-Marc; Rue Montmartre; Rue Saint-Honoré.

DELESPINE Nicolas (II)
'Doyen des experts' in 1704. Academician 1724.
Maison Claude Le Bas de Montargis, Rue Neuve-des-Petits-Champs, 1715. Houses: Rue Sainte-Anne, Rue de Cléry, Rue Thérèse. Chapelle des Enfants-Trouvés.
Ref.: Arch. Nat. Z ij 531, 536, 572, 578.
Bibl.: Mireille Rambaud, 'Une famille d'architectes: les Delespine', in *BSHAF*, 1968.

DELESPINE Louis-Jules
Pupil of Jossenay in 1745. 'Expert-bourgeois.' Died 1796.
Chapelle des Bénédictines du Saint-Sacrement, Rue de Turenne, about 1780; drawings: Arch. Nat. S 4757. H 4143–6. N III, Seine 459.

DELONDRES François
Architect in charge of the demolition of the royal Château de Clagny, 1769.
Hôtel de la Bélinaye, Rue de la Ville-l'Evêque. Tenements Omer Talon, 42 Faubourg Saint-Honoré.
Ref.: Arch. de Seine-et-Oise, A 72. Thierry, Watin.

DELVINCOURT
'Expert-bourgeois' from 1739. Rue des Fossés-Monsieur-le-Prince in 1759.
Works for the Comte de Vienne in 1743.

DERVILLE Louis-Henri
Died before 5 August 1757. 'Inspecteur des Bâtiments du Roi.'

DESAMSON Pierre-Antoine
House, Rue de Verdelet, 1752.
Ref.: Arch. Nat. Z 1j 806–26.

DESARNOD Joseph-François
Architect from Lyon. Inventor of a heating system. Appears to have settled in Paris about 1790.
Tenements, Rigod de Terrebasse, Lyon. Chapter-house of Largentière. Works at Salles-en-Beaujolais.
Publ.: *Mémoires sur les foyers économiques et salubres*, Paris, 1789.

DESBEUFS De ST-LAURENT Laurent
Pupil of the Academy, debarred in 1765, recommended by the *Almanach des artistes* of 1776 as architect of 'petites maisons de plaisance' and of gardens. Opponent of Soufflot. Opposition scheme for the church of Sainte-Geneviève, engraved by Moreau in 1767. Altar decoration of the church of Saint-Louis (formerly des Jésuites), given to the priory of the Val des Ecoliers, 1771. Work for the Chevalier des Bordes, 1775.
Publ.: *3ᵉ cahier de pièces de serrurie*, 1765.
Ref.: Arch. Nat. Z 1j 940, 1003.

DESBŒUFS
Family of architects:

DESBŒUFS Henri-Quentin
Pupil of the Academy 1728. 'Expert-bourgeois', 1732. Rue Sainte-Croix-de-la-Bretonnerie in 1759.
Maison Bonin, 19 Rue Sainte-Croix-de-la-Bretonnerie (contract approved, 1734). Ecole d'Auxonne, 1734. Maison Moreau de Saint-Just, Rue de la Monnaie, 1746. Work for the Abbé de Hacqueville at le Mont-Saint-Hilaire. Desbœufs house, Rue Saint-Martin. Tartarin house, Rue de la Harpe, opposite the Rue Serpente, 1750. The Dalençon-Dorville house, 70 Rue des Gravilliers, was reconstructed after a *devis judiciaire* drawn up by H.-Q. D., 10 April 1737. Maison Pouget, Rues de la Grande-Truanderie and Mondétour, 1775. Maison Morin, Rue de la Chanvrerie, 1736.
Ref.: Arch. Nat. Z 1j 627, 658, 659, 668, 693, 755, 762, 776, 1005.

DESCOUTURES
Quantity surveyor, employed by the architect C.-E. Briseux.
Publ.: *L'Architecture pratique*, 1762.

DESENNE Michel
Died 16 February 1742. 'Intendant des Bâtiments du Prince de Condé.'

DESGODETZ Antoine
Born in Paris 1653, died Paris 20 May 1728. Rome scholar 1674. Prisoner of the Barbary pirates, 1674–76. 'Contrôleur des Bâtiments du Roi' at Chambord, 1680. Academician 1694. Professor at the Academy in 1719.
Works for the Collège de Beauvais, 1717–26. Maison Belhomme and Duval, Rue and Porte Montmartre, 1717. Houses in the precinct of Saint-Germain-l'Auxerrois, 1712, 1724. Work for Mme Lombard d'Ermenonville, Rue Bourg-l'Abbé, 1722. House in the precinct of the Val-de-Grâce, 1724.
Publ.: *Les édifices antiques de Rome*, 1682 (2 édition, 1779); London edition, 1771–75; Rome edition, 1822.
Bibl.: Lunsing-Scheurler, 'Sur le Traité de la Commodité de l'Architecture, connu par les notes de Jean Pinard, élève de Desgodetz', in *Mélanges Ozinga*.
Ref.: Arch. Nat. Z 1j 522, 530, 555. M. Rambaud, *Doc.* 1, pp. 464, 466.

DESGOTS Claude
Died 1732. Landscape architect, nephew of Le Nôtre.
Châteaux de Perrigny in Burgundy, and de Sablé (Maine), built in 1712–15, for Colbert de Torcy. Staircase at Anet. Gardens of the Palais-Royal, of Bagnolet, of Saint-Maur.
Publ.: *Abrégé de la vie d'André Le Nôtre*, 1759.
Bibl.: Runar Strandberg, 'Claude Desgots und sein Projekt für den Garten in Schleissheim', in *Münchener Jahrbuch der bildenen Kunst*, 1964.

DESJARDINS
'Expert-bourgeois' from 1782 to 1792. Living Rue Vieille-du-Temple, near the Rue du Roi de Sicile, 1792.

DESMAISONS
Family of architects:

DESMAISONS André

DESMAISONS Nicolas
Maison Pinson, Rue de Cléry. Hôtel de Charny, Rue des Barrées, 1720. Maison Gabriel Allegrain, Rue Meslay, 1723. Work at the Hôtel de Matignon, 57 Rue de Varenne. Maison du Noble Artisan, Rues de la Lune and Sainte-Barbe, 1733. Three houses, Cul-de-sac du Crucifix and Rue Montorgueil, 1738.

DESMAISONS Jean-Nicolas

DESMAISONS Robert
Practising in 1733.

DESMAISONS DE JOUY Jean-François
'Expert-entrepreneur' in 1752.
Houses: Hébert, Rues de Seine and de Bucy; Marguerite Roullier, Rues de Sèvres and du Bac; Desmaisons, Rue de Jouy.

DESMAISONS Pierre
Born in Paris in 1711, died Palaiseau 1795. Academician 1762.
Hôtel de Jaucourt, 1 Rue de la Vrillière, 1733. Buildings for the Théatins: entrance on the Quai Malaquais, 1747; court, 26 Rue de Lille, 1754 (engraved by de la Marquade).

Buildings for the Grands Augustins, about 1740. Buildings of the Saint-Honoré chapter, Rue des Petits-Champs (site of the Banque de France), about 1745. Desmaisons house, Rues de Lille and de Verneuil, 1760. Tenements at 1 Rue des Bons-Enfants, 1755. Montholon tenements, 58 Rue Dauphine, 1771. Choppin-d'Arnouville tenements, 61 Rue Dauphine, 1769. Staircase and salons of the Archbishop's palace, 1772. Hôtel Lepaige de Quincy, Rue Sainte-Apolline, 1772. Three tenements in the precinct of Saint-Denis de l'Estrée, Saint-Denis, 1780. Tenements, Cul-de-sac Dauphin (engraved in the 'Cours de Blondel'). Work at the Château de Conflans, 1776–78. Cour du Mai at the Palais de Justice. Gallery '*mercière*' and vestries of the Sainte-Chapelle, 1776–85. Prison de la Petite Force, Rue Pavée du Marais, 1786–91. Place du Palais de Justice, 1788–90. Passage between the Louvre and Saint-Germain-l'Auxerrois, 1789. Work at the prisons of the Abbaye and Sainte-Pélagie, at the Courneuve and at Moisselles.
Ref.: Arch. Nat. Z 1j 964, 985, 1029, 1058, 1090. Z 1F 449.
Bibl.: Hébert, *Dictionnaire pittoresque*. Roze de Chantoiseau, Essai *d'indication pour 1790* (maisons de Jaucourt et Montholon). M. Gallet, L'Œuvre de P. Desmaisons', in *BSHAF*, 1959.

DESMARETS
Grand Prix 1728. 'Architecte du Roi.'
Works in developing the Parc-aux-Cerfs, Versailles, 1740. Work at the Hôtel de Rivié. Desmarets house, Rue Princesse, 1758. Maisons Doria, Rue des Bourdonnais, 1748
May not be the same as the DESMARAIS or BOUCHER-DESMARAIS, who built the Hôtel d'Avejan, Rue Saint-Thomas-du-Louvre, 1743.
Ref.: Arch. Nat. Z 1F 468. Z 1j 629, 698. Bauchal, *Dictionnaire des architectes*. M. Rambaud, *Doc.* 1, p. 407.

DESTOUCHES Laurent
'Huissier de la Chambre' and 'Contrôleur des Bâtiments du Roi'. 'Maître des Bâtiments de la Ville' 1751.
'Maître des Bâtiments de la Ville 1751.'
Hôtel de Surbeck, Rue du Doyenné. Hôtel de Novion, Rue des Bons-Enfants (contract approved by Maître Hachette, June 1741). Alterations to the Hôtel d'Armenonville for the postal administration (Rues Platrière) Verdelet and Coq-Héron, 1755.
Ref.: Bachaumont, Manuscrit 4044 de l'Arsenal, fol. 121.

DEVAL
Hôtel de l'Abbé de la Villéon, at the east corner of the Rue de Grammont and the boulevard, 1768–69.
Ref.: Arch. Nat. Z 1j 927.

DEVARENNE Claude-Etienne
'Expert-entrepreneur' from 1737.
Architect of the Saint-Gervais manufactory, and the Harmant house, Quai de Grève and Rue Pernelle, 1741.

DEVILLERS Eustache-Robert
Martin tenements, Rue du Pont-aux-Choux and 113 Boulevard Beaumarchais, 1775.

DEVILLIERS de MAISONROUGE Joseph
Pupil of the Academy in 1746.
Work for the Marquis de Livry at the Château de Bénouville (Calvados), 1774. Projected hôtel in the Rue Saint-Dominique, abutting on to the Abbaye de Panthémont, for the Marquise de la Rivière, 1780–82.
Ref.: Arch. Nat. Z 1j 1057, 1096.

DEVOUGES Michel
'Expert-entrepreneur' from 1752. Living Rue Sainte-Avoye, at the corner of the Rue du Plâtre, in 1760.
Tenements at the corner of the Place Maubert and the Rue des Lavandières, 1767.

DE WAILLY Charles
Born in Paris 9 November 1730, died 2 November 1798. Pupil of Blondel and Lejeay. Grand Prix 1752. Member of the Academy of Architecture in 1767, and of the Academy of Painting in 1771.
Proposed portal for the Abbaye-aux-Bois, 1761. Design for a table decorated in bronze and lapis lazuli, mentioned in 1761. Chapelle du Reposoir at Versailles, Rue Hoche, engraved by Leprince. Work at Saint-Bénigne, Dijon, 1763. Decoration of the Palazzo Serra, Via Garibaldi, Genoa; designs in the *Bibliothèque des arts décoratifs*, Paris, and engravings in the *Encyclopédie de Diderot*, 1772–73. Work at Saint-Sulpice: decoration of the chapel of the Virgin, squinch over the Rue Garancière (1774), pulpit (1789); designs in the library of the Cooper Union, New York. Château de Montmusard, near Dijon; painting by Lallemand (Dijon museum), and engraving by Krafft based on proposals only partly carried out. Château des Ormes, near Chatellerault: *corps de logis* and circular balcony, known from a painting belonging to M. le Marquis d'Argenson (before 1774). Alterations to the Hôtel de Villette, 1 Rue de Beaune (before 1774, according to the *Almanach Dauphin*). Houses, Rue de la Pépinière, 1776–79. Château de Rocquencourt, for the Comtesse de Provence, 1781–86. Crypt of Saint-Leu–Saint-Gilles, about 1781. House for Mme Denis, Voltaire's niece, remarried to M. Duvivier, Rue Richelieu; model of the oval staircase exhibited at the Salon of 1785 and offered to the Academy of Architecture. Théâtre Français (l'Odéon), in collaboration with M.-J. Peyre, 1773–85; drawings in the Bibliothèque Nationale, Collection Destailleur; in the Musée Carnavalet, and the Archives Nationales, series O 1; in the archives of the Comédie-Française, and at Waddesdon Manor; models in wood at the Academy of Architecture in 1792. Development of Port-Vendres; obelisk engraved in 1780. Transformation of the Chancellerie d'Orléans, Rue des Bons-Enfants, 1784. Portal of the abbey of Saint-Denis, 1782. Theatre in the park of Seneffe, 1787. Pavillon d'Hingène, near Antwerp, 1790. Plan for transforming the Salon Carré of the Louvre, 1789, Musée Carnavalet. Projected palace for the Prince Galitzine and Count Cheremetov, and theatre at St Petersburg. Alterations to the Salle des Cariatides for the meetings of the Institut de France (engraving in Clarac's galerie des Antiques). Project for an opera-house, surrounded by 9 temples, 9 palaces and 312 houses on the site of the Capucines, about 1797. Theatre in Brussels.

MS.: Observations sur la forme la plus avantageuse à donner aux salles de spectacle, Bibliothèque de Bruxelles.
Publ.: Suite de Vases, n.d. *Le Temple de Salomon.*
Ref.: Sketches in Paris by Sir William Chambers, RIBA library.
Bibl.: L.H. vol. IV, pp. 232–42. J. Mayor, *GBA*, 1916. Réau, *Histoire de l'expansion de l'art français.* G. Gaillard, *BSHAF*, 1954, pp. 80–4 and 1957, pp. 55–9. Sylvia Pressouyre, 'Un ensemble néo-classique à Port-Vendres', in *Monuments historiques de la France*, 1963.

DEZAIGRE Nicolas
Died 1726. Craftsman in marble and architect.
Hôtel Pujol, 5 Rue Béranger (contract approved by Maître Larsonnier, 11 July 1715). Maison 'Dezègre', at the corner of the Rue du Gros-Chenet and of the boulevard; date of project March 1726.
Ref.: Arch. Nat. H 2127; Z 1j 599.

DHERBELOT
'Expert-bourgeois' from 1785 to 1792. Living at 15 Rue Percée Saint-André in 1792.

DOBILLY
Architect of the Prieuré Saint-Martin-des-Champs, 1756–66.
Ref.: Arch. Nat. N II Seine, 68, 238. Musée Carnavalet, Topo. XIV.

DORLÉANS Pierre
Born at Sceaux. Pupil of Perronnet. Grand Prix 1767. 6 Rue Montparnasse in 1789, and at Sceaux, 31 Rue des Imbergères.
Pavillon du Marquis de Sinéty, Rue Notre-Dame-des-Champs, today in the garden of the Collège Stanislas, 1776–77. Design for a waterfall in the Parc de Sceaux, Musée de l'Ile de France.
Ref.: Watin, Arch. Nat. Z 1j 1009.

DOSMOND Pierre
'Expert-bourgeois' from 1769 to 1792. Living Rue Trousse-vache, later Quai Pelletier (1790).

DOUCET Jacques
Spire of Saint-Louis-en-l'Ile, 1726. Buildings in the Rue Pastourelle, 1730; and on l'Ile Saint-Louis.

DOUCET Henri-Prosper
Practising in 1772.

DOUCET Prosper-Nicolas-Charles-François
Pupil of Rousset.
Practising in 1780.
Publ.: Projet de place devant Saint-Germain-l'Auxerrois, engraved.
Ref.: Arch. Nat. Z 1j 1063.
Bibl.: Diderot, *Mémoire pour Catherine II* (the publishers wrongly identified Doucet with P.-N. Rousset).

DOUSSIN Isaac
Died 1755. Difficult to distinguish from DOUSSIN Charles-François.

Work at the Hôtel de Romanet (today Maison de la Chasse), 1732. Houses, Rues des Tournelles and du Pas-de-la-Mule, 1746. Maison Grimod du Fort, Rue Neuve-Saint-Augustin, 1748.

DUBLIN (DEBLINE) Jean-Baptiste-Benoît
Practising between 1766 and 1786.
Chateau de Courtomer (Orne).
Ref.: Catalogue du Salon de Saint-Luc, 1756. Arch. Nat. Z 1j 1147.

DUBOIS Jean
'Syndic des experts-entrepreneurs' in 1720. Rue de Gindre. Probably the same as J.-B. Dubois.
Work in the Rue du Temple, 1729.
Ref.: Arch. Nat. Z 1j 602.

DUBOISTERF Sébastien-Jean
'Architecte-expert.' Living Rue Meslée in 1789.
Foundations and load-bearing elements of the Hôtel de Botterel-Quintin, 44 Rue des Petites-Ecuries, 1790.

DUCHESNE
Practising in 1748–52.

DUCRET Nicolas
'Expert-juré.' Working at Bolbec (Calvados) and at La Rochelle in 1774.
Tenements, Rue du Faubourg Montmartre, 1769. Tenements, Rues de la Jouaillerie and du Pied de Bœuf, 1769. Tenements, Rue de Paradis, 1779. Tenements, Rue du Coq Saint-Honoré, 1779. Tenements, Rue de la Huchette and du Chat qui Pèche, 1767. Château de Buzay (Charente), 1770. Tenements, Rue de la Michodière.
Ref.: Arch. Nat. T 129 12. N III Seine 714. *Congrès archéologique*, 1956, p. 24.

DUFOUR
Practising in 1735.
Ref.: Arch. Nat. Z 1j 657.

DULLIN (d'Ullin or d'Hullin)
Family of painters and architects:

DULLIN Nicolas
Born in Paris about 1670. Academician 1718.
Hôtel d'Etampes, Rue de Varenne (later Hôtel de Vendôme, de Mazarin, de Talmont and de Rohan-Chabot). Pavillon Dunoyer, Rue de la Roquette, 1708. Pavillon Galpin, Auteuil. Hôtel Soning, 87 Rue de Richelieu (contract dated 7 March 1711; Arch. de la Seine, DE 2, portfolio 5). Wings and main entrance of the Hôtel du Plessis-Châtillon, Rue des Bons-Enfants, 1721. Transformation of the Hôtel de Richelieu, 21 Place des Vosges, 1724 (contract dated 14 January 1724; Etude LXXXIX; work continued by Jean-René Billaudel and Nicolas d'Orbay). Hôtel de Locmaria (later de Lambert and d'Harcourt, site of 102 Rue de l'Université), 1730. Dullin house, Rues des Fourreurs and des Déchargeurs, 1726. Work at the Château de

Crosne, 1730–32. Château de Villegenis, near Massy. Restoration of the Hôtel Jabach, Rue Saint-Merry.
Ref.: PVARA, vols. II, IV. *NAAF*, 1885, vol. IX, p. 134. Blondel, *Architecture française*, vol. I, p. 215. Portefeuille de Bachaumont, Bibl. de l'Arsenal. Arch. Nat. Y 9505, 14.797; Z 1J 629. Minutier, Etude LXXXIX and CXXII: N. Dullin's will, 12 January 1751. M. Rambaud, *Doc.* I, p. 416.

DULLIN fils
Contant d'Ivry's son-in-law. Attacked Couture's modifications to Contant's (subsequently abandoned) scheme for the Madeleine.
Ref.: PV, vol. IX, pp. 151–92, *passim*.

DUMAS
Pupil of P. Hélin.
Halle aux cuirs, Rue du Petit Carreau, 1781. Halle à la Marée, Rue Mauconseil, 1784.

DUMESNIL Paul
Practising between 1722 and 1741.
Maison L'héritier, 'au Marteau d'Or', Rue Saint-Denis, 1735. Buildings for a M Girault and the Abbé de Preuilly.
Ref.: Arch. Nat. Z 1J 566, 627, 646, 653, 706, 710.

DUMONT Charles
Distinct from the other two of this name. Professor of architecture in 1773.

DUMONT Gabriel-Pierre-Martin
Born in Paris about 1720, died after 1790. Grand Prix 1737. 'Académicien de Saint-Luc' in Rome, Florence, Bologna and Paris. Living Rue Neuve-Saint-Merry, Hôtel Jobert, in 1765.
Chapel in the vicinity of Rome, 1761. Tenements, 14 Rue de Tournon. Proposed gateway for the town of Caen. Designs (possibly executed) for tenements, Rue Saint-Martin, and for a hôtel at Versailles. All these schemes were engraved.
Publ.: Plans des trois temples de Paestum, 1764 – Paestum or Possidonia; English text by Th. Major, French translation by Jacques de Varenne, Paris, London, 1768. *Recueil de plusieurs parties d'architecture sacrée et profane de différents maîtres, tant d'Italie que de France: entablements, charpentes, croisées de Rome, ruines antiques*, Paris, 1767; with Dumont's portrait engraved after Kucharsky. *Détail des plus intéressantes parties d'architecture de la Basilique St-Pierre*, Paris, 1763. *Parallèle des plus belles salles de spectacle d'Italie et de France. Projects détaillés de salles de spectacle particulières.*

DUMONT Jean-Charles
'Expert-entrepreneur' from 1755 to 1792. Rue de la Mortellerie, near the Rue des Barres, in 1792.

DUMONTIER Pierre-Jean
Mentioned 1773–78.

DUPARC de FONDJOUR Antoine-Nicolas
Born 1744. Inspector of mines. 55 Rue Rochechouart in 1789.

DUPUIS Charles
Architect at Versailles.
Publ.: Recueil de Vases; 12 sheets. *Nouveau traité des cinq ordres d'architecture*, Paris 1768; reissue of a work published in collaboration with his brother Etienne. Project de reconstruction de l'église paroissiale Saint-Paul. Décoration d'un tombeau dédié au Marquis de Beringhen. *Planches du 'Recueil d'architecture' de Michel d'Ixnard*, Strasbourg, 1791.

DURAND
Born in Paris 18 September 1760, died Thiais 31 December 1834. 2e Grand Prix 1779 and 1780. Professor at the Ecole Polytechnique from its inception.
Maison La Thuile, Faubourg Poissonnière, 1788 (engraved by Krafft and Ransonnette, *Recueil d'architecture*; Landon, *Description de Paris*, 1818, vol. I, p. 209; and Durand, *Leçons*, vol. II, pl. 23). Decorations for the Festival of Unity at the Panthéon, with Thibaut. Maison Lermina at Chézy, near Lagny (Durand, *Précis*, vol. II, pl. 31). Projects submitted to the Convention: temple 'décadaire', temple of public felicity, *maison commune*, fountains and public wash-houses (engraved by Destournelle), column for the interior of the Panthéon, *assemblées primaires*, *palais de justice* (law-courts), *justice de paix* (court of reconciliation), prison, public baths (engraved), primary school.
Publ.: Recueil et parallèle des édifices en tous genres, 1800. *Précis et leçons d'architecture*, 1802–05. Partie graphique du Cours d'architecture fait à l'Ecole Polytechnique.

DUTILLET Pierre
Mentioned 1783.

DUVAL Alexandre
Mentioned 1781–89.

DUVAL Charles
'Expert-entrepreneur' in 1715. Living Rue Sainte-Croix-de-la-Bretonnerie, 1720.

EGRESSET Guillaume
'Expert-entrepreneur' from 1752 to 1792. 'Architecte de la Police.' Associate member of the Académie de Saint-Luc in 1775. Quai Saint-Paul in 1792; Rue des Nonnains-d'Hyères in 1771.

FAUCARD J.-B.
Mentioned 1777.

FAUVEL
Family of architects:

FAUVEL François
Practising in 1727.

FAUVEL Jacques

FAUVEL Maurice-Michel
Practising in 1735.

FAUVEL DE VILLIERS Jean
Died in 1763 at the Château de Villiers. 'Expert-entre-preneur.' Living Rue des Deux-Ecus in 1730.
Houses: du chapitre Saint-Benoît, 1735; Josset, Rue de la Parcheminerie, 1739; Testard du Lys, Rue Saint-Martin; de Guchery, Rue de la Harpe, 1743. Pavilion in the park of the Hôtel de Matignon. Work at the Hôtel de Monaco, Versailles, about 1743–60.
Some of these buildings were erected to the designs of Chevotet.
Ref.: Arch. Nat. N II Seine, 920. Z IJ 651, 685, 702, 704.
Bibl.: Labande, 'L'Hôtel de Matignon', in *GBA*, 1935.

FERROUSSAT de CASTELBON Etienne-Humbert
Died after 1773. Inspector of buildings and farms to the Prince de Conti.

FINOT
Landscape architect, practising before 1784.

FOACIER Nicolas-Martial
Sometime Rome scholar. 'Contrôleur des Bâtiments du Roi.' Public baths, Versailles, 1785.
Bibl.: Corresp. des dir., 29 July 1774, E XIII, p. 12. Thierry.

FORTIN
'Expert-entrepreneur' in 1766. Rue de Seine.
Maison Brayer de la Motte, Rue Saint-Honoré and Rue de la Tonnellerie, 1740. Maison Bailly, Rue des Arcis and Rue Saint-Jacques de la Boucherie, 1742.

FOUCHEROT
Practising in 1781.

FOUGEROUX (FAUGEROUX)
'Expert-entrepreneur' from 1788 to 1792. Rue Le Regra-tier, Ile-Saint-Louis.

FOUGERON
Tenements for the Baronne de Traverse, Rue Notre-Dame-des-Champs, 1769.

FOURCROY Louis
Died 8 July 1735. Rue Neuve Saint-Michel.
House, Rue Saint-Antoine and Cul-de-sac de la Guépine, 1727. Hôtel Samuël-Bernard, 46 Rue du Bac, work begun 1730 (contract approved by Maître Tessier). Maison Dambrun, Quai Dauphin (contract approved by Maître Junot, 20 January 1730).
Ref.: Arch. Nat. Z IJ 594, 596, 613, 615.

FOURRÉ (le Chevalier Antoine)
Pupil of Servandoni. Architect to the Prince de Conti. Rue Meslée in 1759. In Strasbourg in 1776.
Salle des machines and galerie d'histoire naturelle in the precinct of the Temple, 1760–72.
F.-N. Sellier engraved after A. Fourré the setting for '*Le seigneur de village.*'
Ref.: Mémoires secrets, 22 September 1772.

FOURRIER Edme
'Expert-entrepreneur.' Practising about 1705–20. Rue Culture Sainte-Catherine, opposite les Filles Bleues.
Hôtel Barrenton de Villeneuve de la Motte-Josserand, Rue de l'Arbre-Sec, 1719 (contract approved by Maître Ave-line).

FRANÇOIS Honoré
May be the same as the Nancy architect who directed the funeral of King Stanislas.
Burial chapel of Marie-Louise de Croy, wife of Gaspard Grimod d'Orsay, at the church of Orsay; sculptures by Clodion, 1772–78. Tenements, Rue Saint-Martin, 1771.

FRANQUE François
Born at Avignon 1710, died after 1792. Son of architect J.-B. Franque. Rome scholar 1733. Academician 1755.
Main entrance of seminary at Bourges, 1740 (Blondel, *Cours d'architecture*, vol. III, p. 143 and pl. XXV). Château de Magnanville, near Mantes, 1753 (Argenville, *Environs de Paris*, 1779, p. 216). Abbaye de Corbie (*Encyclopédie*, vol. I des planches, 1762; *Architecture*, p. 8, note a; and *PVARA*, vol. IX, p. 345). Abbaye de Vauluisant, diocese of Troyes (staircase engraved in the *Encyclopédie*, vol. I des planches, XXXIX). Project for the Collège de Narbonne, 1757 (Arch. Nat. Z IJ 836 and N III Seine 428 1–2–9–10; see also notes on Le Carpentier). Maison Franque, 12 Rue Guénégaud, 1758 (Arch. Nat. Z IF 469). Tenements of les Célestins, Rue du Coq Saint-Honoré (Blondel, *Cours d'architecture*, vol. III, p. 454 and pl. LXXI). 'Château dans le Bourbonnais', 1768 (*PVARA*, vol. IX). De Crillon tene-ments, Rues de la Verrerie and du Renard, 1775–77 (Arch. Seine, DE 1). Entrance-gate of the d'Argenson house at Neuilly. Project for the Abbaye de Panthémont (*Encyclo-pédie*; see notes on Contant d'Ivry, and Legrand-Landon, *Description de Paris*, 1818, vol. I, p. 211). Abbey buildings of Saint-Benoît-sur-Loire, and of the order of Prémontrés of Villers-Cotterets (today Hôtel de Ville) (Blondel, *Cours d'architecture*, vol. IV, p. 357 and pl. XLVI). House at Amiens, about 1774 (Blondel, *Cours d'architecture* vol. IV, p. 361 and pl. XLVII). Projects for the abbeys of Saint-Denis and Notre-Dame de Soissons, and for the Esplanade du Peyrou at Montpellier (engraved) Collège de Dombes, 1771. Château in Les Dombes. Château near the Tour de Crouÿ. Abbey of Saint-Pierre d'Abbeville. At Avignon: Hôtel de Villefranche (*Encyclopédie,* vol. I des planches, XXIV, XXV), Hôtel des Invalides and transformation of the Palais Colonna.
Publ.: Account of Servandoni, inserted in the Nécrologe, and reproduced in the *Vies d'Architectes* by Milizia and Pingeron. Eulogy of Jacques-François Blondel, in the *Journal des Beaux-Arts et des Sciences de l'Abbé Aubert.*
Bibl.: See above notes, also *Catalogue de l'exposition de St-Luc*, 1753.

FRÉMIOT Nicolas
Died 1738. Architecte des Bâtiments du Roi. Rue Neuve Saint-Martin.

FROSNE Jean-Luc
'Expert.' Living Rue Thibaut-aux-Dés in 1715, then Rue des Lavandières.

GABRIEL
Family of architects:

GABRIEL Jacques (V)
Born in Paris 6 April 1667, died Fontainebleau 23 June 1742. Academician 1699. Premier ingénieur des Ponts et Chaussées, 1716. Premier Architecte du Roi, 1735.
Hôtel de Varangeville, Rue Saint-Dominique (contract approved by Maitre Dupuis le Jeune, 22 February 1704). Hôtel Blouin, 31 Rue du Faubourg Saint-Honoré, 1718. Wing and staircase of the Hôtel d'Etampes, Rue de Varenne (contract approved by Maître Dulion, 22 February 1722). Hôtels Gabriel, Place Vendôme, built on sites distrained upon John Law (contract approved by Maître Perret, 12 February 1724). Works at the Hôtel de Mesme, Rue Sainte-Avoye; at the Hôtel Poulletier, 7 Rue de Sévigné; at the Palais Bourbon; and the Hôtel de Lassay, 1724. Chambre des Comptes, 1737–39. Bâtiment des Bacheliers at the Collège de Navarre, Rue de la Harpe. Maison Camuset, 14 Rue François-Miron, 1737.
Bishop's palace, Blois, 1725. Stalls of Orléans cathedral, today at the Seminary. Chapel of the Hôtel-Dieu, Orléans. Cathedral of La Rochelle (completed after 1742).
Wing of the Palais des Etats, Dijon, on the Rue de Condé: staircase, Members' chapel, after 1731. The works were supervised by Le Mousseux. (Jacques Hardouin-Mansart de Sagonne bore the title, at this period, of 'architecte des Etats de Bourgogne'.)
General plans for Nantes, and Rennes, after 1731. Hôtel de Ville, Rennes. Place Royale, Bordeaux: Hôtel des Fermes, 1738–45; central pavilion and Hôtel de la Bourse, both built after 1742.
Pont de la Guillotière, Lyon. Bridges at Pontoise, Charenton, Pont-Sainte-Maxence, l'Isle Adam, Poissy. Pont des Belles Fontaines at Juvisy (?). Work at Fontaine-bleau and Chambord. The official jobs of Jacques V Gabriel – considered by his contemporaries a poor de-signer – are difficult to distinguish from those of Robert de Cotte and of Jacques-Ange Gabriel, his son.
Bibl.: P. Courtault: *La place royale de Bordeaux*, 1924. F. Bergot: *L'hôtel de ville de Rennes*, 1953. J. Brachet: *L'hôtel de la Chambre des Comptes* 1966.

GABRIEL Jacques-Ange
Son of Jacques V. 'Premier Architecte du Roi' from 1741 to 1774.
VERSAILLES
The Queen's bedroom, 1735. The King's bedroom and cabinet de la Pendule, 1738. The Dauphin's suite on the ground floor, 1746–47. Cabinet d'angle, 1753. Cabinet du Conseil, 1755–56. Cabinet de Mme Adélaïde, 1767. Cabinet de Mme Victoire, 1761–63. Louis XV's bath-room, 1770–71. Petits appartements de Mme du Barry, 1770. The King's Library, 1775. Salle de l'Opéra, 1748–70. Scheme for the general reconstruction of the

palace, initiated in 1772–73 by the building of the Gabriel wing between the chapel and the Cour de Marbre.
TRIANON
Salon frais du Grand Trianon; ménagerie, 1749–50. Pavillon Français, 1751. Petit Trianon: preliminary studies, 1761; foundations and masonry elements, 1764; panelling, 1765–68.
FONTAINEBLEAU
Grands appartements: the Queen's bedroom, 1746–47 (re-taining an earlier ceiling). The King's staircase, 1750 (retaining, at the top of the well, the stucco-work of the former bedroom of the Duchesse d'Etampes, by Prima-ticcio). The Dauphine's suite, towards the Cour des Princes. King's bedroom; cabinet du Conseil, 1751–52. Anterooms of the Cour ovale, 1757. Escalier de la Reine or des Chasses, 1767–68.
Petits appartements of the King, the Queen, and of Mmes de Pompadour and du Barry, between the Cour de la Fontaine and the Jardin de Diane. Octagonal salon of Mme du Barry, on the Terrace de Diane, 1772–73, destroyed 1774.
South wing of the Cour du Cheval Blanc, begun by Jacques Gabriel in 1738, completed by the Gros-Pavillon, by the Etang des carpes, 1751 (suite of Mesdames the daughters of Louis XV). Schemes for the general recon-struction of the château, 1750 and 1773. Ermitage de Mme de Pompadour, proposals of 1749.
LA MUETTE (Bois de Boulogne): work after 1742.
COMPIÈGNE
Schemes of 1751 and 1756. Left wing built in 1751–53. Pavilion on the right-hand side of the Place d'Armes, 1764. Terrace facing the park, 1756. Façade on the park side, completed during Louis XVI's reign by Ledreux de la Chartre (who built the main staircase of the right wing). Ermitage, 1754.
CHOISY
Entrance pavilions of the Cour Royale, 1748; enlarge-ment of the main *corps de logis*, 1752–53. Gallery on the Paris side, 1745–47. Wings of the *gouverneur* and of the *seigneurs*, 1746–73. Theatre, 1750–63. Petit Château, 1754–56. Ménagerie, 1745. Glass-houses and peristyle sheltering Bouchardon's Cupid, 1753. Parish church, 1748–60. Presbytery, 1764–66. Drawings: Musée Carnavalet.
BELLEVUE; *Grand salon*
SAINT-HUBERT
Louis XV's hunting-lodge in the forest of Les Yvelines 1755. *Grand salon* decorated by Pigalle, Falconet and the stucco-craftsman Clerici, 1757.
Hunting-lodges of la Muette, in the forest of Saint-Germain (Ganay, *Ile de France*, vol. IV, pl. 95); of le Butard, in the wood of Les Hubies, 1750; of Les Fosses-Reposes, 1756 (copied in the pavilion of Le Pont Colbert in 1778). Designs: Arch. Nat. O 1 1870–71.
ECOLE MILITAIRE: 1751–88
Drawings of elevations: Arch. Nat. K 150–52, and Musée Carnavalet.
PLACE LOUIS XV
Scheme of 20 July 1753: Arch. Nat. H 2 2162; Album, Arch. Nat. O 1 1546; Album 58 of the transference of the Bâtiments Civils to the Arch. Nat. Final scheme of 9

December 1755: Arch. Nat. O 1 1585 290. Part elevation, Olivier Le Fuel collection.

Bibl.: Comte de Fels, *Ange-Jacques Gabriel, Premier Architecte du Roi*, Paris, 1924. Pierre Pradel, 'Les projects de Gabriel pour l'Opéra de Versailles', in *GBA*, February 1937. Robert Laulan, *L'Ecole Militaire de Paris — le Monument*, 1950. Georges Poisson, 'Un édifice de Gabriel retrouvé: le petit château de Choisy', in *BSHAF*, 1954, pp. 10–15. Yves Bottineau, *L'Art d'Ange-Jacques Gabriel à Fontainebleau*, 1962. Solange Granet, *La Place de la Concorde*, Paris, 1963.

GABRIEL Ange-Antoine
Son of Jacques-Ange. Born 15 September 1735, died 1781. Academician 1761. Contrôleur des Bâtiments du Roi at Marly, 1761–75.

GABRIEL Nicolas-Toussaint
'Expert-bourgeois' from 1768 to 1792. Living Rue de la Croix, near the Temple, in 1792.

GALLAND Nicolas
'Contrôleur' de l'Ecole Militaire in 1762, then Premier Architecte to the Comte d'Artois, retiring in 1776.
Completion of the Hôtel des Gardes-du Corps at Versailles.
Bibl.: D'Argenville. *NAAF*, 1894.

GALLIMARD Guillaume
Landscape architect.
Gardens of the Sieur Dogeron, 1772. Houses, Rue Verte-Saint-Antoine, 1774. Work for M. Moreau de la Brosse, 1787. Work for M. Baudard at the Folie Sainte-James, 1770–78. Work at the Palais-Royal, in the Valois wing, in 1792.
Ref.: Arch. Nat. Z 1J 982, 1012, 1065, 1202.
A Gallimard fils published in Paris in 1750 a series of sixty-nine plates of flower-beds, orangeries, shrubberies, mazes and trellises, etc.

GALLOIS
Mentioned in 1760.

GALLOT
Grand Prix 1727.
Difficult to identify. Probable works: portal of the Trinité, Fécamp, 1744; choir of the church of Bully, 1742. Work for the Marquis d'Allonville, before 1755.
Bibl.: Bauchal. Joan Evans, *Monastic Architecture in France.*

GARNIER
House for the Chevalier Lefèvre at Chaillot, 1770.

GARNIER d'ISLE Jean-Charles
Academician 1724. 'Dessinateur des jardins du Roi.'

GARNIER d'ISLE Charles-Hippolyte
Son of above. Contrôleur-général des Bâtiments du Roi.

GARTNER Jean
Mentioned in 1781.

162

GAUBIER
Family of architects and building contractors:

GAUBIER Sulpice
Died 21 May 1754. 'Expert-entrepreneur' in 1734. Rue Daguesseau.
Work at the Chaillot foundry, 1720. Maisons Daguesseau and Girardin, Rue du Faubourg Saint-Honoré. Six Gaubier houses, Rue Daguesseau, 1725. Hôtel de Choiseul, Rue Saint-Romain, 1729. Bonnet house, Faubourg Saint-Honoré and Rue d'Anjou, 1728. Work at the Hôtel de La Rochefoucauld for the Comtesse de Rupelmonde, 1732. House, Rue du Petit-Lion-Saint-Sulpice and Rue du Brave, 1735. Maison Bourgeois, Rues Saint-Honoré and Traversine, 1736.
Ref.: Arch. Nat. Y 9505. Z 1F 401; Z 1J 521, 533, 633, 637, 672.

GAUBIER Edme, le Jeune
Practising 1733–50.

GAUDEBERT
In 1782 submitted a scheme, with accompanying brochure, for the development of Les Catacombes (Mémoires secrets).

GELOT Nicolas
Pupil of the Academy in 1774.
Buildings for the Marquis de Seignelay, Rue Saint-Dominique, 1786–87.
Ref.: Arch. Nat. Z 1J 1175.

GENTILS
Landscape architect.
Gardens for M. d'Espagnac, Rue d'Anjou, and for the Duc d'Harcourt at Chaillot (Lerouge, *Jardins anglo-chinois*, XIe cahier).

GERARD DE MONTBROUARD
'Expert-bourgeois.' Parvis Notre-Dame in 1730, then Rue Tiquetonne in 1755, later at Deuil-la-Barre.

GILBERT Florentin
Architect to the University. Rue d'Orléans Saint-Honoré. 'Architecte des Eaux et Forêts de la Champagne et du Nivernais' in 1789. Practising in 1778–93 (see Arch. Nat. Z 1J 1175).
Publ.: Adresse à tous les corps administratifs de la France et à tous les connaisseurs dans l'art de l'architecture, Paris, L. Jorry, 1790.

GILLET Jean-Fleurimont
Pupil of the Academy in 1762. Practising in 1777.

GILLET François
Hôtel de Saint-Florentin, Rue de la Ville-l'Evêque (contract approved, 8 April 1742).
Ref.: Arch. Nat. Z 1J 782.

GILLET Pierre-Eutrope
Tenements, Rue de Bourgogne, 1777–81.
Ref.: Arch. Nat. Z 1J 1007, 1027, 1074.

GILLET DE LA FONTAINE Jacques
'Expert-bourgeois' from 1727. Rue Sainte-Anne in 1740. Maison Gillet de la Chaussée, Rue de Bourgogne, 1739. House for the Marquis de la Pallun, Rue de Condé (contract approved by Maître Laideguives, Etude LXV, 16 July 1737). Bell-towers of the churches of Jaulnes and Paron.
Ref.: Arch. Nat. Z 1J 676, 685. Bauchal.

GIRARDIN Nicolas-Claude
Died September 1786. Pupil of the Academy, 3e prix 1772. Maison Giambonne, 62–64 Rue de Bondy, 1778. Glasshouses of the Elysée. Pavillon de la Chartreuse-Beaujon. Bathing pavilion in the garden of the Chartreuse, and chapel of Saint-Nicolas-du-Roule. Transformation of the Basilique Saint-Martin-de-Tours, 1780–86. Hôpital Beaujon, Faubourg Saint-Honoré. Works for M. Taillepied de Bondy, and for Lepelletier de la Garenne at Villemomble, about 1785. Château des Boulayes at Tournan (S. & M.), 1785–86.
Bibl.: M. Gallet, 'Le Château des Boulayes', in *GBA*, January 1962.

GIRAUD Louis-Alexandre
Born 1725. Architect of the Menus Plaisirs about 1775. Decoration of the cathedral and Archbishop's Palace of Reims, for the coronation of Louis XVI (engravings by Patas). Hôtel des Menus Plaisirs, Faubourg Poissonnière. Design for the Théâtre Français: Arch. Nat. N III Seine 1142, 87 sheets.
Bibl.: 'Papillon de La Ferté', in *Journal des Menus Plaisirs*, *passim*.

GIRAUD Pierre
Died in 1814. Architect of the Palais de Justice and prisons. Proposal for a *place* to the north of the Pont-au-Change (Musée Carnavalet).

GITTARD
Family of architects:

GITTARD Pierre
Academician 1699. Gentleman, Chevalier de Saint-Louis, Chief Engineer to the town of Lille.

GOBIN Jean-François
Died 1725. 'Expert-bourgeois' in 1704. Living Rue des Prêtres-Saint-Gervais in 1720.

GOBIN Jean-Léonard
Died 1786. Hospital architect.

GODOT Pierre-François
Academician 1739. Contrôleur des Bâtiments du Roi. Rue Saint-Honoré and at Compiègne.
Maison Eynaud, 52 Rue de l'Arbre-Sec, 1717. House for the Marquis de Harville, Rue Saint-Martin, near the Rue Saint-Julien, 1729. Monasteries of La Merci, Lyon, 1727–31; and in Paris, 45 Rue des Archives. Choir of Saint-Médard, Soissons, 1729. (?) Château of Vic-sur-Aisne. Bishop's Palace, Chartres (staircase, 'Italian' hall;

the chapel is by P.-N. Rousset). Maison Siré, Rue de l'Arche Marion and Quai de la Mégisserie, 1739. Hôtel de Clermont d'Amboise, Rue Saint-Honoré, near the Orangerie, 1741. Choir of Noyon cathedral, 1752. Works at the Abbaye de Faremoutiers.
Ref.: M. Rambaud, *Doc.* I, pp. 74, 397, 489. Other contracts: Etude XXIX, 1 September 1739. Etude Prévost l'Aîné, 1 February 1749. Etude Laideguive, 24 July 1741. Arch. Nat. Z 1J 528, 529, 553, 557, 631, 712.

GONDOIN Jacques
Born at Saint-Omer 7 June 1737, died 29 December 1818. 2e prix 1758. Rome scholar. Academician 1774. 'Designer of the Crown furniture.' Member of the Institute. School of Surgery (the present Ecole de Médecine) 1769–75. Project for the church of Saint-Côme. Completion scheme for the Palais de Justice, about 1782. Interior fittings of the Garde-Meubles, about 1772. Vendôme column, 1806. Villa des Eaux-Vives, near Meulun (about 1795) Unclassified drawings in the Bibliothèque Nationale.
Publ.: *Description des Ecoles de Chirurgie*, 1780.
Bibl.: Jean Adhémar, 'L'Ecole de Médecine', in *L'Architecture*, 15 May 1934. P. Verlet in *Connaissance des arts*, May 1958, pp. 92–7. Marguerite Jallut in *GBA*, May–June 1964, p. 307.

GOUBELY
Family of 'vérificateurs' and architects.
Michel Goubely was practising in 1786.

GOULET
'Expert-entrepreneur' from 1786 to 1792. Rue Quincampoix in 1792.

GOUPY
Family of architects:

GOUPY Martin
'Expert-bourgeois', 1728. Living Rue Saint-Jacques, near Saint-Yves, 1728; Rue de la Truanderie, 1740.
Maison Goupy, Rue Saint-Jacques and Rue de la Bretonnerie, 1729. Robillard house, 15 Rue Montorgueil; Dunet house, 17 Rue Montorgueil, 1729–30. House, Rue de Beauvais and Rue Jean-Saint-Denis, 1736. Dubuisson house, Rue de la Parcheminerie, 1729. Maison Goupy, Rue des Prouvaires, 1739 (contract, etc., approved by Maître Tournois, 15 September 1739). Maison Goupy, Rue Marie-Stuart, 1742. Proposed *place publique*, near the Quai Conti, Musée Carnavalet.
Ref.: Arch. Nat. Z 1F 417, fol. 132, 433, fol. 26v, 437, fol. 99v, 443, fol. 38v and 120v. Z 1J 604, 606, 620, 633, 659, 667. Minutier, LXVI, 437.

GOUPY Jean-Pierre
Practising in 1749.

GOUPY André

GOUPY Claude-Martin
Architect and 'expert-bourgeois' (from 1766 to 1792).

Hôtel Cardon, 50 Rue du Faubourg Poissonnière, 1773. Maison Deleuse, 52 Faubourg Poissonnière, 1774. Tenements, Chaussée d'Antin, 1772. Presbytery of Les Saints-Innocents, 1770–71. Barracks of the Gardes Françaises, Faubourg Poissonnière, 1771–72. House at La Grande Pinte, near Bercy, 1772. Barracks of La Pépinière, 1775. Work for the Duc de Penthièvre at Armainvilliers, about 1780. Tenements, Rue de Choiseul, 1782–83. Cl.-M. Goupy worked as contractor under the direction of Louis at the Hôtel de Richelieu, Lenoir at Saint-Antoine-des-Champs, Bélisard at the Palais-Bourbon, and Rousset.

Ref.: Arch. Nat. series R. Z 1J 924, 939, 953, 954, 956, 968, 971, 980, 993, 994, 1090.

GOUJON Louis-Alexandre
'Expert-bourgeois.' Living Enclos du Temple, later Rue des Vieilles Garnisons, behind the Saint-Esprit.

GOURLIER Charles-Pierre
Born 1726. Practising in 1783.

GRANDHOMME
Family of architects and building contractors:

GRANDHOMME Pierre
Hôtel du Président Chevallier, Rue Saint-Honoré (contract approved by Maître Dutartre, 20 July 1714), building altered by Chevotet (Blondel, *Architecture française*). Houses: Desperriers, Rue Sainte-Croix; Desperriers, Rue de Richelieu, 1717; Lallemand de Betz, Rue Neuve-Saint-Augustin; Yvon, Rue Neuve-Saint-Roch; Terray, Rue de Richelieu; Rodot, Rue Vieille-du-Temple and Sainte-Croix-de-la-Bretonnerie, 1735; Coustou, Rues des Deux-Portes and Saint-Sauveur, 1735; Gautier de Beauvais, Rue de Surène, at the corner of the Boulevard, 1735.

GRANDHOMME Eloi
Son of above. Practising in 1750.

Ref.: Z 1J 528, 533, 572, 576, 584, 711.

GRANGERET
Family of architects:

GRANGERET Charles
Practising about 1730–40.

GRANGERET Louis-Barthélémy
Born 1747. Mentioned in 1783.

GRISOT Jean
'Expert-bourgeois' from 1756. Rue du Chantre, later Rue Chapon.

GUERNE Jacques-Jacob
Grand Prix 1769. Among his 'picturesque' drawings, *Le Temple de la Sibylle à Tivoli* is in the Musée de Besançon. Interior decoration of Senlis cathedral, about 1785.
Ref.: Arch. Nat. Z 1J 1150.

GUILLAUMOT Charles-Axel
Born in Stockholm 27 February 1730, died Paris 7 October

1807. Chief Engineer to the Généralité de Paris, 1761. Academician 1773. Director of the Gobelins, Inspector of Quarries.
Porte Dauphine at Sens. Abbey buildings of Vézelay. Châteaux de Sauvigny, and de la Brosse, near Montereau. Fenestration of the Salon Carré of the Louvre, 1789. Barracks of the Swiss guards, Rueil, 1754; Joigny, 1769; Saint-Denis, Courbevoie (Caserne Charras). See Durand, *Recueil d'architecture*, and *VP*, April 1926 and photo.
Publ.: Remarques sur un livre . . . de M. l'Abbé Laugier, Paris, 1768. Mémoire sur la manière d'éclairer les galeries du Louvre, Paris, 1794. Considérations sur l'état des arts à Paris, 1802. Essai sur les moyens qui constituent la beauté essentielle en architecture, 1802. Considérations sur les connaissances et les qualités nécessaires à un architecte. Observations sur le tort que font à l'architecture les déclamations exagérées contre la dépense qu'occasionne la construction des monuments publics.

GUILLAIN Philippe
'Expert-entrepreneur' in 1715. Rue des Gravilliers.

GINGAUD de BUFFEIX
Transformation of the Hôtel de Terrat-Brancas, Rue de Tournon, 1760. Work at Saint-Denis to Mique's orders, and at the Palais-Bourbon, 1788.

GUILLOT-AUBRY Claude
Died 1771. 2e prix 1721. Academician 1737. Rue du Temple and at Bagnolet. 'Inspecteur-général du Pavé de Paris.'

GUYON Jean-Baptiste
'Expert-bourgeois' from 1755. Rue Sainte-Avoye in 1760, later Rue du Monceau Saint-Gervais.

HABERT-TIBERGE
Perhaps related to Gillet-Habert, building contractor about 1760. Saint-Vrain dairy, 1794. Plans in the B.N., Est.

HALLET Sulpice
Architect, 'expert-bourgeois' from 1785 to 1792. Rue des Juifs au Marais in 1792, the following year in Washington. Design for the Capitol, Washington, 1793.

HALLOT Etienne
Died 3 November 1721. 'Expert-entrepreneur' in 1715. Rue Saint-Martin, near the Rue Grenier-Saint-Lazare, in 1712.

HANARD Martin
'Inspecteur des Bâtiments du Roi' in 1718.

HANEUSE Jacques
Died 1770.
Work for Balthazar Durand de Belleval at the Château de Chauvry, 1743.
Ref.: PVARA, vol. v.

HAPPE Célestin-Joseph
'Vérificateur' of the City of Paris, before 1790. Architect to the Préfecture de Police in the year XII.

Richomme tenements, 12 Rue du Sentier, 1782–84. Houses: Dubreuil, 1785; Brasdor, Rue Comtesse d'Artois (Montorgueil), 1786; Happe, Rue d'Angoulême au Marais, 1786. Works, Rue de la Michodière, 1790. Group of tenements, called Cour Batave, Rue Saint-Denis (near the Passage de Venise), 1790. Transformation of the Hôtel Sainte-Foix, Rue Basse du Rempart, 1800. Maison Moitte at Mantes (Krafft, pls. 17–18). Poultry market, Quai des Augustins, 1809–12. Abattoir de Popincourt, 1810.
Ref.: Arch. Nat. Z 1J 1088, 1097, 1111, 1125, 1146, 1150, 1194, 1240. Krafft.

HARDOUIN
Family of architects:

HARDOUIN Jules-Michel-Alexandre
Died 1737. Academician 1720. Contrôleur des Bâtiments du Roi.
Reconstruction of Châteaudun after the fire of 1723. Decoration of the Grand Salon of the Elysée, 1723 (trophies carved by Michel Lange). House, Rue des Chantres, 1727. Work at the former Hôtel de Conti, Rue des Poulies, 1725, for Gaspard de Réal, Marquis de Colombières.

HARDOUIN-MANSART de JOUY Jean (known as MANSART The Elder)
Château de Brunoy, built for Pâris de Montmartel: forecourt buildings and interior decoration (D'Argenville, *Voyage pittoresque*, 1st ed., attributes these to Boscry, a mistake corrected in the three subsequent editions of 1762, 1768 and 1779). Hôtel d'Herbouville, 13 Rue Pavée, 1737. Entrance level of portal of Saint-Eustache (first stone laid 22 May 1754). Design for the Place Saint-Eustache (perspective view engraved by J.-B. de Poilly, dedicated to the Duc de Choiseul). Ecole paroissiale for boys, Rue Tirechappe, 1750. Presbytery, Rue Traînée, about 1758. Maison Mansart de Jouy, Rue Saint-Honoré, near the Rue Tirechappe, 1745.
Publ.: Suite de Cheminées, gravées par Poilly. Suite de la décoration de Brunoy.
It is difficult to determine whether the Château d'Asnières is by Mansart de Jouy or Mansart de Sagonne (below).

HARDOUIN-MANSART de LEVI Jacques, Comte de SAGONNE
1700–62. Academician 1735.
Maison des Dames de Saint-Chaumont, Boulevard de Sébastopol, 1734. Maison de Cintray, Rue Péquay, 1735. Work at the Château de Seine-Port, for Mlle Benoist de Collemie, 1738. Decoration of the Château de Saint-Non-la-Bretêche, for Marie-Anne de Boullongne, widow of J.-P. Richard de Saint-Non, 1738–48. Transformation of the Hôtel de Lesdiguières, Rue de la Cerisaie, for M. Parot de Puisneuf, 1739–47. Church of Saint-Louis de Versailles, today cathedral; first stone laid on 12 June 1743. Presbytery, same date. Work at the Hôtel Bazin de Bezons, Rue de Richelieu, 1743. Work on the first floor of the house at 52 Rue de l'Arbre-Sec, 1743. Maison Clostrier, 56 Rue des Francs-Bourgeois, 1752. Hospital at Marseille, 1753. Various schemes

for the Place Louis XV. Dominican abbey of Prouilles in Languedoc. (?) Palace of Commerce, Tours. Maison Mansart de Levi, Rue Montorgueil, near the Cul-de-sac de la Bouteille, 1756. Embellishments to the Hôtel Mansart de Sagonne, 28 Rue des Tournelles, before 1743.
Bibl.: D'Argenville. Argenson. Paul Lacroix, 'Un concours d'architecture en 1753, *Revue universelle des arts*, 1858. Deshairs, *Les Dessins de Nicolas Pineau*. G. Huard, *Nicolas Pineau*, 1930. Angèle Payen, in *Positions des thèses de l'Ecole du Louvre*, 1959, p. 175. Solange Granet, *La Place de la Concorde*. Mireille Rambaud, *Doc. 1*.
Ref.: Arch. Nat. Z 1J 568, 587, 627, 629, 645, 659, 675, 687, 688, 697, 712, 726, 728, 733, 750, 751, 753, 763, 768, 795, 803. Z 1F 450, fol. 135v; 460, fol. 36.

HAZON Michel-Barthélémy
Grand Prix 1745. Academician 1775. Intendant des Bâtiments du Roi.

HECQUAN
Family of architects:

HECQUAN Marie-Claude
Died before April 1779.

HECQUAN Pierre
'Expert-entrepreneur' in 1720. Rue Neuve-Saint-Laurent.

HÉLIE André-Michel
Living Cloître Saint-Merry in 1788, Rue Saint Avoye in 1793. Practising in 1775.

HÉLIN Pierre-Louis
Born at Versailles 26 September 1734, died in Paris 23 May 1791. Grand Prix 1754. Sub-inspector at the Ecole Militaire in 1752. Rue du Bac in 1776, Rue Vivienne in 1778.
Chartreuse de Bourbon-lez-Gaillon, 1769–74. Chapelle des Visitandines de la Rue du Bac, 1775–80. Abbey of Notre-Dame de Soissons, 1779–81. Church of the Priory of Hautes-Bruyères, near Rambouillet, 1778–80. Work at the Hôtel de Hautes-Bruyères, Rue des Prêtres Saint-Germain-l'Auxerrois. Work for the Prince de Soubise, before 1778, and for Louis-Joseph Amable d'Albert de Luynes, about 1789.
Publ.: *Compositions diverses d'architecture*, Paris, Chéreau, n.d. I^e, IIe and IIIe *cahiers d'etudes de Croisées faites d'après les plus beaux édifices de Rome et d'Italie, ouvrage utile aux gens de Bâtiment*, Paris, Chéreau, n.d. Miscellaneous engravings, including *Une entrée de Palais* (Prix de Rome 1754), and *Chartreuse de Gaillon*.
Bibl.: M. Gallet, P.-L. Helin, *Art de France*, 1963, pp. 187–94.
Ref.: Inventory of P.-L. Helin, see Minutes de Maître Péan de Saint-Gilles.

HENRY known as Henri Trou
Rue de la Michodière in the year XII.
Church of Saint-Cloud (portal), not completed, 1776. Théâtre des Jeunes-Artistes, Boulevard du Temple, built

in 1778 for Tessier-Abraham. Tenements: Lewal (Contrôleur-général de la Maison du Comte d'Artois), Rue Cadet.
Ref.: Arch. Nat. Z 1J 1012, 1021, 1137; Z 2 2461. Krafft and Ransonnette. Watin. Alexis Donnet.

HERBET Michel
'Expert-entrepreneur', 'voyer-général' of the Notre-Dame chapter in 1720.

HEURTIER Jean-François
Born Paris 6 March 1739, died 16 April 1822. Grand Prix 1765. Academician 1776. Member of the Institute at its inauguration.
Théâtre italien (site of the Opéra-Comique), 1780. Prefecture and theatre, Versailles.
Bibl.: Account of Heurtier by Quatremère de Quincy, 1822.

HOULIER François-Simon
Consultant to the Cardinal de Rohan for the restoration of Strasbourg cathedral, about 1770.
Maison d'Arginy at Chatou, 1772. Tenements, Boulevard Saint-Martin, 1779.
Ref.: Arch. Nat. Z 1J 967, 1016; H 2123 3. *PVARA*, vol. VII, pp. 34–7.

HOURSE Charles-François
Died 22 August 1760.
Brother-in-law of the architect Sulpice Gaubier. Architect to the Dauphine. Candidate for the Academy 1755–56.
Maison Hourse, Rue Daguesseau, 1758.
Ref.: Arch. Nat. Z 1J 468.

HOUVET de SECOURET
Practising in 1773. Living Rue de la Bûcherie.

HUET Antoine
Born 1745. Mentioned in 1782.

HUPEAU
'Architecte du Roi.' Premier ingénieur des Ponts et Chaussées. Academician 1757.
Bridge, and houses in the Rue Royale, Orléans.

HUVÉ
Family of architects:

HUVÉ Jean-Jacques
Born at Magnanville 1742, died 24 May 1808. Pupil of Blondel. Grand Prix 1770.
Aqueduct for the Prince Biscari over the Etna. Public baths, Luchon. Decoration of the château of Mme Elisabeth, and garden of Montreuil. Hôtels de la Suze and de la Rochefoucauld, 65-67 Rue de Varenne, 1777–80 (interior and exterior views, Archives phot. d'art et d'histoire). Château of the Président Hornois in Normandy, 1780. Theatre of Magnanville, 1780 (drawings, Musée Carnavalet). Hôtels de Martinville and de Bosquillon, Rue de Provence. Huvé house at le Bas-Meudon. Chapels at les Récollets de Versailles. Châteaux of Hornoy and Bécon; house for the painter Noël Hallé;

sepulchral chapel of the Montmorency family and belvedere at the Château de Montmirail; church of Saint-Gaudens.
Ref.: Krafft.
Bibl.: Lenormand, *Notice biographique sur J.-J. Huvé membre de l'Institut*, 1843. L. Serbat, 'Le voyage d'Italie et les dessins de J.-J. Huvé', in *BSHAF*, 1924.

ITASSE Pierre-Henri
Living Rue de la Grande Truanderie in 1788.
Hôtel de Tamnay, Rue Chauchat, 1789 (engraved by Krafft, Gaite and Prieur; Krafft and Ransonnette, pls. 8 and 94).

JACOB
Architect, 'expert'.
Hapey tenements, Rue du Mail, 1784.
Ref.: Arch. Nat. Z 1J 1108.

JACQUIN
Author of a development plan for the Choiseul district, 1780.

JALLIERS de SAVAULT Claude-Jean-Baptiste
Born 1738, died 12 October 1807. 2e Grand Prix 1760. Rome scholar 1761. Living Rue Meslée in 1774 and 1790. Scheme for the Place Royale, Brest, approved in 1786; model displayed Rue Meslée in 1788; perspective in the Cabinet des Dessins of the Louvre. Design for the Caisse d'Escompte to be built in the Rue Louvois, approved in 1789; execution interrupted by the Revolution.
Work at the Conservatoire des Arts et Métiers, 1805.
Watercolours by Jalliers are preserved in the museums of l'Ile de France and Besançon (and in the O. LeFuel collection).

JARDIN Nicolas-Henri
Born at Saint-Germain des Noyers 22 March 1720, died in Paris 31 August 1799. Grand Prix 1741. Academician of Bologna, Florence, Marseille and Copenhagen. Member of the Royal Academy of Architecture in 1771; Chevalier des ordres du Roi.
The architect's long career in Denmark (1754–71) places him largely outside the scope of this book.
Château near Dammartin (under the direction of Tannevot), about 1750. Hospital of Lagny, 1772–86. House and gardens of Mme Vieillard at Ivry. Façade of the Hôtel de Ville, Cambrai (with Antoine), finished about 1786.

JAUNEZ
Pupil of the Academy 1764–65. Rue d'Anjou in the year XII.
Hôtel Grimod de la Loube, Porte du Temple, 1775–78. Work at the colleges of Saint-Barbe and Les Cholets, and at the archbishop's palace for Mgr de Juigné; for M. d'Espagnac, 1791, and at the abbey of Maubuisson.
Ref.: Arch. Nat. Z 1J 990, 1070, 1129, 1141, 1215. Archives de Seine-et-Oise, III, Q 88.

JOLLIVET Maurice-Louis

JOLLIVET Philippe
Died before May 1748.

JOSSENAY Denis
Died 1748. Academician 1717. Professor at the Academy 1738. Work at the Château de Villeroy, 1732. Plans for the Hôtel-Dieu, Troyes, 1728. Design for wood panelling of the choir of Saint-Thomas d'Aquin (carved by Roumier).
Ref.: Arch. Nat. Z 1J 590, 630. Bauchal.

JOUBERT
Family of architects:

JOUBERT Charles
Born 10 March 1640, died 30 November 1721.
'Doyen des experts-jurés'.
Amphithéâtre Saint-Côme, today Institut d'Anglais, Rue de l'Ecole de Médecine, 1710.

JOUBERT d'ORGEMENT Louis
Trésorier de la Chancellerie, Bordeaux.
De Jean house, Rues Bertin-Poirée and Saint-Germain-l'Auxerrois, 1724. Monastic buildings and portal of la Trinité, Rue des Mathurins, 1728. Joubert house, Rues de la Tannerie and des Teinturiers, 1730. De Noireterre house, Rues Saint-Denis and Courtalon, 1733. House, Rue de la Coutellerie (contract approved by Maître Boursier, 1740). Maison des chapelains de la Sainte-Chapelle at Picpus. Maison du Collège des Trente-Trois, Rue Perdue (7 Rue Maître Albert), 1741. Maison Godot, Rue Montmartre, opposite the Rue de la Jussienne. Work for the Saint-Benoît chapter, 1740.
Ref.: Blondel, *Architecture française*, vol. III, p. 84. Arch. Nat. Y 9504; Z 1J 708, 717, 735, 736, 752; Z 1F 433, fol. 93.

JU Charles
Architect-in-ordinary to the Regent.
Work for Mlle de Séry, about 1712. Work at Bagnolet, about 1720.

JU Louis

KAUFFER
Hôtel de la Régie, Rue Saint-Augustin, 1780.

LABBÉ Jean-François
Died 1750. Inspecteur des bâtiments du Roi.
Scheme for the reconstruction of the hospital des Quinze-Vingts, 1750, executed by P.-H. Martin (model in the new Hôpital des Quinze-Vingts).

De LABRIÉRE Jean-Jacques
Born 15 March 1716, died 25 July 1785.

De LABRIÉRE Alexandre-Louis
It is difficult to distinguish between these architects before 1785. One or other filled the following positions: Contrôleur des Bâtiments du Roi at Fontainebleau in 1772, and at Meudon in 1778; architect to the Comte d'Artois, architect to Mme Elisabeth. Alexandre-Louis emigrated to England during the Revolution.
Hôtel de Gamache, Rue des Martyrs, 1762. Hôtels at

7, 9 and 11 Rue de la Chaise. Abbaye de Notre-Dame aux Nonains, Troyes, 1778–81. Gardens of Gennevilliers, 1785. Work at Bellevue, 1791. Préponnier house at Boissy-Saint-Léger, 1783. Château de Montreuil for Mme Elisabeth. Work at Bagatelle for the Comte d'Artois. Théâtre des Petits Comédiens, Passy. Work for the Prince of Wales at Carlton House. Boudoir at Southill, about 1795.
Publ.: *Projet de portail pour St-Germain-l'Auxerrois*, 1757. Mémoire sur la nécessité de mettre les sépultures hors la ville de Paris. Plan d'un Temple pour la sépulture de nos rois (*Journal de la République des lettres et des arts*, texte transcrit dans la *Revue universelle des arts*, 1855, vol. xx).
Ref.: Arch. Nat. Z 2 2459; R 4 433. Archives de Seine-et-Oise: *VP*, vol. IX, 189. Thiéry.
Bibl.: F. J. B. Watson; Southill, *A Regency House*, London, 1951.

LA GUÊPIÈRE Jacques de
Died 1744. Academician 1720. Contrôleur des Bâtiments du Roi.
Decoration of the Château de Bercy (attributed by Fiske Kimball to Pierre Lepautre, today distributed between the Hôtel de la Rochefoucauld-Doudeauville, former Hôtel de Janvry, 47 Rue de Varenne; La Maison de la Pensée française, 2 Rue de l'Elysée; La Maison de la Chasse et de la Nature, 50 Rue des Archives, etc.).
Ménagerie de Sceaux. Transformation of the Abbaye Sainte-Geneviève (library, today dormitory of the Lycée Henri IV). Work at the Petit Hôtel d'Aumont, Rue de Jouy, 1721–23. Partial reconstruction of the Hôtel de la Ferté, 12 Rue de Richelieu, 1712.
Ref.: Mireille Rambaud, *Doc.* I. Brice, Mariette, etc.

LANCRET François-Nicolas
2e Grand Prix. Associate of the Academy of Saint-Luc in 1775. Living Rue de la Calendre.
Château de la Motte-Tilly (Aube), built for the Abbé Terray and his brother in 1755. Hôtel de Ville de Château-villain, 1780–84. Hôtel de Ville de Chaumont, 1787–90.
Bibl.: H. Ronot, 'Les Œuvres de l'architecte F.-N. Lancret', in *BSHAF*, 1961.

LANOUE DE LA COUPERIE Jean-Julien
Died May 1788. Rue de la Clef.
Hôtel de la Marquise de l'Hôpital, Boulevard du Temple, 1761. (?) Hospital of Lagny.
Ref.: Arch. Nat. Y 9507; H 2124; Z 1J 888–9 (design for the Grecian banisters of the Hôtel de l'Hôpital, executed by Jacques Lucotte).

LARDANT Pierre-François
'Expert-entrepreneur' from 1770 to 1792. Passage des Petits-Pères in 1781.
Tenements: Faubourg Saint-Honoré, between the Hôtel Beauveau and the Rue Verte, 1773; Passage des Petits-Pères, 1780; Rue de Grammont, about 1780.
Ref.: Arch. Nat. Z 1J 1059.

LASSURANCE (CAILLETEAU known as)
Academician 1699.

Château de Petit-Bourg (destroyed in 1750). Hôtels de Rothelin, Rue de Grenelle, 1700; de Béthune-Neuchâtel, Rue Saint-Dominique; de Montbason, Rue Saint-Honoré; de Maisons-Soyecourt, 51 Rue de l'Université; d'Auvergne, Rue de l'Université; de Noailles, 211 Rue Saint-Honoré; Desmarets, Rue Saint-Marc (later Montmorency); de Roquelaure, Boulevard Saint-Germain, 1722 (Ministry of Public Works). Palais Bourbon, with Giardini, 1722.
Ref.: Blondel, *Architecture Française*.

LASSURANCE Jean
Academician 1723. Son of above.
Work for Mme de Pompadour at Crécy, near Dreux, and at Aunay, La Celle, Fontainebleau, Compiègne, Versailles and Paris (decoration of the Elysée).

LAURENT Louis-Jean
Architect to the Prince de Condé in 1783.

LAURENT Pierre, known as LAURENT de TROYES
Grand Prix 1735. Architect and engraver.
Design (engraved) for the organ-case of Saint-Sulpice. Etching of the court of the Hôtel de Ville on the occasion of the marriage of Madame Première to the Infante, Duque de Parma, 1738. Laurent took over the work at Saint-Sulpice after Servadoni's death (Blondel, *Cours d'architecture*, vol. III, p. 330, and *Architecture française*, vol. III, p. 39).

LEBÈGUE Pierre
'Expert-bourgeois' from 1733. Living Rue Saint-Martin, near the Fontaine Maubué.
Château de Beauregard-en-Brie, 1714. Maison Gourdon, Rue François Miron, opposite the Rue Clocheperce, 1732. House for the Comte de Maleyssie, Cul-de-Sac Férou, 1733. House, Rue de l'Hirondelle. Work at the Hôtel de Hautes-Bruyères, Rue Saint-Germain-l'Auxerrois, 1734.
Ref.: Arch. Nat. Z 1J 578, 638, 651, 653.

LE BLOND Alexandre Jean-Baptiste
Born in Paris 1679, died in St Petersburg 1719.
Archbishop's palace of Auch (unfinished). Gardens of le Cannet, near Narbonne. Hôtel de Vendôme, Rue d'Enfer, today Ecole des Mines, built in 1706–7, enlarged in 1715 (built by Le Blond according to Brice, Pigagnol, Hurtaut-Magny, Mariette – Blondel, in the Daviler of 1738, Blondel in *Architecture française*, 1752, vol. I, p. 55. Built by Courtonne; enlarged by Le Blond, according to Patte, *Cours d'architecture*, 1777, vol. VI, pp. 465–7. Built by Le Blond, enlarged by Courtonne, according to D'Argenville fils, 1757. Built by Le Blond, and probably enlarged by Le Blond also, according to B. Lossky in *GBA*, 1934. 'Courtonne a effectivement contribué à la construction d'un bâtiment à l'Hôtel de Vendôme en 1715', cf. M. Rambaud, *Doc. I*, p. 39.) Maison Regnault at Châtillon-sous-Bagneux. Garden of the Hoguer house, same place (probably La maison des Dominicains, photographed in Jarry, *La Guirlande de Paris*, vol. II, pls. 25–6. The attribution of the latter house to Le Blond, accepted by L. Hautecœur, is not generally supported). Hôtel de Saissac, 69 Rue de Varenne, 1708–14. Designs for the castle of Strelna (built by Michetti), and for the Peterhof palace (built by Rastrelli the younger).

Publ.: Illustrations for the *Histoire de l'Abbaye de Saint-Denis* by M. Félibien. Drawings for *La Théorie et la pratique du jardinage* by Dézallier d'Argenville père, 1709 (in the name of Le Blond in the 1722 edition); and for the second and third editions of the *Cours d'architecture* by Daviler, 1710 and 1720 (the fourth by Mariette and Blondel, 1738).
Bibl.: P.-J. Mariette, *Abecedario*, vol. III. D'Argenville fils, *Vies des architectes*, p. 440. B. Lossky, 'L'Hôtel de Vendôme et son architecte Alexandre Le Blond', followed by an additional note on the erroneous attribution of the Hôtel de Vendôme to Courtonne, in *GBA*, 1934, vol. I, pp. 30–41. B. Lossky, 'J.-B. A. Le Blond, architecte de Pierre le Grand, son œuvre en France', in *Bulletin de l'association russe pour les recherches scientifiques*, Prague, vol. III, No. 17, 1936.

LEBON Pierre-Etienne
Pupil of Cartaud. Sometime 'pensionnaire du Roi' in Rome.
Works for the Cardinal de Rohan in Paris and Strasbourg, about 1740. He was Boullée's first teacher.

LEBOSSU J.-B.
Inspector of Quarries 1784–90.

LEBOURSIER Jean-Baptiste-Louis-Elisabeth
Pupil of the Academy. Owner of the Hôtel Lamoignon, Rue Pavée, in 1774.
Hôtel du Prince Xavier de Saxe, Faubourg Saint-Honoré, 1779. Hôtel Thiroux de Montsauge, 1777–78, today Rue du Faubourg Saint-Jacques. Hôtel de Broglie, 73 Rue de Varenne, 1782–84. Hôtel de Périgord, Rue de l'Université (disappeared).
Engravings of various schemes: entrance of an opera-house (Musée Carnavalet); a temple to the muses; a building dedicated to peace.
Ref.: Arch. Nat. F 17 1265 10.

LE BRUN
Died October 1729.

LE BRUN Charles-François
'Expert' in 1740.

LEBRUN Jean-Pierre
'Expert du Roi' in the Provostship of the Household.

LE CAMUS Louis-Denis
(Referred to as Lecamus-Choiseul in the *Almanach Dauphin* of 1774.)
2e prix 1742. Contrôleur at the Invalides, later architect to the Duc de Choiseul.
Transformation of the Château and *fabriques* (in the park) of Chantelou. Plan for the Choiseul quarter (carried out by Sandrier, Roland, Renaud and Durand, Delarbre, Briand and Delanoé, Armand and Roche), 1780.
Ref.: Arch. Nat. Z 1J 1072, 1085.

LE CAMUS de MÉZIÈRES Nicolas
Architect, 'expert-bourgeois' from 1751 to 1792.
Maison de Varenne, Rue Mouffetard, 1766 (*PVARA*, vol.

VII, p. 250). La Halle au Blé (1763–66). Le Colysée (hall of entertainments), Champs-Elysées, 1771–74. Hôtel de Beauveau, Faubourg Saint-Honoré. Barracks of the Rue Mouffetard. Pavillon, 5 Rue Saint-Blaise, Charonne (demolished in 1929). Work at the Free School of Drawing (cf. *GBA*, 1920, vol. I, p. 205). Several houses in the Quartier des Halles.

Publ.: Recueil de différents plans concernant la nouvelle halle aux grains, 1768. Le Génie de l'architecture ou l'analogie des arts avec nos sensations, 1780. Le guide de ceux qui veulent bâtir, 1781. Traité de la force des bois, 1782. Description de Chantilly et des jardins.

LE CARPENTIER Antoine-Mathieu

Born at Rouen 15 July 1709, died in Paris 13 July 1773. Academician 1756.

Work at the Cour des Comptes, under Jacques (V) Gabriel, 1738–40. Church of the Collège de Grandmont, Rue Mignon. Collège de Navarre, Rue de la Harpe (contract approved by Maître Mouette, 16 June 1759, Arch. Nat. Min. LXXVI, 371, with nine drawings). Main entrance of the archbishop's palace of Rouen. Design for the choir screen of Rouen cathedral. Building for the abbey of Clairvaux. Building for the Arsenal. Main entrance of the Palais Bourbon (Patte, *Cours d'architecture*, vol. IV, p. 153). Château de Courteilles (Eure), built for Jacques de Barberie, Marquis de Courteilles, 1754–62. Château de la Ferté Vidame (Eure), for J.-J. de La Borde. Château de Ballainvilliers (Seine-et-Oise), for Jacques Samuël Bernard. Château for the Comte de Waldner in Alsace. Pavillon de Croix-Fontaine en Forêt de Sénart, for Michel Bouret (about 1755). Transformation of the Château d'Ormesson. Pavillon de la Boissière, Rue de Clichy, 1751 (enlarged by Couture the younger, pupil of Le Carpentier, about 1770).

Hôtel Bouret, Rue Grange-Batelière (later Hôtel de La Borde, de La Reynière and de Choiseul; contract approved by Maître Alléaume, 30 May 1752). Oval dining-room and bath suite of the Hôtel Montmorency-Luxembourg (former Hôtel Desmarets, built by Lassurance), Rue Saint-Marc. Extension of the Hôtel de Choiseul, Rue de Richelieu (former Hôtel Pierre Crozat, built by Cartaud). Hôtel de Boulainvilliers, Rue Bergère. Maison Le Père (?), same street. Hôtel de Lassay or de La Guiche, Rue du Regard, 1752 (Arch. Nat. Z 1F 459, fols. 59–60); façade rebuilt in a court of the Caisse d'Epargne. Hôtel de Barillon in the Marais (Rue des Vieilles Haudriettes or Rue de Birague?). Maison Bauche, same quarter. Gallery in the Hôtel du Contrôle général (former Hôtel de Lionne, Rue Neuve-des-Petits-Champs, built by Louis Le Vau). Hôtel d'Harcourt-Beuvron (Rue de Grenelle?). Work for the Marquis de Brou, 1769. Maison Le Carpentier, Boulevard Saint-Martin, 1770 (Arch. Nat. H 2131).

LECHANGEUR Pierre-Jean-Charles

'Architecte breveté of His late Majesty the King of Poland.' Churches of Lagesse and Villemaux in Lorraine, about 1766–70. Building of the Café Anglais, Boulevard du Temple, 1780.

Ref.: Arch. Nat. Z 1J 1064.

LE CHAUVE

Family of architects:

LE CHAUVE Brice

'Expert-bourgeois.' Architect to the Prince de Condé. Living Rue des Quatre-Vents in 1730, later at the Palais Bourbon.

LE CHAUVE Claude known as BRICE LE CHAUVE

Juliot house, Rue du Saint-Sépulcre; work for a Sr le Rat, Rue Taranne; and at the Hôtel de Varsovie, Rue de Seine, 1777. He may also be the architect of the Hôtel de Montmorency, 87 Rue du Cherche-Midi, 1757; cf. inventory after the death of the Maréchal de Montmorency-Bours, étude I, p. 491, 20 March 1759: 'Brise le Jeune': elevation of the hôtel in Banister-Fletcher (Cordingley edition 1961), *A History of Architecture*, p. 788 E.

Ref.: Arch. Nat. Z 1J 644, 705, 1032, 1037.

LEDOUX Claude-Nicolas

Born at Dormans (Marne) 21 March 1736, died in Paris 18 November 1806. Pupil of Blondel (1757) and of L.-F. Trouard (1760). Academician 1770.

Works in Burgundy, Champagne and Bassigny; church, Pont Prégibert; restoration of the old bridge at Rolampont (Haute-Marne); fountains and drinking-trough at Neuilly-l'Evêque; pulpit and choir of the church of Corgirnon; churches of Fouvent-le-Haut and Roche-sur-Vannon (Haute-Saône); work at Culmont (Haute-Marne), 1764. Bridge of Marac (Haute-Marne); chapel and bell-tower at Villadin (Aube); church of Cruzy-le-Châtel (Yonne) – first order of the portal and first five bays of the nave; work at Rigny-le-Ferron (Aube), at the abbey of Les Echarlys (Yonne) and its dependent buildings, and at La Celle-Saint-Cyr and Précy-le-Sec. Bridges at Sainte-Colombe de Sens, 1765.

Decoration of the Café Militaire, 1762. Château d'Eaubonne, 1762–63. Work at the cathedral of Auxerre: design for the decoration of the sanctuary and organ-loft, 29 April 1765 (fees received in 1771). Hôtel d'Hallwyl, 28 Rue Michel Le Comte; scheme submitted to Caqué, 'expert', and Foucard, 'greffier des bâtiments', 14 June 1766. Hôtel d'Uzès (site of the Rue d'Uzès, 1768; sculptures by Félix Lecomte. Enlargement of the Château de Montfermeil, about 1765. Hôtel Hocquart de Montfermeil, 68 Chaussée d'Antin, 1765–67. Work at Sens cathedral: probably the door made in March 1768 between the left-hand lateral aisle and the chapter-house. Hôtel de Montmorency (Lenormand de Mézières, 'bare owner'), at the west corner of the Boulevard and the Chaussée d'Antin; building line, etc., fixed 16 May 1769; programme decided 5 January 1770; work accepted 1771. Hôtel Tabary, Faubourg Poissonnière, opposite the Menus Plaisirs; programme settled before 1 June 1771; stucco-work by Feuillet and Métivier accepted 19 June 1773. Château de Bénouville (Calvados), 1770–77. Pavillon of Mlle Guimart, Chaussée d'Antin; programme decided June 1770; work accepted 1773; fees 1776. Maison Lenormand de Mézières (little château) at Eaubonne (built for the poet Saint-Lambert); acceptance of sculptures by

Feuillet and Méthivier June–July 1773. Pavillon de Mme du Barry at Louveciennes, begun in 1771, completed during the summer of 1773. Stables for Mme du Barry, 5 Avenue de Paris, Versailles; Grand Château de Louveciennes (unfinished). Project for a palace for Mme du Barry in Paris, Rue d'Artois (Rue Laffitte). Ledoux house, Rue de l'Université, scheme of 6 September 1773. House for Mlle de Saint-Germain at Les Porcherons, about 1772. Hôtels d'Attilly et d'Espinchal, Faubourg Poissonnière; de Jarnac, Rue des Petites Ecuries; d'Evry, Rue Ventadour, about 1772–80. Design for the Château de Saint-Vrain, between Corbeil and Arpajon, 1776, for Mme du Barry. Salt-works of Arc-et-Senans (Doubs); designed 1774, built 1775–79. Projects for triumphal arch and library, Cassel, 1775. Hôtel Thélusson, Rue de Provence, 1778–83. Château (and *fabriques* in the park) de Maupertuis, near Coulommiers, for the Marquis Anne-Pierre de Montesquiou, about 1780. Proposed house for M. de Witt, 1781. Salt store, Compiègne, 1783. Theatre of Besançon; date of project 24 August 1775; foundations and masonry 1778–81; opening 9 April 1784. Proposed Hôtel de Ville for Neuchâtel, 1783. Paris toll-houses, 1785–89. Proposed Palais de Justice and prisons at Aix-en-Provence, 1786. Hôtel des Fermes Générales, Rue du Bouloir, unfinished, 1786. Maisons Saisseval at La Grenouillère, 1788. Hosten houses, Rue Saint-Georges, 1792. Scheme for the Caisse d'Escompte, 1789.

BUILDINGS AND PROJECTS OF UNCERTAIN DATE OR LOCATION
House in the park of Bellevue. Country-house for M. Schmidt (near Paris, according to Gaite). House for M. Lauzon at Chavigny, in Poitou. House for the Chevalier de Mannery at Salins (according to Ramée), near Paris (according to Gaite). Château d'Aiguières.
Château for the Comte de Barail. Design for the bishop's palace, Sisteron. Drinking-trough, wash-house and rural school, Meilland. '*Ferme parée*' of La Roche-Bernard. Project for theatre of Marseille. Commercial building, Rue Saint-Denis. *Fabriques* in the park of Bourneville (gateway to park, chapel, temple of Zephyr and Flora). Subsidiary chapels of Clichy and Monceau.
Publ.: De l'architecture considérée sous le rapport de l'art, des mœurs et de la législation, 1804, vol. I, vol. II, edited by Daniel Ramée, 1847.
Bibl.: Geneviève Levallet-Haug, *Cl.-N. Ledoux*, Paris-Strasbourg, 1954. Emil Kaufmann, 'Three Revolutionary Architects: Boullée, Ledoux and Lequeu', in *Transactions of the American Philosophical Society*, Philadelphia, 1952, vol. 42. Helen Rosenau, *The Ideal City*, London, 1959. Marcel Raval and Jean-Ch. Moreux, *C.-N. Ledoux*, Paris, 1945. Johannes Langner, *Cl.-N. Ledoux, die erste Schaffenzeit, 1762–1774*, thesis, Freiburg-im-Breisgau, 1959. Yvan Christ, in *Arts*, 26 April–2 May 1967. Yvan Christ, *Projets et divagations de C.-N. Ledoux*, 1961. J. Langner, 'Ledoux – Redaktion der eigenen Werke für die Veröffentlichung', in *Zeitschrift für Kunstgeschichte*, 1960. W. Herrmann, 'The Problem of Chronology in C.-N. Ledoux's engraved work', in *Art Bulletin*, 1960. M. Gallet, 'La Jeunesse de Ledoux', in *GBA*, 1970.
Ref.: Arch. Nat. Z IJ 902, 936, 939, 949, 954, 970, 974, 975, 998, 1000, 1086, 1118, 1221. Arch. Nat. 265 AP 421,

No. 161: Etat de dépenses et mémoires de la construction de l'hôtel d'Uzès; No. 162: Contrôle des fournitures pour le même Bâtiment – 1768–74. Arch. Nat. AB XIX, 213–14: Mémoires de la construction de l'hôtel Thélusson. N III Seine 1265: Dessins pour la chambre de Mme d'Hallwyl; dessins pour l'hôtel d'Uzès. Arch. Nat. Minutier LII, 479, 5 January 1770: Projet d'architecture et de décoration de l'hôtel de Montmorency. Arch. Nat. Z IF 501, fol. 50: permission de construire, pour l'hôtel Thélusson, au nom de Haudry du Souci, 25 September 1778.

LEDREUX de la CHARTRE Louis
Accessit in Rome competition 1760. Contrôleur des Bâtiments du Roi at Compiègne.
Grand staircase of the palace of Compiègne and elevation facing park. Hôtel de la Surintendance and private building in the town.

LEFÈVRE
Family of building contractors and architects:

LEFÈVRE senior
Houses in the precincts of the Halle au Blé, 1764. Hôtel, Place du Palais-Royal, 1770. Hôtel de Malanville, Rue d'Angoulême Saint-Honoré (with Armand and Paris).

LEFÈVRE junior
Probably eldest son of the above.
Arthur's wallpaper manufactory, Boulevard de la Chaussée d'Antin and Rue Louis le Grand. *Fabriques* in the Thierry garden at Ville d'Avray. Clémon house at Etampes, etc.
Ref.: Krafft, *Architecture civile*.

LEFÈVRE J.-B. Louis
A son of the first-mentioned. Pupil of Paris. Grand Prix 1789.
Ref.: Eulogy of M. Lefèvre by Legrand.

LEFOULLON Guillaume-Elie
'Expert-entrepreneur' from 1773 to 1792. Living Rue et Barrière de la Chaussée d'Antin in 1792.

LE FRANC D'ÉTRECHY Charles
Died 1762. Pupil of the Academy 1732. Academician 1755. Rue Monsieur le Prince.
Maison du Collège d'Harcourt, Rue des Francs-Bourgeois and Rue Monsieur le Prince, 1743. Maison Le Franc, Villejuif, 1746. Work for M. d'Epinay at la Chevrette, 1755.
Ref.: Arch. Nat. Y 4613; Z IJ 727, 768, 820. *PVARA*, vols. V and VI.
This architect is not to be confused with

LE FRANC Louis-Thibaut
Living Rue du Vieux-Colombier in 1776.

LEGRAND
Several architects of this name occur in eighteenth-century records, but it is often difficult to distinguish between them.

1 (a) Pierre LEGRAND who died before 1730.
 (b) Etienne LEGRAND, son of the above. 'Expert-bourgeois' from 1727. Architect to the police. Rue Levêque in 1730, Rue Française in 1740; property owner, Rue de Grenelle, the same year.
Maison Thuin, Rue aux Ours, 1735. Work for M. Bouret at Croix-Fontaine, 1750.
 (c) Etienne-François LEGRAND. Son of the above.
Work at Orléans cathedral. Work at Montmagny for the Comtesse de la Rochefoucauld, 1780. Tenements in the Gros Caillou district and, in particular, the Maison Cardon, adorned with a monumental colonnade, by the Seine, 1786. Hôtel de Gallifet, 75 Rue de Grenelle, 1775–92. Hôtel de Jarnac, 8 Rue Monsieur, 1784.

2 (a) Germain-Eloi LEGRAND. Died April 1751. Academician 1728. Rue du Hasard 1728–40.
Work for the Abbé Larcher, Quartier de la Villeneuve. Maison Lombard d'Ermenonville, Rue Bourg-l'Abbé, 1725. Maison d'Argenson, Rue des Tournelles. Scheme for les maisons de l'Orme Saint-Gervais, 1733. Séminaire des Trente-Trois, 35 Rue de la Montagne Sainte-Geneviève, 1737.
 (b) Pierre-Germain LEGRAND. Associate of the Académie de Saint-Luc 1775. Architect to the Duc d'Orléans 1775–80.

3 Jean LEGRAND
Maison Morel, Rue de Bretagne, 1736.
This architect may be the same as. (i) Jean-Jacques LEGRAND, a patron of Saint-André-des-Arts in 1754; (ii) LEGRAND L'AÎNÉ.
Maison Regnault, Rue Montorgueil and Rue Leopold-Bellan, 1744–45. Engraving of a triumphal arch, dedicated to the Duchesse du Maine.

4 Pierre-Antoine LEGRAND. Affiliated to the lodge of the Douce Union in 1788.

5 Jacques-Guillaume LEGRAND
Born in Paris 9 May 1753, died Saint-Denis 8 November 1809. Pupil of Perronet and Blondel. Son-in-law of Ch.-L. Clérisseau.
In charge of works for the bridge of Tours, about 1775. Dome of the Halle au Blé, 1793 (in collaboration with Molinos). Slipway for the port of Brest. Marché des Innocents, Paris. Monument known as 'Lantern of Diogenes' in the park of Saint-Cloud. Transformation of the Fontaine des Innocents, 1786. House at 6 Rue Saint-Florentin 1789. Théâtre Feydeau, 1789; design, Arch. Nat. Z 1J 1205. Façade to court and decoration of the Hôtel Marbeuf, Faubourg Saint-Honoré, 1789. Work at Saint-Denis, 1807–9.

Publ.: *Parallèle de l'architecture ancienne et moderne*, 1789. Text of *Les Antiquités de la France* by Clérisseau, 1804. *Galerie Antique*, 1806. *L'Architecture*, 1809–10. *Description de Paris*, in collaboration with Landon, 1818.
MSS.: Biography of Piranesi; Bibl. Nat. nouv. acq. fr. 5968, published in G. Morazzoni and G. B. Piranesi, *Notizie Biografiche*, Milan, 1921.

Bibl.: Jean Adhémar, 'La Coupole de la Halle au Blé et l'influence de Ph. Delorme au XVIIIe siècle', in *L'Architecture*, 1933, p. 249.
A Legrand was a candidate for the Academy in 1756 and 1758.

LE HAIN
'Expert-bourgeois' from 1739. Rue de la Verrerie.

LE JUGE Nicolas
Sometime 'avocat en Parlement'. 'Expert-bourgeois' in 1715. Rue du Gindre-Saint-Germain in 1720.

LE MASSON Louis
1743–1819 (?1829). Ingénieur des Ponts et Chaussées. Brother of the sculptor Fr. Le Masson.
Château abbatial of Royaumont, 1785–89. Courbevoie church, 1789. Plans for Guitrancourt church, 1787.
L. Le Masson was the author of a panorama of Rome, depicted from San Pietro in Montorio, engraved on five plates. The original watercolour (5 m × 0.75 m) has been preserved by the family.
Bibl.: J.-Ch. Moreux, Le Masson (1743–1830), in *Revue des arts*, 1951, pp. 31–6. Henri Lemoine in *Bulletin de la Société des Antiquaires de France*, 1945–47, p. 28. Emilio Terry, 'Le Palais abbatial de Royaumont', in *Art et style*, No. 5, 1906, pp. 41–54.

LEMIT Louis
Practising in 1789.

LEMIT Pierre-Henri-René
'Expert-bourgeois' from 1778 to 1792. Rue Saint-Anne.

LEMOINE de COUZON Jean-Philippe
Born in Paris. Pupil of Mansart de Sagonne. Grand Prix 1768. Candidate for the Academy from 1784 to 1792. Rue de Vaugirard, near the Hôtel de Condé, in 1776.
Monument in honour of the Comte d'Artois at the Château de Long (Somme), 1777 (sculpture by Pfaff von Pfaffenhoffen). Restoration scheme for Sens cathedral. Immeubles d'Argenson, Faubourg Saint-Honoré. Hôtel d'Argenson, 38 Avenue Gabriel, 1780–87. Restoration of Les appartements de la Meilleraie, at the Arsenal, 1784. Project for the institution of deaf-mutes at Les Célestins, 1784. House for M. de Châlus (occupied by the Comtesse d'Artois) at Saint-Cloud, 1788. Work for the Comte de Mercy-Argenteau; perhaps at the Château de Neuville-sur-Oise.
Ref.: Arch. Nat. Z 1J 1050, 1082, 1133, 1163, 1221. R 1 379. O 1 1932 8.

LEMOINE Paul-Guillaume
Known as Lemoine le Jeune, Lemoine le Romain and, later, Lemoine-Beaumarchais. Grand Prix 1775. Inspector at the Colysée in 1774. Contrôleur at the Théâtre Français in 1790. Contractor for work on the Madeleine, 1806.
Project for Saint-Sauveur. Hôtel de Beaumarchais, Porte Saint-Antoine, 1790 (Krafft.).
Ref.: Settlement of fees between Pierre-Augustin Caron de Beaumarchais and Guillaume-Paul Lemoine, through the 'expertise' of Nicolas Toussaint Gabriel and Sylvain Marie Moyreau, dated 7 Prairial, year IV (private records).

LEMOINE Pierre-Hippolyte
Son of the sculptor J.-B. Lemoyne. Pupil of Chalgrin.

LEMONNIER Louis-Philippe
Contractor and architect.
Roger de Beaulieu tenements, Rue d'Anjou Saint-Germain and Cul-de-sac de Nevers, 1787. Tenements at 2 and 4 Rue de Tournon, 1779–80. Hôtel Cassini, Rue de Babylone, to the designs of Bélisard. Restoration of the Palais Bourbon, 1788.
Ref.: Arch. Nat. Z 1J 948, 975, 1205.
Bibl.: G. Macon, *Les Arts dans la Maison de Condé.*

LENOIR LE ROMAIN Samson-Nicolas
Born at Saint-Germain (according to *Corresp. des dir.*) or in Paris (according to *Les Biographies bourguignonnes* of L.-B. Baudot). Died in Paris 29 June 1810. Pupil of Blondel in 1751. In Rome, under the protection of the Marquis de Marigny, in May 1753.
Works at Dijon and in the neighbourhood: Hôtel Bouhier de Lantenay (prefecture), engravings of plans; public fountain opposite Les Bernadines; façade of the Hôtel (inn) de Saint-André, Rue Saint-Nicolas (today, Rue J.-J. Rousseau); Hôtel de Loisy, 3 Rue Buffon. Dependent buildings of the Château de Pouilly-lès-Dijon. Work at the Château de Longecourt and at the abbey of Cherlieu. Hôtel du Marquis Bénigne (III) Bouhier de Lantenay, before 1760 (three engraved plans). Hôtel Berbisey, Rue Berbisey (scheme engraved, but not completely carried out). Obelisk, paid for by the Président Fyot, in the garden of the Hôtel Berbisey. Public fountain opposite Les Bernadins (engraved). Hôtel de Loisy, 3 Rue Buuffon.
Porte Saint-Nicolas at Beaune (engraved), 1762.
Building for the abbey of Cîteaux (general scheme in the Library of Dijon, reproduced by Joan Evans in *Monastic Architecture*); also engraving by De Neufforge.
Parish church, and buildings constructed for Voltaire, at Ferney. Works in Paris: Abbey of Saint-Antoine des Champs (Hôpital Saint-Antoine), project of 1763; Arch. Nat. N II Seine 18. Maison de Pondeveyle, corner of the Rues Bourbon-le-Château and de l'Echaudé, 1764. Vauxhall de la Foire Saint-Germain, 1769. Vauxhall at Bordeaux, 1774 (*Almanach Dauphin*). Hôtel Benoist Sainte-Paule, 30 Faubourg Poissonnière, 1773. Halle aux veaux, between the Quai de la Tournelle and Les Bernardins, 1773–75. Shops of the Foire Saint-Laurent, 1774–75. Hôtel Rigoley de Juvigny, later Giambonne, Rue de Bondy, 1776. Bimont tenements, Rue Notre-Dame-des-Victoires and Place de la Bourse, 1776. Improvement scheme for the enclos du Temple, 1777; Arch. Nat. N II Seine 97. Group of tenements, Rue de Bourbon (Lille), 1777. Tenements at the south corner of the Rue de Saintonage and of the Boulevard, 1778. Entrance design for the abbey of Saint-Denis, 1778. Development plan for the Hôtel de Choiseul. Marché Saint-Antoine, 1775–79. Tenements at the south corner of the Rues Montmartre and Buffault, 1780. Temporary Opéra, known as Théâtre de la Porte Saint-Martin, 2 August–27 October 1781. Magasin des Menus-Plaisirs, Rue Richer, 1781. Tenements, Rues Saint-Augustin and de la Michodière, 1780–83. Choiseul Gouffier tenements, Rue Pagevin, 1780. Tenements, Rue Taitbout, 1781, one of which was for Talbot, silversmith to Monsieur. Group of eighteen tenements forming the Rue d'Angivillers, on the site of the former Quinze-Vingt, and scheme for a semicircular *place* in front of the Palais-Royal, 1781; Arch. Nat. N III Seine 406. Giroux de Villette tenements, Rue Saint-Antoine, 1783. Tenement building for the Comte de Tracy, at the corner of the Rues Saint-Denis and de Tracy, 1783–84. Completion of the Hôtel de la Régie Générale, Rue Saint-Augustin. Vauxhall of the Rue Saint-Thomas du Louvre, 1785–88. Tenements of the Rue Bleue. Design for the theatre of Montpellier, executed by Jacques Donnat, 1786. Etablissement des Bains-Chinois, 1787; model in the Musée Carnavalet. Hôtel Margantin, rue Richer, 1786. Bagnolet church. Transformation of the Château des Ternes. Théâtre de la Cité, 1790. Abattoir, Villejuif.
Ref.: Arch. Nat. Y 9506; Z 1F* 481, fol. 58; T 153 2; Z 1J 901, 973, 975, 991, 994, 1008, 1018, 1022, 1050, 1055, 1060, 1064, 1068, 1070, 1073, 1074, 1079, 1097, 1104, 1120, 1122, 1123, 1131, 1195. *Corresp. des dir.* vol. x, p. 450.
Bibl.: Ch. Oursel, in *Annales de Bourgogne*, 1946, vol. XVIII, pp. 133–6. Joan Evans, *Monastic Architecture in France*, 1964. Other sources: Martin Meade and Pierre Quarré.

LENOIR de VERNON
Practising in 1789.
Ref.: Arch. Nat. Z 1J 1189.

LEPAREUR Nicolas
Transformation of the Hôtel de Jassaud, Quai d'Orléans (contract approved by Maître Junot, 24 October 1733).
Ref.: Arch. Nat. Z 1J 644, 647.

LEPAS-DUBUISSON
Family of architects:

DUBUISSON Senior
Church of the Foreign Missions, Rue du Bac, 1696.

LEPAS-DUBUISSON Charles-Nicolas
Hôtels at 118 and 120 Rue du Bac, 1716. Work at the Royal Library for the Abbé Bignon, 1716. Maison Lepas-Dubuisson, Rue de la Lanterne, 1719. Maison Lepas-Dubuisson, 151 bis, Rue Saint-Jacques, 1720. Maison Aubin, Rue Saint-Denis, 1735.
Ref.: *Journal des Savants*, 10 August 1716. Arch. Nat. Z 1F 390, 393; Z 1J 525, 526, 528, 530, 541, 543, 547, 563.

LEPRINCE
Pupil of Rousset in 1766. Practising in 1784–85.
Tenements at la Pointe Saint-Eustache, 1785.
Ref.: Arch. Nat. Z 1J 1240.

LEPROUST Roland
'Expert-bourgeois' in 1720. Living Rue Bardubec.

LEQUEU Jean-Jacques
Born at Rouen 14 September 1757.
Scheme for Saint-Sauveur, about 1780. Country-house in Burgundy. Work at the Château de Montgermont. 'Maison à l'antique' for the Comte de Bouville at Neuilly.

Casino de Mme Molonaer at Saint-Grawensol. Maison S., *fermier-général*, at Boulogne. Maison Thowet, Romainville. Gothic gallery at the Château de Gaillon. Design for pulpit for Saint-Sulpice. Projects for the Hôtel de Ville, Rouen; and for the Capuchins of Marseille. Decoration, Rue de la Chaussée d'Antin (Krafft, *Recueil des habitations*, pl. 101). Work for the Comte d'Espagnac. Chinese pavilion for M. Mertin at Chatou.
Drawings and MSS.: Architecture of J.-J. Lequeu; B.N. Est. Ha 80 to Ha 80c, 4 vols.
Travels in Italy, MS.; B.N. Est. Vb 43.
Publ.: Précis méthodique pour apprendre à graver au lavis à l'eau forte, 1789; MS. in B.N. Est. Ad 64. Nouvelle méthode appliquée aux principes élémentaires du dessin tendant à perfectionner graphiquement le dessin de la tête de l'homme . . . 1792; B.N. Est. Kc A. Lettre sur le savonnage . . . adressée aux mères de famille; B.N. Est. Lh 34.
Bibl.: Günther Mekten, 'Jean-Jacques Lequeu ou l'architecture rêvée', in *GBA*, 1965, vol. I.
Jacques Guillerme, 'Lequeu et l'invention du mauvais goût', in *GBA*, 1965, vol. II.

LERIDDE
Practising in 1790.

LE ROUX Jean-Baptiste
Born about 1677, died 13 July 1746. Academician 1720.
Maison Fradet, Rue Sainte-Anne, 1714 (Arch. Nat. Z 1J 587). Hôtel de Serre de Rieux, Place Saint-Michel; Maison Anne Pinon, Rues Saint-Antoine and Culture Sainte-Catherine (2 Rue de Sévigné): the commemorative plaques found in the foundations of these two buildings appear in *Inscriptions de Paris* by Guilhermy). Hôtel d'Avaray, 85 Rue de Grenelle, 1721 (Arch. Nat. Z 1J 605). Hôtel du Prat, 60 Rue de Varenne, 1731 (Arch. Nat. Z 1J 624). Enlargement of the Hôtel de Roquelaure, 246 Boulevard Saint-Germain, 1732. Gallery of the Hôtel de Villars, 116 Rue de Grenelle, 1732 (commemorative plaque in the former collection of Baron Pichon, reproduction in the Musée Carnavalet). Transformation of the Hôtel d'Etampes, Rue de Varenne, for the Duchesse de Mazarin (Blondel and Bastide, *L'Homme du monde éclairé par les arts*, 1774; contract attested by Maître Camuset, 19 June 1736 – see Arch. Nat. Z 1J 683–4). Enlargement of the Hôtel Desmares-Villeroy, 78 Rue de Varenne. 'An infinity of fine "maisons de plaisance"' (Blondel). Hôtel Bourgeois de Boignes, 3 Rue d'Antin, 1729. (Banque de Paris et des Pays-Bas. Decoration by Nicolas Pineau.)
Ref.: Record (of affixing seals) after the death of J.-B. Le Roux – see *NAAF*, 1785, vol. II, p. 92.

LEROUX
'Expert-entrepreneur' from 1789 to 1792. Rue de Bondy.

LEROY Etienne
Born Versailles 1737. Pupil of Soufflot.
Bishop's palace, Agen (today, prefecture). Château d'Aiguillon.
Bibl.: Bauchal. Information supplied by P. Lavedan.

LEROY Etienne-Martial
'Expert-bourgeois' 1704–23. Rue du Bout-du-Monde in 1720.
A Leroy was building on his own behalf in the Rue de l'Egout-du-Ponceau in 1742.

LEROY Jean-François
Born at Chantilly 24 September 1729, died 17 May 1791. Architect of the Château de Chantilly and the Palais Bourbon, under the direction of Bélisard. Château d'Enghien, 1769–70. Work at the Palais Bourbon and the Hôtel de Lassay. *Fabriques* in the park of Betz-en-Multien, for the Princesse de Monaco: pavilion of rest and temple of friendship.
Bibl.: C.-M. Dugas, 'Une Dynastie d'architectes: les Le Roy', in *Société d'histoire et archéologie de Senlis*, 1959.

LEROY Julien-David
Born in Paris 6 May 1724, died 27 January 1803. Grand Prix 1751. Professor at the Royal Academy. Member of the Académie des Inscriptions and of the Académie de Marine.
Publ.: Les Ruines des plus beaux monuments de la Grèce, 1758. Histoire des formes différents que les Chrétiens ont données a leurs temples, 1764. Observations sur les édifices des anciens peuples, 1767.

LE ROY Jean-Joseph
Mentioned in 1772.

LESEIGNEUR Martin
Living Rue de la Pépinière in 1787. Contractor and architect. Working to the designs of Pérard de Montreuil in 1782.
Tenement building, Rue de la Pépinière, 1788.

LESNAY François-Etienne
'Expert-entrepreneur.' Rue des Francs-Bourgeois in 1715, later Cul-de-sac de la Rue Beaubourg.

de LESPÉE Jacques-François
Died 1762. Academician 1728.
Church of Sainte-Marguerite de Charonne, 1737.

de LESPÉE the younger
Died 1792. Academician 1747.

LESTRADE Gabriel de
Died 1770. Academician.
Project of 1770 for the Château de la Brosse, near Coulommiers.
Bibl.: E. de Ganay, *Les Jardins classiques au XVIIIe siècle*.

LE SUEUR Adrien
'Expert-bourgeois.' Rue Pastourelle in 1734.

LE SUEUR Jean-Charles
Rue Phélipeau in 1759.
Another LE SUEUR was a pupil of the Academy in 1769, and practising in 1785.

LE TAILLEUR DE BONCOURT Jean-Pierre
Died 1 August 1757. Rue des Vieux Augustins. Probably the same as BONCOURT, a Grand-Prix winner of 1724 and candidate for the Academy in 1735.
Work for les Pères de Nazareth in 1745.
Ref.: Arch. Nat. Z 1J 753. *PVARA*, vols. IV and V.

LE TELLIER Antoine-Nicolas
Rue Quincampoix in 1775.

LE TELLIER Louis
Contrôleur du domaine de Versailles. Rue Grenéta in 1784.
Hôtel Le Maître, 7 Rue Saint-Florentin, 1768. Hôtel de Ségur, 9 Rue Saint-Florentin, 1768. Hôtels Le Roy de Senneville and La Tour-du-Pin-Gouvernet, 6 and 8 Rue Royale, 1769. Tenements: 9, 11 and 13 Rue Royale, after 1781; panelling and stucco-work by Pierre or Louis-Pierre Fixon (those from 11 at the Museum of Decorative Arts in Buenos Aires and at the Musée Nissim de Camondo, Paris; from 13 at the Pennsylvania Museum of Art). Staircase, salon de Flore and des Zéphirs in the Hôtel de Hollande, 47 Rue Vieille-du-Temple, 1759–62; sculpture by Guibert, painting by Vien.
Bibl.: Paul Brenot, *Un vieil hôtel du Marais du XIVᵉ au XVIIIᵉ siècle*, 1939. Ch. des Courtils, *Les hôtels Le Tellier de la Rue Royale* (limited edition), 1958.

LE TELLIER Pierre-Louis
Died 3 June 1786.

LE TORDEUR Jacques
'Expert-bourgeois' from 1729. Living Rue de la Haumerie in 1730, and Rue de la Pelleterie in 1760.

LHUILLIER DE LA TOUR Nicolas
Died 20 March 1754. Rue des Gravilliers.
Tenements for les Théatins, 1720 and 1730. Building for the Abbaye Saint-Martin-des-Champs, 1743.
Ref.: Arch. Nat. Z 1J 736.
Bibl.: *La France littéraire (de l'Abbé de La Porte)*. M. Rambaud, *Doc.* I, pp. 406–73.

LIÉGEON Denis-Claude
Died after 1801. Third prize at the Roman Academy of Saint Luke in 1754, where the four sheets of his design, a cathedral, are preserved under the numbers 805–8. Candidate for the Académie Royale in 1780. Château de Ballincourt, in the valley of the Sauceron, near Pontoise. Tenements, 2 Rue Chabannais. Hôtel de Ballincourt, Rue Neuve-Saint-Charles (La Boétie). Hôtel Bersin, 11 Rue Saint-Florentin. Hôtel de Lapalu, Rue de la Pépinière. Project for a *théâtre français* at the Carrefour Buci (B.N. Est. Va 263). Doric temple for Mme d'Auberville, near Yerre. Pavilion and bath suite at the Château de Plessis Saint-Pair, near Longjumeau; work for M. Randon de Lucenay, 1790. Tenements and hôtels in the Quartier d'Antin.
Bibl. and Ref.: Jean Boyer, *BSHAF* 1957, p. 279. Dulaure, *Environs de Paris*, 1786. Watin, *Le Provincial à Paris*, 1790.

Papillon de la Ferté, *Journal des Menus-Plaisirs*, pp. 315–46. *Almanach historique*, 1777. Arch. Nat. Z 1J 963, 988, 1017, 1020, 1030, 1039, 1239.

LIEUTAUD Jacques-François
Dessinateur des Bâtiments du Roi in 1725.

LIEVAIN Denis-Louis
'Expert-entrepreneur.' Rue Michel-le-Comte in 1720. Work at the church of Les Théatains, and at the Hôtel Amelot de Chaillou (Tallard), 78 Rue des Archives.

LINDET Laurent
2ᵉ Grand Prix 1737. Architecture des Bâtiments du Roi. Manufacture de Sèvres (today Centre National d'Etudes Pédagogiques), 1760.

LOIR Jean-Baptiste
Died 22 January 1755. 'Expert' in 1715. Rue Neuve-Saint-Merry in 1730.

LOIR Denis
Died 1770. 'Expert-entrepreneur' from 1727. Living Rue Simon-le-Franc in 1740. Rue de la Verrerie, near the Rue des Coquilles in 1760.

LORIOT Louis-Adam
Academician 1735. Professor at the Academy.
Triumphal arch at Versailles, Avenue de Paris, for the peace of 1748. Gateway of the Château de Dampierre. Both engraved.

LOUCHET Joseph
Died 20 August 1790.
Professor at the Academy.
Ref.: *PVARA*, vol. IX.

LOUIS Nicolas known as Victor
Grand Prix 1755.
Most of the drawings by Louis were lost during the nineteenth century or destroyed in a fire at the Archives Municipales de Bordeaux in 1862; analyses were published by L. Gaullieur l'Hardy in 1828 and by Detcheverry in 1860. His Italian drawings have disappeared except for a few sanguines of Rome; the Louvre has an interior view of Saint Peter's, with figures by Amand.
Chapel of Notre-Dame de Bon Secours, Rue de Charonne, 1760: a scheme for this building was in the Legrix de Tustal collection in 1880; descriptions in the *Année littéraire*, vol. V, pp. 211–16, *Observateur littéraire*, vol. V, pp. 65–72, and the Guide de Thiéry, do not agree; the ballroom in the monastery buildings is not Louis's work, but a later addition by Richard Lenoir. Chapelle des Ames du Purgatoire, Sainte-Marguerite-de-Charonne, decorations painted in trompe-l'œil by Brunetti. Decorations for peace celebrations, 1763, engraved by Poulleau. Works for the King of Poland; the University Library of Warsaw possesses fifty-eight sheets of sketches and schemes done in Warsaw in 1765 and Paris in 1766. Furniture and panelling for the King's bedroom, and the portrait and throne-rooms were executed in Paris, to the designs of Louis and Prieur, by

the cabinet-maker Jadot. The costing of these items took place in the former Noviciat des Jésuites in 1768. Work on the periphery of the choir, Chartres cathedral, 1767; a drawing for the choir screen belonged to Legrix de Tustal in 1880. Church of Saint-Vincent, Metz. Façade of Saint-Clément, Metz. 'Vauxhall' de Toré, Boulevard Saint-Martin, 1770; an interior view was engraved by Poulleau. Decorations for the entertainment given by the Spanish ambassador for the marriage of the Dauphin, 1770. Project for a 'Vauxhall' in the Bois de Boulogne, engraved by Taraval, 1770. Transformation of the Hôtel de Richelieu: the Corinthian peristyle of the court is shown on a sketch preserved at the Archives Nationales, Z 1J; the work was carried out by Goupy in 1772–73; several drawings were burnt in 1862; Legrix de Tustal owned *L'Elévation d'une nouvelle entrée pour le pavillon de l'Hôtel de Richelieu* (Pavillon de Hanovre). Intendance de Franche-Comté, today the Prefecture of Besançon; nine drawings belonging to the Archives of the Doubs. Theatre of Bordeaux, 1778; album of engravings; Salle de Spectacle, Bordeaux, 1780; drawings and documents in the Archives of the Gironde, cartons k227 et seq.; in the municipal archives and in the 'bureau des plans' of the Hôtel de Ville de Bordeaux, and in the former Jules Lafargue and Puifferrat collections. Other work at Bordeaux: hôtels and maisons Saige, Fontfrède, Legrix, de la Molère, de Rolly, de Nairac, *grille* of the Chapeau-Rouge; Château de Virasel, near Marmande, 1774, for the Président Daugeard; Château de Bouilh (Gironde) for the Marquis de la Tour du Pin, 1786, drawings in the former collections of Ch. Durand, Legrix de Tustal, Marionneau and in the municipal archives. Project, Château d'Argent (Cher), for M. Dupré de Saint-Maur. Tenements in Paris, Rue de la Michodière, 1780 and 1787. Peristyle and interior decoration, Saint-Eloi, Dunkerque, 1783, engraving by the brothers Varin. Galleries of the Palais-Royal and project for a building between the Cour d'Honneur and the garden, 1781; a hundred drawings bought by the Duc d'Orléans (Louis-Philippe) from M. Latus, of Bordeaux, have vanished. Théâtre du Palais-Royal (today Théâtre Français), reconstructed in the present century by Guadet, father and son. Project for the Place Louis XVI at Bordeaux; drawing in the Louvre, plans in the municipal archives of Bordeaux and in the former Durand collection. Project for barracks on the site of the Fort du Ha; library of Bordeaux, Clouzet endowment. Project for a corn-market at Bordeaux. Projects for a triumphal bridge in Paris, and for alterations to the Luxembourg. Projects 'd'additions aux préparations du Panthéon'. Alterations to the interior of the Hôtel Titon, 58 Faubourg Poissonnière, 1797. Work at Rouen.

Bibl.: Ch. Marionneau, *Victor Louis, sa vie, ses travaux, sa correspondance*. Paul Courteault, 'Les Dernières années de Victor Louis', in *Revue historique de Bordeaux*, 1921. F. G. Pariset, *Notes sur l'architecte Victor Louis; Proceedings of the 87th congress of learned societies*, Bordeaux, 1957 (1959), archaeological section, pp. 197–202. F. G. Pariset and S. Lorenz, *Victor Louis et Varsovie*, catalogue of exhibition presented at Bordeaux and at the Musée Jacquemart-André, 1958; review by L. Hautecœur in *Les Mémoires de l'Académie des Beaux-Arts*, 1959, pp. 95 et seq. F. G. Pariset,

BSHAF, 1959. Barbara Krol, 'Projet du théâtre pour le Château Royal de Varsovie, par V. Louis, *c.* 1766, in *Revue d'histoire du théâtre, 1960*.

LUCOTTE J.-Raymond
Professor of architecture. Collaborated on the plates for *L'Encyclopédie*. Rue Saint-Sauveur in 1787.
Publ.: Le Vignole moderne; dédié au Comte d'Artois, Paris, 1784.

LUSSAULT
Buisson house, Rue des Quatre-Vents, 1753.

de LUZY
Academician 1733. Died 1773.
Abbey of Jouarre.

MACLAURIN
According to Roze de Chantoiseau, Maclaurin built the Hôtel de Chestret, Rue de Bondy (see notice on Lenoir le Romain).

MALDENC
Robert house, Rues Boucherat and de Normandie, 1724. Hôtel Le Peletier de la Houssaye, Rue Séguier, 1737–38 and 1756.
Ref.: Arch. Nat. 589, 727, 831.

MALHORTIE
Pupil of Blondel.
Private teacher of architecture, Rue de Grenelle Saint-Honoré in 1761.

MANGIN
'Expert-bourgeois' from 1777 to 1792. Rue des Mathurins in 1792.

MARCHAND Marc
'Expert-bourgeois' in 1716. At la Villeneuve 1715–20.

MAROLLES the Chevalier de
Architect and engineer. Rue du Cherche-Midi, at the Bureau de la Petite Poste, in 1775.
Decorations for celebrations in honour of the Duke of Württemburg, Stuttgart, 1763–64; and for coronation of the Emperor, Frankfurt, 1764. Project for a new castle and embellishments to the gardens of Schwetzingen, for the Elector Palatine, 1764. Work at Sans-Souci, 1765. Plans for draining the marshes of Bourgouin, Crémieux and la Verpillère, in Dauphiné, 1766. Renovation of the Episcopal palace of Saintes, 1768, for Mgr de la Chataigneraie. Château de Bar-sur-Seine, 1769. Draining the *étang* of Ferrières, near Montargis, 1773.
Ref.: Arch. Nat. o 1 1913 1 (curriculum vitae du 13 mars 1775).

MARQUIS
Grand Prix 1772. 'Premier dessinateur' in the agence du Théâtre Français, after 1 November 1773. An architect of this name was building at La Rapée for a M. Lemire in 1790.
Ref.: Z 1J 190; H 2 2177 (Arch. Nat.)

MARTEAU
Family of cabinet-makers and architects:

MARTEAU Jean-Baptiste
Thévenot house, Cul-de-sac de l'Etoile and Rue Thévenot 1715–17 (contract approved by Maître Gourdin, 10 May 1716), early photograph in *GBA*, March 1966. Ridoy house, Rue d'Aboukir, 1723.
Ref.: Arch. Nat. Z 1F 400; Z 1J 562, 565, 577.

MASSON Etienne
'Expert-entrepreneur' in 1720. Rue Clocheperce.
Project for the Hôtel des Abbés de la Victoire, Rue Saint-Germain l'Auxerrois, 1723; see Arch. Nat. Z 1J 562.

MATHIEU Claude
Died 7 April 1732. Engineer, architect 'des Bâtiments du Roi'. Academician 1717. Rue du Roi Doré.
Work on the bridge of Moulins, 1685. Bridges in the Marche and the Bourbonnais (Saint-Pourçain), 1687. Bridges at Lyon, 1689.

MAZIN Antoine
'Ingénieur du Roi', director of plans of the royal houses and fortifications of France. Knight of Saint-Louis.
Maison des Filles du Calvaire, Rue de Vaugirard, 1714. Maison Girardin de Vauvré, Rue Monsieur-le-Prince, 1718. Building for the Abbaye-aux-Bois, 1718. Completion of the Hôtel Matignon, 1724. Houses, Rue d'Anjou (including No. 8, Hôtel de la Fayette), 1727. Hôtel de Charost, 39 Faubourg Saint-Honoré (British Embassy). Scheme, partly carried out, for the Cour du Dragon, 50 Rue de Rennes. Schloss Asfeld.
Ref.: Arch. Nat. Z 1J 575, 605. N III Seine 754, 951. Archives de Monaco.
Bibl.: Courtonne, *Architecture moderne*, 1725. Labande, 'L'Hôtel de Matignon', in *GBA*, 1935. Monique Hébert and Jacques Thirion, *Catalogue des plans . . .*, vols. I and II.

MELLAN Michel
Rue Coquillère in 1786. 'Architecte du Roi' in Corsica.
Tenements for the Marquis de Faudoas, on the site of the Hôtel d'Aligre, Rue Bailleul, 1780. 'Vauxhall' du Boulevard Saint-Martin, 1785 (original design: Arch. Nat. Z 1J 1132 – engravings by Donnet and another). Chinese pavilion, Rue Saint-Lazare (view by Lavreince, in *GBA*, April 1923).
Ref.: Arch. Nat. Z 1J 1009, 1082, 1132, 1194.

MÉTIVIER Joseph
Rue Notre-Dame de Nazareth in 1780.
Tenements and Hôtel Gouthière, Faubourg Saint-Martin, 1780 (6 Rue P. Bullet). Petit and Métivier tenements, Boulevard Saint-Denis, 1789.
Ref.: Arch. Nat. Z 1J 994, 1013, 1060; H 2135.

MEZERETS
Family of lawyers and architects:

MEZERETS Michel de
Died 1749.

MEZERETS Charles-Philippe de
Died 6 May 1769
Mariette engraved (after one or other of the above): principal entrance-door of the Dumas house, Rue Pavée, in the Marais.

MICHÉE Jacques
'Expert-entrepreneur' in 1715. Rue du Murier, near Saint-Nicolas-du-Chardonneret.

MIQUE Richard
Born at Nancy 1728, executed in Paris 8 July 1794. Pupil of Blondel. Adviser to King Stanislas, 1759. Ennobled 1761. Chief engineer for the bridges and highways of Lorraine and Le Barrois, 1762. Academician 1775. Director of the Académie Royale 1782–92.
Portes Stanislas and Sainte-Catherine, barracks of Sainte-Catherine, Nancy. Couvent des Augustines, today Lycée Hoche, Versailles, 1767–72. Eglise des Carmélites, Saint-Denis, today 'Petite Paroisse' Saint-Denis, 1775. Chapel of the Hospice de Saint-Cloud, 1788. Theatre and *fabriques* of the Petit-Trianon; octagonal belvedere, Temple of Love, 'Hameau' (drawings in the library of Modena). *Cabinet doré* and library of the Queen, Versailles, 1785–90.
Ref.: Arch. Nat. F 17 1265 8: Inventory of Mique's papers.
Bibl.: Alfred Hachette, *L'Affaire Mique*, 1923; *Le Couvent de la reine à Versailles*, 1923. Pierre Le Lièvre, 'La Bibliothèque de Richard Mique', in *Les Mélanges F. Calot*, 1960.

MOISY Dominique Madeleine
Landscape architect, practising in 1770.
Garden of the Hôtel Biron, Rue de Varenne. Gardens, Rue des Amandiers. The plan of a garden in the Rue des Amandiers (Wrightsman collection) may be in his hand.

MOLINOS Jacques
Born in Lyon 4 June 1743, died 19 January 1831. 'Architecte de la Ville de Paris' during the Empire. Member of the Institute 1829.
Jacquin house and gardens in Les Près-Saint-Gervais, 1775. Château de Puisieux, for the Marquis de Vasan, near Villers-Cotterets, 1780–85. Julien garden, Epinay – see Krafft, pl. 71. Works in collaboration with J.-C. Legrand (see latter). Orangerie du Muséum (Krafft). Decorations for 'les fêtes de la Ville de Paris' during the Empire. Fontaine Valhubert. Marché Saint-Honoré, 1809. Rag market, Enclos du Temple, 1809–11. Barrière de Rochechouart, 1826. Marché Popincourt, 1829–31.
Ref.: B.N. Est. Va 255, Va 257.

MOLLET
Family of architects:

MOLLET Armand-Claude
'Maître des Jardins du Louvre.' Academician 1699. Knight of Saint Michael 1732.
Hôtel d'Humières, Rue de Bourbon. The Elysée 1719–22. Work at the 'Grand Hôtel' du Maine, Rue de Bourbon. Gallery of the Hôtel de Bullion, Rue Plâtrière, for the Marquis de Fervaques, 1720. Enlargement of the Hôtel de la Rochefoucauld, Rue de Seine, 1720. Outbuildings

of the Château de Roissy, 1720. Main entrance of the Hôtel de Mazarin (today Bibliothèque Nationale), Rue Neuve-des-Petits-Champs. Château de Stains. Mollet houses, Rue d'Anjou and Rue de La Ville-l'Evêque 1739, Rue de Bourbon 1741.

MOLLET André-Armand
Died 1742. Academician 1718.

MOLLET Armand-Louis
Died 1747. Academician 1734.

MONOT Jean-Guillaume-Hubert
Mentioned before 1789.

MONTGOLFIER Etienne de
1745–1810. Pupil of Soufflot.
Parish church of Faremoutier; Chambre de la Papeterie, Annonay.

MONROY Jean-François
'Inspecteur et toiseur' of the King's buildings.
Publ.: Traité d'architecture pratique, 1785.
Not to be confused with:

MONROY Jean-Baptiste Séraphin
Rue Coquenard in 1792.

MONTIGNY
Family of contractors and architects:
Hôtel Choppin d'Arnouville, Rue de la Michodière, 1780.
Bourbant tenements, Rue Lenoir Saint-Antoine, 1785.
Tenements, Rue de Provence, 1786.
Ref.: Arch. Nat. Z 1J 1049, 1120.

MORANZEL Louis-François THOUROUX de
1709–1785. Academician 1756.
'Contrôleur' of the King's buildings at Fontainebleau.

MOREAU Jean
Grand Prix 1743. Academician of Florence and Bologna.
Design for the portal of Saint-Merry, engraved in 1754 – B.N. Est. Va 247f.

MOREAU-DESPROUX Pierre-Louis
2e Prix 1750–51–52. 'Pensionnaire du Roi.' 'Maître des Bâtiments de la Ville de Paris', 1763; resigned 1787.
Hôtel de Chabanne, Porte du Temple (design in Musée Carnavalet). Work on the fabric of Saint-Eustache: upper level of portal, bell-towers, gallery for the great organs; presbytery (Impasse Saint-Eustache); sacristy and treasure (today Chapelle des catéchismes), 1782. Fontaine des Haudriettes, Rues des Archives and des Haudriettes, 1764. Théâtre de l'Opéra, at the Palais-Royal, 1763–70. Pavillon Carré de Beaudoin, Rue de Ménilmontant (the alleged Folie-Favart), 1770. Proposals for reconstruction of Hôtel de Ville, before 1771 – cf. Blondel, *Cours d'architecture*, vol. I, p. 110. Decorations for Hôtels de Marsan and de Luynes (state bedroom, now in Louvre), Hôtels de Gontaut, Rue Louis-le-Grand, 1772 (see Krafft), and Saint-Julien, Rue d'Artois. Chimney-piece, Hôtel de Mazarin, Quai Malaquais. Design for the Théâtre Français, 1773.

Elevations of the Palais-Royal, facing the *Place* and the first court, 1765. Decorations for the celebrations of 1762, 1763 and 1782 (drawing Arch. Nat. K 1014 151 – Musée Carnavalet). Decorations of the ship *Ville de Paris*, launched in 1764, destroyed at the battle of Dominica, 12 April 1782.
Bibl.: M. Gallet, 'Dessins de P. L. Moreau-Desproux pour des Edifices Parisiens', in *Bulletin du Musée Carnavalet*, 1962.

MOREL Jean-Marie
Born in Lyon 1728, died 10 August 1810. Architect to the Prince de Conti 1745. Garden designer.
Chartraire de Montigny house and garden, Montmartre. Château de Gressy at Montlignon, near Claye, for the Comte de Pont-Saint-Maurice, 1777. Parc de l'Isle-Adam. Gardens: Nicolaï at Berry, Girardin at Ermenonville, d'Aumont at Guiscard, de la Reine Hortense at Saint-Leu-Taverny; de la Malmaison, and of Mme de Brienne at Limours; Maison Chartraire de Montigny, Montmartre.
Publ.: La Théorie des jardins, 1774; 2nd edition 1802.

MOUCHELET
'Expert-bourgeois' from 1778 to 1790. Rue de l'Oseille, in the Marais.

MOUCHET André
'Expert-entrepreneur' 1739 to 1792. Rue des Poulies in 1792.
Construction work at the Hôtel de Mortemart, Rue de l'Université, opposite the Rue de Beaune.
Ref.: Arch. Nat. Z 1J 724, 741, 818, 828.

MOUILLEFARINE Junior
Garden architect. Practising at the end of the century.
Ref.: Krafft. Arch. Nat. N IV Seine 87. Ed. de Ganay, *Les Jardins de France*.

MOULY
Author of the model of a theatre, preserved in the museum of the Opéra, 1780.

MOURET (Mourette)
Family of architects, often difficult to distinguish:

MOURET Louis
Pupil of the Academy. 2e Prix 1725.
Maison Regnault, Rue Guérin-Boisseau, 1738. (?) Maison Boutteville, Rue Jean-Robert (des Gravilliers), 1742. House, Rue de la Mortellerie, 1741.

Ref.: PVARA, vols. IV, V. Arch. Nat. Z 1J 723, 733.

MOURET Pierre
Born at Moussy-le-Vieux 1705.
Royal ribbon manufactory of La Villette, 1746–47. Manufacture du Bon-Teint at Saint-Denis, 1736–37. Work at the Hôtel de Bauffremont, Rue Taranne (contract approved by Maître de Savigny, March 1743). Enlargement of the Hôtel de Broglie, Rue de Varenne, 1752. Alterations to the Hôtel d'Estiaux, 1 Rue de Lille and 6 Rue des Saints-Pères (contract approved by Maître Dutartre, 22 December 1753). Enlargement of the Hôtel de Maisons-Soyecourt, 51 Rue de l'Université.

Enlargement of the Hôtel d'Auvergne, 28 Rue Saint-Dominique (completed 1756). Design for the high altar of Reims cathedral, 1744. Château of the de Bauffremont family, near Besançon. Hôtel-Dieu (hospital) de Madrid, begun in 1751.
Ref.: Blondel, *Architecture française*, vol. I, p. 257, note a. Musée Carnavalet, topographie, inscriptions. Arch. Nat. T 188 1; Z 1J 674, 678, 709, 723, 819, 832.

MOUTIZON
An architect concerned with the demolition of the Bastille in 1790.

MOUTON Adrien
Grand Prix 1764. Practising in 1775.
Works for the family of Brûlart of Genlis.
Ref.: Archives de Seine-et-Oise.

MOYREAU Sylvain-Marie
'Contrôleur' of the King's Buildings, of the City of Paris, and 'des affaires de bâtiments attribuées au cours de judicature'. 'Contrôleur' of the Buildings of the Comte d'Artois.
Ref.: Arch. Nat. R 1 379.

MULLART Louis-Jacques
'Inspecteur' of Buildings of the Comte d'Artois.
Tenements for Les Pères de l'Oratoire. Quai Saint-Michel, Rue de la Huchette and Rue des Trois-Chandeliers (Xavier-Privas), about 1767. Hôtel d'Orgement, Place Beauveau, at the corner of the Rue Miromesnil, 1777, altered 1913. Rocher tenements, Rue Cassette, 1775.
Ref.: Arch. Nat. Z 1J 926, 990, 1009, 1066.

MUNSTER
Rue Grange-Batelière in 1776.
Hôtel du Marquis de Gouffier, 51 Rue de Paradis, 1779 (altered during Empire, height increased about 1930).
Ref.: Arch. Nat. Z 1J 1045. *Almanach historique de Le Brun.*

NATIVELLE Pierre
Died 29 June 1729.

NAVIER
Prize for architecture, Ecole Spéciale de Dessin, 1777.
Ref.: Arch. Nat. Z 1J 1213.

NEVEU
Family of architects:

NEVEU Charles
'Expert-entrepreneur', practising in 1775. Rue de Tournon in 1780.
Le Maistre house, Rue du Petit-Bourbon, Saint-Sulpice. Tenements, 12 Rue de Tournon, 1777.

NEVEU Michel
Rue du Four in 1776.
Ref.: Arch. Nat. O 1 846 178.

NOEL Philippe-Jacques
Tenements for the Duc de Mortemart, Rue de Saintonge, in the Marais, 1773. Works for the Marquis de Boulain-villiers, at the former Hôtel des Mousquetaires, Rue du Bac, 1784.
Ref.: Arch. Nat. Z 1J 968, 1140.

NORMAND
'Expert-bourgeois' from 1777 to 1792. Living Parvis Notre-Dame.

OPPENORD Gilles-Marie
Born 27 July 1676 in Paris, died 13 March 1742. Pupil of Jules Hardouin-Mansart. Rome scholar 1692–97. 'Intendant' of the buildings of the Regent.
Work for Innocent XII at Nettuno, about 1698. Monument of the Ducs de Bouillon at the abbey of Cluny, not completed (design engraved by Audran in *L'Histoire de la Maison d'Auvergne*, by Baluze. The work was suspended in 1710. Fragments preserved at the hospital of Cluny. A plaster bas-relief is mentioned at the Museum of Mâcon, before 1954). Tomb of the Comtesse de Relingue in the church of Saint-Thomas d'Aquin. Epitaph inscription of Marie-Anne des Essarts, wife of bookseller Frédéric Léonard, in Saint-Benoît le Bétourné (engraved by Millin, after alterations). Holy-water basins and commemorative slab in the monastery church of the Carmelites. High altar of Saint-Germain-des-Prés (design, B.N. Est. Va 669; engraving in the *History of Saint-Germain-des-Prés* by Dom Bouillard; drawing attributed to G. Palmkrantz, after Oppenord, Museum of Stockholm). Chapelle du Chef-Saint-Jean in Amiens cathedral (B.N. Est. Va 401a). Projects for the choir of Saint-Victor (before 1707), for the high altar of Saint-Jacques de la Boucherie, c. 1712, engraved. High altar of the Abbaye de Jouarre, c. 1721–29 (B.N. Est. 342). High altar of the cathedral of Meaux, between 1723 and 1731, engraved. Schemes for the portal of the Oratoire (Paris, Ecole des Beaux-Arts). Work at Saint-Sulpice, 1719–40: former Communion chapel, main altar (disappeared); south portal, reverse side of north portal; galleries of transept arms (balconies in Musée Carnavalet), crossing arches, 'sacristie des mariages' (drawings, Ecole des Beaux-Arts).
Work at the Palais-Royal: transformation of Mansart's gallery, suite of the Duchesse d'Orléans, 'grand appartement' (sketches at the Cooper Union, New York, and prints in 'Le Grand Oppenord'). Work at the Hôtel du Grand Prieur du Temple. Chinese room of the Schloss at Bonn, mirror room at Falkenlust, designs for Brühl (sketches among the papers of Robert de Cotte, B.N. Est.).
Decorations for the festivities of Villers-Cotterets, November 1722. Stables of the Château d'Enghien. Orangery of the Château de Montmorency (engraved). Main entrance of the Château de la Bôve en Laonnais (Ecole des Beaux-Arts). Work for Mme Chaumont. Salon of the château of M. Cazes de la Bôve at Torcy (notes in album OS 2712 gr of the Staatliche Kunstbibliothek of Berlin). Salon of the Château de la Grange-du-Milieu (drawings, Tessin-Harleman collection, Stockholm; the paintings by Caze and Fr. de Troy have disappeared).
Work at the Hôtel de Saint-Albin, Place des Victoires (panelling reassembled in a hôtel on the Boulevard Delessert). Salon of the Hôtel de Chavaudon, 58-*bis* Rue des Francs-Bourgeois.

Drawings by Oppenord: Tessin-Harleman collection, Museum of Stockholm; Staatliche Kunstbibliothek, Berlin; Decloux collection, Cooper Union, New York; album formerly belonging to the Abbé Chagny, President of the Academy of Lyon; Musée du Louvre; Chantilly; B.N. Est.; library of the Ecole des Beaux-Arts; Musée des Arts décoratifs; Musée Carnavalet. Drawings at the Royal Institute of British Architects and at Waddesdon Manor.

Bibl.: Brice, *Description de Paris*, 1713 edition, pp. 182–3. Orlandi, *Abecedario*. Dézallier d'Argenville, *Vie des plus fameux architectes*, 1787. A. Mahieu, in *L'Architecture*, 1914, pp. 129–31. P. Alfassa, in *Musées de France*, 1914, pp. 123–31. G. Huard, Oppenord, in Dimier, *Les Peintres français du XVIIIᵉ siècle* 1928, vol. I, pp. 311–29. Abbé Emile Malbois, 'Oppenord et l'Eglise Saint-Sulpice', in *GBA*, 1933, vol. I. Fiske Kimball, 'Oppenord reconnu', in *GBA*, 1935. Fiske Kimball, 'Oppenord au Palais-Royal', in *GBA*, 1936. Yves Bruant, Gabriel Huquier, in *GBA*, 1950 (printed in 1959). Mathey and Nordenfalk, Watteau and Oppenord, in *Burlington Magazine*, 1955. Beate Sydoff, in *L'Information d'histoire de l'art*, 1963, pp. 85–90; and in *Konsthistorisk Tidskrift*. Carl Hernmark, in *Svensk Sjuttonhundratal*, 1953. Wanda Bouleau-Rabaud, in *L'Art français au XVIIIᵉ siècle*, catalogue, 1965. Runar Strandberg, in *GBA*, January 1968. M. Gallet, 'Oppenord au Château de la Grange-du-Milieu', in *Revue de l'art*, 1968. J.-P. Babelon, 'L'Hôtel d'Assy, Rue des Francs-Bourgeois', in *MFSHP*, 1963. Tony Sauvel, 'Les Travaux exécutés au Palais-Royal par Monsieur, frère de Louis XIV', *BSHAF*, 1963. T. Sauvel, 'Le Palais-Royal, de la mort de Richelieu à l'incendie de 1763', in *Bulletin Monumental*, 1962.

ORBAY Nicolas d'
Died 1742. Academician 1705. 'Contrôleur' of the King's Buildings.

OSSELIN Jean-Louis
Rue Neuve-des-Petits-Champs in 1780.

OUDOT de MACLAURIN
South tower of Saint-Sulpice. Entrance of cemetery of Saint-Sulpice (engraved). Completion of church of Saint-Nicolas de Nérac.

PALAISEAU
Architect of the Palais-Royal in 1792.

PALLOY
Contractor for the demolition of the Bastille. Hôtel de Saisseval, Place du Palais Bourbon. Tenements, Rue des Imbergères, Sceaux.

PANSERON Pierre
Born in the neighbourhood of Provins. Pupil of the Academy 1765.
3ᵉ Prix 1770. 'Inspecteur' of the Buildings of the Prince de Conti.
Publ.: Projet pour l'Eglise Sainte-Marguerite, engraved. *Etudes de lavis*, 1781. *Eléments d'architecture*, 1775–80 (the second devoted to 'English' gardens). *Jardins anglais et chinois*, 1783. *Grand et Nouveau Vignole*, n.d. *Recueil de profils d'architecture*, 1787.

PARIS Pierre-Adrien
Born 1747 at Besançon, died 1 August 1819. Pupil of L.-F. Trouard. 3ᵉ Prix 1765, 1766, 1768, 1789. Pensionnaire du Roi 1772. Academician 1780. Dessinateur du Cabinet du Roi. Architect of the 'Menus-Plaisirs', 1783. Knight of Saint Michael 1787.
Supervision of buildings designed by Louis, Bordeaux, 1774. Suite of the Duc d'Aumont, Place Louis XV; decorations transferred to the Hôtel de la Tour d'Auvergne, 2 Avenue de la Motte-Picquet, and at the Metropolitan Museum, New York. Cabinet du Comte de Broglie, 1779. Workhouse, Bourges. Hôtel de Chastenoye, 120 Faubourg Saint-Honoré. Hôtel Boulogne de Malanville, Rue d'Angoulême-Saint-Honoré (built by Armand and Lefèvre, contractors). Hôtel de Richebourg, Rue de Courcelles. Work at the Folie Beaujon, for Bergeret fils, after 1786: the mill and perhaps the two rotundas (flanking) of the pavilion of the Chartreuse. Funeral settings of Marie-Theresa of Austria at Notre-Dame; of Mme Sophie, of the Duc d'Orléans, of Carlos III of Spain. Opera stage-sets: L'Amant Sylphe, Le Droit du Seigneur, etc. Design for reconstruction of Palace of Versailles. Town hall, Neuchâtel, executed in modified form, 1784. Hospital of Bourg-en-Bresse. Palace of the Prince de Bâle at Porrentruy (work suspended by the Revolution). Top sections of the towers of Orléans cathedral. Hôtel Tassin, Orléans. 'Thermal Establishment' of Bourbonne. Salle des Notables and of the Estates General, Hôtel des Menus-Plaisirs, Versailles, 1787. Château de Colmoulin, near Le Havre. Picturesque garden at Le Valasse, near Le Havre, for the Comte de Bégouen. Paris house at Vauclusotte (Doubs). Château of M. Amertot, Lillebonne. Designs for the Château de Neuilly-sur-Eure. Project for a château for M. de Montendre.
Italian drawings and other designs, Library of Besançon; cf. Inventaire des richesses d'art de la France, Monuments Civils, Province, vol. II, Library of Besançon.
Bibl.: L.H. vol. IV. E. de Ganay, *RAAM*, 1924, vol. II, p. 253. J.-Ch. Moreux in *Revue des arts*, September 1952. Dr Ronot in *BSHAF* 1959. G. Levallet-Haug in *BSHAF* 1933, pp. 88–99. Alain Grüber, *Le Projet de P.-A. Paris pour le Palais . . . de Porrentruy*.

PARVY de la REGNIARDIÈRE Nicolas
'Expert-entrepreneur'. Parvis Notre-Dame in 1777.

PASQUIER J.-B. Mathias
Contractor for the portal of Saint-Eustache in 1767. Berry tenements, at the corner of the Rues de Grenelle and de Bourgogne, 1769. Tenements at the corner of the Rues de la Banque and des-Petits-Champs, 1778. Tenements, Rue Sainte-Croix, 1787.

PATTE Pierre
Born 3 January 1723 in Paris, died at Mantes 18 August 1814.
Salon of city hall (Hôtel de Ville), Grenoble, 1763. Plan of theatre, Grenoble, 1768. Decorations of the Hôtel de Charost, Faubourg Saint-Honoré (British Embassy). Hôtel de Charost, site of the Mairie of the VIᵉ arr., c. 1764. Church of Bolbec, 1776–84. Decorations of the Hôtel de Deux-Ponts, Rue Saint-Augustin, after 1767 (alcove

described in Patte *Cours d'architecture*, vol. V, p. 109, and reproduced pl. LII). Schloss Jaegersburg. Hunting-lodge, Petersheim, for the Duc de Deux-Ponts.

Publ.: Discours sur l'architecture, avec un abrégé de la vie de Boffrand, 1754. 'Observations sur la manière dont sont décorés les extérieurs de nos eglises', in *Mercure de France*, 1755. *Architecture singulière, l'éléphant triomphal, grand kiosque à la gloire du roi*, par M. Ribart, 1758. *Etudes d'architecture*, 1755. *Mémoires de Ch. Perrault*, Avignon, 1759. 'Dénonciation d'un plagiat à M. Fréron', in *L'Année littéraire*, 1760. *Monuments érigés en France à la gloire de Louis XV*, 1764–71. *De la manière la plus avantageuse d'éclairer les rues*, 1766. 'Lettres sur les greniers d'abondance établis depuis peu à Corbeil', in *L'Année littéraire*, 1766. *Mémoire sur l'achèvement du grand portail de Sainte-Sulpice*, 1767. *Mémoires sur les objets les plus importants de l'architecture*, 1769. *Mémoires sur la construction de la Coupole projetée pour couronner l'eglise Sainte-Geneviève*, 1770. *Suite du 'Cours d'architecture' (de Blondel)*, 1777. *Description du théâtre de la ville de Vicence*, 1780. *Essai sur l'architecture théâtrale*, 1782. *Mémoires qui intéressent particulièrement Paris*, 1801.

PAULIK Jean-Népomucène
Living at the Hôtel de Soissons. Practising after 1764.

PAUMIER Nicolas
'Expert-entrepreneur' from 1723. Rue du Jardin-Saint-Antoine in 1740.

PAYEN Jacques-Antoine
Died in 1795.
Pawnshop, bâtiments de la Rue des Blancs-Manteaux, 1777. Main entrance of the Salpêtrière, 1780.

PÉCOUL Ch.-Pierre
Contractor for the Hôtel de Salm. Uncle of J.-L. David.

PÉRARD
Family of architects:

PÉRARD Nicolas-Antoine
Fégueur tenements, Faubourg du Roule, 1776. Work at the Hôtel de Marigny, Quai d'Anjou, 1779.

PÉRARD de MONTREUIL François-Victor
Hôtel, Rue de la Chaussée d'Antin, 1772–75. Three hôtels, Rue Chantereine, 1776–77. Reconstruction scheme for the Palais de Justice, 1776. Hôtel de Créqui. Porticos of the Temple. Hôtel Botterel-Quintin, 44 Rue des Petites-Ecuries (basic structural work). Hôtels in the Saint-Honoré district.

Ref.: Arch. Nat. Z 1J 970, 988, 1008, 1019, 1070, 1088.

PERCENET L.-N.
Major construction for the monastery of Saint-Joseph, Rue Saint-Dominique, 1774 (Arch. Nat. N III Seine 518–20).
Publ.: Ière et IIème suites de vases, 1762. *Recueil de différents ornements*. *6e Cahier des Rosaces*.
Ref.: Arch. Nat. N III Seine. 518–520.

PÉRIAC
Family of architects:

PÉRIAC Louis

PÉRIAC Antoine
Théâtre d'Audinot, and house, Boulevard du Temple, 1770. Théâtre de la Foire Saint-Germain, 1770. Two houses, Rue d'Aguesseau (Rue Montalivet), 1778. Tenements, Rue Chabannais. Designs for a theatre, Rue Guisarde, *c.* 1775.

PERLIN Firmin
Died before 24 July 1783. Rue Sainte-Anne in 1780. Candidate for the Academy in 1780. Author of 'dessins pitoresques' (*Cabinet Harenc de Presles*, 1785): *Une partie de bains*, dedicated to the Comte d'Angiviller, 1778, engraved by Sellier; *Invocation à un Héros*, New York, Cooper Union. Two pendant designs sold at the Palais Galliéra, 5 December 1961.
Hôtel du Baron de Breteuil, Rue de Provence, 1777. Hôtel de Mercy-Argenteau, 16 Boulevard Montmartre, 1778. Elevation facing the court of the Hôtel de Montmorency, Boulevard Montmartre. House of the Duc de Montmorency, Place du Tertre. Work at the Château de Seignelay, *c.* 1780.
Ref.: Arch. Nat. N III Seine 1290 2, Y 14573; Z 1J 1020, 1147; Z 2 2461. *Mercure de France*, February 1778, p. 184; testament du 20 janvier 1783 chez Lambot, étude 83 (Julien). Projet de l'Hôtel de Breteuil, B.N. Est. Ha 110. Papiers Mercy-Argenteau, Vienna Court and State Archives.

PERRAULT André
Died March 1723. 'Expert.' Rue Beaurepaire in 1715.

PERRICHON Simon
Dumée house, Rue du Plâtre Sainte-Avoye, 1752.
Ref.: Arch. Nat. Z 1J 807.

PERRIER Claude-Joseph
Practising in 1778

PERRONET Jean-Rodolphe
Born at Suresnes 1708, died in Paris 1794. Academician 1756. Inspector-General of Bridges and Highways.
Reconstruction of the choir of the cathedral of Alençon, 1745. Bridges of Mantes, Nogent-sur-Seine, Neuilly, Pont-Sainte-Maxence. Pont Louis XVI (de la Concorde), 1787–92.

PERROT Vincent-Louis
Died before 27 October 1766.

PERROT Lazare-Antoine
Rue des Tournelles, at the former Hôtel de Sagonne in 1786.

PETIT
'Expert-entrepreneur' from 1780 to 1792. 'Architecte des domaines nationaux' in 1792. Rue des Juifs in 1792.

PETIT-RADEL Louis-François
Born in Paris 1740, died 1808. 3e Prix 1763. 'Expert-bourgeois' from 1770 to 1792. Inspector-General of Civil Buildings during the Empire.
Tabary tenements, Faubourg Poissonnière. Choir of Saint-Médard. Abattoir, Le Roule.

PEYRE the Elder, Marie-Joseph
Born 1730, died 11 August 1788. Grand Prix 1751. Academician 1767.
Folie Leprêtre de Neubourg au Clos Payen (Boulevard de L'Hôpital), 1762. Works concerned with the royal canal of Provins (undertaken by the Prince de Salm), 1780. Reconstruction scheme for the Hôtel de Bourbon (site of the Odéon). Church of the Visitation Saint-Jacques and enlargement of monastic buildings; plans of 1767 implemented by the contractor Barrat, c. 1780; for the Church of the Visitation: 'Tablettes de Renommée', 1777; sketch in the Musée Carnavalet, engravings by Janninet; demolished in 1906. Hôtel de Nivernais, 10 Rue de Tournon, today a barracks (building authorization, Arch. Nat. Z 1F 494). Théâtre Français (Odéon), 1772–82.
Publ.: Œuvres d'architecture, 1765.

PEYRE the Younger, Antoine-François
Born in Paris 5 April 1739, died 7 March 1823. Grand Prix 1762.
House on the site of the former Monnaie. Wings of the Hôtel Caron (Benoist de Sainte-Paule), 30 Faubourg Poissonnière, 1778. Chapels of the Charité and of Saint-Thomas de Villeneuve at Saint-Germain (the latter impaired by the later addition of two bell-towers), 1784 to 1786. Parish church and farm of Deniécourt for the Vicomte d'Hervilly, near Péronne, after 1781. Designs for La Trinité, Saint-Germain. Two designs for Les Jacobins, Rue Saint-Jacques. Electoral palace of Koblenz. Pavilion and farm of Tiburg, near Trèves (Trier).
Publ.: Antiquités de la ville de Trèves, 1789. *Mémoires sur l'achèvement du Louvre*, 1795. *Restauration du Panthéon français*, 1799. *Œuvres d'architecture*, 1818, 1819, 1820.

PEYTOURAUD
Family of architects:

PEYTOURAUD Martin

PEYTOURAUD Michel
Rue Cassette in 1780. Architect of the Seminary of Saint-Sulpice, 1789.

PHAROUX
'Expert-bourgeois', from 1789 to 1792. Rue de Cléry, No. 1.

PICARD François
Rue des Fossés Saint-Germain-l'Auxerrois. Huzard house, Chaussée d'Antin, 1766.

PIÈTRE
Family of architects:

PIÈTRE Henri
Pupil of Cartaut. 'Premier architecte du Duc d'Orléans' in 1777.

Work at the Palais-Royal: decoration of the Hôtel Mélusine, elevation facing the Hôtel d'Argenson, 1766; observatory in the Cour des Fontaines, 1775; library, 1769; Madame de Blot's suite (to the west of the second court); salon contrived from the former Galerie des Hommes Illustres; ballroom replacing the Salle de Gombaud (1777); scheme for new palace, between the second court and the gardens, 1781.
Works, Rue de Provence: gallery and suite for Mme de Valence, linking the Hôtel de Montesson and that of the Duc d'Orléans (circular salon); alterations to the Hôtel d'Orléans (circular salon); alterations to the Hôtel de Breteuil, assigned to the Orléans stables. Works at Le Raincy: Salon des Glaces in the right wing of the château, round chapel with Ionic orders 'with the capital of Michelangelo' and pierced dome, 1773; after the fire, central dining-room of the château. Design for the Capuchin church d'Antin.
Ref.: Arch. Nat. H 5 3612; N III Seine 897, 548, 549, 547, 897, 899, 188, 501, 903, 914, 1292, 1290; N II Seine 189; N III Seine-et-Oise 572, 574; O 1 1913 204. Curriculum vitae, Bibliothèque des Arts décoratifs et de l'Ecole des Beaux-Arts. Cabinet des Dessins du Musée Carnavalet.

PIÈTRE Henri-Médard
Contractor

PIÈTRE Jean-Baptiste-Marie
Architect to the Duc d'Orléans in 1782.

Bibl.: M. Gallet, *Les Dessins de l'architecte Henri Piètre pour la décoration du Palais-Royal; Bulletin du Musée Carnavalet*, 1960. Monique Hébert, 'Les Hôtels du Duc d'Orléans et de Mme de Montesson à la Chaussée d'Antin', in *GBA*, September 1964.

PILET Jean-Baptiste
Garden architect, practising before 1761.

PINARD Jean
'Expert-entrepreneur' from 1730. Grand Prix 1723 (prize design at the Ecole des Beaux-Arts). 'Maître-général' of the Buildings, Bridges and Highways of France. Maison Pinard, Rue Neuve Saint-Merry, 1740. Maison La Peyre at Champlan, 1740.
Bibl.: Manuscrit illustré du *Cours d'architecture* de Desgodetz par J. Pinard (B.N. Est. Ha 23 and 23a; another copy in a private collection in Amsterdam).

PIRETOUY Jacques
'Expert' 1704–20. Rue Vieille-du-Temple.

PITET
Mentioned in 1772.

PITROU
Inspector-General of Bridges and Highways. Design for the Place Louis XV, 1750.

PLACONNET Alexandre
Raibaut tenements, Rue Neuve des Capucins (20 Rue Joubert), 1783.

PLOU
Practising in 1790.

PLUYETTE Hubert

POIRIN Jean-Michel
'Expert-bourgeois' from 1724. Rue Saint-Martin in 1740, later Rue Sainte-Avoye.

POLLEVERT Jean-C.
Died in 1766. 2ᵉ Grand Prix 1756. 'Contrôleur' des Bâtiments du Prince de Condé.

PORQUET Claude-Joseph
'Expert-bourgeois' from 1766 to 1792. 'Premier expert du Roi', associate of the Academy of Saint-Luc in 1775. Rue Hautefeuille 30. Work for the Chevalier d'Arcy, *c.* 1768. Hôtel de Pille, 14 Rue de Grammont, 1776–77.

POTAIN Nicolas-Marie
1713–96. Grand Prix 1738. Academician 1756. 'Contrôleur' des Bâtiments de Fontainebleau.
In charge of the works, Place Louis xv, 1754–70. Rennes cathedral (design of 1763, executed from 1786 onwards, revised by Soufflot). Church of Saint-Germain-en-Laye, begun in 1766, work suspended, then restarted in 1787, but stopped at the Revolution (the present church was built by Moutier and Malpièce in 1824 – Arch. Nat. O 1 1718).
Publ.: Traité des ordres d'architecture, 1767.

POTHENOT
Family of architects:

  POTHENOT Gabriel
  Died 1765. 'Expert-bourgeois.' Rue de Saintonge.

  POTHENOT Nicolas
  Son of above.

POULAIN J.-B. Martial
'Expert-bourgeois' from 1768 to 1792. Rue du Jardinet, near the Rue Mignon.

POYET Bernard
Born Dijon 3 May 1742, died Paris 6 December 1824. Pupil of De Wailly.
2ᵉ Prix 1768. 'Contrôleur' des Bâtiments de la Ville de Paris.
Maison des enfants d'Orléans, Rue de Bellechasse, 1778. Hôtel for Antoine Callet, the King's painter, Boulevard Montparnasse, 1777; sketch in the Archives Nationales; engraving in Krafft et Ransonnette; description in *L'Encyclopédie d'architecture*, pls. 994–6; photograph of the dining-room in the library of the Arts Décoratifs. Design for the reconstruction of Saint-Sauveur. Stables for the Duc de Chartres, Rue Saint-Thomas-du-Louvre, 1780. Design for Hôtel-Dieu (hospital) to be built on the Ile des Cygnes, 1785. Designs for a National Column, 1798, 1816 (with a museum of French history). Peristyle of the Palais Bourbon, 1806–7. Hôpital Sainte-Anne, unfinished; engraved plan in the collection of Durand. Houses on the

Quai de Corse, scheme of 1788. Project for a theatre in the grounds of the Capucins Saint-Honoré (with Cellerier), 1777.
Bibl.: Bellier and Auvray, *Dictionnaire des artistes de l'Ecole française.*
Ref.: Arch. Nat. Z 1J 1023, 1125.

PRÉTREL Philippe-Laurent
Pupil of Blondel. Rue Bourbon Villeneuve in 1780. Architect to les Filles de Saint-Sauveur in 1782. Houses in the Rue Pétrelle (or Prétrel).

PRUNEAU de MONTLOUIS Jean-Louis
'Expert-bourgeois' from 1752. Rue Beaubourg in 1760, later Rue du Sentier.

PUISIEUX the Elder, J.-B. de
?1679–1776. Collaborated with Soufflot.
Publ.: Eléments de géométrie, 1765.

PUISIEUX the Younger
Publ.: Elévations de Cheminées dans le Goût Antique. Plans et élévations de portes cochères. Autels.

QUÉAU Jean-Charles
Died 31 May 1777. Pupil of the Academy in 1728–29.

QUIN Jean-Baptiste-Nicolas
Avenue des Invalides in 1793.
Hôtel de Pompignan, Rue Monsieur, 1782. Drawing, B.N. Va 248.

QUIROT (occasionally written Guirot or Guérot)
Family of architects and clerks of works:

  QUIROT Etienne
  Calville house, Rue des Gravilliers, 1730.

  QUIROT Denis, known as QUIROT le Jeune
  Died 1775.
  'Expert-bourgeois' from 1729. Living successively at Rue Jean-Pain-Mollet, Rue du Coq Saint-Jean, Rue de la Verrerie, Rue de la Jussienne, Rue du Hasard, Hôtel du Pérou.
  Hôtel Quirot, Rue des Capucines, near the Boulevard, 1746. Quirot houses, 2 bis Rue de la Jussienne and Rue Montmartre, 1752. Tenement buildings, 73 Rue des Saints-Pères, and 21 Rue du Faubourg Saint-Honoré are designed in this architect's manner.
  One of the above designed in 1731 the main entrance, staircase and cantilevered *cabinet* of the Hôtel de Bersan, former Hôtel d'Epernon, 110 Rue Vieille-du-Temple.
  An architect, identified by the name of Guérot, designed about 1780 the altar, and the pulpit of the church of Andrezel (Seine-et-Marne).

  QUIROT Pierre
  Died 1743. 'Expert-bourgeois' from 1706, 'Syndic des Experts' 1730, 'Doyen' 1742.
  Quirot house, Rue de la Mortellerie, 1723.

Ref.: Arch. Nat. Z 1F 4000 (Pierre Q.); Z 1F 549, p. 98r, and Z 1F 460, p. 68r (Denis Q.); H 2128–2 (Denis Q.) – information supplied by M. Jean Queguiner.

RAUX
Free-lance teacher of architecture in 1776. Practising between 1758 and 1778.
Engravings: public fountains. Interior of a monastery. Decorated transept. Sepulchral monuments, etc.

RAYMOND
'Expert-bourgeois' in 1720. Rue de la Verrerie.
This architect may have built the Hôtel Gouffier de Thoix, 56 Rue de Varenne. He appeared as the 'expert' of the Marquis de Gouffier on the occasion of the 'visites de mitoyenneté', 16 May 1720, and of the 'toisé général', 21 August 1721. Louis Benoist was the contractors' 'expert' at the time.
Ref.: Arch. Nat. Z 1J 458, 537, 543.

RAYMOND Etienne-Hubert
'Expert-entrepreneur' from 1741. Rue Sainte-Foy in 1760, later Rue Saint-Martin.

RAYMOND Jean-Arnaud
Born Toulouse 9 April 1742, died Paris 28 January 1811. Pupil of Lescuyer, Blondel and Soufflot. Grand Prix 1766. Works for the Archbishop of Narbonne, 1768. Scheme for draining the Pontine Marshes, 1776. Decoration of the Place du Peyrou and designs for the Palais des Etats at Montpellier. Designs for the prisons of Montpellier and Toulouse, 1783–86. Reconstruction schemes for La Daurade de Toulouse, and for Saint-Remy de Bordeaux, 1783. Chambre souveraine du Clergé and repository for the Diocesan Archives, Place Sainte-Scarbe and Place Montoulieu-Saint-Jacques, Toulouse. Decoration of the Archiepiscopal Palace of Toulouse for Mgr Loménie de Brienne. Church of l'Ile Jourdain. Hôtel de Saint-Priest, 170 Faubourg Saint-Honoré. Hôtel and sale-room for Lebrun, Rues du Gros-Chenet and de Cléry, 1785–86. Work at the Hôpital Saint-Louis, 1790. Rooms of Graeco-Roman antiquities in the Louvre (decoration of the Queen-mother's summer apartment and structural work of the bath suite). Design for the Arc de Triomphe de l'Etoile, engraved by Normand.
Bibl.: Paul Mesplé, 'Une œuvre Toulousaine de Raymond', in *L'Auta*, April 1949. M. Gallet, 'La Maison de Mme Vigée-Lebrun', in *GBA*, November 1960.

RÈGEMORTES Louis de
Engineer of dikes and embankments. Academician 1765. Bridge of Moulins. Died 1776.

REGNARD de BARENTIN
'Expert-entrepreneur' from 1768 to 1792. Rue Neuve Saint-Laurent.

RENARD Jean-Augustin
Born Paris 1744, died 24 January 1807. Grand Prix 1773. Academician 1792. Member of the consultative committee 'des Bâtiments Impériaux'. Restoration of the Observatory of Paris, 1786. Royal stables of Sèvres and Saint-Germain. Work at the Hôtel Grimod d'Orsay, 69 Rue de Varenne. Gallery in the Hôtel Gallifet (Hôtel of Foreign Affairs under Talleyrand's ministry). Enlargement of the Château de Valençay, and *fabriques* in the park: Egyptian temple, pavilion, Turkish kiosk, cottages. Three designs for the Château de Rambouillet, 1785. *Fabriques* in the park of the Duc de Penthièvre, at Armainvilliers (Krafft, pls. 93–5).
Publ.: Picturesque drawings in *Le Voyage en Italie et en Sicile* by the Abbé de Saint-Non. *Ornements d'Architecture tirés des Monuments Antiques.*

RICHARD Claude-Alexandre
'Inspector of the King's Buildings.'

RICHARD Jean

RICHARD Pierre-Louis
'Expert-entrepreneur' from 1732. 'Surveyor to the fabric' of Saint-Merry.
House, Rue Saint-Martin. Presbytery of Saint-Merry, begun by Jean-François Blondel, 1732; Communion chapel, begun by Boffrand.

RIVET Alexandre
Died November 1720. Academician 1700.
Laujon house, Rue de Bourbon and Rue Saint-Philippe, 1719.
Ref.: Arch. Nat. Z 1J 548.

ROCHE
'Expert-bourgeois' from 1789 to 1792. Rue de la Monnaie 41.

ROHAIS Toussaint
'Expert-entrepreneur' in 1715. Rue des Boucheries-Saint-Germain.

ROLAND LE VIRLOYS Charles-François
Born Paris 2 October 1716, died 19 May 1772. Theatre at Metz, 1738–52. Patiot tenements, Rue de Grenelle, 1770.
Publ.: *Dictionnaire d'architecture civile, militaire et navale*, Paris, 1770–71, 3 volumes.

RONDELET Jean-Baptiste
Born Lyon 4 June 1743, died 26 September 1829. Member of the Institute in 1815.
'Continuator' of Soufflot's work on the construction of Sainte-Geneviève.
Publ.: *Traité sur l'art de bâtir*, 1802.

ROUGEVIN Jean
Rue des Fossés Saint-Germain in 1795.
Hôtel de Sandrouin, Rue Chantereine, 1785–88. Tenements 10–12 Rue de l'Odéon and Rue de Condé, 1788.
Ref.: Arch. Nat. Z 1J 1174, 1195.

ROUSSEAU Alexandre-Julien
Mentioned in 1786.

ROUSSEAU Pierre
Baptised Nantes 1 June 1751, died Paris 1810. 2e Prix. 'Pensionnaire du Roi' 1773. Living 25 Quai Voltaire.

Hôtel des Gardes de la Porte du Roi, Fontainebleau. Les Théatins tenements, Rue de Lille, 1778–80. Tenements, Rues Royale and de Bellechasse. Hotel de Dreuneuc, Rue de Provence. Hôtel, 26 Rue de la Rochefoucauld, 1788 (building authorisation, Arch. Nat. Z 1F 520). Hôtel de Salm (Palace of the Legion of Honour), 1783. Church of Saint-Germain (rebuilt in 1824). Muniment room and Chinese pavilion of the Hôtel de Montmorency, Boulevard Montmartre; model of pavilion in Gontaut-Biron collection. Design for National Assembly – Arch. Nat. N II Seine 190.
Bibl.: RAAM, July 1933; GBA, 5 June 1955.

ROUSSET Pierre-Noël
Died 1795. 2e Prix 1731 and 1732. Academician 1757. Academician of Florence and Bologna.
Decoration of the Danger house and Hôtel de Meulan, Rue des Capucines (former Hôtel Legendre d'Armini, later d'Antin), 1749; of the Hôtel de Bourbon, 46–50 Rue Neuve-des-Petits-Champs; house for M. Boucher, Rue Vivienne. Hôtels de Tessé, 1 Quai Voltaire, and Brochant des Tourterelles, Rue Perrault, 1768. Organs for the Sainte-Chapelle.
Château for M. Larcher on the Ile Saint-Denis, 1753. House at Viry-Chatillon. Kitchens of the Château de Livry. Chapel of the Bishop's Palace, Chartres. Work at Brunoy; and for the Duc de Rohan Chabot at Athys including gate and salon. Project for the Hôtel d'Uzès, 1776. Town hall, Uzès, about 1770.
Bibl.: Blondel, *Arch. française*, vol. III, p. 117. *Cours d'architecture*, vol. III, p. 368. PVARA, Hurtaut-Magny, vol. III, p. 413. Jusselin, in *Bulletin de la Société Archéologique d'Eure-et-Loir*, vol. XVIII, 1950, pp. 77–121. Archives of the family d'Uzès. Minutier XCI, 1336.

ROZE
Rue Neuve Saint-Martin in 1792. Architect practising in Paris in 1782. Received fees from M. de Ligray.

SAINT-FAR Jean-Baptiste-Eustache
Hospital architect.
Main doorway of the Hôpital des Vénériens, Boulevard de Port Royal, about 1785.

SAINT-MARTIN Pierre-Henri de
Born in Paris 1710, died 1780. Candidate for the Academy in 1762. 'Architecte-expert.'
Alterations to the Hôtel de Rohan, 1749–52. Hôtel de Rohan at Versailles, 1754. Completion of Les Quinze-Vingt, Rue St-Nicaise, 1750–56. Jesuits' College and Seminary, Strasbourg, 1757. Suite of the Marquis d'Argenson at the Arsenal (office of the Keeper of the Library), *c.* 1775. Servants' wing of the Hôtel de Toulouse (Banque de France), at the corner of the Rues de la Vrillière and Radziwill, 1760.
Bibl.: J.-P. Babelon, *Historique des bâtiments des archives*, 1958.

SALIOR
Practising in 1790. Rue Saint-Pierre de Montmartre.

SANDRIER
Family of speculative builders and architects; including a Sandrier de Bièvres, and a Sandrier des Fossés.

SANDRIER Jerôme
Hôtel de la Mark, Rues de Suresnes and Daguesseau, today Belgian Embassy, 1760; houses in the Rue Thiroux.
Bibl.: L'Avant-coureur, 1762, pp. 153–4.

SARNÈQUE Antoine
Work at the Château de Verneuil, near Meulan, for M. Randon de Lucenay, 1778.

SEDAINE
Family of architects, of which the writer Jean-Michel Sedaine was also a member. A Sedaine, living Rue des Ecouffes, was an 'expert-bourgeois' in 1730. Another built the Château de Verneuil-sur-Indre, *c.* 1770.

SERIN
A pavilion in the 'parc de Bagnolet', *c.* 1720 (engraved), which may well be the one still standing in the precinct of the Hospice Debrousse, 108 Rue de Bagnolet.
Bibl.: Mauban, *L'Architecture française de Mariette*, 1945.

SEROUGE Jean
'Expert-entrepreneur' in 1715. Rue et Porte Montmartre.

SERVANDONI Giovanni Niccolo
Born Florence 2 May 1695, died Paris 19 January 1766. Pupil of Pannini and of Giuseppe-Ignazio Rossi. 'Premier peintre-décorateur' of the Royal Academy of Music, 1728. Architectural works, based on the obituary notice of Fr. Franque: portal, organ gallery, chapel of the Virgin of Saint-Sulpice (work continued by Laurent, de Wailly and Chalgrin). Door of La Maison de l'Enfant Jésus, barrière de Vaugirard. Church of Coulanges-la-Vineuse (Yonne). High altar of the cathedral of Sens. High altar of Saint-Bruno, Lyon. Staircase of the Hôtel d'Auvergne (contract approved by Maître Bapteste, 22 July 1738, Etude CXVII, 421). Chapel in the gardens of the Hôtel de La Live de Jully, Rue Cambon. Temple in the park of Gennevilliers (engraved by Le Rouge, photograph of 1896 in the Museum of Sceaux). Fountain in the cloister of Sainte-Croix de la Bretonnerie (drawing reproduced in the catalogue of the exhibition 'Le Marais, Age d'Or et Renouveau', Musée Carnavalet, 1963, p. 39). House at 6 Place Saint-Sulpice and general scheme for the Place, 1752. Château de Balaine, 'four leagues from Paris' (=Balagny?). Main staircase of the new Palace of Madrid. Buildings in Brussels for the Marquis of Leyden, and the Dukes of Aremberg and Ursel.

SIGUY
'Expert-entrepreneur' from 1779 to 1792. Rue des Vieux-Augustins, near the Rue Coquillière in 1792.

SILVY
Independent teacher of architecture. Porte Saint-Bernard, near Les Miramiones, in 1762.
Ref.: L'Avant-coureur – Essai général d'indication.

SIMON Mathurin
'Syndic des experts-entrepreneurs' in 1730.

SIMON René-Auguste
'Expert-entrepreneur' from 1730. Rue des Quatre-Vents in 1769.

SIMONNET Nicolas
Died 1742. 'Expert-bourgeois.' Academician 1735. Rue Le Regrattier.
Work for the Prémontrés de la Rue Hautefeuille. Enlargement of the Hôtel de la Vrillière-Conti, Rue Sainte-Dominique.

SOBRE Jean-Nicolas
Pupil of Ledoux.
Masonic Lodge, Rue et Carré Saint-Martin 16, 1788. Group of tenements of the 'Cour Batave', Rue Saint-Denis (in collaboration with Happe), 1790. Théâtre des Jeunes Elèves. Château de Saint-Assise (Krafft, pls. 77–8). Decoration for Mme H(amelin?), Rue Vivienne (Krafft, pl. 87). Plans and elevations of the Château of M. de Caumartin, near Moret (destroyed before 1812), 'communicated by Sobre' were reproduced in Krafft., pls. 61–2. Engraved design for a city hall for Paris. Project for a temple to Immortality.

SOISSONS Senior
Rue des Rosiers in 1771.

SOISSONS Junior (son)
Rue de Suresnes in 1792. Tenements, Rue des Ecouffes, 1772. Jubault house, Rue du Coq-Héron, 1786. House, Place du Palais-Bourbon, 1790.
Ref.: Arch. Nat. 968, 969; M 47, 1191.

SOUFFLOT Jacques-Germain
Born Yrancy (Yonne) 22 July 1713, died Paris 29 August 1780. Pensionnaire du Roi 1734. Academician 1749. Academician of San Luca, Rome. 'Contrôleur des Travaux' de Paris, 1755–76. 'Intendant-Général' of the King's Buildings, 1776. Director of the Gobelins. Ennobled in 1753.
Work in the Lyonnais: Decoration of Saint-Bruno-des-Chartreux. Elevation, facing the Rhône of the Hôtel-Dieu, after 1741. Hôtel de la Croix-Laval. Parent tenements. Merlino house, L'Ile Barbe. Court of the Archbishop's Palace. Loge du Change, 1747–49. Former Grand Théâtre.
Work in Paris: Treasure and sacristy of Notre-Dame, 1756; original designs, Arch. Nat. O 1 1690 101–4; engravings by Chauffard and Charpentier. Church of Sainte-Geneviève (Panthéon), executed by Soufflot up to the base of the dome; designs, manuscripts and plans of details — Oudet sale, 1866; Arch. Nat. O 1 1695, N III Seine 213; Musée Carnavalet, Topographie 95 B (1757); B.N. Est. Va 259b; Arch. Nat. O 1 1694 25 (1764), O 1 1695 2–3–5 (c. 1770), O 1 1694 43 (*dessins d'exécution* by Brébion c. 1780); Angoulvent collection (c. 1770 and 1775). Engraved designs: six prints by Bellicart and three by Charpentier, 1757. Portal engraved by Panseron, 1764.

Plan of the Place by Le Rouge, 1767. Engravings by Pouleau, Sellier and Taraval, after Dumont and Lequeu. Ecole de Droit; design of 1763, Arch. Nat. N III Seine 543. Hôtel de Marigny, Rue Saint-Thomas-du-Louvre, *c.* 1767. Hôtel de Marigny at Le Roule, 1769; design at the Musée Carnavalet. Terrace, orangery and nymphaeum of the Château de Ménars, after 1764. Nymphaeum in the gardens of M. Bertin at Chatou. Shops in the *demi-lunes* of the Pont-Neuf. Water-tower of the Place Louis XV. Fountain of the Arbre-Sec, Rue Saint-Honoré, 1775. Scheme for enlarging the Luxembourg, 1776; Arch. Nat. N III Seine 1205. Church of the Visitation. Le Mans.
Uncertain attributions: La Charité, Mâcon. The Hôtel-Dieu, Mâcon, was built to the plans of Munet, perhaps in consultation with Soufflot.
MSS.: Mémoire sur les proportions de l'architecture, 1739. Mémoires sur l'architecture gothique. De l'identité du goût et des règles de l'architecture. Bibliothèque de l'Académie de Lyon.
Publ.: Suite de plans . . . de trois temples antiques à Paestum, Paris 1764. Recueil de plusieurs parties d'architecture, Paris 1767.
Bibl.: J. Monval, *Soufflot, sa vie, son œuvre, son esthétique*, Paris 1919. Michael Petzet, *Soufflots Sainte-Geneviève und der französische Kirchenbau des 18. Jahrhunderts*. P. Lavedan in *BSHAF*, 1954.

SOUFFLOT le ROMAIN François
Son of J.-B. Soufflot, Mayor of Vermenton, cousin of Jacques-Germain Soufflot. Rome scholar July 1761. Married Marie-Sophie Antoine, niece of J.-D. Antoine, 17 February 1789. Living Place de l'Estrapade at this period. 'Inspecteur des Travaux' de Sainte-Geneviève.
Work at the priory of Sainte-Radegonde at Le Plessis-Chenet. Staircase of the priory of Saint-Martin-des-Champs, 1786; about 1880 the designs were in the possession of Brother Arcadius of the 'doctrine chrétienne'. Hôtel de Montholon, 21 Boulevard Montmartre, 1785. Maison d'Epinay, Sceaux (Krafft, pl. 16). Proposed portal for Sens cathedral. Pavilion, 32 Rues des Bois, Bagnolet; demolished 1901. Decoration of the Château de Montgermont, engraved by La Hure in 1786.
MSS.: Album of drawings of the Hôtel de Montholon; B.N. Est. Ve 92 fol.
Bibl.: Chartraire, *La Cathédrale de Sens*, p. 32.
Ref.: Corresp. des dir., vol. XI, p. 389. *NAAF*, 1892. *VP*, 13 March 1902.

TANNEVOT
Family of architects:

TANNEVOT Michel
Died 1762. Academician 1718.
Hôtels des Vieux et Castanier, 15–19 Rue des Capucines, 1726. House, 26 Rue Cambon, 1742. Château de Dammartin. Wooden pavilion in the park of Bagnolet. Alterations to the Hôtel de Montbazon for M. Richard, Rue Saint-Honoré, 1751. Alterations to the Hôtel Sonning, Rue de Richelieu, for M. de Pontferrière, after 1740.
Bibl.: Mauban, *L'Architecture française de Mariette*, 1945. L.H. Jean Féray, 'L'Hôtel Tannevot', in *BSHAF*, 1963. Blondel, *Architecture française*.

TARAVAL Louis-Gustave
Born Stockholm 1738, died Paris 15 October 1794. Pupil
of Boullée. 'Inspector of the King's Buildings'. Architectural draughtsman and engraver. Collaborated in published
works of Contant d'Ivry, Dumont, Chalgrin, Cauvet,
Viel, etc. Drawings in the libraries of the Arts Décoratifs de
Paris, and Berlin, the Institut Tessin in Paris, etc.

TERRIER
'Expert-bourgeois' in 1770.

THÉVENIN Louis-Hercule
'Expert-bourgeois' from 1735. Rue de Seine in 1740.
Maison Poinsin de Buras, Rues de Cléry et des Petits-
Carreaux, 1742.
Ref.: Arch. Nat. Z 1J 723.

THÉVENIN Jacques-Jean
'Architecte-entrepreneur' of the King's Buildings. 'Expert-
entrepreneur' from 1787 to 1792. Rue Lévêque in 1782.
Contractor for Sainte-Geneviève.
Barracks for the Gardes françaises, Rue Saint-Honoré, 1770;
Rues de Babylone and Plumé, 1771. Pavilion for the
brothers Perrier, Chaussée d'Antin, 1773–74. Two hôtels,
Rue d'Artois (Laffitte), 1782. House, Rue de Provence,
1789. Works at Rambouillet: Hôtel du Gouvernement;
new stables; experimental farm; royal dairy, 1788.
Bibl.: J. Langner, 'Architecture pastorale sous Louis XVI',
in *Art de France*, 1963.

THIERRY ?Jacques-Etienne
Pupil of Contant. 3e Prix 1773. Practising in 1782. Profes-
seur at the Ecole Royale de Dessin.
The museum of the Ordre des Avocats possesses a drawing.
Bibl.: Stein, *Le Palais de Justice*, p. 67.
Ref.: Arch. Nat. Z 1J 1092.

THUNOT Edme-Jean
Instructor in surveying. Rue Michel-le-Comte in 1790.
Brétignère tenements, Place de l'Odéon (between the Rues
Crébillon and du Théâtre Français); elevation to Peyre's
designs.
Ref.: Arch. Nat. Z 1J 1100, 1116.

TIERCELET
Family of Architects:

TIERCELET Gilles
Died before 1763. Practising in 1719.

TIERCELET Augustin-Claude
Died 8 May 1769.

Publ.: one of the above was the author of *L'Architecture
moderne* 1st edition by Jombert, 1729; also attributed sometimes to Jombert himself, and to C.-E. Briseux. According
to Blondel, *Architecture française*, vol. I, p. 255, note a; and
Cours d'architecture, vol. III, p. 233: 'Le Muet a été imité par
feu M. Tiercelet dans *L'Architecture moderne*, éditée chez
Jombert en 1729.'

TOUFFAIRE Pierre
Rue du Faubourg-Saint-Honoré in 1764.
Château du Bullou, for the Président de Murard, 1764.
Town hall, Chateaudun, 1776. Hospital, Rochefort;
fountain, Rochefort, 1782–88. Barracks, Libourne, 1776.

TOTTIN Jean-Baptiste.
Practising in 1740.
Many houses for the Hôtel-Dieu; wings of the Hôtel de
Rottenbourg, Rue du Regard, 1734.

TREFFEUILLE
Gobin tenements, Rue Comtesse d'Artois (19 Rue Montorgueil), 1776.

TREPSAT
Family of architects:

TREPSAT Guillaume
Died in Paris 25 or 26 December 1800.
Twin hôtels of M. Pasquier, 46–48 Rue de Bourgogne,
1776. Château de Saint-Brice. Théâtre du Marais, 11
Rue Sévigné, 1790. Villiot house, au Gros-Caillou 'face
à la rivière', 1768–73.

TROUARD Louis-François
Born Paris 1729, died 1794. Grand Prix 1753.
Maison Trouard, 9 Faubourg Poissonnière, 1758; Maison
Trouard, 1 Faubourg Poissonnière (disappeared), 1762;
Maison Trouard, Rue de Provence, 1778. Château de
Carlepont, near Noyon, 1762. Salon of the Château de
Savigny. Barracks of the Place d'Armes, Versailles. Church
of Saint-Symphorien de Montreuil, c. 1765–70. Chapelle
des Catéchismes at Saint-Louis de Versailles, 1764–70.
Work at the cathedral of Orléans, 1766–73.
Bibl.: M. Gallet, *GBA*, February 1970.

TUBEUF Jean
Born at Etiolles c. 1745. Prix de l'Académie de Rouen 1770.
2e Prix of the Académie Royale.
Proposed opera-house at the Carrousel, included among the
works of 'Architecture de J. J. Le Queu' – B.N. Est. Ha 89a.
Ref.: Arch. Nat. O 1 629.

VANNEMBRAS de FOURNEAUX Yves de
Born c. 1733, died after 1793. Rue de Sèvres.
Work at the Hôtel de Soyecourt, Rue Saint-Dominique.
Entrance building for the monastery of Le Bon Pasteur,
1784 (Arch. Nat. N III Seine 523); three schemes, one bear-
ing the approval of the Duchesse de Mouchy.
Ref.: Arch. Nat. Z 1J 1170. La Chesnaye des Bois, *Diction-
naire de la noblesse. Almanach national*, 1793, pp. 376 and 397.

VARIN Pierre
Neo-gothic design for the portal of Saint-Sulpice, 1726.
'Château de M. de Bréchaud', a project of 1724; B.N. Est.
Hd 205. Antoine Ange house, Rues du Gros-Chenet and
du Croissant (contract approved by Maître Pattu, 30
April 1731). *Petit appartement* at the Hôtel de Thiers, 19
Place Vendôme.
Bibl.: Blondel, *Architecture française*. G. Lemesle, in *L'Archi-
tecture*, 1913, p. 105.

VARIN Pierre-Jean
Died 1742.
Hôtel de Jaucourt, 2 Rue de la Vrillière, to the designs of
P. Desmaisons, 1733. Hôtel d'Ecquevilly, 60 Rue de
Turenne, to the designs of J.-B. A. Beausire, 1734. Varin
house, Rue de Seine, 1741.

VARIN Bénigne-Joseph
'Expert-bourgeois' from 1786 to 1792. Rue Vieille-du-
Temple, near the Cul-de-Sac d'Argenson in 1792; may
have built the Directoire house on this site (which belonged
to him in 1792).

VAUCHELET Claude-(or Charles) Nicolas
Died in 1780. Pupil of the Academy 1762. Appears in
Almanach historique, 1776. Cul-de-Sac Coquerelle.
Tenements, Pic de la Mirandole, Rues des Fossés-Saint-
Germain l'Auxerrois and de l'Arbre-Sec, c. 1779. Satenz
tenements, Rue du Renard Saint-Sauveur, c. 1779.
Ref.: Arch. Nat. Z IJ 1072, 1081.

VAUGOYON Jean-Vincent (le Jeune)
Born 1740. Mentioned in 1774.

VAUTRAIN Jean-Baptiste
Died 26 June 1753. 'Expert-bourgeois.'
Maison Lallié (contract approved by Maître Prévost le
Jeune, 7 October 1747). House for the Abbé Tricot, Rue
du Petit-Lion-Saint-Germain (contract approved by Me
Gouvion 18 December 1737). Bellon-Watard house, 31
Rue de Cléry, 1738. Grand et petit Hôtels du Tillet, 29–31
Rue des Francs-Bourgeois, 1740. Vautrain house, Rues
de Beauvais and Champfleury, 1747.
Ref.: Arch. Nat. Z IF 451, fol. 42; Z IJ 673, 674, 716, 721,
738. Extraits des Criées au Châtelet, Bibl. Nat. Imp. F
14.449, March 1738, p. 5.

VAVASSEUR des PERRIÈRES
'Expert-entrepreneur' from 1773 to 1792. Rue Saint-Paul
in 1792. Lucotte tenements, Rue Royale, 1770.

VAVIN
Practising in 1789. Rue de la Harpe in 1792.
House, Rue Montparnasse (Krafft, pl. II, p. 26).
Ref.: Arch. Nat. Z IJ 1192.

VÉDY Julien
Died 10 December 1780. 'Expert-entrepreneur' from 1730.
Rue et Barrière de Charenton.

VERNIQUET Edme
Born Chatillon-sur-Seine 9 October 1727, died Paris 26
November 1804. Rue Michel-le-Comte in 1775. Practised
in Burgundy, Maine and Poitou before 1774.
Houses in Châtillon-sur-Seine, Laigues, Lugny, Semur,
Dijon, Roanne, Marcigny, Bourbon-Lancy, Arrinthes, Le
Mans, Paris. Châteaux of Gémeaux (Côte d'Or), Terrans
à Pierre (Saône-et-Loire), Arcy (S. et L.), Le Vigneau à
Bourbon-Lancy, Digoine à Palinges (S. et L.), Chanceaux
(Côte d'Or), Saint Vincent de Boisset (Loire). Works in
Saint-Seine-sur-Vingeanne, Montmusard, La Boulaye, Le

Mée. Abbey of Marcigny sur Loiret. Church of Latrecey
(Haute-Marne). In Paris: Hôtel de La Queuille, 51 Rue
de Babylone, hôtel d'Avrincourt, 23–25 Rue Saint-
Dominique. Bâtiment des Dames pensionnaires à l'Abbaye
aux Bois (engraved). Kiosk and house in the Jardin des
Plantes.
Publ.: Plan of Paris in 70 sheets, 1790.
Bibl.: Mauclaire, 'La vie et l'œuvre d'Edme Verniquet', in
Société des VIII et XVIe arrondissements, 1936–38.
Ref.: Arch. Nat. F 17 950–51.

VIEL Charles-François
Born Paris 12 June 1745, died Paris 1 December 1819.
Pupil of Chalgrin, and supervisor of his work at the Collège
de France and at Saint-Sulpice, 1775–80.
Hôpital Cochin, 1780. Hôpital la Rochefoucauld, Avenue
d'Orléans, 1781 (completed by J.-J. Huvé). Main building
for the Hôpital de la Pitié, 1785–91. Pawn-offices, Rue des
Francs-Bourgeois. Organ-loft of Saint-Jacques du Haut-
Pas. Main sewer of Bicêtre, 1791. Large amphitheatre of the
Hôtel-Dieu. Work at the Salpétrière, at Bicêtre, at the
Enfants-Trouvés, and the Pharmacie Centrale des Hôpi-
taux, Rue de la Bûcherie. Corn-market hall, Corbeil, 1780.
Entrance of the Deaf-Mutes, Rue Saint-Jacques. Perron of
the Château de Bellegarde, near Montargis.
Publ.: *Projet d'un monument consacré à l'histoire naturelle*, 1778.
De l'architecture des anciens et de celle des modernes, 1787.
Décadence de l'architecture à la fin du XVIIIe siècle, 1800. *De
la construction des edifices publics sans l'emploi du fer*, 1803. *De
l'impuissance des mathématiques pour assurer la solidité des
bâtiments*, 1805. *Des anciennes études de l'architecture*, 1809.
Des principes de l'ordonnance et de la construction des bâtiments.
De la chute imminente de la science de la construction, 1818. *Des
points d'appui indirects en architecture*, 1802.
Bibl.: J.-M.-Pérouse de Montclos, in *BSHAF*, 1967.

VIGNÉ de VIGNY Pierre
Born Nantes 30 May 1690, died Paris 1772. Academician
1723; resigned 1758. Société des Arts et des Sciences, c.
1730–35. Royal Society, London, 1741. 'Architecte des
Domaines.' Architect to the police. 'Intendant' of the
buildings of the Duc d'Orléans. French Embassy, Constantinople (suburb of Pera), Drawings Bibl. Nat. Est. H 2 18a
(IV, vol. II), 1720–22. Work at Versailles, Meaux, Valen-
ciennes, Notre-Dame de Nantilly. Choir of Saint-Pierre de
Saumur (metalwork executed in Paris by Robert and
preserved at the orphanage of Saint-Joseph de Saumur).
Hôtel de Chenizot, 51 Rue Saint-Louis-en-l'Ile, 1726–30.
Cour du Dragon, 50 Rue de Rennes (work begun by
Antoine Mazin), 1729–34. Works for the Canal de Picardie,
c. 1732. Works for the Luynes family: *cabinet* of the Duchesse
de Chevreuse at the Hôtel de Longueville; alterations, Rue
Saint-Dominique; stable of the Garde du Corps at Coulom-
miers.
De la Faille tenements, Rues Poissonnière, Beauregard and
Notre-Dame de Recouvrance, 1730 (altered in nineteenth
century). (?) Hôtel de Luteaux, 27 Rue Lhomond, 1736.
General hospital, today Hospice Général, Boulevard du
Peuple Belge, Lille, from 1740.
Delamaire tenements, Rue Saint-Honoré, 1740. Restora-
tion of Reims cathedral, 1741 (ironwork by Antoine

Ramel). Works for La Communauté des Orfèvres, l'Abbaye Saint-Martin-des-Champs, and Les Filles de l'Union Chrétienne, Rue de la Lune. Tenements of La Barre de Carroy, 42 Rue François Miron, 1742 (sculptures of Ph. Cayeux, ironwork by Mathieu Debauve). De Beauny tenements, Cimetière de Saint-Jean, 1749. Plan for the extension of Nantes; design for a commercial exchange at the point of the Ile Feydeau. Design for the Place Louis XV in Paris. Work at Rennes, 1754.

Publ.: 'Dissertation sur l'architecture', in *Journal economique*, March 1752. 'Dissertation sur le four à briques,' *ibid*.

Ref.: *Journal Book of the Royal Society, London*, vol. XVII, pp. 250, 287, 298. Archives du Nord, 195 H 1, 195 H 2. Archives Nat. O 1 1908–12 fol. 28; O 1 1930; Y 15.972; Z 1F 404, fol. 86v.; Z 1F 405, fol. 9v.; Z 1J 610, 696, 697, 725, 731, 758, 763, 793. Minutier central, vol. XII, p. 469; vol. LXXVIII, p. 645. Archives de la Seine DC 6 254, fol. 245.

Bibl.: *Journal economique*, March 1752, pp. 68–107. Abbé Lambert, Bricaire de la Dixmerie, Jacques-François Blondel: works quoted elsewhere. Ch. de Beaumont, 'Pierre Vigné de Vigny', in *Réunion des Sociétés des Beaux-Arts des Départements*, 1894 (portrait of the artist); also, 'Nouveaux documents sur Pierre de Vigny', ibid., 1898. V. Advielle, *Notice sur Philippe Cayeux, sculpteur*, Paris, 1895. Leclair, 'Pose de la Première Pierre de l'Hôpital Général de Lille en 1739', in *Bulletin de la Société d'Etudes de la Province de Cambrai*, 1906, vol. VI, p. 79. Montaiglon, Corresp. des dir. 1896, vol. VI, pp. 187 et seq. François Boucher, 'Quelques exemples de la valeur documentaire des catalogues de ventes anciens', in *Bulletin de la Société de l'Histoire de l'Art Francais*, 1938. Pierre Lelièvre, *L'Architecture et l'urbanisme à Nantes au XVIIIe siècle*, 1942; and *BSHAF*, 1941, p. 33. Pierre et Anne-Marie Piétresson de Saint-Aubin, 'Bibliographie de l'Hôpital Général de Lille', in Archives du Nord, Inventaire de la Série H 2, 1943, pp. 509–10. Fritz Lugt, *Répertoire des catalogues de ventes d'art*. Runar Strandberg, 'La Réception de C.-J. Cronstedt dans la Société des Arts et des Sciences de Paris', in *Konsthistorisk Tidskrift*, Stockholm, 1963. Mireille Rambaud, *Documents du Minutier Central concernant l'histoire de l'art*, 1964, vol. I, p. 411. Wolfgang Herrmann, *Laugier and XVIII Century French Theory*, London, 1964, pp. 64 et seq., 84 et seq. M. Gallet, 'Quelques etapes du rococo dans l'architecture parisienne', in *GBA*, March 1966. 'L'Architecte Pierre de Vigny et son temps', in the album of *Le Festival du Marais*, 1968.

de VILLENEUVE
'Expert-bourgeois' in 1720. Rue Saint-Sauveur.

VILLETARD
Family of architects:

VILLETARD Etienne (Senior) ..
'Expert-entrepreneur' from 1767 to 1792. Rue des Barres in 1792.

VILLETARD (son)
'Expert-bourgeois' from 1785 to 1792. Rue des Barres in 1792. House, Rue Fer, Moulins. House for M. de V(ilmorin?), Verrières. Berfoy house, Malabry, on the road from Choisy to Versailles – Krafft *Arch. Civile*, pls. 88, 89, 90. Château de Mareuil, 1812 – ibid, pls. 85–6.

VILLIET Guillaume
Sometime 'Inspector' of the King's Buildings (1767).

VINAGE Jacques
Died 1735. Academician 1730. 'Conseiller du Roi.' 'Maître des Bâtiments' of Bridges and Highways.
House, Rue Saint-Victor, 1732. Maisons de l'Orme Saint-Gervais, Place Baudoyer, 1733. Hôtel de Breteuil-Fontenay, 56 Rue des Francs-Bourgeois, 1733–34.
Bibl.: J.-P. Babelon, 'L'Hôtel de Breteuil-Fontenay', in *BSHAF*, 1964.

VIVENEL Jean-Louis
Augier house, Rue de l'Echiquier, 1789.
Ref.: Arch. Nat. Z 1J 1210.

VUIET
Family of architects, connected with that of the painter Nocret.

VUIET Girard
'Expert-bourgeois' in 1703. Living 'hors la Porte Richelieu' in 1703; Enclos du Temple in 1716.
Hôtel de Langlée, Rue Neuve-des-Petits-Champs.
Bibl.: Germain Brice, *Description de la ville de Paris*, 1752, vol. I, p. 421.

YVERT
'Expert-entrepreneur' from 1789 to 1792. Rue des Boulets Saint-Antoine.

Bibliography

Principal Printed Sources

L'almanach royal, 1715–92.

Les curiosités de Paris, editions of 1716 and 1717.

Tiercelet: *Architecture pratique*, Paris, Jombert, 1728 (called *L'Architecture de Jombert*).

Chevotet, Prévotel and Blondel: *L'Architecture francaise*, Paris, Mariette (called *L'Architecture de Mariette*).

Abbés Antonini et Raynal: *Mémorial de Paris*, 4th edition, 1747.

De Jèze: *Etat de Paris*, 1750.

Germain Brice: *Description de la Ville de Paris*, 9 editions, the last of which was completed by P.-J. Mariette and Abbé Pérau, 1752.

Jacques-François Blondel: *L'Architecture francaise*, Paris, Jombert, 1752–56

G.-L. Le Rouge: *Jardins anglo-chinois*, 1755–88, 9 vols.

Soret, Boudier de Villemert, Meusnier de Querlon, Jonval, Le Comte and Bricaire de La Dixmerie: *La Feuille nécessaire*, followed by *L'Avant-coureur*, 1759–73.

Hébert and Alletz: *Almanach parisien en faveur des étrangers*, 1762–94.

Pigagnol de La Force: *Description de Paris*, edition post-humously completed by La Font de Saint-Yenne and Abbé Pérau, 1765.

Roze de Chantoiseau: *Essai sur l'almanach général d'indication*, followed by *Tablettes de renommée*, about 1769–89.

J.-F. Blondel: *Cours d'architecture*, continued by P. Patte, 1771–77.

Lebrun: *Almanach historique et raisonné des architectes, peintres, sculpteurs, graveurs et ciseleurs*, 1776–77.

A.-N. Dézallier d'Argenville: *Voyage pittoresque de Paris*, 6th edition, 1778.

Hébert: *Almanach pittoresque et historique*, forming a continuation of *Almanach des Beaux-Arts*, 1770–80.

A.-N. Dézallier d'Argenville: *Voyage pittoresque des environs de Paris*, 1768 and 1779.

P.-Th. Hurtaut and P. Magny: *Dictionnaire de Paris*, 1779.

Journault: *Almanach des Bâtiments*, 1780–90.

L.-V. Thiéry: *Almanach du voyageur à Paris*, Paris, Hardouin, 1783–87.

J.-A. Dulaure: *Nouvelle description des curiosités de Paris*, 1785, 1787, 1791.

J.-A. Dulaure: *Description des environs de Paris*, 1786.

A.-N. Dézallier d'Argenville: *Vie des fameux architectes, avec la description de leurs ouvrages, depuis la Renaissance des arts*, 1787.

Prévost de Saint-Lucien: *Le Provincial à Paris*: Paris, Watin fils, 1785–90.

Hardouin: *Le Voyageur à Paris*, 1788–89.

Thiery: *Guide des amateurs et des étrangers à Paris*, 1787.

Thiery: *Guide des amateurs et des étrangers . . . aux environs de Paris*, 1788.

Guyot, Roger and Le Campion, engravers after Testard and Sergent: *Vues pittoresques des principaux édifices de Paris*, 'chez les Campion', 1789.

Janinet: *Vues des principaux édifices de Paris*, Lamy, 1792.

P.-L. Van Cleemputte and P. Prieur: *Petites maisons de Paris*, collection comprising 24 engravings dated 1796.

Jean-B. de La Borde: *Voyage pittoresque de la France*, 1781–84.

Gaitte: *Recueil des plus belles maisons et des plus beaux édifices de Paris*, Paris, Jean, n.d.

J.-Ch. Krafft and N. Ransonnette: *Nouvelle Architecture francaise ou collection des édifices publics et maisons particulières bâties à Paris depuis 25 à 30 ans*, Paris, n.d.

Krafft: *Recueil d'architecture civile contenant les plans . . . des châteaux, maisons . . . situés aux environs de Paris*, Paris, 1829.

Landon: *Annales du Musée*, 1800–9.

A. Donnet: *Description des environs de Paris*, 1810.

Legrand and Landon: *Description de Paris et de ses édifices*, 2nd edition, 1818.

J.-B. Bins de Saint-Victor and La Croix de Marlès: *Tableau historique et pittoresque de Paris*.

D. Guilmart: *Les maîtres ornemanistes*, 1880.

C. Daly: *Motifs historiques d'Architecture*, Paris. Morel 1869; 2nd series, Paris, Duché, 1880.

Ch. Bauchal: *Nouveau dictionnaire des architectes francais*, 1887.

Correspondence des directeurs de l'Académie de France à Rome, edition A. de Montaiglon, 1887 and after.

Planat: *Encyclopédie de l'architecture et de la construction*, 1888–92.

A. de Champeaux: *L'Art décoratif dans le vieux Paris*, 1898.

E. Rouyer and A. Darcel: *L'art architectural en France*, 4th edition, 1904.

Procès verbaux de l'Académie royale d'Architecture, edited by H. Lemonnier, 1911 (*PVARA*).

Jules Guiffrey: *Histoire de l'Académie de Saint-Luc*, 1916.

Vial, Marcel and Girodie: *Les artistes décorateurs du bois*, 1912.

J. Vacquier, P. Jarry, H. Soulange Bodin: *Les vieux hôtels de Paris*, 1914 and after (22 vols.).

P. Jarry: *La guirlande de Paris*, 1931.

Armand Brette: *Atlas de la censive de l'archevêché*, 1906.

R.-A. Weigert: *Jean Ier Bérain*, 1937.

L. Hautecœur: *Histoire de l'architecture classique en France*, 1943–57.

A. Mauban: *L'architecture français de Jean Mariette*, 1945.

Fiske Kimball: *The Creation of the Rococo*, Philadelphia, 1943, also paperback, French translation by Jeanne Marie (*Le style Louis XV, origine et évolution du rococo*), Paris, 1950.

E. Kaufmann: *Architecture in the age of reason*, Cambridge (U.S.A.), 1955, French translation by O. Bernier, Paris, 1963.

M. Hébert, J. Thirion, S. Olivier: *Catalogue . . . des plans de la série N, des Archives nationales*, vol. I, Paris, 1958.

F.-J.-B. Watson: *Louis XVI French Furniture*, London & New York, 1960; French translation by R. de Michaux, Paris, 1963.

P. Verlet: *Versailles*, Paris, 1961.

W. Herrmann: *Laugier and eighteenth century French Theory*, London, 1962.

R.-A. Weigert: *L'époque Louis XIV*, Paris, 1962.

Mireille Rambaud: *Documents du Minutier central concernant L'histoire de l'art (1700–1750)* (publication of deeds excerpted from studies Nos. 36, 68, 70, 91, 92, 113, 115, 118), Paris, 1964.

F.-G. Pariset: *L'art classique*, Paris, 1965.

Ph. Minguet: *L'esthétique du rococo*, Paris, 1966.

P. Verlet: *La maison du XVIIIe siècle en France*, Paris, 1966. English translation by George Savage: *French Furniture and Interior Decoration of the 18th Century*, London, 1967.

Jeanne Pronteau: *La numérotation des rues de Paris, de XVe siècle à nos jours*, Paris, 1966.

J.-P. Babelon: *Les relevés d'architecture du quartier des Halles avant les destructions de 1852–54*, Paris, 1967.

M. Le Moël: *Catalogue général . . . des plans cadastraux de Paris . . . levés de 1809 à 1854*, Paris, 1969.

Fr. Souchal: *Les Slodtz*, Paris, 1969.

Principal Manuscript Sources

Archives nationales:

H 2123 à 2146: Autorisations de bâtir délivrées par le Bureau de la Ville.

Y 9505 à 9507: Autorisations de bâtir aux coins des rues, délivrées par le Châtelet.

Z 1F* 382 à 520 (registres): Autorisations de bâtir délivrées par les Trésoriers de France.

Z 1J 517 à 1222: Papiers de la Chambre des bâtiments (expertises, réceptions de travaux, autorisations de bâtir).

Z 2 2456 à 2461: Autorisations de bâtir du Baillage de Montmartre.

Q I 1134 à 1363: Titres de propriété et permissions de bâtir.

Q 1* 1099 (registres): Plan cadastral de Paris en 1705, dit 'Plan terrier du roi'.

Q 2* 188 à 215 (registres): Etat général des propriétaires de Paris en 1790, dit 'Sommier des rentes nationales'.

Y *passim*: 'Avis de parents' ou autorisations de bâtir accordées à des personnes mineures ou interdites.

R: Papiers des princes.

T 'Séquestre': papiers des émigrés, saisis vers 1792.

N III: Collection de plans d'origines diverses.

F 31 3 à 72: Plans au rez-de-chaussée de toutes les maisons de Paris, levés de 1809 à 1854.

H: Biens des communautés religieuses.

O I: Maison du Roi: papiers des architectes du roi.

Minutier central: Archives des 130 notariats parisiens, déposées aux Archives Nationales depuis 1926 (contrats d'emprunts, marchés de construction, inventaires après décès, successions, unions de créanciers).

Les projets ici reproduits le sont avec la permission de MM. les Notaires.

Archives de la Seine: DC 6, DQ 10, DQ 18.

Principal Public Collection Containing Designs by Parisian Architects

Ecole des Beaux-Arts, Paris: Fonds de l'ancienne Académie d'architecture, collections Masson et Lesoufaché.

Bibliothèque de l'Union centrale des Arts décoratifs, Paris.

Bibliothèque Nationale, Estampes.

Bibliothèque d'Art et d'Archéologie de l'Université, Paris.

Musée du Louvre: Cabinet des dessins.

Bibliothèque de l'Institut.

Musée Condé, Chantilly.

Musée Carnavalet, cabinet des Estampes.

Musée de l'Ile de France au château de Sceaux.

Bibliothèque de Besançon, collection Pâris.

British Museum.

Royal Institute of British Architects, London.

Victoria and Albert Museum.

Rothschild Collection at Waddesdon Manor.

The Cooper Union, New York, collection De Cloux.

Library of Warsaw University, prints collection.

Bayerische Staatsbibliothek Munich.

Staatliche Museen, Kunstbibliothek, Berlin.

Nationalmuseum, Stockholm: collection Cronstedt-Tessin-Hårleman.

Abbreviations

AAF: Archives de l'art francais.

NAAF: Nouvelles archives de l'art francais.

BSHAF: Bulletin de la Société de l'histoire de l'art francais.

MSHP: Mémoires de la Société de l'Histoire de Paris.

BSHP: Bulletin de la Société de l'Histoire de Paris.

MFSHP: Mémoires de la Fédération des Sociétés historiques . . . de Paris.

PV or VP: Procès-verbaux de la Commission du Vieux Paris.

Index to Text

N.B. As the Register of Architects is arranged alphabetically it is not included in this index.

A

Adam, James, 28, 54, 56, 68
  Lambert-Sigisbert, 84
  Robert, 28, 53, 54, 55–6, 68, 76, 102, 106
Alberti, Leone Battista, 50, 51, 73
Albi, Mme d', 97
Algarotti, Count Francesco, 28, 52
Alincourt, Duchess d', 125
Amalienburg, pavilion, 84
Andlau, Comte d', 29
Angivillers, d', 61
Antoine, Jacques-Denis, 14, 55, 68, 82
Argenson, Marquis d', 5, 38, 97, 113
Argenton, Mme d', 134
Arnoult, Mlle, 23
Arnouville, 23
Arthur, 65, 130
Artois, Comte d', 6, 7, 91, 103, 119
Aubert, André, 6, 67, 76
  Jean, 24, 40, 70, 84
Audran, Claude, 41, 43, 86, 105, 110, 130
Aumont, Duc d', 21
L'Aurore, pavilion, 76
Auteuil, 96, 102
Auvergne, Cardinal d', 34
Avenue Gabriel (No. 38), 6

B

Bachaumont, Louis Petit de, 28, 33, 98
Bachelier, 99
Bagatelle, 85, 102, 103, 119
Bagnolet, 95, 96, 98
Balletti, Marie-Anne, 24
Barbier, François, 35
Barré, Jean-Benoît Vincent, 23
Barreau de Chefdeville, François-Dominique, 54, 57, 59, 60
Barry, Comtesse Du, 32, 107, 118
Barthélémy, Abbé, 53, 54
Bartolini, 35, 118
Bastide, Jean-François de, 32, 98, 100, 134

Beaudoin, 67
Beaujon, 19, 22, 35, 85, 92
  folie, 76
Beaumarchais, Pierre-Augustin Caron de, 18, 104, 107, 108
Beaumont, Monsiegneur de, 82, 102
Beausire family, 24, 43
Bechameil, Marquis de, 27
Bedford, Duchess of, 55
Bélanger, François-Joseph, 6, 18, 23, 31, 68, 76, 84, 102–3, 108, 129
Bélisard, Claude Billard, 5, 73
Bellechasse, 107
Delle-Isle, Marquis de, 20, 33
Bellevue, 60, 97, 131
Bellotto, Bernardo, 1
Bérain, Jean, 41, 43, 45, 130
Bergeret de Grandcourt, 54
Bergeret, junior, 76
Bergevin, L.-C. 66
Bernard, 90
  Jacques-Samuel, 84, 125
  Samuel, 43
Bernini, Giovanni Lorenzo, 37, 42, 43
Besenval, Baron de, 114, 121
Bibliothèque Nationale, 91
Blain de Fontenay J.-B., 121, 130
Blève, Jean-Louis, 24, 67
Blondel, Jacques-François, 2, 14, 23, 24, 26, 31, 32, 37, 43, 49, 50, 51, 52, 55, 63, 65, 67, 70, 76, 79, 81, 82, 93, 111, 112, 114, 124, 131
  Jean-François, 42, 48
  Nicolas-François, 20, 22
Blondel de Gagny, 91
Boffrand, Germain, 2, 14, 18, 22, 24, 33, 40, 49, 70, 76, 79, 81, 83, 84, 89, 124
Boixière, de la, 98, 135
Bonnet de Boisguillaume, Pierre Alexis, 24, 74
Bordeaux, Intendance de, 59
Borromini, Francesco, 42, 43, 45, 46, 49
Boscry, Charles, 48
  Pierre, 48

Bouchardon, Edme, 28, 110
Boucher, François, 89, 91, 99, 105, 121, 135
Bouchu, Paul-Antoine, 67
Boufflers, Marquise de, 74, 102
Bouillon, Duc de, 28
Boulevard Delessert, 123
  Saint-Germain, 66, 70, 89
  du Temple (No. 17), 67
Boulle, Charles-André, 92, 131
Boullée, Etienne-Louis, 6, 14, 19, 22, 28, 35, 52, 61, 70, 71, 76, 108
Boulogne, senior, 96
Bouret, 10, 29, 54
Bourgogne, Duchesse de, 41
Boutin, 7, 54, 60, 86, 95, 101
Brancas, Duchesse de, 97
Bretez, Louis, 2, 14
Breteuil, Baron de, 74
Brice, Germain, 131
Brienne, Cardinal de, 20
Briseux, Charles-Etienne, 48, 50, 94
Broglie, Victor François, Duc de, 70
Brongniart, Alexandre-Théodore, 6, 18, 24, 61, 73, 107, 121, 129
Brosse, Salomon de, 101
Bruandet, Lazare, 102
Bruant, Libéral, 21, 22, 27, 37
Brûlé, Jean-Baptiste, 67
Brunet family, 15
Brunetti family, 131
  Gaetano, 89, 131, 133
Brunoy, Mme de, 6, 119
Budlet, Denis, 113
Buirette, Sebastien, 21
Bullet, Pierre, 37
Bullet de Chamblain, 21
Burlington, Earl of, 28, 53, 55

C

Caffiéri, Philippe, 57, 133
Café Turc, 61
Cailleteau, see Lassurance
Calderari, Antonio, 55
Callet, Antoine, 85, 105, 107
Cameron, Charles, 54
Campbell, Colen, 49, 55

Canale, Antonio, 1
Carmontelle, 102
Caron, 6, 67
Carré de Beaudoin, Nicolas, 100
  "Carré Marigny", 6
Carroy, Labarre de, 46
Cartaud, Jean-Sylvain, 23, 28, 33,
  46, 63, 76, 83, 93
Cauvet, Gilles-Paul, 29, 35, 60, 129
Cayeux, Ph., 28, 113
Caylus, Comte de, 31, 33, 53, 54, 58,
  134
Cellerier, Jacques 5, 6, 18, 23, 100
Chabannes, 118
Chalgrin, Jean-François-Thérèse, 22,
  24
Chambers, Sir William, 52, 54, 55
Champaigne, Philippe de, 90
Champs-Elysées, 3, 6–8, 84
Chantilly, 115, 134
Chapelle, de la, 28
Charny, 28, 113
Chartraire de Montigny, 134
Chartres, Duc de, 7, 10, 24, 90, 91,
  102, 107
Château d'Asnières, 113
  de Bénouville, 73
  des Boulayes, 73, 118
  de Champltreux, 113, 128
  de Champs, 21
  de Cheverny, 31
  de la Chevrette, 30
  de Combreux, 76
  de l'Ermitage, 33
  de la Grange-du-Milieu, 45, 83, 90
  de Mesnil-Riant, 76
  de Moncanisy, 28
  de la Muette, 130
  de Navarre, 28
  of Queluz, Portugal, 93
  de Surville, 76
  de Vanves, 32
  de Villarceaux, 128
  de Voré, 29
Châteauxroux, Duchesse de, 4, 112,
  115
Châtel, Du, 28
Châtelet, Marquise Du, 26, 125
Chaussard, Jean-Baptiste, 33
Chaussée d'Antin, 79, 105, 129
Chavannes, de, 59, 115
Chéradame, 8
Cherpitel, Mathurin, 23, 29, 52, 70,
  86
Chevalier de Beauregard, 100
Chevallier, see Monsiau
Chevotet, Jean-Michel, 10fn, 19, 23,
  24, 31, 33, 46, 57, 98, 101, 114,
  124
Choiseul-Gouffier, Comte de, 10, 60,
  93
Choisy, 112, 115
Cirey, 26, 110, 125
Claustrier house, 48, 57
Clérisseau, Charles-Louis, 23, 25, 53,
  56, 57
Clérissy, 99

Clermont, Comte de, 23, 96
Clodion, Claude-Michel, 54, 105,
  121, 129
Coatnizan, Marquis de, 28
Cochin, Charles-Nicholas, junior, 48,
  57, 58, 91
Colbert, Jean-Baptiste, 17, 34, 37
Collins (of Brussels), 113
Condé family, 115
  Prince de (Louis II de Bourbon), 80
  Prince de (Louis Joseph de
    Bourbon), 22, 32, 92, 95
Condillac, Etienne Bonnet de, 32
Contant d'Ivry, Pierre, 3, 23, 28,
  33, 57, 82, 89, 133
Conti, Prince de, 24
Corbin, 15, 133
Corneille, Michel, 136
Cortona, Pietro da, 40
Cotelle house, 12
Cottard, 79
Cotte, Robert de, 22, 38, 40, 46, 70,
  89–90
Couet, Pierre-Michel, 45
Coulanges, Abbé de, 21
Courcillon, Sophie de, 89
Cour d'Aligre, 66
Cour du Dragon, 34, 46, 66
Courman house, 100
Courtonne, Jean, 22, 70, 91
Coypel Antoine, 83, 96, 134
  Charles-Antoine, 89, 134
Crillon Comte de, 16–17
Crosnier, 35, 101
Croy, Prince de, 4, 23, 29, 33
Crozat, Antoine, 34, 46–7, 66
  Pierre, 17, 45, 83
Cuvilliès, 84
Coyer, Abbé, 100

D

Dailly, Victor-Thierry, 47, 66
Damun, Jean, 15, 21, 23
Dandrillon, 99
Dangeau, 40
Daviler, Claude-Louis, 47, 124
Debesse, Claude-Guillaume, 23
Debias-Aubry, François, 21
Delafosse, Jean Charles, 22, 60, 61,
  70, 71, 119
Delamair, Pierre-Alexis, 2, 38
Dervieux, Mlle, 32, 120
Désarnaud, J.-F., 65, 118
Desboeufs, Henri-Quentin, 47
Deschamps, Mlle, 134
Desgodetz, Antoine, 22
Desgots, Claude, 101
Desmaisons, Pierre, 5, 14, 47, 67, 76,
  82, 83
Desportes, 130
Desprez, Louis-Jean, 61
Diderot, Denis, 16, 23, 24, 51, 105,
  112, 135
Doni, A. F., 100
Doucet, Prosper, 23
Dresden gallery, 28

Ducret, Nicolas, 67
Dugoulon, 123
Dullin, Nicolas, 23, 70, 98
  Pierre, 134
Dumont, Gabriel-Pierre-Martin, 53
Dupain, Louis, 123
Dupin, 121
Duras, Duc de, 21
Duvaux, Lazare, 57, 113–14

E

Ecole de Chirurgie, 32, 55
  Militaire, 4, 15, 61
Elysée, 14, 19, 35, 93, 118, 123
Enfants Trouvés, chapel of, 131
Enseigne de Gersaint, 26
Epinay, d', 30 (Louise Tardieu
  d'Esclavelles, Mme)
Eriksen, S., 59
Ermenonville, Mme Lombard d', 22
Escalier des Ambassadeurs, 80, 93
Espagnac, Baronne d', 89, 118
Estève, P., 48
Eynaud, house, 113

F

Falconet, 98
Falconieri, Paolo, 28
Farsetti, Abbot, 28
Faubourg Poissonnière (Nos. 58 and
  60), 70–1
  Saint-Denis (Nos. 99–105), 66
  Saint-Germain, 64, 65, 115
  Saint-Honoré, 29, 113
  Saint-Jacques, 6, 12
  Saint-Marcel, 23
  Saint-Martin, 105
  du Temple, 35
Faudoas, Comte de, 66
Fayet (master-smith), 15
Feuillet, 67, 129
Fischer von Erlach, J. B., 47
Folie Cornu, 95
  Favart, 100
  Méricourt 95,
  Sainte-James, 102, 103
  Soubise, 107
  Titon, 96
Fontainebleau, 60, 86, 103
Fontana, Giovanni, 46
Fontenelle, 23, 46
Fornaro, Duca di, 27
Foucou, 107
Fouquet, 19
Fouquier-Tinville, Antoine-Quentin,
  7
Fournier, Pierre, 123
Fragonard, Jean-Honoré, 23, 54, 101
Francastel, Pierre, 42
François (known as Tourangeau), 19
Franque, François, 16, 63, 65
Frémin, de, 35
Fréron, Elie (or Jean by Voltaire),
  23, 130
Frézier, 50

G

Gabriel family, 40
  Jacques (V), 18, 22, 32, 38, 123
  Jacques-Ange, 3, 4, 6, 15, 18, 29, 76, 93, 95, 102, 124
Galerie d'Enée, 83, 89
  des Glaces, Versailles, 38, 123
  des Hommes illustres, 90–1
Gallifet, Marquis de, 79
Garnier, 90
  Charles, 80
  Pierre, 60
Gaudion house, 45
Gaudreaux, 47
Genlis, Mme de, 107, 115, 129
Gennevilliers, 10, 76, 98
Geoffrin, Mme, 23
Germain, Thomas, 42, 47, 110, 124
Girardin, Nicolas-Claude, 23, 52, 73, 76
Godot, Pierre-François, 47
Gondoin, Jacques, 55
Gouffier, Comte de, *see* Comte de Choiseul-Gouffier
Goujon, Jean, 21, 104–5
Goupy family, 14
  Claude-Martin, 7, 76
  Martin, Senior, 47
Gouthière, 10, 105
Goutheinze, 15, 67, 129
Graffigny, Mme de, 110
Grange Batelière, 79
Grenard, 65, 130
Grignan, Mme de, 21, 27,
Grimod de La Reynière, 7, 25, 105
Gudin de la Brenellerie, 36
Guerchy, de, 55
Guerne, Abraham, 15
Guibert, 113
Guimard, Mlle, 32, 79

H

Halle au Blé, 5, 15, 68
Hamilton, Gavin, 53
Happe, Célestin-Joseph, 67
Harcourt, Duc d', 31
Hardouin-Mansart, *see* Mansart
Harlay, 18
Hårleman, 46
Hébert, architect, 6
Hébert, merchant, 113
Helin, Pierre-Louis, 54
Helvetius, Mme, 96, 102
Henri IV, 82
Henry, *see* Trou
Herpin, Louis-Jacques, 123
Holbach, Baron d', 99
Holkham Hall, 55
Hollande, D', 15, 67, 129
Hosten, 66, 67
Hôtel Alexandre, 70
  d'Andelot, *see* Julliennet house
  d'Antin, 98
  d'Argerton, later d'Argenson, 61, 83, 134

Hôtel d'Armenonville, 93
  d'Assy, 45
  d'Augny, 50
  d'Aumont, 87
  d'Auvergne, 81
  Beaumarchais, 85
  de Beauvais, 79
  de Belle-Isle, 123
  de Besenval, 118, 121
  Biron, 40, 79, 83-4, 93
  de Biseuil or de Hollande, 79, 135, 136
  Bonnier, 123
  de Boullongne, 130
  Boutin, 59
  de Brancas, 84, 123
  de Breteuil, 119
  de Broglie, 70
  de Bullion, 89, 93,113
  de Canillac, 83
  de Carignan, 123
  Carnavalet, 21, 27, 80
  Du Châtelet, 70, 86
  de Chavannes, 59, 74
  Chenizot, 46, 73
  de Choiseul-Gouffier, 5, 93
  de Clermont d'Amboise, 93, 131
  de Courcelles, 86
  Crozet de Thiers, 82, 133
  Deshayes, 61, 84
  Dodun, 82
  de Duret, 131
  d'Ecquevilly, 82
  d'Etampes, 93
  d'Evreux, 45
  de Feuquières, 48
  de Gallifet, 105, 129
  Goix, 70, 119
  de Gournay, 40, 70
  de la Grange, 10, 16, 82
  Grimod de la Loube, 73
  d'Hallwyl, 20, 57, 60, 134
  d'Harcourt, 31, 135
  d'Havré, 93
  de Hollande, *see* Bissenil
  d'Humières, 79
  des Invalides, 21, 95
  de Jarnac, 129
  de Jaucourt, 14, 47, 83, 130
  Lambert, 121
  de Lassay, 40, 80
  de La Live, 93
  de Lorges, 38, 79
  de Lubert, 105–7, 108
  de Luynes, 89, 131
  du Maine, 40, 131
  de Marigny, 60
  de la Mark, 79
  de Marsilly, 124
  de Matignon, 14, 70, 80, 81, 93, 123
  de Mercy-Argentau, 73
  de Monaco, 73
  des Monnaies, 82
  de Montesquiou d'Artagnan, 76
  de Montholon, 74
  de Montmorency, 19, 20, 61, 120
  de Montsauge, 6

Hôtel de Monville, 108, 115
  de Nesmond, 69
  de Noailles, 38, 69, 79, 80, 93
  d'Orléans, 84
  d'Ormesson, 123
  d'Orrouer, 48, 123, 124
  Perrotin de Barmond, 119
  Pierre Crozat, 17, 28
  de Polisy, 33
  Poulpry, 130
  de La Reynière, 6, 57, 60
  de Rohan, 130
  de Roquelaure-Molé, 80, 113, 123
  de Rothelin, 40
  de Saint-Albin, 45, 46
  de Saint-Florentin, 60
  de Sainte-Foix, 79
  de Saint-Prest, 76, 82, 108
  de Salm, 28, 75, 79, 85
  de Sérilly, 57
  Soubise, 131
  de Tamnay, 85, 134
  de Tessé, 89, 118
  Thélusson, 12, 21, 32, 75, 76, 79, 84, 85, 87, 115, 118, 130
  de Thiers, 82, 133
  du Tillet, 15, 46–7, 73, 131
  Titon, 70
  de Toulouse, 89, 90, 123
  de la Trémouille, 123
  d'Uzès, 32, 57, 70
  de Vendôme, 22
  de Villars, 90, 134
  de Villette, 61
  de la Vrillière, 75, 82
Huet, Christophe, 57, 99, 130
  J. B., 65, 130
Huquier, Gabriel, 45
Huxelles, Marquise d', 134

I

Invalides, 38, 40
Isenghien, Prince d', 28, 86

J

Jacquin, 5
Jardin, Nicolas-Henri, 59
Jaucourt, Mme de, 76
  Jaunez, 73
Jefferson, Thomas, 28, 54, 75
Jones, Inigo, 55
Jouasse, Alexandre, 123
Journal du Garde-meubles, 113
  des Menus-Plaisirs, 20
  de Paris, 120
Jouvenet, 96
Juliance, Pierre, 123
Julliennet house, 73
Jullienne, Jean de, 91

K

Kent, William, 53, 55
Kimball, Fiske, 40, 41, 45, 60, 76
Kinsky, Mme de, 118
Kolly, Fermier-Général, 134
Kornmann, 18

L

La Boissière, 7, 57
Laborde, 5, 6, 18, 19
La Bretêche, 35
La Chapelle, 101
La Dixmerie, 38
Ladoireau (goldsmith), 123
Lafon, Pierre, 14
La Fond de Saint-Yenne,
La Grange family, 10
la Grange du Milieu, 124
La Guêpière, Jacques de La, 101
Lajoue, 47, 91
La Live de Jully, 57-9, 60
La Londe, 60
La Muette, 97, 102
Lancret, François-Nicolas, 83, 130
Lange, Michel, 45, 113, 123, 124
Langelier, 35
Langlée, de, 27
Lante, Duchessa, 28
La Popelinière, 96
La Porte, Roland de, 31, 130
Largillière, 105
La Salle, Philippe de, 60
Lassay, Marquis de, 28, 95
Lassurance, 38, 40, 41, 70, 118
La Tour, Quentin, 82, 96
Laugier, Abbé, 2, 50-2, 57, 59, 70,
    73, 82, 114, 118, 135
Launay de, 28, 113
Lauraguais, Comte de, 23, 84
La Vallée-Poussin, 57, 130
La Ville l'Evêque, 97
La Vrillière, duc de, 89-90
Law, John, 96
Leblanc, Abbé, 50, 55
Le Boeuf, Abbé, 93
Le Bon, Pierre-Etienne, 33
Le Boursier, J.-B., 70
Lebrun, 26, 41, 135, 136
    J.-B. Pierre, 93, 105-6, 108,
    113
    Mme, see Vigée-Lebrun
Le Butard, 76
Le Camus, Louis-Denis, 5, 66, 79,
    80, 118, 121
    de Mézières, Nicolas, 5,
    21, 23, 32, 84, 128
Le Carpentier, Antoine-Mathieu, 10,
    23, 29, 48, 57, 98, 99, 120
Leclerc, 101
Le Cler-du-Brillet, 66
Le Cloître Saint-Merry, 105
Lecomte, Felix, 79
Le Cour, 21
Ledoux, Claude-Nicolas, 5, 6, 8, 12,
    18, 19, 20, 21, 22, 23, 25, 29,
    32, 52, 57, 60, 68, 70, 71, 73,
    75, 76, 79, 84, 118, 129, 134
Lefranc, 30
Le Geay, 19, 54
Le Goupil, 123
Legrand, Jacques-Guillaume, 15, 21,
    105
Le Lorrain (Louis), 59-135

Lemoine, François, 134
    Paul-Guillaume, 108
Lemonnier, Louis-Philippe, 73
Lemoyne, Jean-Baptiste, 84
    junior, 28
Lenoir le Romain, Samson-Nicolas,
    5, 81, 20, 23, 67, 68
Le Normand d'Etioles, 86
Le Normand de Mézières, 19
Le Nôtre, André, 2, 28, 101
Léopold, duc de Lorraine, 40
Lepas, Martin, 12
Le Pas-Dubuisson, Cl.-N., the elder,
    19, 43, 65
Le Pautre, Antoine, 79, 119
Lepautre, Jean, 41
    Pierre, 41, 118
Leroux, Jean-Baptiste, 48, 90
Leroy, Julien-David, 53, 55, 57, 59
Le Sueur, 28
Le Tellier, 6
Le Vau, 37, 83
Lezay-Marnézia, 103
Lieutaud, Balthazar, 60
Ligne, Prince de, 23, 31-2, 55, 105
Lille, hospital of, 46, 55
Livry, Suzanne de, 110
Louis XIV, 28, 29, 31, 37, 38, 41,
    79, 80, 82, 88, 95, 109
Louis XV, 2-4, 10, 16, 24, 29, 82,
    95, 97, 98, 102, 111, 112, 115,
    118, 135
Louis XVI, 6, 9, 105
Louis XVIII, 5
Louis-Philippe, 102
Louis, Victor, 23, 30, 54, 60, 73, 91
Louvre, 3, 37, 98, 107, 123, 135
Lubersac, Abbé de, 2
Lubert, Chevalier de, 105
Lunéville, palace of, 40, 79
Luxembourg, 23, 26, 115, 131
Luynes, Duc de, 32, 46, 128

M

Machy, de, 1, 16, 133
Mansart family, 22, 49
    François, 34, 37, 38, 51,
    70, 75, 89
    Jacques Hardouin-, de Levi,
    (Comte de Sagonne), 24, 48, 57
    Jean Hardouin-, de Jouy, 48, 115
    Jules Hardouin-, 18, 22, 27, 31,
    37, 38, 40, 41, 48, 69, 70, 79,
    89, 123
Mansart, Jules-Michel-Alexander
    Hardouin-, 45, 123
Machard, 113
Madeleine, The (church) 3, 108
Magny, 97
Maine, Duchesse du, 41, 79
Maison Carrée, 28
Marcel, Etienne, 12
Marie, Alfred, 40, 41
Marie Antoinette, 23, 60, 91,107
Marigny, Marquis de, 29, 31, 50, 55,
    60

Marivaux, 32
Marly, 32, 37, 38, 41, 95, 123
Mariette, Jean, 33, 49, 58, 63, 70
Marteau, Jean-Baptiste, 45
Massé, J.-B., 105
Mazarin, Jules, 91, 115
    Duchesse de, 93
Meissonier, Juste-Aurèle, 33, 42, 43,
    47, 124
Mellan, Michel, 61, 66
Mengs, Raphaël, 53
Mercier, Sébastien, 4, 9, 12, 14, 109
Méricourt folie, 95
Mesme, Président de, 27
Métivier, Joseph, 129
Meudon, 37, 41, 45
Michel, Georges, 7
Middelbourg, Comte de, 124
Mignard, 26
Mique, Richard, 55
Mirabeau, Marquis de, 109, 110,
    112
Molé, Président, 43, 113
Molinos, Jacques, 21, 105
Mollet, Armand-Claude, 89
Monaco, Princesse de, 29
Monceau, parc, 104
Monicault, 66
Monnoyer, Jean-Baptiste, 130
Monsiau (known as Chevallier), 90,
    129
Montaigu, de, 121
Montesquieu, Baron de, 49, 101,
    109, 112
Montesson, Mme de, 129
Montmartre, 67, 97, 104
Montmorency, Prince de, 19
Montreuil, 134.
Montsauge, de 35
Monville, de, 35, 99
Moreau, the elder, 102
    -Desproux, Pierre-Louis, 2,
    5, 19, 23, 54, 59, 61, 74, 76, 89,
    100, 115, 118
Mullart, 67
Musée Carnavalet, 91, 119, 131

N

Nadeau, Martin, 16
Nancy town hall, 134
Natoire, Charles-Joseph, 84, 136
Necker, Jacques, 9
Neuchâteau, 131,
Neuilly, 48, 97, 102, 103
Neveu, Charles, 67, 86
Nivernais, Duc de, 31, 54, 87
Noailles, Louis de, Maréchal, 105
    Louis-Antoine, Cardinal, 93
Nordenfalk, 60

O

Oberkampf, Christophe-Philippe,
    130
d'Oberkirch, Baronne, 32, 95
Oeben, J.-F., 60

Opéra, 43, 115, 134
-Comique, 5
Versailles, 15
Oppenord, Gilles-Marie, 15, 23, 33, 40, 42, 43, 45–6, 83, 89, 91, 93, 110, 123, 124
senior, 42
Orbay, François d', 37, 93
Nicolas, 98
Orrouer, Marquis d', 10 see also Hôtel d'Orrouer
Orsay, Comte d', 54
Oudry, Jean-Baptiste, 29, 96, 105, 130
Outrequin, 2, 8

P

Paillet, 93, 113
Paine, 55
Pajou, Augustin, 104–5, 129
Palacio de Alba y Berwick, 82
Palais Abbatial de Royaumont, 118
Bourbon, 28, 40, 83, 85, 95, 118
de Justice, 15
Royal, 15, 45, 57, 68, 73, 75, 80, 82, 83, 87, 88, 89, 90, 92, 93, 124, 129, 133, 135
Soubise, 84, 86, 89, 123, 124
Palladio, 26, 38, 54, 100, 107, 131
Palazzo Mancini, 53, 54
Spinola, 54, 104
Palloy, 5
Papillon de La Ferté, 20
Paris, Pierre-Adrien, 23, 54, 115
Pâris, the brothers, 96
Pariset, F.-G., 59
Parme, Julien de, 129
Pasquier, J.-B. Mathias, 15
'Pâté-Pâris', 96
Pater, Jean-Baptiste, 130
Patte, Pierre, 120
Pavillon d'Argenson, 6
de la Boissière, 57, 98, 101
Carré de Beaudouin, 100
de Croix-Fontaine, 10, 98
Français de Trianon, 29
Gouthière, 79
de Hanovre, 57, 98, 101, 114
de Langeac, 6
de Louveciennes, 29, 118
Payen, 9, 14
Percier, Charles, 93, 119
Périer, François, 89
Perlin, Firmin, 6, 19, 73
Perrault, Claude, 3, 22, 26, 42, 49, 50
Perronet, Jean-Rodolphe, 15
La petite maison, 98–100
Petitot, Ennemond-Alexandre, 60
Peyre, Marie–Joseph, 5, 54, 55, 60
Peyrotte, 57, 99, 130
Philippe Egalité, see Duc de Chartres
Pichon, Baron, 19, 90
Picquiny, Duc de, 91
Pierre, J.-B., 110, 035
Piètre (Italian painter), 134
Henri, 90, 91, 116

Pilon, Germain, 104
Pineau, Nicholas, 43, 47–8, 50, 86, 90, 121, 123, 124
Pinot-Duclos, Charles, 97
Piranesi, Giambattista, 53, 54, 59, 102
Place Baudoyer, 66
de la Concorde, 2–4
Dauphine, 105
de l'Etoile, 8
de Grève, 100
Louis XV, 6, 60, 87
Monge, 66
du Palais Bourbon, 5
du Palais Royal, 5
Royale, 134
Saint-Sulpice (No. 6), 81
Vendôme, 38, 82, 111, 123
(No. 23), 130
des Victoires, 45
Polignac, Melchior de, Cardinal, 49
Pompadour, Marquise de, 4, 6, 29, 40, 50, 57, 60, 86, 97, 98, 113, 118
Pont de Neuilly, 102
Notre-Dame, 113
Porquet, Claude-Joseph, 67
Saint-Martin, 43
Poyet, Bernard, 54, 107
Prétrel, Philippe-Laurent, 67
Prévost, Abbé, 96
Provence, Comte de, 24
Prud'hon, Pierre-Paul, 129
Puget, Pierre, 43

Q

Quai de la Mégisserie, 113
Quillard, 130
Quirot family, 47
Denis, le jeune, 104

R

Rambouillet, Marquise de, 27, 80, 109
Raymond, Jean-Arnaud, 15, 20, 23, 54, 76, 79, 93
Regnault folie, 95
Restout, Jean, 89
Réveillon, 65, 96, 130
Riboutté, 18
Ricci, Sebastiano, 122
Richard, Pierre-Louis, 93
Richelieu, Armand-Jean du Plessis de, Cardinal, 90, 92
Armand de Vignerot, Duc de, 4, 10, 57, 94, 97–8, 110, 114, 115, 131, 133, 134
Richomme house, 65
Rigaud, Hyacinthe, 1
Rivarol, Antoine de, 105
Robert, 65, 130
family, 120
Hubert, 23, 87, 108
Robillon, 93

Roland (Philippe-Laurent), 79
Rondelet, Jean-Baptiste, 15
Rougevin, Jean, 67
Roquet, François, 17
Rothelin, Marquis de, 49
Rougé, Mme de, 105
Rousseau, Jean-Jacques, 6, 102, 121, 134
Pierre, 10, 75, 104, 130
Rubens, Pierre-Paul, 26, 134
Ruckers, 86
Rue Amelot (No. 136), 76
du Bac, 125
(Nos. 118 and 120), 19, 43
Cambon (No. 26), 124, 125
Caumartin (No. 4), 67
de la Chaise (No. 10), 129
du Faubourg-Poissonnière, 59, 70–1
(No. 60), 119
des Francs-Bourgeois, 46, 83
(No. 56), 48, 57
des Lions (No. 3), 64
du Mail (No. 1), 67
des Mauvaises Paroles, 63
Mazarine (No. 51), 67
Montmartre (No. 51), 64
Neuve des Petits-Champs (No. 1), 67
de l'Odéon (Nos, 1-3), 67
Saint-André-des-Arts (No. 52), 12, 47, 73
(No. 27), 104
Saint Antoine (No. 133), 15
Saint-Florentin (No. 6), 21, 105
Saint-Jacques (No. 151 bis), 65
du Sentier (No. 12), 65
de Tournon, 67
(Nos. 2 and 4), 73
(No. 12), 86
Vieille-du-Temple (No. 102), 119
de la Ville l'Evêque (No. 16), 70

S

Sabran, Mme de, 105
Saint-Cloud, 26, 27, 37
Sainte-Croix, M., 6
Saint-Eustache, 15, 48, 115
Saint-Florentin, Comte de, 22
Sainte Geneviève, 4, 16, 20
Sainte-James, Baudard de, 103
Saint-Leu, Dufort de, 31
Sainte-Marguerite de Charonne, 131
Saint-Martin, P.-H. de, 98
Saint-Maur, Dupré de, 30
Saint-Merry, 92
Sainte-Paule, Benoist de, 7, 18
Saint-Philippe du Roule, 15
Saint-Simon, Duc de, 40, 69
Saint-Simon, Duchesse de, 94
Saint-Sulpice, 14, 42, 54, 61
Salm, Prince de, 10–11
Salpétrière, 21
Sandrier, 6, 18
Santerre, Jean-Baptiste, 42
Sauvage, 129
Saxe, Maréchal de, 90

Scamozzi, 26, 50, 91
Scudéry, Mlle de, 83
Secousse, Abbé, 118
Seignelay, Abbé Colbert de, 19
Seissac, Mme de, 93
Seminary of Foreign Missions, 19, 43
  of the Irish, 48
Sens, Mlle de, 115
Servandoni, Giovanni Niccolò, 10,
  15, 24, 33–4, 42, 43, 76, 81, 93,
  98, 115
Sévigné, de, 27
  Marquise de, 21, 80
Simonnet, Nicolas, 104
Simony, Dominique, 123
Slodtz, family 42, 43, 86
Sobre, Jean-Nicolas, 67
Soldini, 131, 133
Soubise, Prince de, 87, 93, 97, 100,
  121
  Princesse de, 84, 136
Souchal, François, 42
Soufflot, Jacques-Germain, 2, 4, 15,
  20, 22, 29, 31, 50, 53, 54, 55,
  60, 67
Spinola, Marchese, 104
Stanguier, Martin-Jacques, 163
Suffolk, Countess of, 87

T

Tannevot, Michel, 48
Taupin, 123
Temporitti, 42
Tessé, Mme de, 28, 75
  folie, 70
Tessin, N., the younger, 46
Teyssèdre, Bernard, 42
Théâtre Français, 5, 23, 108
  Porte Saint-Martin, 23
Thélusson, Mme, 32, 85, 105

Thévenin, 10
Thiers, Baron de, 111
Thiéry, 23, 102
Thornhill, Sir James, 131
Tiercelet, 63–4, 65
'Tivoli', 96, 101
Toiles de Jouy, 65
Toro, Bernard, 43
Toulouse, Comte de, 45, 90
Tourangeau, *see* François, 19
Tramblin, André, 130
  Charles-André, 130, 131
Trémollières, 89, 135
Trianon, 37, 38, 41, 60, 76, 95, 113
Trois-Chapelets, house of the, 47,
  104
Tranoy, 115
Trou, Henri, 75
Trouard, Louis-François, 21, 59
Troy, Jean-François de, 86
Tuileries, 3, 75
Turgot, Anne-Robert-Jacques, 9
  Etienne-Michel (father), 1, 14

V

Vandiéres, Marquis de, 50, 54 (*see*
  also Marigny)
Van Loo, Carle, 135
Varin, 111
  Pierre-Jean, 15, 47, 83, 104
  Philippe, 123
Vassé, senior, 45, 46, 90, 123
Vatard house, 21, 46
Vautrain, Jean-Baptiste, 15, 21-2, 46
Vavasseur-Despérièrs, 6
Vélye, Machet de, 18
Vendôme, Duc de, 41
Verberckt, Jacques, 124
Verlet, Pierre, 29

Vernet family, 24, 26
  Carle, 23
  Claude-Joseph, 113
Versailles, 26, 37, 38, 41, 69, 70, 80,
  82, 83, 88, 93, 95, 111, 113, 115,
  118, 123
Vézelay, Bouret de, 7
Vien, Joseph-Marie, 135
Vigée-Lebrun, Mme, 79, 93, 105,
  107, 119, 129
Vigné de Vigny, Pierre, 23, 24, 34,
  46, 55, 82
Vignola, 26, 54,
Villayer, Marquis de, 115
Villarceaux, de, 24
Vintimille, Mgr de, 93
Vitruvius, 51, 54, 112
Voltaire, Jean, 2, 24, 49, 63, 98, 110,
  115, 131
Vouet, 89, 90, 135

W

Waddesdon, 90
Wailly, Charles De, 5, 14, 19, 24, 54,
  55, 61, 79, 104, 108, 115
Walpole, Horace, 28, 55, 70, 86
Ware, Isaac, 55
Watteau, 23, 26, 38, 45, 56, 57, 91,
  109, 113, 122, 130
Weigert, Roger-Armand, 43
Weinlig, Christian, 52
Winckelmann, Johann Joachim, 53,
  54
Witt, de, 20
Wolmar, de, 102
Wood, Robert, 53, 56
Wren, Sir Christopher, 55

Z

Zelotti, Battista, 122